Herman Friedrich Grimm, Sarah Holland Adams

The Life and Times of Goethe

Herman Friedrich Grimm, Sarah Holland Adams

The Life and Times of Goethe

ISBN/EAN: 9783741101441

Manufactured in Europe, USA, Canada, Australia, Japa

Cover: Foto ©Andreas Hilbeck / pixelio.de

Manufactured and distributed by brebook publishing software (www.brebook.com)

Herman Friedrich Grimm, Sarah Holland Adams

The Life and Times of Goethe

THE LIFE AND TIMES OF GOETHE.

BY

HERMAN GRIMM.

TRANSLATED BY

SARAH HOLLAND ADAMS.

FIFTH EDITION.

BOSTON:
LITTLE, BROWN, AND COMPANY.
1902.

THIS TRANSLATION

IS RESPECTFULLY DEDICATED TO

RALPH WALDO EMERSON,

THE FRIEND OF THE AUTHOR, THE FRIEND OF TRANSLATORS AND
TRANSLATIONS, AND THE INSPIRATION OF MANY
GREAT MEN IN ALL COUNTRIES.

THESE lectures are not intended to give a biography of Goethe, but to show in what sense he was at once the most real, as well as the most ideal, man and poet that ever lived.

I ask for the labor bestowed on this translation the mercy of the reader, and a measure of gratitude that even so much of the intrinsic meaning of a very valuable work can be shared by another public than the one for which it was written.

A perfect translation would be simply a re-creation, possible only to the genius of the author. Zeller, of Berlin, says Hegel could be translated into Greek, but never into English. No translation can ever bring out the fine psychological differences imbedded in the deposits of language; but what enthusiasm, sympathy, and earnest study can do toward rendering a clear translation, I have devoted to this work, — the fruit of my visit to Germany, and of the honor, as well as advantage, derived from personal acquaintance with its author.

S. H. A.

BERLIN, August, 1880.

TO THE TRANSLATOR.

I RETURN to you herewith the manuscript of your translation of my book, which you intrusted to me. I have compared it carefully, and find it excellent. It will be a pleasure to me if your work is printed in your fatherland.

I am very much indebted to America. I can indeed say that no author, with whose writings I have lately become acquainted, has had such an influence upon me as Emerson. The manner of writing of this man, whom I hold to be the greatest of all living authors, has revealed to me a new way of expressing thought. Although I grew up in the study of Goethe, and had had much intercourse with those who have known him personally, I am indebted to Emerson for the historical view of Goethe, which taught me to regard him as the great phenomenon in the development of mankind. In this sense I have sought in these lectures to represent him.

Should you give this letter a place in the introduction to your translation, permit me to add a few words which are addressed to my countrymen in America.

I have been told that many Germans in America undervalue their own language, and read only English books. Without doubt it is right and necessary to speak the language in which are decided the fortunes of the country where one lives, and which one calls his fatherland. But how much would he lose who would thereby forget his own language! Should my book, as an English translation, enter the household of such a German, it may be that he and his family will learn what a man Goethe was, and what an inestimable benefit it is to be able to read his works in his own language.

May this book help to draw still nearer together the two nations of the earth which have before them the most glorious future!

HERMAN GRIMM.

BERLIN, May, 1880.

CONTENTS.

LECTURE.		PAGE
I.	INTRODUCTION	1
II.	PLAN OF THE LECTURES. — GOETHE'S FIRST FRANKFORT DAYS. — STUDY OF LAW IN LEIPSIÇ. — CHANGE TO STRASBURG	18
III.	LIFE IN STRASBURG. — HERDER. — NEW IDEAS OF THE NINETEENTH CENTURY	38
IV.	FREDERIKA IN SESENHEIM. — DOCTOR'S DEGREE. — RETURN TO FRANKFORT	57
V.	PRACTISING LAW. — HIS PARENTS. — MERCK. — "GÖTZ VON BERLICHINGEN"	77
VI.	GÖTZ VON BERLICHINGEN	98
VII.	THE SORROWS OF YOUNG WERTHER	117
VIII.	"WERTHER"	140
IX.	LAVATER	167
X.	FRITZ JACOBI. — SPINOZA	184
XI.	LILLI SCHOENEMANN	210
XII.	WEIMAR. — ANNA AMALIA. — VON FRITSCH. — WIELAND	231
XIII.	FRAU VON STEIN	247
XIV.	CARL AUGUST AND GOETHE IN THE TEN YEARS	264
XV.	THE GERMAN AND THE ROMAN IPHIGENIA	283

CONTENTS.

LECTURE.		PAGE
XVI.	ROME	302
XVII.	THE END OF "IPHIGENIA." — "TASSO." — CHRISTIANE. — "ROMAN ELEGIES"	321
XVIII.	ROME. — SICILY. — NAPLES. — PHILIPP HACKERT. — SECOND SOJOURN IN ROME. — RETURN TO WEIMAR. — SCHILLER	343
XIX.	SCHILLER AND GOETHE. — THEIR ESTRANGEMENT	364
XX.	GOETHE'S SECLUSION. — THE UNION WITH SCHILLER. — SCHILLER'S WIFE	383
XXI.	GOETHE AND SCHILLER IN WEIMAR	404
XXII.	SCHILLER AND GOETHE	420
XXIII.	STUDY OF NATURAL SCIENCE. — "THE NATURAL DAUGHTER." — "ELECTIVE AFFINITIES"	442
XXIV.	GOETHE AS A POLITICIAN. — NAPOLEON. — "FAUST"	475
XXV.	"FAUST." — CONCLUSION	500

CHRONOLOGICAL TABLE 527
INDEX 537

LIFE AND TIMES OF GOETHE.

LECTURE I.

INTRODUCTION.

IT is ninety-nine years, almost to a day, since GOETHE appeared for the first time in Weimar. It was on the seventh of November, 1775, when, in his twenty-sixth year, he responded to the call of the Duke, who had himself hardly reached his twentieth year.

Goethe, although even then enjoying the reputation of a poet, both in and out of Germany, was just entering that higher region of intellectual activity, and beginning that career in which for himself and for us he became what he is, and what is comprehended in the single word Goethe. From his advent in Weimar the century moves on, stamped with the name of Goethe.

Goethe has worked in the intellectual life of Germany as some great physical phenomenon might work in the realm of Nature. Our coal formations tell of times of tropic warmth, when palms grew in this land. Recently explored caverns speak of ice-periods, when the reindeer was at home among us. In enormous spaces of time radical changes have been produced in the German soil, which in its present condition bears so much the appearance of eternal unchangeableness. And, to carry our simile further, Goethe has affected the spiritual atmos-there much like some telluric event, which should raise the average climatic warmth a certain number of degrees. If this were to happen we should have another vegetation, another kind of cultivation, and with this an entirely new foundation for our whole existence.

Goethe has created our language and literature. Before his time both were valueless in the world-market of the European nations. Such statements must, however, be received as referring not to the exceptions but to the average product. In the year 1801, when Goethe and his followers had already accomplished the principal part of that which could be done for the regeneration of the German language, Karl August still speaks of the " pitiful German tongue from which Schiller has wrung the sweetest melody." Goethe himself, fifteen years earlier, had spoken much more severely of the German language.

When Goethe began to write, the German language was as limited in its general influence as the German national interest in our politics. The nation existed, had a silent consciousness of its worth, and a presentiment of its future course; but that was all. Among the criticisms which Goethe wrote in the beginning of his literary career, he speaks of the meaning of patriotism, and asks how one could demand of us such a feeling as inspired the Romans, who felt themselves to be citizens of a world-embracing empire. Any influence beyond our own borders seemed to us impossible. The English, French, and Italian critics noticed German literary productions only so far as our authors (by way of addition to foreign literature) allowed their works to appear as a part of the same. Frederick the Great, if perchance he had the honor to be named at all, was counted in Paris among French authors, and regarded himself as such

INTRODUCTION. 3

French was spoken in all circles of North Germany, and it ranked as the second mother-tongue. In Austria the Italian language prevailed. Voltaire discusses, in the article "Langue" of the Encyclopedia, the peculiarities of different languages as forms of literary expression; and in this the German is not mentioned at all. Not until Goethe's "Werther" had been devoured by the French and English, and had penetrated even into Italy, was the possibility conceded in foreign countries of German literature of a higher rank.

Attempts had often been made before Goethe's time so far to perfect the German language that expression might be found in it for the finer shades of thought; but beyond a personal circle these efforts were unsuccessful. Klopstock, Lessing, and Winckelmann, while they availed themselves of the forms of the classic languages and of French and Italian, sought to create their own German; but all without radical effect. Herder had been more successful in giving higher qualities to German prose than any other writer, save Goethe. Herder, more than any one, assisted Goethe in producing a true living German language, which later authors have been taught by him to write. This Goethe did by collecting together and turning to advantage the work of all those who had preceded him. Goethe would ascribe this service to Wieland, but he has himself in reality cast all other attempts into the shade. It was Goethe's verses which made Schiller's flow; and he lent to Schlegel the fulness whereby he converted Shakspeare almost into a German poet.

Goethe's prose has become by degrees, in all departments of intellectual life, the standard form of expression. Through Schelling it has penetrated into philosophy; through Savigny into jurisprudence; through

Alexander von Humboldt into natural science; and through Wilhelm von Humboldt into philology. We are even indebted to Goethe for our present style of letter-writing. Innumerable expressions which we now use without questioning their source, because they seem to stand so naturally at our command, would without him have been sealed to us.

Out of this unity of the language arose among us the true fellowship in higher intellectual enjoyment to which we are solely indebted for our political unity,— a unity which could never have been achieved without the unceasing activity of those whom we, in the highest sense, call "the educated," and to whom Goethe first gave the common direction.

Before Goethe there were three great poets, who exerted over the nations from which they sprung a power which may be compared with the influence of Goethe in Germany,— Homer, Dante, and Shakspeare. All that is comprehended in the term "spiritual influence" is especially to be claimed as the effect wrought by these men on Greeks, Italians, and English: each in a different way, it is true; but the success of each places them in almost equal rank. In every single Greek, Italian, and Englishman can the chain, as it were, be traced which binds him irrevocably to one of these three great leaders of the people. Without them Greece and Italy would be cold political abstractions. Homer and Dante have called into being the higher unity of Greece and Italy, which stands far above the political. And who knows what an exalted rôle Shakspeare may yet play, if the fragments of English-speaking peoples, the world over, shall at some time seek for a supreme authority in whose word they may feel themselves united? And who knows what offices are reserved for Goethe in Germany in the future changes of our destiny? But let us speak of what he has already accomplished. No poet or thinker since the time of Luther has worked in so many different directions at once, and permeated with his influence four successive generations, as Goethe has done. How wholly unlike was Voltaire's work in France! So far as quantity is concerned, Voltaire embraced far more; certainly he worked more intensively than Goethe. Also during his life his writings penetrated more instantaneously, deeply, and widely among the people. But he was not so unresistingly believed in; he did not stand upon the same moral height with Goethe. Voltaire destroyed; Goethe built up. Again, Goethe never tried to create a party for a momentary aim; he always granted his rivals full scope; his immortal weapons were too precious to be used against mortals. Goethe worked quietly and imperceptibly, like Nature herself. We see him everywhere recognized, without envy, as a man raised above men: " an Olympian, enthroned over the world," Jean Paul calls him; to whom no one could give anything, who was enough to himself. Goethe stands lifted above love and aversion. The few who have acknowledged themselves his enemies appear from the outset to have much trouble in maintaining their stand-point, while to-day they seem utterly incomprehensible. And, even as regards these, it was good fortune for any one to have been in relation with Goethe; and it was impossible to ignore him.

Almost too much appears to have been said about Goethe even now. An entire library of publications concerning him exists. This increases daily; latterly scarcely a week has passed in which, either here or there, something new about him has not been printed. And yet these labors dedicated to him are but the faint beginnings of a work which must stretch on to a boundless future. Goethe's first century only has elapsed; but to none of the following, so far as the future can be foretold, will be spared the trouble of ever anew reshaping Goethe for themselves. The German people must change their nature before they will cease to do this. For thousands of years there has been a science called Homeric, which has had its disciples in uninterrupted succession; for hundreds of years, one that bears the name of Dante, and one that bears Shakspeare's name : henceforth there will be one called Goethean. Indeed, Goethe's name long since designated not his person alone, but the circumference of a whole domain. Each generation will believe that it comprehends his nature better : never, until now, does the right stand-point seem to have been attained from which Goethe can be impartially studied. Opinions in regard to his work will vary ; he will appear to stand nearer to, or farther from, the German people, according to the character of the times : but he will never be wholly dethroned, never be resolved into himself,— never melt as a glacier, of which, when the last drop has run away, nothing remains. If, however, that should happen which has happened to Homer, that after the lapse of thousands of years, when our German shall have ceased to be a living language, wholly distant generations may be unable to conceive that a single man could have created so many and such various kinds of works,— then may the learned men, who will certainly for a time be believed, affirm that Goethe is to be interpreted only as a mythical name, under which the entire intellectual work of his age was comprehended.

It would seem as if already the time approached in which the German people, after having gone too far in their adoration of Goethe, were inclined in some degree to withdraw their homage. But this is only an appearance. A few have tried to represent Goethe as a discarded aristocrat, who had rendered his service and might rest. Such things have been said; but what begins to be strange to us about him is not what Goethe is in himself, but the image bearing his name which the last generation formed of him. We live in a new era, which must create anew its own image of him: it overthrows the old one, but does not touch *him*. To-day, more than ever, it is important that our attention should be turned to him; but another stand-point must be accepted.

This change of stand-point is the natural result of the different position we occupy in Germany to-day towards all historical inquiry. Before Germany was united and free, and stood politically on her own feet, the aim of our historical labor was to burrow into the past, out of which, as secret advocates of a course of proceeding which we did not dare openly to call by the right name, we ventured to initiate for ourselves a better Present. All historical work bore the secret motto, "It is impossible that things in Germany should remain as they are."

But within the last twenty-five years, with the aid of this scholarly labor, the revolution has been accomplished which we may now regard as finished. We possess a Present far exceeding our expectations. Its benefits are no longer something to be struggled after or hoped for, but to be held fast, developed, and utilized. With the light of this freshly dawning day, the times which lie behind us take on a new aspect. We no longer seek in them the weapons which might avail us in obtaining freedom, but we seek after those which, the struggle for liberty being successfully ended, will strengthen us in the position won, and render permanent the possession of the blessings gained. We seek to fathom the nature of historical movements, and to regulate our own in conformity to them. Many things so contemplated take on a wholly new meaning. Splendors fade, and things which were despised rise into undreamed-of importance. Goethe, to whose nature every form of agitation was foreign, and who — especially in his later years, when his opinion was most frequently asked — had the appearance and seemed to have the style of thinking of a comfortable conservative, now takes a new position as statesman and historian. We perceive in him one of those who most confidently foresaw our present freedom, and prepared the ground for it. We read with astonishment how accurately he prophesied the revolutionary agitation of the latter half of the nineteenth century. We understand how he came to look upon the dead calm in which his last years fell as an unavoidable necessity; we see how he held steadfastly in view the free future of his country, and quietly gave to his works the material needed for these days. Goethe's labor helped to create the soil on which we to-day sow and reap; he belongs among the foremost founders of German freedom; without him, in spite of all our conquests, we should be wanting in the ideas which enable us to derive the noblest benefits from them.

Naturally, when things of this kind come before us as a new discovery, the career of such a man is to be historically reconstructed.

What, then, was Goethe in his main characteristics? Among the many who struggled and aspired with him, he was the most powerful and the most successful: one for whom Fate manifestly smoothed the way; a husbandman cultivating the field of the mind, with never a sterile year, but ever the full harvest. It might be a dry or a rainy year, but Goethe always had his seed sown in the very field to which the weather was favorable. His progress was never interrupted by useless delays, to which he must look back as upon so much lost time. He was healthy, handsome, and vigorous. He always lived fully in the present and in his surroundings, and was at the same time far in advance of the general progress of mankind. With an ever-upward development, even to his latest days, he experienced the whole destiny of man on earth. It is well to consider the sum-total of his years.

Goethe had a twofold life measured out to him, whose latter half, indeed, proved most important to the full completion of that which he had begun in the earlier part. He was allowed to enter into the enjoyment of a secure and undisturbed inheritance of the conquests of his youth, as if he were his own heir and successor to the throne. To how few has been granted this privilege! The latter half of the lives of Lessing and Herder were blighted. Schiller began gradually to die just as he was beginning really to live; just as he had begun to unfold his capacities, and freely to make the most of his creative power. We recall the names of many others, whose career was interrupted before their fortieth year, although they seemed to possess a vigor which should not have been exhausted in double that number of years. It is curious to reflect with what doubtful aspects Goethe himself entered on the second portion of his life. He seemed to be intellectually exhausted. We gather from many observations made at the close of the last century and the beginning of this, that his friends in Weimar and his admirers all over Germany had resigned themselves to the idea that he had passed his prime. The cool, reserved Privy Councillor with the double chin, more and more inclining to rest; past the fiery days of youth, — in stately ease he keeps aloof from men and things; he turns aside from whatever reminds him of the old times. He sees again his friends the Jacobis in Düsseldorf, and will read something aloud to them: they put "Iphigenia" into his hand, but he lays the book aside; it is disagreeable to him to touch again the old feelings. It is only an accident if something in the verses which he now writes here and there reminds us of what once charmed in his poetry. Even those who stand nearest to him realize this change. They pity him, but they must regard it as a change in some degree common to all men. Around him, also, has grown up a new generation (about whom he scarcely troubles himself), who would like nothing better than to shake off the burdensome authority of the old Dictator. As a result of the French Revolution there prevailed in Germany new and unfavorable conditions, with which Goethe was unwilling to have anything to do, or indeed even to try to understand. Schiller was the man of the day; and, after he had passed away, there seemed no one left to fill his and the former Goethe's place.

But Goethe soars again! "Faust" appears. With this poem, in the new century, Goethe thrills all Germany as if for the first time. No one had expected anything so great. Once more he carries the young away with him, while their elders return to their allegiance. Not until this time had he taken complete possession of Germany. There had always been men among us who had not felt drawn to him. Baron Von Stein until now had never read any of Goethe's works, and now first makes his acquaintance. Goethe's influence manifests itself after this in quite a different way from what it had done earlier. On all sides he gains the ascendancy. It now seems as if he only needed to stretch out his hand to have his power realized.

Goethe had enjoyed what are called the best gifts of Fate : he had come at the right time, and the right time had lasted for him as long as is permitted to mortal man. But we pass on now to speak of the higher gifts, — the highest gifts of Fate ; and here we see an harmonious development of spiritual power, which had perhaps fallen to the share of others before him, but which we have never been able to observe in any one as we may observe it in him. It seemed as if Providence had placed him in the simplest circumstances, in order that nothing should impede his perfect unfolding. With a very few words his whole outward life is stated.

The child of rich people in Frankfort, he returns after the ordinary university course is ended to his native town, a gradually declining Free City, to practise law. Meeting by accident a Prince, who himself had but just attained his majority, he wins his confidence, almost in a childlike way, and follows him to Weimar, there to take his position as Prime Minister and Court Poet.

To the end, Goethe was never anything but Prime Minister and Court Poet of Weimar. He lived there almost uninterruptedly, and his whole story is included in this.

But now we see how, in the course of years, he moulds and shapes these at first merely outward circumstances until they are exactly adapted to his necessities ; and then how he remodels Weimar itself, until it becomes by degrees a perfectly satisfactory soil to his individual nature, into which he penetrates deeply with wide-spread roots, and out of which he creates finally the principal literary city of Germany. Goethe was the ideal centre of his new Thuringian fatherland from the day of his first appearance in it, and raised it with himself to immortal renown.

And now we can follow, step by step, the way in which this was accomplished.

Goethe was not the poet lost in dreams, nor the writer sitting behind closed doors, whom nobody dared to disturb. His poetical creations imperceptibly perfected themselves, making small demands on his time. Apparently they were merely amusements for leisure hours, of which it was best to say as little as possible, lest they should interfere with that which he considered the proper task of his daily life. Goethe had time for every one. When he was advocate in Frankfort, and also when he was minister in Weimar, in law and government, he attended to everything down to the smallest detail, and threw himself into the breach with the weight of his personal power and his own knowledge of the facts, wherever the carrying through of measures for the public good was under discussion. Goethe was the first member of the administration in Weimar, and remained so after he had nominally withdrawn himself from business affairs. He not only received the salary of a minister, but he gave the fullest possible equivalent for that salary. He always bore in his heart the destiny of the Duke and of the country for which he was responsible. Always, even to the last, his personal authority was next to the Grand Duke's. If he spoke of the scientific institutions of Jena, it was just as natural for him to say " my " institutions as " our."

Added to these labors, as the most responsible officer of the government, was his second work as a scholar. There was no department of knowledge, with perhaps the sole exception of pure mathematics, the progress of which he did not constantly follow. As naturalist as well as historian—meaning by these words to designate, in the most direct way, the extent of all philological and philosophical knowledge — he worked with such zeal and success that his result in either one or the other of these directions would have satisfactorily filled the whole measure of the life of a man. His discoveries are known. The value of his co-operation and sympathy was inestimable to learned men. He was familiar with many languages, and in his old age able to master new ones.

The oversight of a university devolved upon him, which in those days was of far greater importance to Germany than it is now, where he called into existence or promoted institutions for scientific purposes, organized public criticism and prescribed its direction. And to these duties he added for many years the office of director of the Weimar theatre, with here also the most painstaking responsibility in regard to technical and æsthetic details. And finally all these were only subordinate to the duties of his seemingly highest office; namely, personal intercourse with countless people of all ages and in every position, which to his contemporaries appeared to be the real aim of his life.

Goethe, without willing it, forced himself upon the thoughts of men. He was incessantly talked of in Weimar from the first day of his appearance there until the last day of his life. Every one there was conscious of his presence, and kept eyes and ears open for him. If ever he were not talked of in Weimar, it was because it was simply impossible to speak only of him. If we meet with a letter anywhere which in the course of his life was written at Weimar, we seek involuntarily for the mention of Goethe in it, and are surprised if it is omitted. If the people have nothing else to say, they announce at least whether Goethe is at home, or on a journey,— mentioning the last as an abnormal circumstance, as if they had a right to his presence among them.

But his spiritual presence all Germany claimed. From unexpected quarters fresh proofs arise continually of the extent of Goethe's influence with his contemporaries. If one reads his correspondence (of which a great part is still unpublished), one believes he did nothing but receive and answer letters,—and these letters treat of all the interests which were afloat in the course of an epoch. With a tact, conscientiousness, assurance, and dexterity, and at the same time with a hearty enjoyment which never allows him to appear bored, but always in the best humor, he holds all the threads in his hand and continually adds new ones; so that what he achieves in this direction alone seems to prove him endowed with superhuman power. He treats every one according to his nature, often with a touching self-forgetfulness. Every one who comes in contact with him, by the instant surrender of himself, makes the highest demands upon Goethe; and he fulfils them all. He enters into the details of everybody's case as if he were interested in nothing on earth but precisely this. He talks with each one of his specialty as if it were his own. He wins the confidence of all. Men yield themselves to him like children, and he listens to each story as if nothing had ever moved him so deeply. Only once in life to have spoken with Goethe, or to have received a letter from him, was the most brilliant episode in the experience of many whose lives in the main could not be said to have been obscure.

I spoke in the beginning of the second great period in Goethe's life.

Forty years, as intellectual autocrat, Goethe ruled all Germany. He had, as it were, ambassadors at all the Courts who were his champions. He has been sarcastically called *Kunstpabst* (Art Pope); and indeed he did represent something which could be so denominated, taking art in its widest range. There went out from him an irresistible authority. In undertakings of the highest kind, his favor and approval were not likely to be dispensed with. He did not always grant them without hesitation, and he sometimes refused them: he had his fixed policy, his traditional and fundamental convictions. Early in the nineteenth century the language of Goethe began to be generally accepted, and was employed by Goethe himself as an established idiom. And all this power grew slowly in a natural way as the trees grow, and without the slightest reference to literary panegyrics. Goethe had such an aversion to being forced upon the public that he too often incurred the reproach of being intentionally reserved. His calm, self-sustained personality overcame all opposition. There was much spoken and written in Goethe's favor from the beginning, but it could all have remained unsaid and unprinted without in the least affecting his grand position.

So he finally died, after having lived to a great age. The entire land was overwhelmed by his loss. Men felt forlorn and orphaned. But men had to get on without him, and finally they did; for all that we have recounted as Goethe's labor was as mortal as himself.

But now the immortal! As a mighty current on whose surface one neither sows nor reaps is yet the great stream which gives life to the land, and without which the people would be famished and desolate, so the stream of Goethe's poetry still enriches and animates the fields through which it flows. However much he gave himself to the throng of men and affairs, at the same time he was solitary; and nothing shared his solitude save what he there created of his own power to be immortal.

Goethe had the inconceivable capacity of living in two worlds at once,— two worlds which he wholly united, and which he held at the same time wholly distinct. One by one the incidents of his mortal life will contract to our view. With fewer words constantly shall we dispose of it. Ever more alone will he seem to stand, until finally nothing will remain but Goethe, creator of beings of fresh and immortal power.

Whoever speaks as if Goethe's epoch was past should ask himself, Could we in Germany to-day spare Iphigenia, Egmont, Faust, Gretchen, Clärchen, or Dorothea? Do they begin to fade; does what they say sound like old hackneyed melodies; are they puppets with which the children have amused themselves long enough? As little is this so as with Homer's Achilles and Ulysses, or with Shakspeare's Hamlet and Juliet! Goethe lives no more: a very old man, he died half a century ago; Shakspeare two hundred and fifty, Homer three thousand years ago: but they have left behind to their children the dowry of imperishable youth; their blood flows forever warm, and they have lost none of their first power. When we who are here to-day shall sit as old people in the theatre, perhaps some eighteen-year-old Gretchen will come upon the stage, and, as if her sad destiny had never been wept before, draw tears from eyes of which we to-day know nothing. Homer, Shakspeare, and Goethe himself in their immortal creations touch our hearts. So living are their creations that we almost think they are the legitimate children of Nature, instead of having been called out of nothing by the fertile, inventive imagination of a poet.

But the times when Goethe will be such a stranger to us are still far in the future.

In the mean time we rejoice in the overflowing sources

of information with regard to his life. To us a most important task remains, which is to shape out of the abundant testimony that image of Goethe which will be the most helpful, and in which we can have the most confidence. Let us now attempt in these Lectures to form this image.

LECTURE II.

PLAN OF THE LECTURES. — GOETHE'S FIRST FRANKFORT DAYS. — STUDY OF LAW IN LEIPSIC. — CHANGE TO STRASBURG.

GOETHE'S life is divided into two periods, of unequal length, — the Frankfort period, from 1749 to 1776; and the Weimar period, from 1776 to 1832.

Almost all his greatest works were begun in the Frankfort period; "Werther," "Götz," and "Clavigo" were then published.

The Weimar period must also be divided. A complete episode is concluded in the first ten years, extending from his twenty-sixth to his thirty-sixth year. When he went to Weimar, he resigned the idea of devoting himself wholly to poetry. Having accepted a place of great responsibility, he determined to be governed solely by the desire to devote his whole ability to the service of the Prince and the interests of his people. Only his leisure hours were to be reserved for poetry. In this epoch "Iphigenia" was finished in its prose form; and "Tasso," "Egmont," "Wilhelm Meister," and "Faust" (for all of which he had brought materials with him from Frankfort) were carried forward.

Then follows the one striking year in Italy, which divides the Weimar epoch. We may regard this brief period, so rich in its experiences (from 1786 to 1787), either as the conclusion of the first, or as the beginning

MATERIALS FOR THE STUDY. 19

of the second period. In it "Tasso," "Iphigenia," and "Egmont" received a new and perfect form, while "Wilhelm Meister" and "Faust" progressed. Goethe returns to Weimar, and the last and longest period of his life begins. The struggle in his breast as to what he shall demand of himself, and what others have a right to demand of him, is over. Independent of outward co-operation, a calm, steady development goes on within him until he attains absolute intellectual clearness. Even the companionship with Schiller, which for a number of years affected him so deeply, makes no special break in his life. In this long course of years follow, one upon another, the completion of "Wilhelm Meister," "Hermann und Dorothea," "Die Natürliche Tochter," "Das Buch über Winckelmann," "Die Wahlverwandtschaften," "Dichtung und Wahrheit," "Die italiänische Reise,'" "Der westöstliche Divan," and "Faust." At every stage we meet "Faust." Goethe began it as a student, and never ceased to occupy himself with it. Its conclusion was left in manuscript, and not printed until after his death.

In this historical sketch of Goethe, let us connect the incidents of his life with his principal works as they appear in the course of the three epochs, thus adopting the simplest plan for our Lectures. My delineation will be based not on any peculiar arrangement of my own, but will follow the natural divisions of his life and the progress of his works.

The material afforded us for the study of Goethe's life is very extensive; and of this, in order to give an idea of the whole, my division will be somewhat arbitrary. But it is of little moment what categories we accept if only they are comprehensive. I divide the material into two parts, — his own account, and the testimony of others. What a field is opened to our investigation by the extraordinary breadth of his intercourse, which reached to the time of his death, with several generations of contemporaries! During the fifty years in which Goethe was in full possession of his powers scarcely a significant man lived in Germany who was not almost forced, at least once in his life, to describe the relation he bore to Goethe, formed either by his personal intercourse with the poet or through his works. These judgments, confessions, or whatever form their writers gave them, have been often collected, and whole series of such intellectual associations made the subject of special investigation. But we have not yet reached the end of even the preliminary work; and in all directions additional material is being collected.

Goethe's personal evidence is of three kinds: first, his works, as the most important gauge of his growing power; second, his diary and letters, as the most trustworthy records of each day and hour; third, his own biographical attempts, showing how his life, as a completed work, stood in his own eyes.

Our second division of the biographical material here is of immense scope. Its extent is not yet wholly known. Goethe's works lie in many editions before us; but we can follow only certain of them through all the stages of their development. Many letters, and the like, are still wanting. Entire correspondences are missing, or in a mutilated form; and only the smallest part of his diaries is known. But what we possess is so much that it requires some experience to find our way through the labyrinth.

Unceasingly to render an account to himself and others of his thoughts and actions was Goethe's peculiarity. It seems as if Nature had foreseen that every hour of his life would be of importance, and had furnished Goethe with a wholly extraordinary capacity to gratify our desire for knowledge in this respect. Goethe was the greatest reporting genius; pen and paper were his natural tools. In moments of intense enthusiasm, when alone with himself, unless his thoughts become a poem, he knows no better outlet for his emotions than to write down, as faithfully as possible, all he feels. Now-a-days we have so completely lost the habit of committing our thoughts and feelings to paper, that this peculiarity of a former generation calls for especial remark. In the very moment of feeling, people in Goethe's time sought to represent their emotion in words, and thus to enhance their enjoyment, — not consciously for others, but for themselves, and not with the intention of producing a literary effect. They fell upon pen and paper as if it were impossible to feel without recording what was felt.

Of such pages we have a quantity from Goethe's own hand. Many of his works are, as it were, composed of them; and all record inward experiences so transformed by imagination that the individual is eliminated and resolved into the universal. Various persons in the same story are often repetitions of their author; so that, in many dialogues, it is only Goethe talking with himself. Therefore his works, unless abused by indiscreet interpretation, furnish most important material for the story of his life.

I will now proceed to contemplate this life. As a source of information with regard to the first Frankfort period, Dr. Solomon Hirzel, in Leipsic, has published, excellently arranged, the whole series of Goethe's own testimony. Hirzel was in possession of the fullest collection of Goethe's printed and written works. His chronological index of this Goethe library, which appeared in manuscript from time to time, had long been an indispensable source of information. "The Young Goethe" consists of letters and works, chronologically arranged, in three volumes. The works are given in their original form. To-day they are usually read in the form which, at a later period, Goethe himself gave them. The curious, faded manuscripts and printed pages, which in many cases Hirzel's eyes alone had rested on, were now made accessible to everybody.

Still, the principal source for the clear understanding of Goethe's childhood and youth was, and remains, his own narration. Under the title, "Wahrheit und Dichtung," it is in the possession of all the world. We are so accustomed to this title, "Wahrheit und Dichtung," that the form "Dichtung und Wahrheit," which was lately proved to have been the original one, will only slowly be accepted. Goethe's secretary, Riemer, made the inversion, and we next find it in G. von Loeper's latest and best edition of the work. Goethe composed this autobiography on a basis of insufficient material. He was almost sixty years old before he earnestly attempted it. He had been accustomed carefully to collect and place in order everything of importance which he wished to remember; but in spite of this he had to bewail a great gap of his own making. In the year 1797, — previous to a second intended trip to Italy, which was prevented by the war, — he had burned all the letters he had received up to that time. To us the loss does not seem so great, because Goethe's own letters have by degrees come to light, and are now at our service; but he could avail himself of very few of these, as it was not until later that he adopted the habit of retaining copies of his letters. What he drew from sources at present concealed will later become known to the public through the publication of the Goethe Archives, to which at present no one is allowed access. Goethe's heirs, guided by motives not understood, hold the bequest of their great ancestor under lock and key, thereby making it in the highest degree difficult to prepare a thoroughly satisfactory edition of his works. Since these important papers are withheld, and all efforts to obtain them prove fruitless, there remains only the hope that possibly the authorities may buy Goethe's house and its contents for the benefit of the nation.

How much help these family papers afforded Goethe for his work we know not. From his autobiography it is evident that many of the occurrences he relates had taken a mythical form in his memory. Still, we cannot decide whether to assume a sort of organic confusion, such as always arises when memory unaided is called to judge past events, or whether to believe that Goethe, intending to make of his biography a work of art, purposely displaces dates and events; enough that such variation is proved. It might therefore appear that Goethe, conscious of this state of things, chose the title of "Dichtung und Wahrheit" because fiction filled the first place in books. Nevertheless, this was not so. Nowhere can it be proved that Goethe added anything to the actual incidents of his life; nowhere do we perceive any violation of the true coloring. Whatever new fountains of information are open to us confirm for the most part Goethe's narration. What mistakes or transformations are brought to light are trifling by the side of the striking truth with which events and characters are in the main represented. We possess in Goethe's autobiography a narration which can be designated as a most truthful one throughout.

Certainly, the combination of the two words *dichtung* and *wahrheit* sounds like a challenge. This was instantly perceived by Goethe's friends and taken advantage of by his enemies, and finally led him (although he usually took no heed of such things) to explain his meaning. He has done this in several places, so that to-day no doubt exists as to what he intended by the title of "Dichtung und Wahrheit." Goethe declared he had chosen to relate only the circumstances of his life, which, when looking back upon them, seemed to him the steps in his development. Allowing all else to escape, the part chosen by him received a simpler, nobler, more artistic construction, though needing some connecting links; and so far it became a work of fiction. But at the same time the truth was not sacrificed.

This handling increased not only the beauty but the value of the book. It is more important for us to see how Goethe's childhood and youth, as related to his whole life, mirror themselves in his soul, and where he discovers the first steps in his future career, than to have a great mass of authentic detail, which by no skill in mere arrangement could ever become an organic whole.

Goethe, in thus representing his life in "Dichtung und Wahrheit," gives an account of the Frankfort period only. It extends to his departure from Frankfort for Weimar in the year 1775. It seemed to him that he had done enough, perhaps all that was possible, in showing how the child developed into the man. For the representation of his later life he adopted the annalistic form. He then preserved according to a definite method complete records of each year. A comparison of the two methods enables us to realize how much we are indebted to the earlier one.

"Dichtung und Wahrheit" has given the earlier years of Goethe's life their decidedly greater importance, and has placed by the side of the grand, mature Goethe the young Goethe, as a special creation in our literary his-

THE HOME AT FRANKFORT. 25

tory. Without "Dichtung und Wahrheit" Hirzell's three volumes would be scarcely comprehensible. Perhaps it would have been better had Hirzell made a fourth of "Dichtung und Wahrheit." The letters alone do not explain why these early works are presented again in the antique dress which Goethe himself later changed for the form in which he wished them to be read.

Goethe's Weimar life pales by the side of the clear sunbeam which streams from "Dichtung und Wahrheit." Even "Die italiänische Reise," in which Goethe gives an account of what were for him, perhaps, the most important years of his life, is not to be compared with it. So far as I am acquainted with literature, there is only one work which can be said to rival "Dichtung und Wahrheit,"— perhaps the very one whose method Goethe followed, — "The Confessions" of Jean Jacques Rousseau, in which he, too, narrates only the first half of his life, and in which we find the same wonderful blending of the individual with the universal which poets alone have the power to achieve.

It is well known that Goethe was born in Frankfort-on-the-Main, on the 28th of August, 1749. His father's house still stands in the Hirschgraben. It is inwardly and outwardly somewhat changed, but the company which bought it have restored, so far as possible, its early appearance, and have filled it with a variety of relics concerning former changes: the account of the rebuilding ordered by Goethe's father, with the odd pedantry so characteristic of him, is one of the best known episodes in "Dichtung und Wahrheit." Goethe's mother sold the house; and we cannot now say with certainty which was Goethe's room. That it was a Mansard room we know from his autobiography, and from letters dated there. He describes the view from the window, reaching over houses and gardens far as the horizon, and the ever-flowing fountain below in the court. We believe that we breathe the air which he breathed, and watch the same floating clouds which his eyes followed. Through his whole life Goethe loved to describe the spot where he was, — to analyze, as it were, the atmosphere which surrounded him. In his works the locality is described with such exactness, and so kept in view, that maps might be drawn of the paths through which his imaginary beings wandered. The roar of the sea across whose waves Iphigenia's eyes sought her home no one since Homer has brought so distinctly to our ears. The park in which the drama of the "Wahlverwandtschaften" was played is as familiar as if we had trodden every avenue in it. The house in Frankfort stands so vividly before us that we could find our way about it in the dark. In thus building up from the firm earth the story of his childhood, Goethe gives his narration that high degree of credibility which makes it so attractive.

With the same accuracy does he describe his native city. What would the old Frankfort be to-day without this most distinguished of all chroniclers? What "Dichtung und Wahrheit" left untouched Goethe's letters added. At all hours of the day and in all seasons of the year he leads us through the streets of the venerable city. On New Year's Eve we listen with him at the open window; and every sound which breaks upon our ear in the stillness of night thrills us. From the Main bridge we watch the dark waves as they stream toward him in the weird moonlight. At break of day we hear with him the awakening of the city traffic. Goethe is inexhaustible in terms and forms of expression by which he arrests and communicates the fleeting sentiment or presentiment of the moment.

Nevertheless, we now look at these Frankfort things, which Goethe so graphically described, from a greater distance, and more as if in a bird's perspective. We ask about the position which the old and free Reichsstadt occupied in Germany in the middle of the last century. Goethe describes times already too long past for us. Men's minds have no longer any knowledge of the state of things which, when Goethe wrote, were still fresh enough in the memory of all.

Cities are passing historical phenomena. They arise and fade away. To-day, when all boundary lines grow faint, — when in Germany, thanks to railroads, every city seems almost like the suburb of some other city, — we can scarcely conceive the time when, surrounded by immovable walls, a number of independent republics, sole centres of education, covered the German soil. In the thirteenth century these states within the state — the German Free Cities — formed a political alliance. They were fortified; each had its own peculiar constitution; and all resolved to close their gates, even against the Emperor himself, if he should attempt to interfere with their freedom.

Republics have always been based upon the sovereignty of a few powerful families, and this was true of the German Free Cities. Their heroic time was from the thirteenth to the fifteenth century. Their power was destroyed in the age of the Reformation, when it became apparent that great ideas can only gain ground when every individual, even the most insignificant, may be appealed to. Events did not go so far at that time as to give the power to the masses; but the supremacy was placed in the hands of those whom the masses outside the cities willingly obeyed, — the princes of the land. Moreover, the old and powerful families in the cities were dying out, as is always the case when a certain number of generations continue without any influx of fresh blood. This influx failed. The great mass of the people no longer pressed inside the cities to reinvigorate their blood, too fast becoming exhausted, and it appeared more lucrative to serve princes than to obey citizens.

So matters stood in the age of the Reformation. The transition went on slowly and imperceptibly, for the power of the princes grew but gradually; and the strength of the cities was by no means broken when the Thirty Years' War — a frightful malady, brought upon us from without, and artificially nourished — blighted all the young shoots of our development.

The significance of this war in the history of human culture was never so clearly presented to my mind as when, in the retired Boboli Gardens in Florence, I read an inscription on a monument erected in the sixteenth century. It was dedicated to "The Public Felicity" which "permitted all the arts of peace to flourish in Italy, while abroad devastating war had trampled down all the growths of peace to their very roots." The Thirty Years' War left among us both physical and spiritual stagnation, and when peace smiled again on the German waste men found that they had become older, — but nothing more. Principalities and cities still existed, but the first were as much exhausted as the latter. Slowly and gradually the power of the land-princes rose, and that of the cities fell; but, beyond that, everything stood still in Germany. It seemed impossible that anything could hasten the national development.

So we see Goethe born among conditions which a draft of air, such as to-day blows around every corner, would have destroyed, root and branch. And yet they continued as undisturbed as if their pasteboard foundations had actually been hewn out of solid rock. It is this mere fiction of an individual political existence which Goethe represents so vividly in his description of Frankfort, his native city.

The Imperial Cities were, in 1750, still enthroned, free, proud, and unmolested, with walls, towers, and gates. Their " bürgers " still moved majestically, with the pomp of traditional government-machinery clothed with the glimmer of time-honored magnificence. A huge amount of mutual homage in all imaginable forms was daily required and rendered. It was high treason to question any of these forms! But it would have been impossible, even in a dream, to fancy these pompous old citizens really in arms prepared to defend their walls, or to come out in battle array, as the Nürnbergers did under Pyrkheimer, to reinforce the imperial troops. Hard-baked in their own fat like some curious old cake, covered with sugar and dotted with raisins, these gentry believed themselves sufficiently protected if they could find their way amid the intricate maze of rights and privileges on which their existence was based, — the magistrates without initiative, the citizens without a suspicion that anything could possibly be changed! The idea of a political union in Germany, a rising of the whole nation, was inconceivable, — no representation of interests, no rights of debate, no parties in the sense of to-day, not even desires in common! Every city for itself, every house for itself, and each citizen for himself.

This must be considered in order to appreciate the inestimable value of the single independent element among us in those times; namely, literature. There were no political institutions in Germany, where the free, energetic character of a man could be developed; but there was among us the Republic of Letters!

Scholars and poets alone had opportunities of touching the mass of the people. To them alone was it permitted to manifest their enthusiasm publicly and to develop themselves, surrounded by an expectant, sympathetic circle, which at that time — not so indistinct and formless as now, but better disciplined and with purer personal relations — assisted and sustained the men who had once gained its confidence, and who at the same time depended upon its support.

Goethe's narrative of his childhood and youth contains the following: A boy is described, who grows up on the most luxurious soil of this Free-City life. His father — a rich, pedantic, punctilious man — educates and trains his son for the agreeable continuance of a life like his own. From the moment the boy steps out of his childhood coarse and fine threads are laid around him on all sides, from which the net is spun out of which escape seems year by year less possible. But in the boy the desire for freedom becomes ever stronger, as he realizes that the more desperately he exerts himself to escape the more tightly his chains are fastened about him; until at the last moment, when, as we see, it seems impossible for him to gain freedom, he wrenches himself away, and, leaving his native city forever, seeks and finds a soil wholly suited to the development of his nature. To show that this was the purport of his youth seemed to Goethe of the utmost importance. His later experiences have nothing in common with this first grand climax in his life. This is the reason why "Dichtung und Wahrheit" breaks off at the point where Goethe's Frankfort history ends.

Goethe's father was an Imperial Councillor. He had procured this dignity for himself, that he might by a sounding title compensate for his lack of old patrician blood. His family did not belong to the aristocrats. In

HIS EARLY EDUCATION. 31

Krieg's published account of Frankfort life in Goethe's youth new light has lately been thrown on these matters. Goethe's mother's relations were judges and mayors, but his father never held any public office : to the son should be given what to the father had been denied. All the other children had died early. Wolfgang and his sister Cornelia alone remained to be submitted to the father's experiments in education, and the father lived henceforth for this single purpose. They grew up under a guardianship such as is rarely the lot of the children of this generation. Young Goethe was educated with an intensity which would frighten our children, and that not with severity, but through his father's unintermitting watchfulness. No city authorities at that time presumed to decide how children should be treated regarding most important details, as is the case at present, when by a decree of the State a certain quantity of fresh air is pumped into every child's room. Goethe describes amid what curiously conflicting influences his mind was early developed. In the warm lap of his family he felt no rough breath of actual life ; no blasts like those among which Schiller worked his way to eminence ; no trace of the indigence of Lessing, or the wretched poverty of Winckelmann, who, in all weathers, were exposed under an open sky, and only here and there gladdened by a mild sunbeam. In Goethe's case the gifts of this world were in excess ; but united with this abundance was an entire deprivation of personal freedom, against which no resistance seemed possible, because it enveloped him like a fine ether. Goethe was better prepared for intercourse with women than men, owing to the fact that he had been educated for the most part with his sister. In the midst of the all-powerful city gossip, which at that time supplied the place of newspapers and public life, he soon learned to move as a skilled diplomat between the families with whom relationship brought him in contact. He knows how to win his way to the confidence of the many originals who had spun themselves into all sorts of odd webs in out-of-the-way places, where they allowed no strange hands to meddle with them. He ransacks the corners of the city and understands more and more of its organism, of which he considers himself a part. What more natural than that out of this knowledge should arise the conviction that sooner or later it would be his fate to be an active participator in all these whimsical doings? What other plans could Providence have for him? Where but in Frankfort could a future be prepared for him? Germany had then no central point attracting young talent with mysterious and irresistible force. We possessed no Paris, which received Corneille, Racine, and Molière (indifferent whence they came), when their hour struck; no London, to which Shakspeare fled from Stratford; no Berlin, now drawing to itself all rising talent. What city could have enticed from Frankfort the son of a rich bürger? Vienna was far away, — a Catholic, half Italian, half Spanish residence. Berlin was poor, and seemed at that time as far removed from the rich centre of Germany as St. Petersburg is to-day.

And so we see Goethe depart at sixteen years of age to study law at Leipsic, with his plan of life already mapped out. He will take his degree, return home, enter on his practice as a lawyer, marry a rich patrician's daughter, take possession of his father's house, receive by degrees the city honors, and possibly once before he dies fill the position of mayor.

We read in " Dichtung und Wahrheit," and find it confirmed in the meagrely-preserved correspondence of these years, that he did little more as a Leipsic student than to continue the narrow life begun in **Frankfort**. Certainly the Elbe and the Pleisse flowed through a land different from the picturesque country watered by the Main and the Rhine. Everything was new in Leipsic, and yet wholly the same. Here, also, stagnation reigned, walled in and protected by a reverence for old customs. It is true that the general intellectual commotion, which, rising in France, thrilled all Europe, vibrated almost imperceptibly in Leipsic. Lessing and Herder were already at work, and had made a sensation in Germany. But Gellert and Gottsched still remained the leading men in Leipsic, the two oracles from whom the student of literature took his cue. Gottsched, the pedantic empty-headed representative of the old French culture, so deliciously sketched by Goethe in his impertinent Grandezza; Gellert, old and inflexible, of somewhat finer mental fibre, — both kept pace with the progress of things, but even while imitating did not understand. Gellert wrought his old-fashioned plots into the new form of sentimental comedy, and composed a panegyric on it. He even made of his own novel, " Die schwedische Gräfin," a perfect extravaganza, which rivals the latest sensation novels. And yet he is in every respect antiquated. I had for Gellert a special personal reverence : he was the favorite writer of my dearly-loved mother, who repeatedly and fervently commended his songs to me. From his works, which I had early received as a gift, I made excerpts for the "Wörter Buch," and thereby obtained a more exact knowledge of them than I should otherwise have had. But I cannot help finding in Gellert's character a mixture of benevolence and humanity with servility and dryness, and an absence of breadth and freedom of thought which is insufferable. Goethe revered Gellert, but never approached him. He was vexed that Gellert ignored the new writers, whom the young generation respected, and, in his lectures on literature, passed them over as if they did not exist. Goethe was indebted to him for calling his attention to his handwriting, the improvement of which Gellert demanded of all his scholars, intimating that it had its moral value.

Goethe was accessible to such admonitions. In spite of all his enjoyments, a conscientious regulation of his inner life was ever conspicuous in his thoughts, and showed itself in his earliest years in the tendency toward Freemasonry and asceticism. His first letter, in the year 1764, contains a request to be admitted to one of the fraternities which at that time rose among us, and whose aim was " Virtue." This word, which to-day (although it has lost nothing of its real nobility) has become less used on account of a certain vagueness bordering on inanity, was at that time full of pregnant meaning, indicating, in an earnest, aspiring, active sense, the highest spiritual good within the reach of man.

We see Goethe in Leipsic continuing to interest himself in all the little city excitements. There prevailed here, heightened by reflection from the court of Dresden, but at the same time as a genuine native specialty, Leipsic " gallantry." The students could not go about rough-shod, like the bullies in Jena and Halle. Goethe adapted himself easily to this more refined life, seeking to visit only the families with whom his intercourse could be as free as it was delightful. He has his acquaintances among women and his love affairs; renders his homage to the ruling taste in poetical effusions; and finally returns home little changed from what he was when he left.

Shakspeare's dramas had already been much admired by Goethe; but they had not, as yet, influenced his writings. He speaks of Wieland and Shakspeare as his instructors in poetry; but, in truth, in his poetry written at that time he proves himself to be a genuine scholar of Gottsched and Gellert. He begins a translation of Corneille's "Menteur." He writes "Die Mitschuldigen"—whose earlier, if not the earliest, printed form Herzel first made known—in Alexandrines. If Goethe were not the author of this work, it would to-day be difficult for any one to read it through. Curiously enough, he had always a certain tenderness for it, and enjoyed reading it aloud.

The beginning of his lyrical productions, on the other hand, was a series of little songs, adapted to musical compositions, which then appeared in print; but it would be no marvel if we should find a French original for each of them. In their time they were little noticed, and accepted only with a half-patronizing air by Goethe's best friends. Such of them as were afterward reprinted underwent great alterations. In these little songs, which contain mere gallantries, Goethe reveals for the first time his enchanting talent for expressing a feeling by a few simple words or combinations, and, while exhausting it, showing it to be inexhaustible. In Goethe's letters, written at this time, the dependence on French taste for forms of expression is very striking. Some are outright French compositions, interspersed with verses of his own in French; and all betraying, in the arrangement as well as in the ideas, the playful French style which was so despotic at that time. Even Voltaire and Frederick, when dealing with the most serious things, could not overcome this manner. Goethe never wrote anything worthy of note in this style. In this correspondence the radiant Leipsic maidens, whom Goethe describes so charmingly in "Dichtung und Wahrheit," assume a character of mediocrity, insipidity, and littleness, which afterward

Goethe himself was obliged to see. After seven years, when he returned to Leipsic, he looked with eyes long since disenchanted on the whole manner of life there.

Otto Jahn and Freiher von Wiedermann have given us the history of Goethe's life in Leipsic. Jahn, for the first time, made Hirzel's collection useful, and justified a very proper local patriotism. The book, adorned with pleasing lithographs, excited at its appearance the liveliest interest, and stimulated an admiration for Goethe as an author in the period previous to the Weimar days, which later, when degenerated, becomes a kind of cultus, — an enthusiasm comparable to the apotheosis of the early days of Raphael in Perugia and Florence. But let us remember that if there had been no Weimar and Rome for Goethe and Raphael, very little would now be said of their youthful works or of the men themselves. He who is too eager to prophesy the grand meaning of the later masterly productions of a genius from his early attempts takes a portion of the glory from the mature powers of the man, which alone are able to create such perfection. Goethe's early works can be rightly estimated only in connection with all he accomplished; and they fall into the shade by the side of the productions of his later years.

Goethe made no acquaintances in Leipsic who had decided influence on his life. He spent three years there, felt himself quite at home, and intended to return thither after passing for the first time his autumn vacation in Frankfort. This was in 1768. He was hurried home, as it seems, because his irregular life had brought on a hemorrhage, the effects of which he could not recover from in Leipsic. Ill, and in a sad frame of mind, he returned to his father's house. He had not studied even law earnestly, and must rest for months before he would be well enough to resume his studies, as was now found advisable in Strasburg. A journey to Paris and into Italy, where his father had been, was proposed at the end of his education.

On the 19th of October, 1765, Goethe matriculated in Leipsic; on the 28th of August, 1768, he leaves for home; and on the 2d of April, 1770, he goes to Strasburg. He was already over twenty years of age.

Now begins the time when every word which drops from Goethe's pen is memorable, as of historical importance. Now, for the first time in his life, he meets a superior nature, a man whom he felt to be greater than himself.

We must now speak directly of the man who, of all his contemporaries, had the most enduring influence upon Goethe. Goethe and Herder met in Strasburg.

LECTURE III.

LIFE IN STRASBURG. — HERDER. — NEW IDEAS OF THE NINE-TEENTH CENTURY.

GOETHE'S Strasburg experiences, as well as those in Leipsic, have been enlarged upon by writers with a sort of local patriotism. He himself describes this short period with loving minuteness.

Again he enters heart and soul into the fulness of life. The inn, "Zum Geist," at which Goethe alighted, no longer exists. But we follow him to-day on his first walk from there to the Cathedral, passing the very same old houses which he passed. Many thousands since then have read from the platform of the tower Goethe's name chiselled high in the stone, and thought of him as they gazed around on the glorious extent of country, and then looked down upon the houses of the crooked city which at that time was so perfectly German that he scarcely felt himself outside his native land.

It was so essential for Goethe to see men, and to hear the world in a certain confusion whirling about him, that he was quickly drawn into a varied intercourse. "My life," as he expresses it in one of his letters, "is like a drive in a sleigh, speeding along with tinkling of bells, but with as little to satisfy the heart as there is much to fill eye and ear." Five years later, when he came to Weimar, he made use of the same figure; and at no time, in the course of his long life, did Goethe fail to have his sleigh-ride. He was always moving forward with sound of cymbals and waving of banners, with a retinue constantly about him whom he ruled, and by whom he in turn allowed himself to be ruled. In this respect Goethe was educated like the child of a prince, about whom, from his first entrance into the world, crowds of men are busy, and by whom he is surrounded to the very end of his life.

This Strasburg life, considered in the light of a sleigh-ride, Goethe has so beautifully and faithfully depicted that his representation of the town, like that of Frankfort and Leipsic, has the value of a chronicle. To-day we observe with some misgivings how the educated classes, from having become almost French, begin to return to German ways; at that time, however, the transition from genuine German to French life was just beginning, and it was hastened on by the first Revolution. In the old French kingdom these Rhine provinces were quite distinct from the others. It would never have occurred to any one at that time to claim Alsace as French soil: the Alsace soldiers were called "les troupes allemandes de sa Majesté," and the Alsace people "les sujets allemands du Roi de France." Goethe had wholly the feeling that he was continuing his studies at a German University, and even somewhat later no soul in Frankfort would have hesitated to recognize the claims of a "Strasburg Doctor."

Goethe does justice to the French as well as to the German element. He describes most charmingly the family of his French dancing-master, and not less pleasingly the costume of the German bürger maidens, — the neat, closely-fitting bodice, and the needle in the hair. He paints the festal procession of Marie Antoinette, the blooming young wife of the Dauphin. He transports us into the very midst of the curious university life, the last remnants of which have been again incorporated with the newly founded university. There is no corner of the city which he does not creep into and describe; and he makes us as familiar with the state of things at that time as if we had ourselves been present and breathed the air of Strasburg in 1770.

He describes the dinner-company of which he was a member. Two old maiden ladies, by the name of Lauth, cooked for a number of people of various ranks and ages. At the head of the table sat Dr. Salzmann, a sort of Gellert in Strasburg; an excellent, irreproachable old gentleman, born in 1722, well-known in the city, and by reason of his good citizenship a man who had won universal confidence, and, although without any special literary merit, not to be banished from literary history. His correspondence with Goethe, preserved in the Strasburg library, was destroyed in the last bombardment of the city. If Salzmann was the most respectable of the company, Lenz was the most brilliant. He, however, joined the circle later, and as tutor to two young noble Lieflanders. Lenz is, of all the friends of Goethe, the one whom he most freely recognized as a poet and his equal, and who afterward was his greatest source of trouble. But the most upright and honorable of them all was Lerse, whom Goethe immortalized in "Götz," although in the first form of the work the tall blue-eyed theologian is converted into a little black-eyed groom. It is possible that Lerse himself demanded better treatment, for, though the black eyes remain, the "little" man is changed into a "stately" one in the rewriting of the drama. Lerse did not live to be old, but died a teacher in the military school at Colmar, in 1800. At the same table sat Leopold Wagner, the first person who in Goethe's opinion was guilty of a literary theft from him, using in his play, "Die Kindermörderin," the idea of "Faust,"—a drama whose passionate, glaringly-portrayed scenes bear so little resemblance to "Faust" that, without Goethe's express declaration of plagiarism, we should scarcely have suspected it. It has been believed that Goethe wished to revenge himself on Wagner by giving to Faust's Famulus, who is the type of the narrow, pedantic bookworm, the name of Wagner; and in all the old puppet-shows we find that Faust's associate is called Wagner. Nor was this the only time that Leopold Wagner came into literary collision with Goethe. He is the only person who, later in life, forced Goethe to give a public explanation concerning some literary matters.

The most prominent man at the table was Jung, better known by his *nom de plume* of "Jung Stilling." His autobiography will always be one of the books no one can repent having read. Jung Stilling, born in 1740, raised himself from the condition of a peasant boy to be a journeyman tailor, a school-master, and lastly to the position of professor and renowned oculist. Jung lived wholly in his idea. He was one of the leading Pietists of the last century, a widely disseminated religious sect, whose members believed themselves to stand in direct intercourse with the ruling powers of Nature.

Goethe had from his childhood a similar tendency, and was only radically cured of it by his experiences with Lavater. But it was only the person from whom he then turned aside, not the thing itself. Fräulein von Klettenberg, who had so great an influence on his early development and whose memory he held dear all his life, was the purest and noblest representative of this form of Christianity, which, by the effect of the French Revolution, was so wholly uprooted among us that the remnant which still exists gives no idea of its earlier significance. The "communications" of the Spiritualists of England and America to-day may be compared with it, bearing in mind the fact that, instead of the prosaic coarseness with which these matters are now handled, they were then treated with the delicacy which was a characteristic of European life before the French Revolution.

Jung Stilling's biography contains one of the earliest remarks of a contemporary about young Goethe. He describes the first meeting with him at 13 Krammergasse, where the gentlewomen Lauth resided. He had gone there with a friend, and, being the first that day at table, watched the company assemble for dinner. "One, especially, with large clear eyes, splendid brow, fine figure, came into the room, full of animation." He impressed them instantly. "He must be an extraordinary man," remarked Jung's companion softly to him. Jung assented, but feared "they might be somewhat annoyed by him, — he seemed such a wild, rolicking fellow;" to which the other added, "Here it is best to withhold one's opinion for a fortnight." No notice, however, was taken of Jung and his friend, except that Goethe "sometimes rolled his eyes toward them." But soon an opportunity occurred for him to do more. An apothecary from Vienna, who was of the dinner-company, gave this opportunity. Jung wore an old round wig, which, for economy, he insisted on retaining to its last hair; and the Vienna man, with a glance at this bit of antiquity, put the question: "Whether they thought Adam had worn a round wig in Paradise?" Goethe now interfered in a way which made Jung his friend for life. Goethe edited Jung's autobiography.

Dr. Salzmann was the founder of the German Association, to which Goethe was admitted. Goethe had gone to Strasburg with the idea of becoming a thorough French scholar, and of going on to Paris later to receive the final polish. He describes how these plans were counteracted. It came over him and his companions like an unexpected discovery, that French literature was insipid. The young people felt that it was old and exhausted, though they were not prejudiced against it by any of the political ideas of to-day. They did not themselves know under what influence they stood. Rousseau's renowned "Contrat Social," which at that time agitated the world, was but indifferent reading to them, and gave them no new ideas. On the other hand, Shakspeare was revered. In power and originality he appeared to surpass everything else in the whole sphere of literature.

Such was the beginning of Goethe's life at Strasburg. From all sides the advantages poured in upon him which ordinary life brings with it to those who have wealth and introductions to the most desirable people, and are also richly endowed by Nature. But how much must be added to such abundance by special accident, if all these favored conditions are really to be made serviceable, is proved also in his case. The man had yet to come who was to teach Goethe to recognize the world as a living whole; who would show him the way whither this whole is moving, and how the individual must exert himself in order to take part in the great work whose result we call the progress of humanity. To render Goethe this service was the mission of Herder, who appeared in Strasburg in the autumn of 1771.

We are accustomed now-a-days to consider Herder only as among those grouped around the pedestal on which Goethe stands in solitary grandeur; but when Herder and Goethe first met in Strasburg, it soon became

Goethe's highest wish merely to revolve around Herder as his planet. What was wanting in Herder's career has already been mentioned: the latter half of his life did not yield him the joyous, prolific harvest which the great result of his early days promised. And yet in his youth he had been marvellously fitted out for this early career. Those privations were his lot which to conquer is an indispensable part of the education of energetic natures, — loneliness and solitude, which develop all the powers of resistance in man, and without which it is almost impossible to attain reliance on oneself, or that stoical bravery, that indifference to the caprices of outward life, which passionate natures need in order to pursue steadfastly their own way. As the best of all the gifts of fate, a friend was early given to Herder; and this friend's doctrines offered worthy problems to test his ability, at a time when his thoughts would not otherwise have been called to them.

Herder was born in Mohrungen, in 1744, into a family not absolutely poor, but in straitened circumstances. At twenty years of age, when Goethe still sat aimless and unprepared for the duties of life in his father's house, Herder, having long passed his student years, had received the position of preacher at Riga on the ground of his "Fragments on German Literature," which had made him famous. During his years of study, 1762 to 1764, he had become acquainted in Königsberg with the man who first directed his thoughts to the highest aims, — Hamann. It is difficult to speak of Hamann. He stands too much outside of the great lines on which the men of the past are drawn up that we may review them. Hamann must be studied; the casual observer finds in him little of general interest or significance. He has been called the "Magus of the North." Goethe said that his writings would be read hereafter like Sibylline books. Hamann sought to embody his thoughts, as it were, in philosophic and magic formulas. A magic formula is one which produces a sudden effect with words seemingly incomprehensible, or even inconsistent. Hamann has written pages which instantly arrest attention, fill us with expectation, and hold us captive, but whose meaning only dawns upon us gradually and after repeated readings. Their deep contents disclose themselves as if a real illumination irradiated them. He who finally understands Hamann ranks him among the heroes of literature, and we constantly meet with eminent scholars who devote their entire faculties to the study of his writings. The story of his outer life is scarcely credible. For the sake of his daily bread he held a subordinate office, lived in continual embarrassment, and showed in all his dealings a mixture of obstinacy and docility which is rarely to be seen. He goes to the bottom of everything.

To a young and fiery mind like Herder's nothing could be more beneficial than intimate communion with such a spirit during the years when he was forming his opinions. The great critic in Germany at this time was Lessing. Herder's criticisms struck a new tone. Lessing knew only one system of tactics, which was with fixed bayonet to run his rival through the body. He made no prisoners. When the work was over, there was nothing left of his antagonist. Herder, on the contrary, never attacks; he seeks from all sides to influence his antagonist and to induce him to retreat. He is inexhaustible in resources. He appears at great disadvantage to-day in comparison with Lessing, whose sharp, concise use of words, pressing directly to their aim, loses nothing of its original perspicuity; while Herder's florid style, his involved periods, and his odd attempts to create a language of his own, in which new and curious words and combinations of words occur, make his style sound antiquated and foreign. Herder was a poet and a theologian : he would convince and rule, but hurt no one. In the depths of his soul lay a quiet mirror, in which the history of humanity was pictured as a work of art. The beauty and the power of his language shows itself most purely when, in hours of rapturous contemplation, he forces into his service the truest and most pertinent words; but it becomes dim and confused when he engages in controversy, which, alas! in his later days he was too often tempted to do.

Herder had, in 1769, published a new work, which added to his renown, called "Die kritischen Wälder," — new fragments of a grand creed, which comprehended the whole world. In a somewhat romantic manner he was then driven to Strasburg. He had given up his position of pastor, and gone by ship from Riga to France. Torn from his former sphere, on a voyage of discovery seeking a new existence, his thoughts given to the contemplation of the infinite, all-surrounding sea, he wrote down all that moved him, trying to make clear the whole horizon of his knowledge, experiences, and expectations. These pages were published long after his death. They give the best idea of his grand theory of life. They disclose an acute and comprehensive mind which includes all phenomena in its system, and a power in the use of language which fills us with astonishment when we think how little our mother-tongue was at that time fitted to express such speculation. We must bear this in mind in order to understand the mass of French words which fill the writings of Lessing, as well as of Herder; and which are also to be found in great numbers in the writings of Schiller and Goethe.

RESULTS OF THE THIRTY YEARS' WAR. 47

From Paris Herder went to Eutin, where he was court preacher. He left there to travel with a young Holstein prince. Herder had an eye disease, necessitating a tedious and painful operation, and chaining him to Strasburg, — "a most wretched, chaotic, disagreeable place," as he wrote Merck. Under these circumstances, needing help and accustomed to command, Goethe's willingness to serve came very opportunely. They became acquainted by accident, and an intimacy sprang up. The enthusiasm at first was all on Goethe's side: he perceived clearly what was to be won, and would not allow Herder to escape him. When Goethe had become older by the few years necessary to cancel the disparity which at their time of life made the difference between the men so striking, there grew up the real attachment which we might say death alone could have severed, if the outward intercourse of the two men had not (apparently through Herder's fault) in later years come to an end. Inwardly they were never estranged.

We shall see that Herder at this time gave to Goethe what no other person in Germany could have given him. It is necessary here again to begin with some general observations.

In speaking of the results of the Thirty Years' War, we have hitherto considered only its effect upon Germany; but the mental stagnation which prevailed among us had, so far as it concerned political life, extended almost all over Europe. The independence of "Bürgership" was destroyed, and the citizens subordinated themselves to the nobles, whose sole aim was to maintain the existing order of things. The ruling lords reigned with absolute authority; and it seemed as if the further development of European history was to consist of incessant struggles to uphold the majesty of the families possessed of power. All public institutions served, directly or indirectly, this single aim. Catholic and Protestant clergy alike sustained, with entire willingness, such views. With all European nobles and officials one question only came to be of importance; namely, whether they were in favor or disfavor at court. To win the former, and to avoid the latter, was the secret of all superior education. An overthrow of such conditions was nowhere attempted; and one may say that in the year 1700 the European world had so conformed to this state of things that it appeared as immutable as the elements, or as man himself. No one could believe that while Europeans lived together they could possibly maintain other social relations than such as had existed. It seemed to have been always so, and that it must ever remain so.

There is an anecdote of a picture of the Flood, in which one of the men swimming for his life is represented bearing in his hand a roll of parchment, while a card hangs from his mouth, on which is written, " Sauvez les papiers de la famille Montmorency." Of course, the Montmorencys were not so far lost as to assert that they actually existed before the Flood; but the hypothesis was that powerful families were of almost any age,—like the great Roman families who derived their origin from the gods themselves. They believed in an eternal continuance as much as Horace did, who, when wishing to express the idea of infinitude, wrôte, "so long as the Tarpeian maiden shall mount the Capitol." Hence the universal unconcern when, in the face of these conditions, the feeling arose that all was not right. Hence, also, sprang up among those looking farther, and seeing the absolute impossibility of continuing these relations, the conviction that men could not by degrees work out of them and pass over to something relatively better; but that a total overthrow must ensue, from the ruins of which, perhaps (as something wholly new), simple natural conditions might be evolved.

These two moods — the one a feeling of absolute security in the enjoyment of the present, the other awaiting a chaos to result in an entirely new creation — characterized the first half of the last century. Men lived merrily on, and regarded the course of things with frivolous irony. This is the meaning of the phrase, "après nous le déluge." Louis XV. — the sublimest representative of this monstrous frivolity, which hurried the people recklessly on — candidly admits the impending end of all things, but commits it to future generations to atone for the sins of their forefathers. But that he himself, or his immediate family, could be concerned in it never occurred to him. He believed in a deluge in the vague future; at all events he calculated on a postponement of the Day of Judgment for at least one or two hundred years. For this reason, and without much anxiety, men left it to the philanthropists (who were beginning to be busy with the subject) to construct new kingdoms in which freedom might find a home, and where philosophers should reign supreme. Attempts of this kind became more significant as the signs increased that not the distant future, but a living generation was to pass through the experience of universal bankruptcy. The history of Robinson Crusoe, who like Adam was forced to begin life anew and alone upon a desolate island, was the embodiment, in the form of an innocent romance, of the thought that each one like Robinson might suffer shipwreck, and with somewhat pitiful household implements be driven to fabricate a new life. Ideas of this kind began to be popular. And now it happened that just in the middle of the century a sudden maturity of the public mind announced itself, and that one morning the hitherto indifferent and frivolous masses were overpowered by the thought, and passionately grappled with the question, of the possible improvement of the world.

The three men who brought about this revolution in France, or rather in Paris, which at that time in quite a different sense from to-day was called "the brain of mankind," were Voltaire, Rousseau, and Diderot.

Voltaire had ploughed up the soil of France, and made it ready for the new seed, which Rousseau began immediately after to sow. Diderot, scarcely to be compared with the two former, must notwithstanding be named, because he was the most able of all the writers of the second rank who, in the spirit of Voltaire and Rousseau, labored to accelerate the growth of the young seed. Diderot succeeded, although he was no poet, in investing these new ideas with an æsthetic literary form. He invented prosaic tragedy, — the so-called "comédie larmoyante," whose representative in Germany was Lessing. Lessing's principal drama in this vein is "Miss Sarah Sampson," and Goethe's chief work upon this model is "Clavigo." Diderot figures to-day, among classic writers, only as a critic and narrator. His theatrical works are insufferable and thrown aside.

Voltaire was best characterized by Goethe, when he said that he was an incarnation of all the qualities of the French nation, good and bad. Voltaire is the most glorious Frenchman to be found in all history. Even the element of personal bravery was not wanting. He once challenged a nobleman who had insulted him, and would not give up the duel until he was imprisoned in the Bastile at the instigation of his antagonist. Goethe has emphatically declared Voltaire to be the originator of the French Revolution, by saying that he loosened all the ties which had hitherto bound men together. Voltaire died before its outbreak. The only circumstance which hindered him from working with even mightier power was that entrance into the highest Parisian circles had been made too easy for him. Had his agitating head been set on the body of a man in the lower ranks of life, whom poverty and destitution had embittered and filled with antipathy to these higher classes, Voltaire might have saved the men coming after him a great part of their revolutionary work. On the other side, it need scarcely be said that an extraordinary opportunity was afforded Voltaire, by his unlimited social intercourse, to spread his ideas in all directions. Never has a writer so entirely governed the epoch in which he lived as Voltaire. Even to-day he is considered one of the greatest of historians.

As a young author, Voltaire, driven from Paris, had taken refuge in England, which, with the United Netherlands, represented in the last century German Protestant freedom. Political independence and undisturbed philosophical convictions were there granted to every one. If it were possible to find a model anywhere for the reconstruction of the rest of Europe, England naturally presented herself as that model.

And it was this which Voltaire perceived on the spot. He studied English philosophy. To him was vouchsafed the marvellous double gift to become quickly imbued with foreign ideas, and then to revolve them with indefatigable care until, having eliminated every superfluous word, he was able to give his writings that ease and grace which all literary form demands in order to be effective. Voltaire added to an unlimited power of production an immense capacity for self-criticism. The works in which he brought the moral and political aspects of English philosophy before the Parisian public produced a tremendous sensation. From that moment began the earnest agitation of mind in France. Voltaire had created with his writings the elements with which Rousseau could work. Rousseau was younger than Voltaire, and found his public ready for him. As an artist, Rousseau stood far below Voltaire's height. But he did not need to adapt and polish his writings so much, for his style naturally possessed the quality — the only one which, perhaps, Voltaire's lacked — of vital heat, penetrating instantly to the heart of the reader, and, where it is a question of success with one generation only, far exceeding any effect of art. Rousseau had raised himself from the dregs of society, and, although intercourse with the highest circles was forced upon him from many directions, he always remained a plebeian. Rousseau moved forward recklessly because it was his nature, and because he so willed it. He had nothing to do with generalizations, but attacked things practically. In colossal literary efforts he discussed, one by one, the seething ideas which disquieted the minds of men, and aroused for himself, far and wide, undisguised hatred and open love. Voltaire, in all his writings, always remained the artist. He had exhibited the existing order of things in such a light, by turning them hither and thither, that finally every one was convinced that their condition was no longer tenable or practicable; but he had addressed himself chiefly to the higher classes. Rousseau, on the contrary, appealed to every one. Each felt him to be like himself.

Voltaire had only been able to *interest* the Germans: Rousseau *agitated* them. His ideas had penetrated Herder's soul. He was related to Rousseau in his whole nature; for as a solitary, poor young man, in the extreme east of Germany, Herder had striven to raise himself in the opinion of the people. He came out against Rousseau and criticised him, but bore him in his soul all the while.

We have seen that in Strasburg Goethe knew not what to make of Rousseau's writings. A great man is not always immediately understood: he needs his prophet. In Rousseau's influence over Herder I refer not so much to definite statements which he accepted from him, but to something which might be compared to electricity, passing through Herder to Goethe, who would not otherwise have come in contact with it. Rousseau saw only one means of freeing the people from their burdensome tyranny: each one of them must be made sensible of the laws and duties imposed upon him by the fact that he is a part of his nation. In his eyes each nation was an individual, responsible for its own fate. Rousseau addressed himself to the French nation as if that alone was in question; but every other nation might apply his theories to itself, and so other countries merely substituted "mankind" for "France." The distinctly national political feeling which now-a-days is thought to belong to a true patriotism, was at that time wholly unknown. Even in France men regarded humanity only as a whole. The development of mankind, which was the fundamental idea in Herder's soul and the basis of all his works, would never have been built up within him without the help of Rousseau. Rousseau's dogma, that all civilization is but deterioration from an originally perfect state, corresponded so exactly to the universal feeling that it was accepted without question: "All is good that comes from the hand of the Creator; all is ruined by man. The way must be found back to our original condition." To-day the theory most widely accepted assumes it to be scientifically proved that mankind has been developed from the animal; and it is not regarded as necessary for the individual to furnish any proof of this before accepting it. In the time of Rousseau the contrary doctrine of original perfection was received with universal credulity. In a certain sense it offered nothing new. Theology has always repeated the story of a lost Paradise; but Rousseau wished to show how, without Christianity, philosophy led back to this Paradise. Herder was the first to draw from these teachings conclusions applicable to poetic art: " The poet should go back to pure Nature." Nature here meant " his own creative power obeying the inward voice." We should go back for teachers to those poets who stood prominent among their people. Winckelmann had pointed to the Greeks, and showed how art with them was the blossom of the entire life of the nation. Herder studied the Psalms, the songs of Homer, Pindar, Ossian, and above all Shakspeare; and with these, like woodland flowers sown by no human hand, but which spring up about the trunks of giant oaks, the Folksongs. While the stormy wind tosses the branches overhead, the grasses beneath are gently stirred by the sighing breath from the yearning heart of Nature. Herder did not present to the people a critically ingenious exegesis of these studies: he was ever the preacher. Herder's writings are intelligible only as sermons. It is not for the preacher to offer on special occasions carefully studied productions afterward to be printed, but at every opportunity to pour out from a full heart living words. We must think of what Herder says as *spoken* words if we would rightly judge him.

Goethe was twenty-one years old when he met Herder. He was in a state of ferment. He sought a master. He had never found anybody who made him say to himself: " This man knows more than I do! He is in the possession of secrets which can help me!" At last came one whose first words were decisive: to him he submit ted. And what strengthened Herder's mastery over Goethe was the manner in which he received his devotion. Herder, accustomed to such submission, saw nothing peculiar in Goethe's homage, and treated him with indifference. Sometimes it almost seemed as if Herder secretly felt Goethe's strength, and perhaps unconsciously tried to hinder his rising too high beside him.

The beginning of Goethe's real productiveness we may date from this time. His previous labors had been only aimless attempts. Goethe had intuitively recognized the right direction: now Herder came to show him the way. Goethe enters that period of joyous, youthful, self-confidence which made him so attractive, and which he so fully sustained in the years which followed.

But now we have something to place in opposition to all this. Goethe, feeling that it was the most important event of his life, has related at some length in "Dichtung und Wahrheit" his meeting with Herder in Strasburg. Yet even this, and his experiences with all his other friends and acquaintances, seem only the frame for an event which was the true centre of his Strasburg life. How he found and loved Frederika Brion in Sesenheim is described with quite another pen. If Goethe had become only a great philosophic statesman or scholar, he would, perhaps, in later years, when recounting and arranging the events of his life, scarcely have mentioned Frederika; but the eye of the poet looked at the matter from a higher point. Goethe felt, when recalling the days of his youth, that in the opening bloom of this love whose long-exhaled perfume had once enchanted him were contained the most precious moments of his life, and knew only too well that it had been more to him than all else. To Frederika he owed most, and to her he was the most grateful. To her his eyes turned back more fondly than to all else, and everything about her he remembers more clearly than all else.

Goethe has shown his utmost skill in painting this maiden in the purest and most beautiful colors. His Leipsic love-affairs seem child's play compared with this. They arose in sport; and when they were ended they were spoken of in a graceful strain of sad despair. She was the first he earnestly loved, — the first whose heart he broke, and whom he never could forget. After a long life, full of much excitement, which had ever more and more dimmed his memory, he was forced, in describing that life, to linger over every moment of this experience. To write is more than merely to remember. In order to surround Frederika with the utmost glamour, Goethe has treated himself with a harshness in which alone is implied, if it were really necessary, a late expiation. Frederika, in Goethe's delineation, is invested with something inexpressibly touching, as if youth had again been given to him and to her, and once more the possibility granted them never to separate.

LECTURE IV.

FREDERIKA IN SESENHEIM. — DOCTOR'S DEGREE. — RETURN TO FRANKFORT.

FREDERIKA, as represented in "Dichtung und Wahrheit," is not, as we say, copied from nature; but Goethe endows the being created in his imagination with so many of the minor features of his friend that it bears a striking resemblance to her. This appearance of reality which the artist lends to his pictures is the highest effect of art. It is as if not he, but Nature, had wrought, and he had only faithfully copied the model. Indeed, the better he succeeds in this the more perfect will his creations be, and the more vivid their effect upon others; while he who does not first carefully go through this process of simply copying what Nature offers will at best produce only an unpleasant counterfeit, dumb and lifeless, because he could not invest it with speech and motion. This is why many portraits which are striking likenesses frighten us; and why photographs reproducing the sharpest reality can never be considered as works of art, however much skill and experience may be expended in preparing them. Photographic portraits, to which the *retoucheur* has not lent a deceitful conventionality, when long examined, give the impression of some one before us in a state of cramp-like rigidity.

As regards Frederika, Goethe has succeeded in an eminent degree in convincing us that the portrait he has drawn is a most faithful likeness of the actual parson's daughter at Sesenheim, whom he once loved. Therefore we are ready to swear that Frederika must have been exactly like this, — only in our secret souls we are inclined to believe her to have been much more charming than Goethe describes her. We think he has not done her justice. And this is the effect produced by truly artistic creations, — that he who contemplates them believes he understands them better than the artist himself; as if the poet had been only a chosen instrument commissioned by Providence to bring a being into the world which lives a life of its own. Like children who as soon as they are individuals show themselves independent of their parents, so creations like Hamlet, Juliet, and Faust appear to assert a certain independence of their creator, and strangers approaching them believe that they understand them better than their authors do. Many of the interpreters of Hamlet seem to imagine that they knew the prince at least as well as Shakspeare himself did. In the representation of this drama the public has objected to the tragic end of the prince; while Alexandre Dumas the Elder, who has rendered the tragedy in French Alexandrines, just at the end makes the ghost of the father appear again and advise Hamlet to seize the reins of government, and wishes him the best success, — which then really happens. I remember that one of my young friends repeatedly insisted that Shakspeare had no right to kill Romeo and Juliet. If similar discussions had gone on in his lifetime, Shakspeare would only have found in them most flattering proofs that he had been so fortunate as to create genuine living beings; and Goethe, when exposed to the severest reproof for having faithlessly deserted such an enchanting creature as Frederika, only found the assurance that the result had been attained which he sought to produce.

THE DANCING-MASTER'S DAUGHTERS.   59

It would be in vain to try to decide how nearly Goethe's Frederika and the original Frederika coincide. Influenced as we are by Goethe's poetry, we find the maiden as captivating as he describes her. I will try, so far as possible, to distinguish the two figures, — the ideal and the real. In order to do this, it is necessary to consider with what artistic means the delineation of his experience at Sesenheim was accomplished.

By way of introduction, in order to excite the anticipation of a tragic end, he relates his adventure with the daughters of the old French dancing-master, — a little narrative complete in itself, whose close makes a thrilling dramatic scene; the whole, in its way, a model for a modern novel. The story runs thus: Of the two daughters of the dancing-master, the younger excites Goethe's interest; while the elder, Lucinda, without his dreaming of it, falls in love with him. Goethe describes how one day Lucinda storms into the room just as he is on the point of committing himself to the younger sister, interrupts them passionately, declares her love, and, after renouncing him in favor of her younger sister, bids him farewell and closes his lips with a kiss, which she avows shall bring ruin to the one next kissed by those lips. Goethe leaves the house, never to enter it again. The reader, with a certain fluttering of the heart, waits to hear on whom this curse will fall.

Before Frederika appears, in order still further to heighten the effect, and at the same time to prepare us to see the inmates of the clergyman's house at Sesenheim as in a mirror, Goethe gives an account of Herder's reading the "Vicar of Wakefield." This romance — only known to-day as an old-fashioned novel, out of which one takes his first lessons in English, as one learns French out of "Paul and Virginia," and Italian out of "I Promessi Sposi" — possessed at that time the charm of perfect novelty. Goethe relates how Herder read it to his young friends, and the conversation which grew out of it exposes a new side of Herder's character. Herder knew how to produce the greatest effect, and at the same time to destroy it again; and, even at this early day, he showed the power to inspire and elevate, and at the same time to depress and dishearten. The Vicar of Wakefield is the head of a family, which, through a series of calamities, sinks into a condition of the greatest misery; but at last, after all the characters have been purified and strengthened by these trials, their hard fate is mitigated, better times come, all obstacles disappear, and we take leave of the family in the full sunshine of the happiness they enjoyed when we first made their acquaintance.

In this way we are prepared for Sesenheim without knowing it. It seems as if we were opening a wholly new chapter, which has nothing to do with the foregoing. It was in the spring of 1771. Herder has left Strasburg. Goethe has every reason to concentrate himself upon the study of law, since he wishes to obtain in the autumn his degree. But the glorious country allures him, and there is also his inborn impulse never to leave a spot of earth on which he has once dwelt without having thoroughly explored it. Alsace between the Rhine and Vosges, a separate province, reminds one, it is said, of Switzerland. People have wandered through the province from end to end, until at last every path in valley or mountain has been traversed. There have always been learned men and lovers of Nature who were at home in Alsace, and who thoroughly knew its history and exact topography. The land has its own history and its peculiar character.

Among Goethe's acquaintances was a born Alsatian,

who was in the habit of enlivening his quiet existence by occasional visits to relatives and friends in the neighborhood: with him Goethe planned a visit to one of his relatives,— the Parson Brion in Sesenheim.

Goethe always had a fancy for presenting himself in disguise, or under a feigned name. According to his tendency to contemplate things objectively, he was most comfortable incognito. When a Leipsic student he made in this manner his renowned journey to Dresden, where he took up his abode with the Socratic shoemaker, whose household he so picturesquely describes. In later years, on his lonely winter journey into the Hartz from Weimar, he allowed himself to be presented under a feigned name to Plessing, in Wernigerode, who had repeatedly appealed to him by letter for advice in his spiritual need. Goethe left him without acknowledging who he was. In Rome he lived the first few weeks unmolested, shielded by a disguise; in Sicily he thus visited the Balsamo family; and the list of his adventures of this kind might be greatly increased.

In his visit to Parson Brion his fancy for assuming a disguise also appears. He resolves to make his *début* in the character of a shabby theological student; borrows a suit of threadbare clothes, brushes his profuse and ornamental locks straight back, and rides off with his friend one morning in May, 1771. The ride is so graphically described that the reader believes himself to be an invisible member of the party, trotting along with them. First of all, in Goethean fashion, we must have firm ground under our feet,— the excellent road, the splendid weather, the Rhine so near, the fruitful country, the plain, with the misty mountains in the distance. Finally, the two riders turn aside from the broad road into the blossoming lane leading to Sesenheim, leave their horses in the village, and betake themselves to the parson's house. How exactly we are informed in regard to every detail of this house! Where building was to be done, Goethe was constantly at hand. A rebuilding of the parson's house was necessary, and Goethe's interest in the plans was one of the ways in which he later won the old parson's favor. He drew sketches for it with his own hand, some of which Riemer — Goethe's amanuensis in the last years of his life — discovered among his papers.

The parson receives the two students alone: the daughters are out. Now we see with what skill Frederika is brought into the scene. Here we recognize, not alone the experienced writer, but the theatre-director. First, he allows the older sister to storm in inquiring for Frederika. A slight impatience seizes us, and with it the expectation to find in Frederika the opposite of this vehemence; but he still holds her back. For a second time must the sister, Salomea, — Goethe calls her Olivia, in remembrance of the oldest daughter in the "Vicar of Wakefield," — come hurriedly into the room again, and ask for Frederika. "Let her alone: she will come back of herself," quietly replies the father. Frederika is belated in her ramble. Now is added to mere expectation the anxiety lest something has befallen her. Finally, she appears; and now, when curiosity is at its highest point, with a few masterly touches he paints the beautiful girl. Frederika is introduced as heroine and principal character, without having done anything more than simply allowing herself to be expected. She wears the German costume — a short white skirt, with a furbelow; "the daintiest feet visible;" a closely-fitting white boddice, and a black taffeta apron, — the whole dress something between a city girl's and a peasant's. Merry blue eyes; pretty nose, slightly *retroussé*; a straw hat, which she bears on her arm, — the whole effect charming. With a **few touches a** lovely picture is here painted.

Father, mother, and daughters **now try to** make the two poor students comfortable. The **sisters begin** an amusing gossip about the entire neighborhood. Frederika then plays on the piano, as one plays in the country, on an out-of-tune instrument. "Let us go out," she said, "and then you shall hear some of my Alsace and Swiss songs."

Now Goethe is struck with the resemblance of the family to that of the Vicar of Wakefield. This completes the picture for the reader, and at the same time hints that stormy days are coming, and that these good, quiet people are to be exposed to trials.

At night, in the tavern, Goethe reviews with his friend the occurrences of the day. The likeness of the family to the one in the romance is talked over, and Goethe's thoughts instantly anticipate all the consequences of such a comparison. Into the family of the Vicar, Thornhill, the seducer of one of the daughters, had also stolen in disguise. Goethe compares himself to this man; and this alone — though without a shadow of guilt — is sufficient to awaken in him the most violent remorse. This is perfectly conceivable. The innocence and truth of the people likewise create in us a feeling of aversion to Goethe's deception. He had observed in his walk through the fields the respect with which the peasants greeted the young maiden. He had walked with Frederika in the moonlight; but "her talk had nothing moonshiny in it, for the clearness with which she expressed herself made the night day." In contrast to all this, he had been acting a part. The next morning, overwhelmed with the unworthiness of his *rôle*, he throws himself upon his horse and rides away. He intends to return to Strasburg; but, as each particular **event of the previous** day recurs to his mind, he rides more slowly, and finally turns back. In Drusenheim he stops. Before the tavern he meets the son of the landlord in his Sunday clothes, with ribbons in his hat, just starting to carry a christening-cake to the parson's wife at Sesenheim. With him Goethe exchanges clothes, to attempt a new masquerade. Bearing the cake in his hand, he soon again reaches the parsonage at Sesenheim. He is not recognized until Frederika comes towards him, and even she at first takes him for the person to whom the dress belongs, and says familiarly, " George, what are you doing here?" Then she suddenly becomes aware of her mistake, and " her delicate cheeks are suffused with the loveliest blushes." We now hear, little by little, what further happens at Sesenheim, — how Goethe fascinates the whole family; how he establishes himself in some special relation to each member of it; and how wildly he surrenders himself to his rapture. We are still touched by the poems he dedicated at this time to Frederika. Herder had been the first to draw his attention to the songs of the people. Now he hears Frederika sing them, collects them from the very mouth of the people, and adds to them his own glorious verses written in the very spirit and tone of the " Volkslied." How conceivable this unrestrained heedlessness in Goethe! How conceivable, also, the artlessness with which Frederika responded to his fancy, as she soon with a sisterly confidence attached herself to him!

And here it is well to consider that at that time such an intimacy was not peculiar. The intercourse between young people at that period was perfectly free and natural. As a young man, when music comes in as a third element, may take a young lady in his arms and move with her to the measure of the dance, so the universal feeling throughout Europe at that time, that all were moving on toward a higher existence, came like music into every relation, and permitted a familiarity which is no longer allowed. People associated, wrote to each other, and talked openly of many things which to-day are no longer discussed among young people; nor was the boundary between affianced and unaffianced at that time so sharply defined. Yet the more freedom allowed, the more necessary in special cases was it to discriminate how far matters might go. It was owing to this that Goethe, who was soon looked upon and treated by Frederika, her parents, and her relatives as her lover, took this position without having declared himself. He was bound to nothing, and could at any moment go as he had come.

Now Goethe describes how, in the fulness of his enthusiasm for Frederika, a consciousness dawned upon him that his love, after all, existed only in imagination. He makes this discovery before one binding word has been said. At a rural feast this struggle reaches its climax. Goethe, who has not decided whether to fly or to remain, brings Frederika to the confession that she loves him; and the first kiss is given and received by the lips upon which the curse had fallen. This recurs directly to Goethe's mind. In the night Lucinda appears to him in a dream and repeats the curse, while Frederika stands opposite to her, stiff and speechless with fright, not comprehending what it all means. The narration is wrought up to the highest dramatic reality, and we await a tragedy.

Instead of this, again an artistic stroke to remind us that this is not a romance, but a simple account of what happened. The story continues in the old calm tone, as the life of the maiden and her parents flows quietly on again. Goethe, considered as Frederika's betrothed lover, enjoys the growing confidence of the family. **He** comes out oftener to Sesenheim, stays there for weeks, and is in constant correspondence with Frederika; but he grows ever more quiet at heart. We have letters from him to Salzmann about these visits to Sesenheim. In one of these he expresses his state of mind: "I am not really in my inmost soul serene. I am too much awake not to realize that I am trying to grasp shadows." The finishing stroke was given by a visit of the sisters to Strasburg, where Goethe saw them torn from their rural life, and transplanted into a society for which they were not educated. But Goethe tells how Frederika conducts herself becomingly notwithstanding, and here discloses a feature of her character which has always seemed to me very touching.

She claimed, as she was justified in doing, what Goethe called his "services," and one evening confides to him that the ladies in the house with whom they are staying wish to hear him read. Goethe takes "Hamlet," and reads it with fire from beginning to end, eliciting great applause. Frederika, it is said, had from time to time breathed deeply, and the color came and went in her cheeks, — the only tokens by which she allowed him to know how proud she was of the applause bestowed upon her Goethe. He tells us further of the elder sister's passionate conduct, who felt much more keenly than Frederika their unfortunate position, and wished to get away from Strasburg. A stone was lifted from his heart when he finally saw them both depart. Goethe had to confess to himself that his dream was ended.

But there was no violent rupture; and this gives to the last moments a peculiar sadness, — like a melody dying gently on the ear! Slowly, leaf by leaf, as the trees in autumn lose their foliage, the early confidence held fast to the very end! No word of reproof when

Goethe, on the point of leaving Strasburg forever, appears before the door for the last time, and, while the tears stand in Frederika's eyes, says farewell, — giving her his hand from his horse! Only later he receives from her a heart-rending letter in answer to his written adieu. Goethe gives us to understand that it remained unanswered.

Goethe's conduct is such that it is almost impossible not to draw from it inferences with regard to his character; and since " Dichtung und Wahrheit " was published this has been done, — many persons on this account having lost their enthusiasm for Goethe. One would forgive him much; but to have broken the heart of such a maiden was inhuman. In that same summer Herder wrote of Goethe that he did not consider him capable of genuine enthusiasm.

Meanwhile the time is past for any personal defence of Goethe. We may to-day revere in him the greatest German poet, without making it a duty to vindicate all he did. We look at things not more coldly, but more critically. We understand him, therefore, when in his own criticism of the Sesenheim affair he says : " The question is not with regard to sentiments and actions, how far they were blamable or praiseworthy, but whether such things could possibly have happened." He seems to say, " Amuse yourselves with the story. So far as I am concerned it was necessary that I should become what I am, with my faults as well as my virtues ! "

To look at the matter in this way is in accordance with our present ideas; and the more so because, when we see men placed as high as mortals can be placed, we are not, psychologically considered, comfortable in mind until we have discovered to a certainty that our heroes have their weak sides like common men, and, above all, like our selves. Then we feel *en famille* with them, and recognize their virtues only so much the more unreservedly.

But before this mental operation is needed for Goethe, we should be sure that all happened as recounted in "Dichtung und Wahrheit." I call attention to one expression: Goethe says, "The question is, whether such thoughts and deeds *could* occur, and not whether they really did." This is a distinction. With the word *could*, the whole Sesenheim story is transferred from the realm of fact to that of possibility. And, indeed, Goethe has not only idealized Frederika's character, but in the whole account of the Sesenheim episode given us a romance, an idyl, as Loeper calls it, in which the fact is proven that the outlines are truth and all the details fiction. In one of the explanations which Goethe has given of the meaning of "Dichtung und Wahrheit," he says: "There is no event related in my autobiography which was not a real experience, but nothing as I really experienced it." Goethe thus stipulates beforehand for the most unlimited freedom in the handling of his facts.

Some minor matters should here be mentioned. It seems quite possible that the Socratic shoemaker with whom Goethe took up his abode on his clandestine trip to Dresden was but a mythical person; and the same may be true with regard to his young friend in Frankfort, whom he called Pylades, and possibly also as regards the two daughters of the dancing-master. But these are only suppositions. Concerning Sesenheim we may say with safety this much, that the affair never *could* have ended as Goethe represents. There is proof also that he did not become acquainted with the parson's family in the manner described; that their circumstances were not exactly as pictured; and, probably, the farewell itself was very different.

I have given you a somewhat detailed account of
Goethe's first appearance at Sesenheim. We have seen
what a part Goldsmith's romance played in it,—how
Goethe recognizes in the Sesenheim family the principal
characters in the "Vicar of Wakefield;" indeed, he even
introduces the names. Two sisters only, according to
Goethe's story, belong to the Brion family,—the elder
Salomea, whom he calls Olivia, and the younger Riekchen. But there were four,—one older, already married;
and another fifteen years of age, and still at home. The
brother, by Goethe called Moses, was named Christian.
All this amounts to very little. Loeper proves that
Goethe's first visit to the village was not in the spring
of 1771, but in October, 1770, when Goethe had not yet
heard of the "Vicar of Wakefield." Accepting this, the
fundamental facts given about the first visit are destroyed.

If this be really so, we are justified in going further.
In Goethe's narrative, we find the events in Sesenheim
from first to last placed in ideal relations,—one coinciding
exactly with another, so that the conclusion follows as a
tragic necessity. In regard to the farewell, Goethe confesses that he did not remember the last days very distinctly, and that in this part of the narrative he made no
attempt to be accurate. Therefore, I believe we know
how to interpret Goethe's remark, "I spoke of deeds and
feelings which *might* have been,"—which means that of
the details he no longer had any knowledge, but they
might have been as he related. Loeper has shown uncommon care in collecting and arranging the notes in
"Dichtung und Wahrheit," which may be considered
authentic regarding the Sesenheim affair. At the first
glance they appear to afford a significant picture to place
by the side of Goethe's description. But, more carefully

studied, they give us only color; often in the most delicate shades, but no outlines. What is needed in outline is found in Goethe's fiction alone. It may possibly happen that some one who could boast an acquaintance with Frederika or her family has left memorials containing confidential communications received directly from them, which one will yet be allowed to read. We have learned quite lately from Goethe's diaries, published by Keil, that he received a letter from Frederika while in Weimar; as we also find, by a letter to Salzmann, that he sent her from Frankfort his newly published works. But what kind of relation continued to exist between them will only become clear when those inform us who knew exactly how things were. Until then, of the actual experience in Sesenheim we know only this: that Goethe met an honest and lovable family, to whom he attached himself as if forever; whom he through his presence brought into embarrassment, and whom he finally deserted in a manner which even he himself could not forgive.

Yet Goethe's own account really loses nothing in value because we are obliged to regard it as a mingling of only dim remembrance with the most vivid poetic fancy. It adds to Goethe's immortal poems one of the finest. The suggestion that the actual Riekchen Brion was another than the Frederika who is so touchingly represented in "Dichtung und Wahrheit," injures her memory as little as Charlotte Buff's has been injured by the certainty that Werther's experience in no wise corresponded to what in truth took place between Goethe and Charlotte in her father's house at Wetzlar. In spite of this, Goethe has given to both maidens a share in his immortality.

Frederika remained unmarried. Goethe saw her again in 1779. The story in "Dichtung und Wahrheit" closes with the account of how, as he rode away from Sesenheim after the farewell, he saw his own figure, dressed in gray clothes trimmed with gold, suddenly coming towards him on a horse. It was a *fantasy* which he interpreted as meaning that he should return to Sesenheim; and so it happened. Of his visit in 1779 we possess only the letter to Frau von Stein, with a description of Alsace scenery, — one of the loveliest Goethe ever wrote, and which shall serve as fitting epilogue to this idyl: "A rarely beautiful day; a charming country, all still green, only here and there a yellow leaf on beech or oak; the willows yet in their silver beauty; a mild, grateful breath over the whole land; grapes with every step, and every day better; each peasant's house vine-clad even to the roof; each door-way a full, rich clustering arbor; the heavenly air, soft, moist, and warm. Man becomes, like the grape, ripe and sweet at heart. Would to God we dwelt here together! — we should not so quickly freeze in winter or dry up in summer. The Rhine and the clear mountains near; the changing woods, meadows, and garden-like fields bespeak refreshment to men, and fill me with a delight I have long missed."

So he writes at mid-day, September 25. In the evening he repairs to Sesenheim, of which, three days later, he gives the following account: "*25th Sept.; toward evening.* — I turned aside from the broad road to go to Sesenheim, while the others straightway continued their journey. I found the family together just as I had left them eight years before, and was received in the most cordial way. As I am now as serene as the air I breathe, the atmosphere of these good and unpretending people was most grateful. The second daughter of the house had formerly loved me much more generously than I deserved, and more than others on whom I have lavished greater passion and loyalty. I was forced to leave her at a moment when it almost cost her her life; but she treated me with consideration, spoke lightly of the remains of the illness she had at that time, and from the first moment when I met her unexpectedly at the door conducted herself in the most lovely manner, and showered upon me such tokens of hearty friendship that I felt quite at ease. I must do her the justice to say that she did not attempt, by the slightest allusion, to awaken in my soul the old feeling. She took me into each arbor, and in each I must sit, and all was pleasing. We had the most beautiful full moon. I inquired about everything. A neighbor who had formerly helped us to make some improvements was called in, who told me he had asked for me only eight days before. And the barber also must come. I found old songs I had composed, a carriage I had painted; we recalled many frolics of that time, and I found my memory as keen about them as if I had only been gone half a year. The old people were true-hearted; they found I had grown younger. I remained overnight, and left the next morning at sunrise. They bade me adieu with friendly faces. And I may now once more think with pleasure of this little nook in the world, and live in a feeling of peace with the spirits of these reconciled ones."

This letter explains something that is not fully explained in "Dichtung und Wahrheit," — Goethe's prolonged despair after the parting and his inward conflicts. He wandered about lonely, stung by remorse, and could find no rest. Nevertheless, Frederika had forgiven him, and what had happened that should awaken in Goethe years after such painful thoughts? From a letter which Goethe wrote to Salzmann at Sesenheim we learn what Frederika's pale cheeks meant, which he said were overspread with such a lovely rose color when she recognized him in the guise of the landlord's son of Drusenheim

The young girl was ailing; she was consumptive. Goethe's leaving her brought on an attack which endangered her life.

It is believed that Gretchen in "Faust" is to be traced back to Frederika; but she bears a closer analogy to Marie Beaumarchais in "Clavigo." All Goethe's reproaches, all that he must say to himself in regard to Frederika, is said by Clavigo; while the heroic gentleness of Marie and her frail human form correspond with what Goethe writes to Frau von Stein of Frederika in the year 1779. By recognizing Marie Beaumarchais as a picture of Frederika, we see her as it were through another perspective, which enhances greatly the idea given of her in "Dichtung und Wahrheit." In reality, the catastrophe of the idyl almost took a tragic turn, and we divine in the real Frederika an admirable character.

And so, as she in truth lived and acted, she was no unworthy sister of the ideal Frederika in "Dichtung und Wahrheit."

In the midst of these excitements Goethe's preparations for taking his degree went on. This must be obtained, and then he would directly begin the practice of law in Frankfort. It was not difficult for Goethe to master the necessary knowledge. His father had early drilled him in law studies. Goethe was good authority in "Corpus Juris." To this fundamental training he was indebted for the knowledge which enabled him so soon to give up the persistent taking of notes, which he began at Leipsic. It tired him to write down what he already knew.

At this point Goethe takes the opportunity to speak of the bad results which follow, when young men have too much professional knowledge before entering the

University. He had chances enough during his long life to acquire from experience trustworthy opinions on this subject.

In Strasburg he submitted himself for the study of jurisprudence to the direction of Salzmann, and pursued it with as much ardor as was necessary to enable him to graduate with honors. In his leisure hours he studied everything possible. Medicine attracted him most. Schöll has printed Goethe's notes on the books he read at this time, as well as his abstracts from them. We see from this how Goethe's early habits made it possible for him every day to read through something like an octavo volume, as he when old boasted to Chancellor Müller he had done. He desired to possess knowledge on all subjects, and gathered into his mental treasury all that it was possible to acquire. Goethe had, also, the genuine impulse of learned men to wish to diffuse his views. If he had had some taste for a University life, and had the power been his to concentrate himself on a specialty, he would scarcely have escaped the destiny of becoming a Professor. But he was more fitted for the position of an author, who from his lonely post addresses the great public, and who is not accountable to any one for anything he may say.

On the 6th of August, 1771, Goethe received his degree of Licentiate, but not of Doctor, although from that time he bore the title. We still have his thesis, *ex officina Henrici Heitzii*. This, although composed in good Latin, which it was easy for him both to speak and write, was never printed. His father had demanded a literary work: the young Doctor should enter the ranks with a respectable volume. The old gentleman had approved of the theme and its treatment; but it had not satisfied the Faculty. Goethe's treatise asserted that it was the duty of the lawgiver to prescribe a certain *cultus*, which the clergy and the laity should be bound to sustain. To this, indeed, Herder and Rousseau had already given their sanction. We see how ideas even at that time had spread in the direction which, twenty years later, produced such mad results. The French republic was not merely destructive, like the Commune in our day: it was constructive. If it abolished the Catholic religion, it was not because the people in general were to be exempted from the trouble of maintaining any kind of worship. French legislation introduced the worship of Reason, for which sacrificial fires were kindled on the public altars. But all this bears to-day too much the appearance of mere eccentricity. We know at present far too little of the positively romantic experiments of this first French republic. They attempted even a costume appropriate to the new age. It was Rousseau who, in the conclusion of his "Émile," first gave an external form to this religion of the future. On blessed islands, purified and regenerated human beings were to find themselves united in Greek temples where the Supreme Being is worshipped. The Greek at that time served as the type of the purely human.

How far Goethe in his treatise presented his own ideas, and how far he sympathized with those of Rousseau, we do not know. Goethe himself has told us that Rousseau asserts the establishment of all religions to be the fruit of legislative enactments, and cites the origin of Protestantism as the strongest evidence of this. That the Dean did not wish this treatise published under the auspices of the University, we believe; since it contains expressions contrary to the fundamental teachings of Christianity. Perhaps we shall, at some future time find this manuscript among his papers.

His graduating day passed off happily. The usual feast was given, and Strasburg was done with.

On the 28th of August, 1771, he presented "Doctor" Goethe's petition begging admission to the bar. Kriegk in his "Deutschen Culturbildern" gives the address:[1] "Wohl und hochedelgeborene vest und hochgelehrte, hoch und wohl fürsichtige inbesonders hochgebietende und hochgeehrteste Herren Gerichtsschultheiss und Schöffen. Ew. Wohl und Edelgeborene, Gestreng und Herrlichkeit, habe ich die Ehre, etc."

Three days later followed his promotion to the bar.

[1] "Well, high and nobly born, vastly-learned and masterly, high and mighty guardians, and especially grand commanders, and highly-honored Lord Mayor, Gentlemen of the Bar and Sheriffs! Your high and nobly born Worships and Magnificences, I have the honor, &c."

LECTURE V.

PRACTISING LAW. — HIS PARENTS. — MERCK. — "GÖTZ VON BERLICHINGEN."

WHEN Goethe had been admitted a member of the bar and enrolled a Frankfort citizen, his father submitted willingly to the coming and going of his literary associates. This gave the whole family the benefit of the friendship of many distinguished men; and as the old man saw with what ease, in the midst of all disturbances, the young Doctor exercised his juridical knowledge, his satisfaction mounted to admiration. He is reported to have said: "As a jurist, I should have envied my son if I had not been his father."

What Goethe said in regard to his legal practice has been fully made known to us of late by Kriegk, who has revised existing documents and brought a series of his legal opinions to light. The stand-point Goethe takes shows how entirely his nature at this time was cast in a certain mould. He works as an advocate with energy and passion.

The result of the Revolution was felt in the administration of public justice as in other departments of mental labor. Instead of the pedantic and scholarly treatment which had hitherto prevailed, the purely human point of view became the standard. Goethe said he had taken the *plaidoyers* among the French lawyers as his models, but he seems to have far outrun his exemplars. In his first lawsuit, the counsel for the opposite party became so excited that the legal strife degenerated into a personal affair. Something bordering on sheer insult was exchanged, until at last both advocates received a reproof from the Court. Theiss, the attorney, afterward claimed that he was wrought into an unusual passion by Goethe's rejoinders; and we can well understand this when we examine the documents given by Kriegk. Goethe won the suit; but in later cases he identified himself less with the party he had to defend.

Seldom, indeed, has a young jurist begun with such glorious prospects. His father studied the briefs as private referee, and prepared them for his son, who analyzed them with a facility which excited his father's admiration. But Goethe evidently began at that time to practise law because he would fain content the old gentleman until he had made up his own mind where he could best apply his talents. He has been censured for the manner in which he criticises his father in "Dichtung und Wahrheit." But Goethe, in recapitulating the events of his life to give them to the world as a work of art, considered only how best to exhibit in the most favorable light the various people who had influenced him in reference to this purpose. He had discovered that when it is intended to present a man as an historical fact, only very little concerning him is worthy of mention. A man may possess the most excellent qualities, and nevertheless fail to create from their combination the harmony which shall stamp itself on posterity as his characteristic feature.

On the contrary, a man, through deeds which neither increase the honor due to him nor require any special gifts for their performance, may yet become a power by

CHARACTERISTICS OF HIS FATHER. 79

means of a certain life which inheres in the deeds themselves. He must be satisfied to be known by this one manifestation of his ability, even while, perhaps, deeds proving nobler tendencies are lost in oblivion. Goethe's sketch of his father was drawn from his experiences and the observation of his own nature in riper years. In his earlier life he had once in a letter to the "Fahlmer," to whom he could speak openly of his parents, written in reference to his father: "Am I then destined by fate to become so narrow-minded?" And later he must have discovered in himself many of the pedantic traits of his father. The habit of recording everything descended to him from this side, as well as the collecting and preserving of trifles. His father forced him to finish what he had begun, less out of interest in the subject than from a love of order. He pasted up his unfinished drawings, and put a border round them. We shall see how this predilection for outward order, which was inherited by Goethe, went so far as to take a peculiar literary form. The hoarding up, to which we are indebted for the bulky romance which "Dichtung und Wahrheit" finally became, must be attributed to this pedantry; and, perhaps, even the disconnected form of "Faust" would admit of the same explanation.

Goethe's father had no spiritual elements in him by which his weak points could be transformed into strong ones. He worried himself more and more about the externals of life. He was in all that concerned the spending of money precise and captious. He even compelled his son at last to give up all free intercourse with him, and to prepare carefully beforehand what he wished to say to him, that he might not be hindered by opposition. If anything was desired of the old man, it had to be asked for in a carefully composed letter. In the little verse in which Goethe explains his nature as an inheritance from father and mother, he attributes to his father his stature and his methodical habits. In Lavater's "Physiognomy" there is a portrait of his father which Goethe considered tolerable.

To his mother he ascribes his buoyant nature and his love of story-telling. And, indeed, this was just what distinguished the "Frau Rath." The mother had in her the material to make an historical personage. Goethe's father can be set aside: we do not need him to understand Goethe. But his mother is inseparable from him: she forms a part of his being. She understood him from the beginning: she divined him. All that Goethe gloriously fulfilled corresponded but to a part of the still greater expectations which this woman cherished.

But who is so truly commissioned, so capable of seeing the beauty and the promise of another, as a mother in judging her son? The most miserable and cast-away man was once found beautiful by one pair of eyes. But what a discovery, what a royal future, when superiority really exists! And here we must say that Goethe's mother had received peculiar gifts for her mission. She had a vein of genius in her nature. An indestructible vitality stood at her command, and her every shade of thought had a deeply-marked originality which only increased with years.

She had, as we say, been given in marriage to Goethe's father; and took her place as companion and housewife to a man whose occupations and individuality were alike indifferent to her. We only see her becoming happy, and more and more roused, as she realizes what a giant she has brought into the world in her son. She understands Goethe's nature fully; most of all in its inconsistencies, because she is a woman. She defends him. She mediates between him and his father. His successes, which never surprise her, fill her with indescribable pride. When Goethe finally left for Weimar, still dependent pecuniarily upon his father, his mother remained behind as commander of a place which must be held. There she was enthroned in state as plenipotentiary, and drew her percentage of the honors which fell to the great Goethe. She later wrote to him in Rome that his Frankfort friends said: "We were, all of us, nothing but his lackeys, you know!"— but they should all have something good to eat at her table when Goethe returned. For his sake she kept open house for all his friends as they passed through Frankfort, and they all called upon her as a matter of course. But especially did she expand when his father at last died. As early as 1779 Goethe, in passing through Frankfort, found his father more quiet, while his mother was as vigorous as ever. In 1782, ten years after the time of which we have been speaking, Merck writes to a friend: "Goethe's father is now out of the way, and his mother at last has a chance to breathe!" And the Frau Rath did not fail to take advantage of it. Mistress of her property and her time, a new era began for her.

Her constitution was like iron. She did what she had to do at once in a fresh, ready way, and swallowed the devil without stopping to look at him. She sells the house with the consent of her son, and moves into a new one. Her first stipulation on hiring was, "No gossip to be repeated." But everything new, great, and world-stirring, especially all of literary significance, she seizes with eagerness. These things were to her a delight. She judges all with cleverness and *naïveté*. She was large and stately, and wore imposing head-dresses; and she had always a circle of young girls about her, who followed her with enthusiastic love. In the theatre she sat in her own box, and applauded as if she had a special commission from Goethe. From there she presented her little grandchildren to the public. She has been described most beautifully and truly, quite in the spirit of "Dichtung und Wahrheit," by Bettina. There are many letters from her,— natural, graphic, true grandmother's letters, with no dead word in them.

But more important than father and mother, Frankfort and law-practice, and next to the Strasburg experience, was the acquaintance with a man who won an influence over Goethe such as Herder only had possessed,— Merck in Darmstadt.

Goethe had been led to Darmstadt by Herder. In Darmstadt lived Caroline Flachsland, to whom Herder had become engaged before he went to Strasburg. "The" Flachsland or "Demoiselle," as was the mode of address at that time, moved in a circle which came much in contact with the Court, and, according to the prevailing standard, was highly educated. It was a species of society such as Jean Paul describes in his romances, and the memory of which is lost together with much else which preceded the French Revolution. A predominance of spiritual life, a soaring among higher contemplations, a mental energy, and withal a simplicity and positive faith such as the world no longer possesses characterized it. In this circle Goethe soon became at home, and here he appeared as poet only. Here he found Merck,— a young man, but much older than himself; and, though not long established in Darmstadt, with an official position. About his past life little was known.

I have spoken of Goethe as an historian. In doing so I did not allude to the fact that Goethe once intended to write the history of Bernhard of Weimar, for which purpose he studied certain archives; neither do I refer to the fact that Goethe, by systematic study, had acquired a thorough knowledge of general history, — but I had the following in mind. Two things constitute the historian: first, that the events of the past should stand before his mind in organic coherence; and, second, that he should be able to reproduce artistically what he has thus seen. Both lay in Goethe's power. It is only necessary to read the introduction to his theory of colors to be convinced that the historical method stood naturally at his command. We need only analyze the language and composition of "Dichtung und Wahrheit" to see with what conscious skill he has sustained the autobiographical form.

In "Dichtung und Wahrheit" Goethe has given a series of characterizations so completely wrought into the text that they attract no special attention. Considered by themselves they strike us as masterpieces, whose handling is so evidently on Roman models that if they were translated into Latin by some one familiar with the language of Tacitus, they would seem genuine fragments stolen from this old Roman author. While Johannes von Müller attempted a superficial imitation, for which he was ridiculed, Goethe has wholly concealed the study of his model. Let us hear what he says of Merck: —

"Of his early education I know but little. Gifted with wit and intellect, he had gained for himself a desirable amount of knowledge, especially of new literature, and was well versed in men and things of all times and countries. His judgment was sound and acute. He was valued as an energetic, decided business man, and a ready reckoner. He entered all social circles with ease, and was thought a very agreeable companion by those who did not fear his biting satire. He was tall and thin in person. A sharp, protruding nose made him conspicuous, while his light blue, or rather gray, eyes, which wandered observantly from one object to another, gave to his whole expression something tigerish. Lavater's 'Physiognomy' has preserved a profile of him. In his character there was the strangest inconsistency. By nature an honest, noble, trustworthy man, he embittered himself toward the world, and so nourished this whimsical frame of mind that he felt irresistibly tempted purposely to play the part of rogue, — yes, even of knave. Sensible, quiet, and good at one moment, in the next it would occur to him, as a snail sticks out its horns, to do a thing which would trouble, wound, or in some way injure another. Yet, as we willingly handle a dangerous thing if we believe ourselves safe, so I felt only the greater inclination to live with him and enjoy his good qualities, feeling confident he would never show me his bad side."

Merck's influence, which he himself says was the greatest, is the more striking because Goethe expressly denies Merck all positive qualities. In his old age, when Merck had long passed from the recollections of men, Goethe refers to him again. In the earlier conversations with Eckermann, and later, he was often the subject of their talk. What motive could Goethe have had to talk to one whose mental range he knew so well about this odd character, whom Eckermann could never have understood? Surely, Merck's character had something in it which, to the last, gave Goethe food for thought, and which needed to be unriddled. He once said to Eckermann: "Such a man coming into the world now, in 1830, could never become what Merck was." What really puzzled Goethe was that Merck, with the most absolute knowledge of men and things, and with marked personal influence over others as well as himself, was in the face of all this, if measured by the highest standard, comparatively a nullity. Goethe asserts this with real severity. He denies, out and out, that Merck was noble. We know how much Goethe meant by this word. To the *noble* he opposed the *base;* and it is the peculiar diabolical quality of Mephistopheles that he lacks all positive, creative power; but, in spite of this, it is so indispensable to Faust that, to produce an effect or even to make his presence felt, he must first put himself in opposition to the thought of another. If this material is wanting, his spirit will not become phosphorescent, and it is as though he did not exist.

Goethe once wrote in his diary that Merck was the only person who wholly appreciated what he did; but Goethe nowhere expressed a longing, or even respect, for Merck. He saw all his hollowness from the beginning; but he could not dispense with him as the incorruptible mirror of things around him. Merck is like an excellent dictionary, in which information is given in regard to every word; while, at the same time, the all-comprising book does not contain a single thought for its own sake.

It has been asserted that Merck did not receive his due at the hand of Goethe. Loeper, in his observations on "Dichtung und Wahrheit," and Haym, in his book about Herder, have refuted this charge on good grounds. It cannot be denied that Goethe speaks with harshness of Merck; yet he acknowledges, at the same time, the obligations which he is under to him. If Goethe's sketch had been written when he was a young man, and in the immediate feeling of what Merck was to him while he was with him, he would perhaps have written more in consonance with the notice in his diary. But when he wrote "Dichtung und Wahrheit" the artistic considerations which decided the point of view from which to characterize the old Rath Goethe influenced him, also, in describing Merck. Goethe saw that Merck, after the power of his presence and the circle of those who had known and felt it had passed away, only continued to exist in the qualities with which he invested Mephistopheles, — impersonal criticism and the incarnation of a spirit whose only power lay in denial. If Goethe in painting Merck had not chosen his colors with this idea in mind, we should have had a portrait much lower in tone, but with blurred outlines, which would have been lost among the millions of good and honest people who lived in Germany then as now, but who were not strong enough to leave behind the faintest trace on the bronze tablets of history. But the most remarkable feature in Goethe's sketch of Merck is that while we have a picture of a thoroughly eccentric individual, which one would believe to be altogether unique, he has at the same time delineated a common type of man to which many a character we have known in life corresponds, and to whom we can imagine ourselves bearing exactly the same relations. Since Goethe has insured Merck's immortality, benevolent people may find excuses for his faults, and try to smooth off his rough angles; but to obliterate what Goethe has said of him would be to shroud his memory with oblivion.

Merck was the centre of Darmstadt society. Such a society first realizes a feeling of entire union, when one among them on whose judgment it places absolute confidence plays the part of unmerciful critic. This was Merck's *rôle* in Darmstadt, and soon also in Frankfort, where he became acquainted with Goethe's parents. In Merck's printing establishment in Langen, near Darmstadt, "Götz" was afterwards printed. The house still stands, and has lately received a commemorative tablet; and an inscription on the rock of the Herrgottsberge, in

Bessungen-wood, marks the spot where Goethe in the circle of his Darmstadt friends wrote, in 1772, the " Dedication of the Rocks to Psyche." These events are described in " Dichtung und Wahrheit" with evident enjoyment, while the letters of Caroline Flachsland add a yet finer and more detailed account of special days. She describes how they read and walked together; shared each other's ecstasies; drank punch together, — a kind of modern nectar, which was offered as a matter of course whenever the gods of this earth assembled; danced together, and, it may be, kissed each other. Caroline Flachsland was not only in the Darmstadt days an important personage to Goethe, but, as Herder's wife, through a long life was ever near him, and one of the women who gave him the most trouble. The mixture of rapturous passion with the most ordinary calculating practicality which formed her character produced, taking all in all, rather an unpleasant result. Nevertheless, in 1772, young, energetic, and elevated by the consciousness of being beloved by one of the first men of Germany, her stormy nature was rather an advantage to her. She was Goethe's particular friend, and his advocate with Herder. She introduced Goethe in Darmstadt, where soon, owing to her and to Merck, he was accepted as a man who, different from and superior to others, had a right to an exceptional position. In Darmstadt he was allowed to sentimentalize over the loss of Frederika. He tells us how on the road thither, which he traversed on foot, striding along through storm and rain, he rehearsed to himself the poems which as spontaneous creations sprang to his lips. Thus arose the " Wanderer's Storm Song," " Wenn du nicht verlässest Genius." Many of his most beautiful verses were written at this time. From few epochs, on the contrary has so little of his correspondence come down to us.

From 1771 to 1772 only three of his letters have been preserved : all his letters to Merck at this time have been destroyed. A change had come over Goethe; his old correspondents were dropped, and no new ones as yet had taken their place. He was still too young for Herder, who had other friends to whom he could open his heart. Herder, moreover, had to cultivate the friendship of people who could help him to a professorship, as he was not happy in Bückeburg. If Caroline Flachsland had not stood between Goethe and Herder, they would perhaps have shaken each other off forever. Herder seems to have had a presentiment of what was later fulfilled, that the weight of Goethe's mind would some day crush him to the earth. Mockingly he calls Goethe in one of his letters "too sparrowlike;" and then again "the great Goethe." Such jokes were not made of empty air.

But Herder at a distance could no longer judge Goethe. When they had separated, Goethe was wanting in much which, like a gift from heaven, came to him after the conclusion of his Strasburg sojourn. "Faust" and "Götz" were considered contraband in Strasburg: his studies were there the principal thing. In Frankfort also, under the eye of his father, he had at first to make a show of pursuing his career as a lawyer; yet he rose from his bed and retired to it with his mind full of literary projects. After his return to his father's house his life was so enlarged, that when he came to the account of this period in "Dichtung und Wahrheit" the chronological thread broke on which the events had previously been strung. Goethe, whose mind now begins to show immense fertility, and who is daily brought into contact with the most superior men in Germany, and who, at the same time reads and assimilates everything which appears in literature, now leaves the usual path, soars into the ether, and, as it were, disappears from our sight.

But who could ever expect to describe adequately a man of such gifts, in the inspired hour of early manhood, — a moment in which even ordinary men are apt to seem endowed with something extraordinary? If all young maidens prove to be what they seem between the ages of sixteen and eighteen, and all the young men what they promise between twenty and twenty-five, then beauty and intellect and genius with inexhaustible vitality would not in later years be regarded of such inestimable value. It is fortunate that every one in the enjoyment of this springtime of life believes it to be enduring. This faith in the inexhaustible power of youth, in a degree commensurate with his superiority, is an essential factor in picturing to ourselves Goethe's extraordinary appearance in the years which now begin. To his ever-increasing power there seemed no limit. Herder knew well that there may be men raised, in this wonderful manner, above the rest of mankind; but, as a critic, he could not make up his mind, without the most decisive tests, to concede to Goethe the right to step forward regally as a favorite of the gods! But now the proofs were given. Goethe wrote " Götz von Berlichingen." The manner in which Herder received this work helps us to understand what, with reference to Goethe, may be called Herder's conversion. We must now speak of " Götz."

" Götz von Berlichingen " was Goethe's first Frankfort work. It is also his first great poem. It raised him, at one stroke, to the very highest rank in Germany. With " Götz" he hit the mark in the centre, and there was no more thought of competition. Homage was paid to him who had taken the first place, and, indeed, before his name was known; for this drama was first published anony mously. His opponents were now only those who envied him, — those who either wilfully closed their eyes, or those who were too old to be moved by the fresh spirit which animated its pages. This accounts for Frederick the Great's opinion of it. Frederick could not be expected, in his old age, to appreciate Shakspeare and Goethe.

In order to understand clearly what Goethe accomplished in this work, we must go back a few hundred years and survey cursorily the development of the drama in Europe. Goethe's "Götz" was the first successful attempt to present to the German people, to whom fate seemed to deny the development of their own drama, an historical play, — although it was no acting-play, but only a drama to be read. We shall see in how far the term reading-drama ("Bücherdrama"), which is now considered reprehensible, was justified, and had for Germans a history.

The present European theatre is no indigenous creation of modern times: it is the theatre of the ancients, which by a series of transformations has come down to us through the ages. The same continuity and legitimate succession which is seen in poetry, painting, sculpture, law, and politics is to be traced here. The Greek drama, taken up by the Romans, was performed both in its own language and in Latin imitations, and passed through the various stages in the history of the Empire, — first flourishing, then stagnant, then in its decline, until at last it only vegetated. But tragedy and comedy will never cease to be read and played so long as Greek and Latin are studied. In the sixth century, when the Goths conquered Gaul, the Gaelic Roman Sidonius Apollinaris, who was a Christian minister, delighted himself and his friends by reading Menander; and among Goths, Franks, and Vandals hexameters were constructed after the model of Virgil, history after that of Suetonius, and the art of conversation was learned from Terence. Einhardt's history of Charlemagne is made up chiefly of Suetonic phrases. The comedies of Terence and Plautus, which bear the stamp of the genuine Greek drama, have certainly been played in Italy in all centuries. Through the darkest years in Italy, — cheerless years, although every spring the roses bloomed and every autumn the wine was pressed out, — the Roman drama was preserved, in a pitiable condition to be sure, but living; so that at the time when classic culture with fresh impulse again sprung up (modestly at first, and then more and more luxuriantly), it was able to take its part in the universal Renaissance. In the fifteenth century the performance of classic plays, often with a vast amount of scenic display, is something quite customary; and in the sixteenth century, the time of Raphael and Ariosto, the Italian stage — with tragedy, comedy, and opera — took its rise. About the middle of this century Italian actors were recognized as a special class; they had their own literature, and began to visit other countries in organized bands, wherever brilliant courts attracted them.

But this was only in three countries, — Spain, France, and England. Germany had no capital, and no nobility educated up to the standard of other nations. This is the primary cause why dramatic art was not developed in Germany as elsewhere. From the union of Italian classic stage-practice with the existing elements of native dramatic art, there arose in each of these three countries a national stage, having its own distinguished poets. This is the soil upon which in Spain Lope da Vega and Calderon, and in England Shakspeare, arose; while Italy and France could at first boast no important names. Corneille's youthful works show the same influences, but he soon rose into his own brilliant style, and drew Molière and Racine after him. Henceforth the supremacy of the French in the drama, as well as in the sphere of politics, æsthetics, and scholarly achievement, was decided. Everywhere the French were imitated ; and, about 1700, the supremacy of France in the drama was so fully established throughout the whole of Europe, that learned men, as well as the general public, believed beyond a doubt that the French drama had thrown even Greek tragedy into the shade. And when, added to all this, the first tragedy of Voltaire appeared, which in the united judgment of all his most competent contemporaries surpassed Corneille, Racine, and all the Greeks put together, it seemed as if such a height had been reached that further steps on this ladder were beyond the power of the wildest imagination. This unanimity of opinion that the highest literary merit had now been attained is in unison with those other symptoms of extreme self-satisfaction which we have already spoken of as the characteristic feature of the first half of the last century. But now came the change here, as elsewhere.

Voltaire, instead of striving to sustain the convictions of his fellow-men who had assigned to him such high rank, became himself the great destroyer of the very convictions upon which his sovereignty was based. Voltaire was not a man of the second rank, who carefully considered only that which would conduce to his personal renown. He stood too high to be so paltry. He would above all things move onward, and he shook the old machinery to pieces without thinking of himself. He prepared the people for that change of opinion in Europe which soon gained ground in all departments of intellectual activity. The stage was too important a factor in the public life at that time not to be affected at once by this change. Here, also, a return to Nature was necessary: the world was tired of the conventional hero raised above the changes of time and the frailties of humanity, and longed for distinct national and historical characters. Voltaire, who has unjustly been called the disparager of Shakspeare, — whom he naturally only so far understood as was possible in his day, and whom he criticised, it is true, with the same overweening confidence which he had shown regarding Corneille, — was the first who attempted to fit Shakspeare's characters into the frame of standard French tragedy; and he initiated the change which took place in France consequent upon the knowledge of the English stage as it was before the autocracy of the French. For though in England the so-called French classic tragedy had been triumphant, it could only be called a *succès d'estime;* and the old English theatre with Shakspeare was never really supplanted. The inherent realism of the English people would not allow their own drama, the natural product of the soil, to perish. They admired the French form, but enjoyed Shakspeare none the less. Voltaire discovered, with astonishment, that Shakspeare had made of Julius Cæsar almost a modern political character, giving to him traits entirely beyond the pale of French stage practice. In proportion as English political theories gained recognition, the English drama also began to be imitated in Paris. Diderot, following the English model, created the *comédie larmoyante*, presenting tragic subjects in modern costume and in prose form.

From Diderot Germany now received her first incentive to the formation of a national stage. The "weeping comedy" just suited us, — a story striking anguish to the hearts of the hearers, but ending in laughter. In France, after a tragedy a farce was played; but the German public prefers to draw this comforting sensation from the last act of the drama itself. We know what Lessing owed to Diderot.

The history of the German stage was first given by Gervinus in his work on German literature. I have known the time when Gervinus was considered among us to be infallible authority in æsthetics. Now, however, we hear him abused, and see the great man's well-deserved renown plucked from him feather by feather, as if his were borrowed plumes. But wherever I look I see others decked out in his feathers. What Gervinus's "History of German Literature" contains about our stage has received additions in the way of facts from many sources; but hitherto every writer has been indebted to Gervinus for the leading points of view. Gervinus is the creator of our literary history. Neither this nor his other valuable services to Germany can ever be cast into the shade, either by his political conduct in the last years of his life, or by the attacks of his opponents who now would deprive him of almost all his merits as a writer. We owe to Gervinus the first scientific analysis of Lessing. This analysis alone comprises almost the entire history of the growth of our national stage in the middle of the last century.

Why no national theatre could be formed in Germany has been already stated. More than any other field of art the stage needs, if it is to rise to a higher level, a never-failing audience representing the real criticism of the people. Only where the theatre is controlled by and dependent on the incessant and minute observation of the educated classes, as well as the more or less noisy applause of the uneducated, whose important share in the general criticism must be recognized, can real growth and the best results be anticipated. This is especially true if the actor is the first consideration: for the poet another element must be added, which is only furnished by great national centres. A real political life must display itself before his eyes in living characters, whose activity is watched over and controlled by this same wide-spread public. Where else should he seek the types for his *dramatis personæ?* The heroes of Corneille are those of the war of the Fronde; those of Racine, the victorious princes of the royal house in the first intoxicating campaigns of Louis XIV. Molière found the models for his characters among the nobility of Paris and Versailles, whose brilliant traits and many foibles were conspicuous before the eyes of the people and the subject of general admiration or derision. In Madrid also the Hapsburg dynasty was developing a monstrous activity, which, in spite of its secretiveness, it could not keep secret; its favorites and generals were lifted up and overthrown, and every kind of human fate bartered and sold. In London, before Shakspeare's eyes, it was the same. Everywhere it was a question of life and death, for the highest as well as the lowest; and everywhere it was understood that the interests of the country were involved in its politics. The people at large were not mere blind spectators. They felt it all. They whispered to each other what might not be said aloud: they could not prevent the outrages of which they were witnesses In France, people disappeared; in Spain, they were burned; in England, they were beheaded. English history, with its formidable apparatus of men and women, passed in a medley before Shakspeare's eyes. If he brought the tower upon the stage, every spectator knew what great lord had last been murdered there. The poet of that time had only to open his eyes; and as in an aquarium the glass walls give us an opportunity to observe the large and little fishes swimming about together, so at every street corner the poet stumbled against nobles and common people just as he wanted them for his plays.

But what material stood at the command of the German poet? With us political life does not come to the surface. Our great developments go on within the heart and brain. We gesticulate little. When we are excited, the hands find a snug place in the pockets; while for an Italian a dozen arms and hands would not be enough. Our fiercest storms often rage without rippling the surface of the waters: they work in the depths. Our nature and our life are wanting in every thing theatrical. Our centres of mental and political excitement, so far as they existed at the time of which we have been speaking, never put all classes of the people in commotion. There were no acting *masses*. That was no genuine national spirit, no real political life, which in the last century showed itself in the court intrigues of Vienna or Dresden, even though all Dresden and Vienna talked of it in the streets. The real decisions were veiled. Our poets had no opportunity to watch important revolutions among the people, in the midst of which the seed-corn of history was shaken out and ground before their eyes, and the bread kneaded and baked on which high and low must live. They were obliged, when they needed heroes, to bring before their fancies the heroes of whom they had read; and they ended by reproducing these paper heroes.

To Lessing only had it been granted to see a bit of the world. He had experienced the camp life of the Seven Years' War, and worked for his daily bread as an author. He had a hard struggle; but he lived through it, and became eminent. There was something aristocratic in his nature and in his appearance which he fully sustained. Lessing was the first who, having obtained a knowledge of the

French, Spanish, and English stage, so far as one can gain an acquaintance with it at home, had added to such knowledge all the experience which the miserable German stage could afford. He wrote "Minna von Barnhelm," a work which reaped the full benefit of all this experience. It was the first truly German production of the class which could be called a drama. Characters were here offered to the actor which appealed to the whole heart.

In spite of this success, Lessing's efforts were frustrated. To understand this we have only to read "Hamburgische Dramaturgie,"—a programme rich in promise; a kindly, painstaking criticism of the representations given at that time; then a gradual turning aside from the subject; and finally mere investigations of literary history, these ending very abruptly. What could Hamburg offer to a mind like his? Lessing was disgusted with the actors and the public. "Emilia Galotti," though prepared for the stage, was accepted only as a "reading-drama;" and "Nathan the Wise" was written as such. Lessing foresaw a possible representation of this play in the distant future; but this was all the connection it had with the stage in his eyes. With these, the condition of theatrical art in Germany had been tested. Lessing, who was born pre-eminently fitted for such a sphere, separated himself most openly from the German stage, and wrote, when he chose the dramatic form for the last time, only a poem for which he needed neither stage nor actor.

LECTURE VI.

GÖTZ VON BERLICHINGEN.

THE portion of Goethe's life in which he appears as stage enthusiast, stage poet, actor in his own plays, critic, and theatrical director can be so minutely followed, that, as in every case where the facts are before us, we can give an account of it in a few words.

It was from French actors in Frankfort that he received his first theatrical impressions. This forms a delightful chapter in "Dichtung und Wahrheit." At Leipsic he found Gottsched as the representative of the French stage, who together with his wife translated many of its productions. The position Goethe himself took in relation to all this is best shown in his "Mitschuldigen." His translation of the "Menteur" of Corneille into Alexandrines was at that time just as natural an undertaking as it would be to-day for a young philologist to imitate Greek hexameters, choruses, or the measures of Horace. In Strasburg, also, he found nothing so attractive as the French theatre, and became acquainted with eminent actors there. Then Shakspeare rose before him; while at the same time he became deeply impressed with the language of the old German stage. But all this did not awaken in him any thought of writing for the stage. He who in writing the "Mitschuldigen" had taken such pains to adapt it to the wants of the stage now undertakes

"Götz," which he writes without plan or regard to the stage, like a romance in dialogue. Goethe would not write for that stage which he had before his eyes. He was not even acquainted with Hamburg or Berlin; but without Lessing's experience, and through his own intuitions, he placed himself on Lessing's stand-point. He felt that he was in opposition to all the existing tendencies. "We are up to our ears in Gottschedism," he says in one of his letters while "Götz" was being printed. We translate this to-day: "We allow ourselves to be led astray by the common stage routine, and are guided by the wishes of the actors, who want only grand climaxes, opportunities for change of costume, and the like." He could never conceive of submitting to such demands in an inspired work. It was, however, no deliberate intention with Goethe: he could write only for that stage which every one builds in his imagination. In this sense his "Götz" was accepted. Goethe was so fully conscious of having used the dramatic form only in a general way, that he did not at first give to his poem even the title of "play," but called it the "Tale of Gottfried of Berlichingen with the Iron Hand, dramatized." In Goethe's "Götz von Berlichingen" four stages of the work are to be considered. The original conception in Strasburg, of which nothing written remains; the first copy in Frankfort, which as a manuscript lay unknown until after Goethe's death, when it was printed; thirdly, the definite form of the drama as it was given to the public in 1773; and, lastly, the attempt to arrange it for the stage in Weimar. An edition of the latter is still extant, but very little known. In Strasburg only the groundwork of the poem was completed.

Gottfried von Berlichingen's autobiography, which appeared in print in Nuremberg in 1731, had fallen into

Goethe's hands. Nothing could have suited his mood of mind better at that time than this unalloyed product of nature, — a simple story, free from art or artifice, which dropped into his hands like ripe fruit from the tree! Rousseau himself could not have given a more convincing proof that authorship must arise spontaneously from the nature of the thing. Götz von Berlichingen, who had known nothing but the roughest military work, who had beaten about in the midst of the endless feuds of his day, his only knowledge being of horses and weapons, doomed at last to involuntary idleness, sits down to write an account of his life from his childhood up, his only thought being to relieve an overburdened heart. Goethe understood this; his own poems had grown out of the same desire: he, too, had sat at his writing-table, and let his pen flow without knowing what would come.

Götz also dashes on, in wild, outspoken German, — no syntax, no punctuation, only pauses, as if in his narration he must stop to breathe; no thought of printing, or even of reading it aloud to others. Only the dim idea that posterity ought to know, truly and candidly, how noble his intentions had been, and how unjustly he had been treated. In this spirit he recalls one adventure after another. No doubt he was ready to strike the table with his iron fist to confirm the truth of every word, to vouch for it that all had happened exactly as he had represented, and to declare that he would prove it, too, in the face of whoever might dare to assert the contrary.

Götz was born in 1480, in Würtemberg, at "Jaxthausen on the Jaxt." The family still exists, and is prosperous. Count Friedrich Wolfgang von Berlichingen (I do not know whether the second name had anything to do with Goethe) republished the history of Götz, with all the documents, in 1861

At fifteen years of age Götz went with his uncle to the Imperial Diet at Worms. He early learned how things went on at these Diets, which allowed the instigators of the strifes and contentions which filled all Germany an opportunity for personal contact, when they could plague and pummel each other. He entered while young into military service, attached himself to various princes, and passed through many campaigns, but always as an independent man, reserving to himself the right to criticise the cause for which he enlisted. At the siege of Landshut, in the war of the Landshutian succession, he lost one of his hands, which he replaced by a most skilfully-wrought iron one.

The Emperor now commanded a general peace in his realm. Orders like these, however, were mere illusions, because the mania for quarrelling among the knights and princes would not allow peace to exist. We see Götz going from one fight to another; imprisoned, and set at liberty; recklessly rushing again and again into the struggle, and earning a reputation as the truest and bravest man in Germany. In 1525 we find him prepared to accept a position, which to us is now incomprehensible, as the chief leader of the rebellious peasants. Towards the end of the war he is taken prisoner, but is set at large on condition that he will appear at the proper time to answer for his share in the rebellion. He accepts these terms, and at the proper time goes to Augsburg to be tried, where he remains two years, and proves clearly that he had only accepted the command of the peasants to avert a greater evil. On this ground, in 1530, he is acquitted, although under conditions. He must remain quietly in his castle of Hornberg, must give full satisfaction to Mentz and Würzburg, or pay twenty-five thousand guilders. As security for all this he leaves many host

.ages, and lives henceforth according to his promise. But once again he appears in arms to join the troops of the Emperor Charles against the Turks, and afterward against France. When a peace is concluded he returns to Hornberg, where he continues to reside until his death, on the 23d of July, 1562, in the eighty-second year of his age.

In this career there is nothing tragic, — only the adventures of a knight, who after a turbulent life dies a peaceful death! So might it have been with Hutten had not a fatal illness brought him to an untimely end; and Luther, who is the best type of the energetic, contending, invincible German of the sixteenth century, closed his life in this way. The motto in that day was, "God help me, I cannot do otherwise;" and then in the universal confusion to press on until strength was exhausted.

The accusation has been brought against the age of the Reformation that nothing was actually accomplished, and that with endless compromises no unity was achieved. But look at particulars and individuals! What hard heads and what hard fists! And when we rightly contemplate and weigh the aggregate, we find with no end of haltings the most satisfactory progress.

What possessed Goethe to give to this long career, ending in the most natural death, a tragic conclusion? Goethe's drama gives us, with such additions and subtractions as pleases him, the life of Götz, up to thirty years before his death; Götz, in the play, reaches Augsburg, and there dies in prison. In the moment of death he receives the news that his sentence has been remitted; but it is too late.

In flagrant violation of the facts, Goethe seems in this conclusion to throw upon the German people the guilt of having sacrificed one of their best men. Can this be allowed?

And here we come to an important subject, — the difference between historic faithfulness and poetic truth.

Why is the charge never brought against Goethe of having falsified history, although we have known, as people knew then, that his drama does not correspond to the course of the actual story? It is because in "Götz" such a graphic picture of German manliness and German life in the age of the Reformation is given, that it has never entered the mind of any one to compare the reality with Goethe's poem. The Götz who wrote his own biography, from which Goethe drew his creation, and the Götz who is the hero of the drama, are two persons whose identity is indifferent to us. When we study the works of a great poet who borrows historical names for his characters, we must stand before them as before the pictures of a great painter whose subjects are taken from history. I use the adjective "great" in both cases, because in such discussions only masterpieces of the first rank are to be considered.

We admire in a picture the composition, the coloring, and the drawing; in a statue, the handling of the marble, the firm moulding of the figure, and the different points of view. When we see a life-like figure, we do not ask if it is a good likeness; but whether it is characteristic, well painted, and effective. There have been thousands of pictures painted of the Madonna, often with marked individual features; but it has never occurred to any one to suggest that they must all be false, because no two of them are alike. We have blond, black-haired, and brunette Madonnas; yet no objection is made to these differences: we only ask if the picture is beautiful, desiring nothing more of it or of the artist. When Michael Angelo had wrought in stone the statues upon the tombs of Giuliano and Lorenzo dei Medici, and was reproved because they bore no resemblance to the two dukes, he answered: "Who in the future is to know how Giuliano or Lorenzo actually looked?" To-day we distinguish one from the other only by the great difference of character expressed in the statues. We experience this oftener than we know. We imagine we find in many historical works the facts accurately and truly stated, while in reality we have only the impressions formed in the mind of the narrator himself. Poems, on the contrary, are often made to serve as historic coin. We know certainly that Schiller's Mary Stuart does not correspond to the actual Mary: this matter has often enough been discussed; but we are not so clear what difference existed between Shakspeare's historical plays and the actual events of English history which he has dramatized.

As soon as we know that we are dealing with a real work of art, the question as to authentic foundation for the facts becomes indifferent. Equally immaterial is the question whether Goethe, in describing the scenery in "Götz," had previously been in Jaxthausen to study the locality. The Jaxthausen which rises before our eyes in the drama, and the trees over whose tops it projects, are as well known and dear to us as a second home; while the actual place as we drive by it has as little interest for us as Romeo and Juliet's tomb at Verona, or Tasso's prison which is to-day exhibited in Ferrara. We would not miss one stone from Goethe's Jaxthausen, even if most convincing proof were given us that the actual castle is wholly different from the one described. The truth of an historical work of art lies not in the exact representation of what was peculiar in the period in which it was laid, but rather in what is comprehensible in all times. The historical costume is only the visible garb in which something is presented which in truth lacks all geographical and chronological foundation. There was never in any century an England in which Shakspeare's Lear or Richard could have lived; only an England raised above time and accident is the native land of both. And the fatherland of Götz von Berlichingen is not the Germany of 1480 and 1562, but our unchangeable Germany whose forests are the same to-day as they were a thousand years ago.

We have seen what harassed Goethe and the younger generation about him; how they saw all progress impeded by omnipotent conventions which ruled the whole order of existence, of whose worthlessness they were thoroughly convinced, and yet to whose laws it was necessary to conform. For there was nothing to take the place of these conventions. In the course of time, indeed, the French Revolution made the desperate attempt to call forth artificially a new and better existence, and where resistance was offered to force it upon mankind by the most extreme measures; but no one dreamed of such things in the days when Goethe in Strasburg or Frankfort found Götz's biography. With amazement he now became aware, as he read, that it was not the first time that these oppressions had weighed upon the German people. He saw in Götz one of the martyrs required by Germany in times like his own, although now long past from remembrance. He saw his fatherland, at the beginning of the Reformation, involved in a boundless web of political intricacies, whose smallest thread was nevertheless carefully and scrupulously guarded from violent hands. He had only to use his eyes to see that the conditions which were so mighty and potential, and at the same time so impotent and powerless, around Götz were still existing in full force. Not Götz's world stirred him, as he read the book, but his own world, whose mirrored image he believed he saw in it.

At the head of all was the Emperor, the highest conceivable power in the land, whose authority was not limited by any written statute, but who nevertheless encountered a justifiable resistance at the slightest exercise of his power. This was also true of the Germany of 1771. Goethe needed only to observe it.

Next to the Emperor was the clergy, theoretically subject to the Emperor and the Pope, but in fact perfectly independent of both; in theory poor and without possessions, yet in reality owning the richest parts of Germany; supposed to be the leaders of all spiritual movements, but in truth mortal enemies to all progress. Goethe had only to look at what was going on around him, on the Rhine or in Strasburg, where that Rohan was Archbishop who was so completely duped by Cagliostro, and where the people lay benumbed in the old superstitions, to see a similar condition of things.

Next to the Emperor and the clergy were the cities, the marrow of Germany; the only powers which represented to the outer world the fatherland, and which were able in their own might to defend their families and possessions. Here also was amassed the money which emperors and princes must borrow, if they were to have any scope in carrying out their undertakings. But these towns, because they had long ceased to act in harmony, were condemned to political stagnation and a sterile conservative existence. This also was still visible in Goethe's time. But the condition of the German cities then has been already discussed.

Next in order were the Secular Princes, whose sole endeavor was to make themselves independent lords of the land, but who had no opportunity to control events in such a way as to increase their power; and, finally, the Knights, — the *enfants terribles,* the proudest, most dangerous, and most indispensable element, — in theory bound in duty to support the Emperor and their liege lords in all their wars; but in fact wild, independent people, who, if their service was to be had, must each be separately won. They reserved to themselves the right to fight on the side which best suited their interests. Carrying on continual feuds with each other, and ever ready to rebel against their superiors, they were nevertheless filled with a tremendous *esprit de corps,* which found expression in the most complicated regulations and ceremonies, to which the Emperor himself must pay the greatest regard, especially if he wished assistance in carrying on a war.

The Princes had found in Frederick the Great their last distinguished representative. Knighthood, it is true, in 1771, was no longer what it had been of yore. But with the spirit of the knights Goethe identified himself and his friends; that is, the young, independent, patriotic generation, who, though ready for action, could not see clearly what they were to assail or where they were to begin the attack. Thus the waves of political excitement rose and fell: no one is presumptuous, but each demands his right; no one willingly injures another, but no one will bear an injury; each submits willingly to the law and to the tribunals which have a right to pass sentence on him, but none will allow law or tribunals to be forced upon him which he does not acknowledge as legitimate; and, finally, each one reserves to himself a revision of the case before his own conscience, and if the public decision does not stand this test he annuls it by his own sovereign right. We ask where, in the midst of such circumstances, lay the solid coherence of Germany? What held the great sea within bounds, and prevented its devastating overflow? What saved each man from blindly attacking and fighting his neighbor?

The elements which had wrought all this confusion possessed also the power to ward off the danger: they were our inborn honesty and the intention to deal justly with every man; the trustworthiness of a person who had once pledged his word; and the controlling influence of a public opinion, always striving to maintain an ideal stand-point, against which vulgar egotism played a losing game. With these elements it was possible to find a way through this maze, and to introduce a reformation which with slowly increasing power was bringing about a new and prosperous order of things, whose last delectable blossom must have borne fruit if it had not been nipped in the bud by the Thirty Years' War. As a political part of our history the Reformation is held in no especial esteem. We see so much intellectual power, so much attempted, so much done, and yet as a whole nothing which took a permanent form. It fills us with impatience to wade through the history of these compromises. It would seem as if Germany should have come out of this chaos a clear crystal with radiant sides and sharply defined outlines; on the contrary, it was the steady but almost imperceptible working on of things which was gradually raising us to a higher level, and without injury to any one of the factors. The Thirty Years' War which put an end to this quiet development is as little to be considered the result of these prosperous conditions as a pestilence which suddenly breaks out and carries off the people.

All these elements of German life in the sixteenth century, without exception, met in and had a perceptible influence over the career of Götz, who was himself in such a measure the product of his age that, although with his memory no important deed is connected, he is yet a striking illustration of the condition of things in his century. Goethe here saw, for the first time, what the peculiar German element was. He recognized how Götz's times resembled his own also in this,— that each man must follow his individual intuitions if he hoped to find the true path in the midst of conditions which were impracticable, and in a state of general disintegration. There was only this difference, that the situation in 1771 was far more difficult than two hundred years earlier.

Goethe, who looked upon his own time as the sequel of the Reformation, must have asked himself how things could have become so wretched among us after such a glorious beginning. No one could explain this better than Götz von Berlichingen. In this time of national confusion and yet of budding hopes Goethe sees foreign views gaining ground among us, and discords arising in the hearts of the German people, by which, according to him, the best men are ruined. His hero, a German of the purest stamp, follows the bent of his own noble nature and moves blamelessly on German earth so long as it is fertilized by its own native fountains; but now treacherous foreign waters suddenly overflow the land and draw from the soil a poisonous crop which springs up all around him. He is bewildered; his ideas grow confused; he becomes a rebel without willing it, and a criminal without knowing it. What did the new Roman law know of that old German legislation in which every village, one might almost say every house, had its own natural laws differing one from another, just as the horizon itself changes to each man when seen from his own doorstep? It thrills us to the heart when Götz, before the Augsburg citizens in the judgment hall, asks, first of all, what has become of his followers. Götz is at his wits' end, thus confronted with a law which acknowledges no distinction in circumstances. Weislingen also is ruined at a court to which foreign subtlety and deceit have found their way. Everything finally succumbs to the charms and intrigues of Adelheid, whose German blood has been corrupted, and whom Goethe has so seductively painted that, as he tells us in " Dichtung und Wahrheit," he became enamored of her himself. Everywhere honesty seems to play a losing game against Machiavellian policy, and the impersonal Roman formula overmasters the recognition of the individual in the German law. The German knight, the peculiar representative of the people in Goethe's thoughts, forsaking the seclusion of rural life forces himself into cities and courts; hence is derived Goethe's motto for his drama: "The heart of the people is trodden in the mire, and they are no longer capable of noble ambitions."

What do we think of these views?

We see Goethe prejudiced by an imperfect knowledge of our history, and we estimate what we owe to foreign nations to-day very differently. We have renounced the idea of indigenous art, poetry, and language in the sense of former generations; we see the great universal progress in the countries around us, and feel that the movement in Germany is in closest sympathy with it. Our reformation in art we owe to the study of the Greeks and Romans, and our present German style to the influence of classic syntax. We should have had no development of our own without the introduction of foreign ideas; and we now see that our national task does not consist in holding on to our traditions and customs because they are German, but in retaining those only which are really good.

At the same time, our history teaches us that there are permanent traits in the German character which constantly reappear, taking their own peculiar line of development; and we are patriotic enough to admire these traits, and to discover in them the foundation of our greatness: and therefore it is that we love and honor what is German. But while this German nature in Goethe's times seemed the sole possession of earlier and almost mythical races, whose vigor no subsequent generation could reach, we to-day postpone our ideal as something only to be attained in the future, and hope to do our part toward the fulfilment of what stands before our eyes as the mission of the German people in the history of the world. Of all this Goethe knew nothing when his drama first awoke in his mind. While he cast his thoughts back to the period of ancient German glory, and saw his own time both politically and æsthetically in such pitiable dependence upon foreign nations, he thought he discovered, captivated by Rousseau's theory of a return to Nature, a fundamental cause for this unhappy change in the adoption of foreign customs and institutions which began in the age of the Reformation.

We do not know how far Goethe advanced with "Götz" in Strasburg. It would seem as if he only worked upon it in imagination. The political element stood foremost in his mind while he wished to give a picture of public and private life in the good old times, — something the Germans should aspire again to arrive at, and such as Rousseau had intended in his "Émile." But this was not enough to tempt Goethe to give his ideas visible shape in a poem. Wholly new and personal elements must be added to the original material before this could be accomplished. If we read thoughtfully "Dichtung und Wahrheit" and his correspondence, we are convinced that the leading incentive in his nature, which like the mainspring of a watch sets all the machinery in motion, was to free himself from all the merely outward and conventional limitations of life. Evidently, as soon as Goethe began to feel himself at home again in Frankfort he saw what his position was and would have to be in his native city, in his father's house, and under his father's authority; and he said to himself that a man was justified in breaking away when he saw the essential rights of his spiritual existence in danger. But circumstances offered no opportunity to act upon this philosophic conclusion. On the contrary, he saw himself pledged as a lawyer to the pursuit of a profession which he never could be satisfied to regard as his life-work. As a Frankfort citizen he saw himself incorporated into a civic body whose very breath was enough to drive him away. To be compelled to live in Frankfort was just as unbearable to Goethe as the forced retirement of Hornberg to Götz. Nevertheless, on quiet reflection he acknowledges to himself that it must be endured, and submits, though his desire for freedom constantly rebels against it. "I, dear fellow," he says in one of his letters, "let my father do as he pleases; and every day he tries to draw me more and more into the web of all these city affairs. So far my submission continues; but one wrench, and all the seven-corded ropes of hemp are severed!"

Two ways presented themselves, one *real* and one *ideal*, to gain the longed-for freedom.

The real was some fine day just to go off. But for this extreme measure I have said already that the opportunity was not to be wilfully taken: it must be offered by the manifest hand of destiny in order to justify his going away to his family and to himself.

The ideal was to seek a fictitious being on whom to heap all his burdens and sufferings. Of this imaginary being he makes a mouthpiece to say all that he is forbidden to utter; its words have the secret import of a manifesto; the more he himself is obliged to conform to circumstances, the more freely he makes his poetical representative give vent to the feelings of his innermost heart. It was always with this end in view that Goethe selected and arranged the material for his poems. He compares the life he actually leads with what he should have led. In imagination he foresees his own ruin, like that of Götz in the prison at Augsburg, if he continues his career under the hitherto depressing circumstances. Foreign conventionalities, wholly alien to his German nature, must gradually crush out in him what he recognizes as best and holiest. Götz now stands before him in a new light. Goethe feels this historical figure draw nearer to him, and assume features resembling his own. Götz's inward struggles become now an image of what he himself is passing through. Early also in the first stage of the drama in Frankfort an added element made the poem assume a prominent place in Goethe's imagination, and the new stimulant came from a wholly different direction. Goethe himself tells us about it. It is no longer his country, nor the situation of Götz von Berlichingen, but quite another figure in his soul which presses forward to be represented. Filled with the consciousness of the wrong he has done Frederika, he seeks relief in whatever way it is to be found, and undertakes to express through another the reproaches he is heaping on himself for the desertion of this maiden and for the faithless betrayal of a heart which was so unwary that it could not even comprehend the meaning of faithlessness. In like manner Weislingen deserts Götz's sister, and Weislingen's character now takes the first place in Goethe's interest. From this moment it has a vital power, and is a living thing in his imagination.

It was curious how he was finally brought to commit to paper the scenes which filled his mind. He cannot resolve to take up his pen, but relates so much of what he is thinking to his sister Cornelia, who is his confidant, that she compels him to go to work. By fits and starts, and hurrying forward with great strides, he now writes the whole play, reading it aloud to her just as it is thrown off. Her praise induces him to continue the work, which in the autumn of 1771 is completed. "I dramatize the story of one of the noblest Germans," he writes in November, 1771, to Salzmann, " to rescue from oblivion the memory of a brave man; and though it costs me much labor it is a real diversion, which I need here, for it is sad to live in a place," etc. In six weeks the work is done. It is all written off-hand. He reads single scenes to Caroline Flachsland, and sends copies of it to Salzmann, Merck, and Herder. Salzmann quickly returns the manuscript with a careful and favorable criticism, and Merck likewise; but not so Herder.

Here Herder's nature shows itself again. That the piece has pleased him we see from what he says to Caroline Flachsland; but at the same time Goethe shall not gain ground. He ridicules Goethe; he jokes about him and his work, but all indirectly. He neither writes to him nor sends the piece back; and when at last he does write, it is in a hard, unfriendly tone, assuming such superiority of judgment that Goethe feels, as he had in Strasburg, that he is standing before a man who is stronger than himself and who must teach him. Whenever real criticism was offered Goethe, we see him always grateful and humble, even if it took the sharpest form; and so it was in this case.

He replies to Herder with a touching submission. The letter is dated July, 1772. He admits all. It is true that Shakspeare has ruined him; that his drama is cold and intellectual. "Enough," he concludes; "it must be melted over, freed from dross, supplied with nobler material, and recast, when it shall again appear before you." This letter contains, also, something which shows how difficult, or rather impossible, it is to grasp the deep symbolic meaning of a poem if the poet himself does not give the clew. We are reminded of the beautiful passage in which George appears before Götz in a suit of armor much too large for him, and expresses his earnest desire to ride with him and fight at his side. To this scene Goethe now refers while characterizing his relation to Herder. He feels that in writing his drama of Götz he is only a beginner, and has no right to go along with Herder whose full-grown shoulders completely fill out his suit of armor. How charming the modesty implied in this parallel! But now did this innermost consciousness of insufficient power which overwhelmed Goethe as he compared himself with Herder, who, a practised combatant, had long held the position he was hoping to reach, really suggest to him the character of George? Is the life-like figure of this youth to be regarded only as the poetical result of this sensitiveness; or did the scene occur to him by chance as he was writing to Herder, and strike him as the most convenient way of expressing what he wished to say? To answer this question is beyond the critic's power.

Without changing anything in the old plot, in a few weeks Goethe rewrote the entire drama. This must have been in the autumn of 1772, a year after the first manuscript was finished. His work amounted chiefly to pruning the piece unmercifully, like a hedge which had thrown out too luxuriant shoots on all sides. In the winter of 1772–73 it was printed, Merck sharing the expense. In the following June the book appears. Now Herder is honest enough openly to confess that he is impressed by the work; and from that time he grants Goethe equality with, and perhaps superiority to, himself.

The applause which the drama received in wider spheres came only by degrees to Goethe's ears. A cunning knave of a printer ran off with the largest share of the profits, and the business was so badly managed that he was forced to ask his friends to help on the sale, because he had not money enough to pay for the paper. He issued a new edition himself; but the profit of all the other editions was pirated by the notorious Berlin bookseller Himburg.

But one thing Goethe must have been assured of, that he had created an excitement of the most extraordinary kind. In August, 1773, he exclaims in one of his letters: "And now my dear Götz! I rely upon his healthy nature: he will continue to make his way. He is a human child with many faults, and yet withal one of the best. Many will take offence at his dress and some rough angles. But already I have received so much applause as to astonish me. And I do not believe I shall again produce anything which will find such favor with the public."

In the mean time, while attempting with broad strokes to picture the origin of " Götz," I have left unmentioned events which independently of this work made the years 1772–73 the most important in Goethe's mental development. When he undertook " Götz," his sister, Caroline Flachsland, Merck, Herder, and a few others formed his whole public; when the work came out this circle was extended in many directions. The personal feeling which Goethe hoped to assuage by this task had long been outgrown, and his heart had formed other ties out of which a new poem arose in his soul, whose success was destined far to exceed that of " Götz."

LECTURE VII.

THE SORROWS OF YOUNG WERTHER.

THE first Frankfort manuscript of "Götz" was just completed and had been given into the hands of his distinguished friends, when it was thought best (in the spring of 1772) that the young lawyer, who had only entered upon his professional career, should be again interrupted that he might for a while be a practitioner in the Imperial Chamber at Wetzlar. This Imperial Chamber was the highest central court for the suits which arose among the countless divisions of the Holy Roman Empire of the German nation. The rulers in these States, owing to their complicated rights and titles, furnished abundant material for fresh disputes. But the number of active jurists did not correspond to the cases; hence arose favoritism and neglect. The chief consideration was simply how to command influence enough to bring the cases on. For one hundred and sixty years had this condition existed, when the Emperor Joseph ordered an investigation which brought to light the most shameful malpractices. There was no better opportunity for a young man ambitious of distinction than to be engaged for a time in this work at Wetzlar; and, added to this, Wetzlar was only a day's journey from Frankfort.

Goethe was so absorbed in his Frankfort and Darmstadt friends that it seemed scarcely possible that new attachments could spring up in his heart, and yet he now fell into a family circle which soon absorbed him as wholly as the clergyman's family at Sesenheim had done. Now begins his friendship for Lotte, which every one interested in Goethe's life believes he fully comprehends. Yielding to his desire to feel himself at home in some agreeable family, Goethe became a frequent visitor at Amtmann (steward) Buff's, in the renowned "Deutsches Haus," which still stands in Wetzlar. Lotte, the eldest daughter, had already as good as plighted her heart and hand to the young Kestner; and the happy man, half her lover, went in and out (it was one of the conscientious connections of those days), and became Goethe's particular friend. Now arose the struggle in Goethe's soul as to whether he could, as perhaps was possible, out-rival Kestner in Lotte's heart. He was true to his friend. The intercourse continues a few months. It becomes necessary for him to leave Wetzlar, and one fine day he goes off like a shot. But there remains as the result of this episode a life-long friendship between him and the whole Buff family, as we are now certain from a correspondence which for a long time was so jealously guarded by the Kestner family that it was only known to exist; but it has now been in print for more than twenty years. These were the simple facts. How was it possible to make out of this experience, which included no passionate or violent scenes, the most beautiful and thrilling German romance which has ever been written? We will make it our task to investigate.

The genesis of this masterpiece is clearly before us. As we became acquainted with the incidents from which the Sesenheim idyl arose, which Goethe transfigured into poetry forty years after they occurred, so we may now follow by degrees Goethe's fancy for Lotte, which, in the course of a single year, shaped itself in his imagination into the "Sorrows of Werther."

It is curious to see Goethe at that time spontaneously converting all the realities of his life into poetry. He seems to us like one upon a chase through the realm of humanity. A consuming desire urges him on continually to new experiences; he surrenders himself wholly to each, and then with pain tears himself free, only restlessly to seek new ties by which to be again made captive. All these anticipations, illusions, and excitements leave behind various images in his soul which enter upon a life of their own, uniting, separating, and changing until they finally come forth glorious creations moulded to completeness; but even then the elements are not quite set at rest, but are subject to endless transformations. He does not always, however, pursue the same method. To represent Frederika poetically, Goethe has exhibited her under different forms. Even before he thought of leaving her, as the first reflected image Gretchen had become detached from her; then Marie Clavigo; perhaps, also, Marie von Götz; and, lastly, the form which bears Frederika's own name in "Dichtung und Wahrheit."

But we find Goethe's imagination taking quite another way to present Lotte as a poetical vision. The Lotte who held sway in the "Deutsches Haus" in Wetzlar, and whom Kestner had married, was not fitted by her simple nature and destiny to be made the heroine of a romance. The suicide must take place of a man who was a perfect stranger both to Goethe and Lotte, to suggest the climax. This suicide happened more than a month after Goethe left Wetzlar; but even this was not sufficient to furnish all the material necessary for the romance. Another figure moving in a sphere apart from Lotte was yet to be added; and from these two the ideal being was created whose romantic beauty shed its lustre finally on the single form of Lotte Buff in Wetzlar.

Let us carefully examine the details of what happened in Wetzlar. From the 9th of June until the 10th of September, 1772 (exactly three months), Goethe lived with Lotte and Kestner in Wetzlar. Kestner belongs so intimately to both that he is not to be separated from Lotte or Goethe. If we compare what the romance tells us about their relation with the statement in "Dichtung und Wahrheit," and also with what Goethe's correspondence contains regarding it, and again with what Goethe as well as Kestner occasionally say about the matter, it follows that not only is the story to be considered merely as a poem, but also that in "Dichtung und Wahrheit" a myth has been created, as in the case of Frederika, although from other motives. Mere friendly consideration for Lotte, whom Goethe would not deprive of the renown she had so long enjoyed of having inspired him in his youth with a beautiful passion, made it impossible for him to state at a later period just what actually occurred.

Indeed, he confesses that he had, like Zeuxis for his Helen, made use of a series of models, and that several Lottes are united in the Lotte of the romance; but even this is so expressed that the glamour is not stolen from Lotte Buff, and she does not lose her lustre because of rival suns. Goethe mentions no name but hers. Still, in the bare exposition of the reason why he left Wetzlar, a contradiction is implied. In one instance, he leads us to think that regard for Kestner had caused his retreat directly he lost his self-control; and then again he tells us that Merck appeared in Wetzlar, and by his criticism cooled his enthusiasm for Lotte. Either the one or the other must be true, for both at the same time seem impossible. Comparing the authentic letters written by Goethe at the time of departure with these two conceptions, we find that he breaks off abruptly in an excited moment as if it were a matter of life and death, and goes away feeling that every additional hour near Lotte is fatal; and he writes, after he is gone, like a desperate man. Yet he writes not to Lotte but to Kestner, to Lotte's betrothed, whom he must have hated. This despairing tone at the loss of Lotte, who should properly have been his, is from this time sustained as his stereotyped mood. In thought he converses with her; he dreams of her; has her *silhouette* over his bed; selects the wedding-rings; is present in imagination at the wedding,—and all in the same tone. But let us compare with this the other incidents connected with Goethe during this not brief period, and we shall find that the Kestner-Buff correspondence really includes very little of it. Lotte and her surroundings form an Arcadian pastoral in Goethe's mind,—a wide, lonely region, where in one spot Lotte and her family dwell in their cottage; and in another Goethe, apart from her, sits in solitude. And now farther we will compare with this what Kestner, who was a pedantic lover of the truth, has recorded in letters and diaries,—as, for instance, his assertion that Goethe behaved much more magnanimously than the romance would lead us to believe; and, again, that Goethe never stood in such close relations to Lotte as did Werther in the fiction. Indeed, it seems as if Goethe was more intimate with Kestner than with Lotte.

Something, at all events, has been withheld which would afford an explanation of these contradictions. Let us recall the fact that, according to his own narration, Goethe was seized when near Frederika with the feeling that he was trying to grasp shadows,—and this even before they had mutually uttered the decisive words that they loved each other. Can it be possible that in Lotte's case he had the same impression, and that Merck like Mephistopheles only finished a work which Goethe, following the law of his nature, had already half done himself? Goethe seems to have begun to criticise his feeling for Lotte before Merck came to Wetzlar: a document showing this to be so has been preserved.

From the beginning of 1772 Goethe was an active critic in the "Frankfurter Gelehrten Anzeiger." The most able of all his articles for this journal was written in Wetzlar, and published Sept. 1, 1772. It must have been composed some days earlier, at least; and even before that have been clearly wrought out in his thought. It is a critique of the poems of a Polish Jew, which were published that same year in Mitau and Leipsic. We pass over what Goethe says of the poems, to come to the close of the essay, which alone interests us. It runs thus:

"O Genius of our Fatherland! May a youth soon arise who, full of youthful merriment and vigor, will in his circle be the most genial companion, suggesting the most pleasing games, singing the most joyful songs, animating the chorus and roundelay; to whom the best dancer will gladly give her hand to dance a series of the newest and most varied figures; before whom the fairest, the wittiest, and the gayest displays her charms to ensnare him; whose sensitive heart is made captive; who in a moment proudly tears himself free again, and on awaking from his poetic dream finds that his goddess is *only* beautiful, *only* witty, *only* gay; or, his vanity offended by the indifference of a reserved maiden, intrudes himself upon her, and by feigned sighs, tears, and tokens of sympathy, added to manifold tender attentions during the day and melting songs and music by night, finally conquers her, only again to leave her because she is *only* coy; who, with the daring freshness of an unsubdued heart, jeers and exults over his defeats or victories,—yes, over all his follies and humiliations!

"But we should glory in this fickle boy, who cannot find a few commonplace feminine charms.

"And, O Genius! be it publicly known that neither shallowness nor weakness is the cause of his fickleness. Let him but find a maiden who is worthy of him! If, led by holier feelings, he seeks a solitude far from the whirl of society, and finds in his wanderings a maiden, whose soul all gentleness, whose form all grace, has harmoniously developed in the quiet circle of active domestic love and duty; the darling, the friend, the support of the mother,— indeed, herself a second mother in the home; whose love-enkindling soul irresistibly attracts all hearts; to whom poet and philosopher would willingly go to school, seeing so much courtesy and grace united to intrinsic virtue: and oh! if she in hours of solitude feels that with all this overflowing love she yet longs for a heart which, young and warm as hers, will anticipate with her the more distant felicities of this world, and in whose animating presence she may hope to realize the golden visions of eternal companionship, lasting union, and immortal, evergrowing love!— should these two find each other, they at once divine what an embodiment of bliss each has secured in the other, and that they never can be parted. Then let him stammer — foreshadowing, hoping, enjoying— what none with words have ever spoken out; none with tears, none with the long, lingering look and the soul in it. Truth and living beauty will then be in his songs, not the glittering baubles floating in so many German melodies. But are there such maidens? Can there possibly be such youths?"

We see thus early the language in which "Werther" was afterward written: it gushes. Undoubtedly Lotte is here sketched, and the closing questions show that Goethe thought it necessary to ward off the suspicion that it was drawn from life. At the same time, however, he speaks again of awaking from the poetic dream: and the question is, whether this awakening had not in the actual case already occurred; so that the ideal picture he has given us is not Lotte as she was, but as she must have been to have really captivated him.

In the mean time, whether I have guessed rightly or not, Merck arrives one day in Wetzlar, and proceeds to test Goethe's extravagant admiration for Lotte. It does not stand the test. He succeeds in so far cooling his enthusiasm that Goethe tranquilly plans his departure, and shortly after Merck's visit actually leaves Wetzlar. If the honest Kestner, in the beginning, had to go through a severe conflict as to whether he ought to surrender his claims to Goethe as being his superior, now at least there was no longer any question about the matter. The relation had reached its natural climax, and exhausted itself without injury to either of the three concerned.

But if Goethe was so very calm when he left Lotte and Wetzlar on the 10th of September, 1772, how are we to account for the letters in which he bade farewell to Lotte and Kestner? If Goethe wished, for Kestner's sake, to maintain his reserve as regards Lotte, why this glowing language, which at the last moment might have taken Lotte's heart by storm and drawn her irresistibly to him? And how is it consistent with the despairing tone of these last hours that Goethe directly after writing the letters should, in the most tranquil frame of mind, wander along the banks of the Lahn, find new friends, and attach himself to them most heartily? This contradiction is only to be explained by trusting Goethe's letters and the assertions he makes at the time of his separation from Lotte, and by setting wholly aside all that is contained in "Dichtung und Wahrheit" and the romance, as has been done by the editor of the Kestner letters.

We give the letters: —

Goethe to Kestner.

Sept. 10, 1772.

He is gone — when you receive this note: he is gone! Give Lotte the enclosed letter. I was quite composed, but the conversation with you tore me all to pieces. I can say nothing to you at this moment but farewell. If I had remained with you an instant longer, I could not have contained myself. Now I am alone, and to-morrow I go. Oh, my poor head!

Goethe to Lotte.
[Enclosed in the above.]

I certainly hope to return, but God knows when! Lotte, what did I feel at your words, when I knew I was with you for the last time! No, not the last time; and yet to-morrow I go away! He is gone! What spirit led you to that discussion? When I might have said all I felt, ah! I only thought of this world, of her hand, — which I was kissing for the last time, — of the room which I shall not see again, and the dear father who accompanied me for the last time!

I am now alone, and may weep. I leave you happy, and do not go away from your heart. And I shall see you again, but not to see you to-morrow seems to me like never. Say to my boys, he is gone! I cannot go on.

Goethe to Lotte.
[Enclosed in the former.]

My things are packed up, and the day breaks. One quarter of an hour more, and I am off! The pictures which I have forgotten, and which you will divide among the children, must be my excuse for writing, when I have nothing to say; for you know all,—know how happy these days have been to me. And I go to the dearest and best of men—but why from you? It is so; and my fate is, that I cannot add to to-day to-morrow and the next day,—what I so often added in joke.

Be always cheerful, dear Lotte: you are happier than hundreds. Only do not be indifferent; and I, dear Lotte, am happy to read in your eyes that you have faith. I shall never change. Adieu, a thousand times adieu!

GOETHE.

To explain these letters we borrow the following passage from a letter written to Kestner six months later, dated "April, 1773":—

"I have had a beautiful day,—so beautiful that labor and joy, striving and attaining, were one. And when the glorious stars appeared in the evening sky my whole heart was full of the rapturous moment when I sat at your feet, and played with the fringe of Lotte's dress; and, ah! with a heart which was to enjoy even that, spoke of the beyond, and did not mean the clouds, but the mountains only."

What, then, had happened? Goethe, fully resigned, sits one evening at Lotte's feet. A conversation carried on by the three suddenly takes a turn which excites him so powerfully that he feels things must be brought to an end. What moves Goethe so deeply is a misconception of Lotte's. He had spoken only of a short absence from her; but in a highly excited, ideal mood. She declares herself prepared to resign Goethe wholly for this life.

But does it not now appear like wounded vanity? At times, when reviewing his past life in later years, Goethe reproached himself for what he called his obtuseness and his predilection for doubtful connections. He had with his passionate nature led himself and others into situations in which a prompt and clear explanation was necessary; but he becomes suddenly like one paralyzed; sees what is before him without being able to take any resolute steps, and lives on, not exactly hoping for a fortuitous solution, but recognizing it as the only possible means of release. Goethe himself speaks of this so openly, and reproaches himself so severely for having yielded to this tendency where important questions were involved, that we are inclined to admit without hesitation that thus matters may have stood in this case.

Goethe, who at the same time had the wonderful gift of following out in all their consequences and of foretelling the slow development of things, had seen a double calamity impending in Lotte's fancy for him and in the generous withdrawal of Kestner in his favor. He perhaps felt himself unable either to respond to the one or to accept the other. Goethe did not trust his own heart. The lot of two human beings would have been uselessly sacrificed for him. He saw just how matters stood, and knew what to do and what not to do. It had been the same in Sesenheim; only there he could not resign the sweet habit of living on in close proximity to the beloved one as he had begun to live.

With Lotte, however, he had felt himself quite safe, until that evening when an experience touched him for which he was not prepared. Sitting together, they had talked of Goethe's approaching departure,— by which Goethe only meant his going to Frankfort. But the indifference which makes Lotte misunderstand him, accept quietly the idea of seeing him in another life, and calmly extend to him her hand, never, as she says, expecting to see him again in this world,— this suddenly kindles in him a feeling of which he had not the slightest conception. He had been strong enough, so long as it lay in his might and choice, to go away from Lotte; but now that it is she who resigns him at once with such equanimity, a demoniac desire is instantly roused to prove to this maiden that a heart like his was not to be thrust aside without ceremony. And now he finds that he has given himself credit for more strength than he possesses; and it becomes clear to him that he must make an end of it at once.

It is this sudden outburst of a comparatively new passion which fills the two notes written on the evening of the 10th of September. Even the next morning he regards the matter more calmly, and adds a few words in an altered tone; while a half year later he speaks with light irony of himself at that time. Nothing of all this is to be found in "Dichtung und Wahrheit."

If I declare Goethe's representation of his love for Lotte in "Dichtung und Wahrheit" to be a myth, I do not mean that it is untrue; but only that he has lent to the whole narration certain figurative universal lineaments, which while betraying the facts still veil them. Goethe prefers to conceal what drove him away from Wetzlar; and who has any right to know it? Hence the somewhat mysterious words: "I separated myself from her not without pain, and yet without repentance."

It was Merck who exerted himself to take Goethe away from Wetzlar,— probably he knew well what he was doing; and it was also Merck who, to work out the cure before Goethe settled himself again in Frankfort, proposed the journey which ultimately led to the writing of the "Sorrows of Werther." He invited Goethe to go with him to Frau von Laroche's on the Rhine, and they agreed to meet at Coblenz. Goethe sent his baggage in advance, and went on foot himself down the Lahn valley. He describes the way he took, which few people to-day, when the convenient railroad is scarcely to be avoided, would be tempted to follow. He saunters along so slowly that he is several days in reaching Ems. From there he proceeds by boat. "Here the 'alte Rhein' revealed itself to me."

There is an earlier and a later Rhine poetry. To the earlier belong the times when Clement Brentano sang the "Lorelei," Gunderode and Bettina rhapsodized on the Rhine, and Goethe himself again visited and described its glorious banks; to the later, the younger Romanticists, whose key-note was sounded by Simrock, and who were localized in Cologne and Dusseldorf, while the former belonged rather to the *Rheingaue* The earlier was more lyrical; the later more political and historical; and to-day, — when the steamboat is scarcely used because the railroad takes one more rapidly along the banks of the river, which is hardly seen from the car-windows, and whose hurrying waves and vessels seem to be lagging idly behind, — even this has come to an end, and the lonely traveller with difficulty works himself up to a fictitious enthusiasm from what he reads about it in the guide-book.

But in 1772, when Goethe was young, no worn-out romantic glamour was needed; for the Rhine was really in its own majesty still the "alte Rhein." All the castles and monasteries mirrored in its waves were then filled with rich ecclesiastical and secular nobles, and all the motley immemorial order of things was filled with a life of which no one remains to-day to tell the tale. How many different lords' territories at that time bordered on the river or were intersected by it! Over its surface, still waved the full, warm breath of South Germany; while to-day it has become North Germany and cool. Goethe tells us about his journey slowly and quietly, for his progress was slow. "Finally, grand and majestic, the castle of Ehrenbreitstein appears."

At his feet in the valley lay the country house of the Privy Councillor von Laroche. The site, the different views from the place, the interior ornamentation, are brought before our eyes with a pleasing garrulousness, as if they must remain so forever.

Goethe, when writing his final description, had himself seen other times, — had lived through the whirlwind in France which had put an end to all this abundance, — but he writes with the certainty with which an aged man may tell how things were on the Rhine in the old days when he was young. These times, and with them Frau von Laroche and the many volumes she then published, are at present forgotten in Germany. Her romances no longer make any eyes moist. Recently, books and magazine-articles have been written about her; but the world at large knows nothing of Sophie von Laroche. Her experiences are antiquated. There is no intrinsic power in them. Fate had, indeed, blown the poor woman hither and thither; but she never encountered the actual storm which might have completely unfolded her nature.

She was engaged in her youth to a handsome Italian, from whom, for her father's sake and on account of his religion, she separated. She next failed in a matrimonial affair with Wieland, whose mother stepped between them, although he remained through life her devoted friend. Ten years later she married, from external motives, Herr von Laroche; and it was not until her children were almost grown up that her first work appeared, edited by Wieland. It was a sensational romance, called "Die Geschichte des Fräulein von Sternheim," which made her known, or, as the phrase is now-a-days, "renowned." In criticising this romance, Goethe gained his first literary spurs.

I have spoken of the "Gelehrten Frankfurter Anzeiger" started by Merck and Schlosser. Goethe's critical essays, long since included in his works, and also to be found in Hirzel's collection, form a considerable series. On the 14th of February, 1772, a discussion as to the merits of this romance appeared, in which the second part, or sequel, was treated in a manner which gave Madame von Laroche nothing to complain of.

Goethe's criticisms showed, as the work of a beginner, perfect facility in the use of language and a wealth of sound thought stated with provoking self-reliance. We feel at once that the older writers, who were a power at that time, must have felt an electric shock at his tone; and it was natural that they should seek to establish some sort of friendly relations with this rising young genius. Although now over a hundred years old, with a few changes in the leading words these essays would maintain their rank among modern productions. In the review of "Die Geschichte des Fräulein von Sternheim," the previous criticism of the first part of the novel is analyzed and refuted. Goethe's judgment of the book was so flattering that he was perhaps indebted to it for his first meeting with Madame von Laroche, which took place in the spring of 1772 before the visit to Wetzlar. She then went to Darmstadt, where they were disappointed in her; for, instead of a simple soul, like the Fräulein von Sternheim, a lady appeared who, with knowledge of the world and not without pretensions to beauty, usurped the first place in the *salon*. Caroline Flachsland, exasperated at this, wrote to Herder. She said Goethe was so sick of Madame already in Frankfort that he would not come with her to Darmstadt; and Fräulein Flachsland, who always painted in strong colors, uses these words: "Goethe was furious as a lion against her."

In "Dichtung und Wahrheit" no reference is made to this journey. Goethe felt, when recording his recollections, that to introduce Madame von Laroche worthily, she should be presented as the presiding genius of a country-house at Thal on the Rhine. He therefore passes over unnoticed what occurred earlier. We receive the impression that on his Rhine journey in 1772 he was struck for the first time with the real charms of Madame von Laroche and the beauty and grace of her daughter Maximiliane, who had also accompanied her mother to Frankfort in the spring. He describes the appearance of Madame von Laroche, whose social position was between noble lady and citizen's wife; her dress always the same, simple but distinguished, corresponding to her manner. Added to this was the tact and friendliness of her husband, and the loveliness of her children. Maximiliane was just entering maidenhood, — rather small than large, with the blackest eyes, and a complexion as fresh and blooming as it is possible to conceive, — still half a child, but through her intercourse with her father, to whom she clung with special tenderness, superior to her years. Maximiliane Laroche was the mother of Bettina and Clement Brentano. These will be spoken of later; and I only call attention to them here as explaining why Bettina, in printing her letters, called them Goethe's "Correspondence with a Child." Maximiliane's children, as formerly Lotte Kestner's, believed themselves to hold a sort of kinship to Goethe.

In the house of Madame Laroche, where friends were constantly coming and going, Goethe came in contact for the first time with the school of the sentimentalists, or what we may call the dominant literature of the time.

In Leipsic he had seen Gellert and Gottsched working as leaders of powerful factions, but was naturally much too young to take part in such things either to co-operate or to oppose. What he wrote himself at that time were only the crude efforts of a student, who does not yet know what direction to follow. In Strasburg he certainly felt more self-reliance; but even there he was not known beyond the circle of his sympathizing friends. In Frankfort, at last, he touched the pulse of the great public. But the "Anzeiger" and its contributors looked upon themselves as a younger generation; their watchword was battle; a path was first to be hewn out; they were a new departure, represented by new people. Madame Laroche on the contrary, under the protection of Wieland, was a member of an old and tried system of power and experience. Wieland was a man of some significance in Germany. His influence was not a thing of yesterday; and, as he felt himself thoroughly safe and strong, so likewise those who were allowed to be partners with him regarded themselves as under his protection. The relations of Goethe to Wieland for the next three years were founded on the maintenance of the different stand-points they had taken. Wieland attempted, with the skill of a real business man, to assert his authority, until it finally dawned upon him that he must submit. But of this we shall speak in its proper place.

Goethe's pleasing description of his visit to the house at Thal hardly allows us to believe that he was only there five days, as Loeper asserts. We feel as if he must have been there at least a fortnight. The different phases of social life there are described, as it were, in organic succession; the different characters of the people who gathered there, sketched; and he finally tells us how near all came to having a bad time at the end. Merck arrives with his family. A ferment directly begins among the guests: incompatibility of temper manifests itself. Merck's sneers, his coldness and restlessness, arouse a feeling of discomfort in the company; so that, just at the right time, the signal for breaking up is given. But note well how Goethe allows that Merck works here, as at Wetzlar, in Mephistophelian fashion. Goethe takes the returning yacht (the representative of the official trade of the Rhine), sails slowly along the stream to Mentz, and reaches home again in the best possible humor. In enthusiastic words he thanks Madame Laroche for the kind attention he has received.

No hint yet of those moods out of which, after Maximiliane's appearance in Frankfort, the second part of "Werther" arose. Goethe had conceived a hearty affection for this clever and fascinating girl; but she was so young that it was of a purely brotherly nature, and the feeling never changed. The circumstances, however, into which Maximiliane was transplanted in Frankfort were of so peculiar a kind, that, combined with the impression he had already received in Wetzlar, it excited ideas in his imagination which formed the romance. Nothing of a thrilling or surprising nature happens, however; things move on slowly, and the effect produced upon Goethe is gradual.

Between him and the Wetzlar friends no shade of misunderstanding had arisen. Kestner came to Frankfort in September, immediately after Goethe's return from his visit to Madame Laroche, and spent most of his time with him. He departs. Goethe's letters give full accounts of the distractions of his life in Frankfort. He is active in helping on Schlosser's engagement to his sister, and is successful. A medley of men press around him to whom, according to his nature, he gives himself up wholly; but at the same time his thoughts are wont to turn to Wetzlar, as the spot where stillness and peace reign. He sends, from time to time, a kind of journal or leaves from his diary, indifferent to whom they go: they are addressed simply to "the Kestners." In these letters he treats of himself and his relation to Lotte as a continuous romance, but one that does not bear the slightest resemblance to the "Sorrows of Werther." In direct contradiction to this his outward behavior was a certain inward mood, revealed to no one, but which might have been guessed by putting together and interpreting certain words which he occasionally dropped.

When Goethe went back from Wetzlar to Frankfort, he shuddered at the thought of the life to which he was returning. At that time "Götz" had not been worked over for the press; and no anticipation of his later fame animated and refreshed him. He saw himself thrust anew into the old swamp, in which it was insufferable to wade about. He felt himself above Frankfort society, and hated it. He hated his father's house, and at the same time could not do without it. He saw his only confidant, his sister Cornelia, through her engagement to Schlosser, already in a certain sense separated from him; and so, while seeming to be in the midst of life's enjoyments, he really brooded over the most despairing thoughts. Some one said to him, at that time, that the curse of Cain was upon him. Goethe relates this himself. His unstable nature was alarmed the more in proportion as he was led to criticise it, and as he became convinced that there was no remedy for it. And this reaches so high a point that he actually wrestles with the temptation to suicide which springs up within him. While in this frame of mind the news reaches him that Jerusalem, a young man of about his own age, and who had worked as he had in the Imperial Chamber at Wetzlar, had shot himself out of disgust with life. Kestner announces it. Kestner had lent Jerusalem the pistols; and the note in which they were asked of him, having been first thrown into the waste-paper basket, was later hunted out, and is in "Goethe and Werther" given in fac-simile. Goethe describes what passed before his fancy when he received Kestner's letter telling of the misfortune.

Jerusalem was the son of an esteemed and renowned theologian. He had studied with Goethe in Leipsic without making much impression on him. Goethe found him again in the Imperial Court at Wetzlar; but there, also, they were only distant acquaintances. Sundry literary productions of Jerusalem's had been published, and among them a letter in which he asserts that he does not like Goethe. Jerusalem was in love with the wife of a Wetzlar official, and shot himself for her sake in October, 1772, — a month after Goethe left Wetzlar, and under circumstances which exactly correspond to what we find related in "Werther."

This occurrence made a tremendous impression on Goethe; but, from reasons which had little to do with Lotte Buff, neither the memory of her, nor even that of Jerusalem, is especially awakened in his soul by this deed. The reasons why it took such hold on his imagination were of a deeper and more personal nature. He and Jerusalem became suddenly one and the same person. He sees himself as in a mirror; and at the same time Jerusalem's beloved one assumes the form and features of Lotte, and he and she, Werther and Lotte, the two characters in the romance, stand before Goethe living creations, divorced from himself, — two finished works of art.

Now begins the serious work of the fiction. In November, a business journey leads him to Wetzlar. He sees Lotte again ; collects exact details of Jerusalem's character and death ; and receives from Kestner, after his departure, full particulars of what he could not find out on the spot. The idea of writing a romance in memory of Jerusalem seems now to have become a fixed plan. But for the present the project is laid aside ; the vision slowly faded again, as wholly other subjects claimed his attention.

At first, he published the little work on the Strasburg cathedral ; then, in the beginning of 1773, he prepared " Götz " for the press. In the spring Lotte and Kestner were married, with Goethe's friendly sympathy. He provided the rings, and took upon himself many other little duties. But after the youthful pair went to Hanover longer intervals in his intercourse with them naturally occurred. Other people engrossed him, and Goethe had no longer as a necessity to fly in thought for repose to the " Deutsches Haus " at Wetzlar. Finally " Götz " appeared ; the fame which attended it turned Goethe in a wholly new direction and roused in him a new desire. Since " Götz " had inspired so much admiration, he would write something which far exceeded " Götz." A letter to Kestner, in which he says he shall find it difficult again to write anything which will elicit so much applause, indicates that even then the idea had sprung up in his mind. On the 15th of September, almost a year after Jerusalem's death, he says to Kestner in a letter : " I am writing a romance ; but it goes slowly." This must have been " Werther ; " for why should Goethe have written to the distant Kestner of a thing only just conceived, to whom he was not in the habit of speaking of such things ? Hints like this are occasionally dropped ; and, in the winter of 1774, Merck was allowed to see the work.

The success of "Götz" had a decisive influence upon Goethe. We feel it directly in the tone of his correspondence. Goethe had gained at last what he needed, and the want of which had made him so restless, — a manifest right to live as he lived, and to be what he was. Until then he had been forced to say to himself that he anticipated future applause, and had staked a considerable sum upon the credit of his coming fame. At last Fate had opened to him unlimited credit. Now he was master in his own house, and a literary career was before him as a matter of course.

In spite of all this, however, the romance did not progress. The elements which had gathered in Goethe's experience showed a void which, owing to his peculiar tendency to nourish his fancy only from the fulness of actual life, was not at that time to be supplied. A suitable conclusion for the second part of the romance was wanting. It needed to take a certain air of tragedy. A type for Albert, as Lotte's husband, was wanting. Goethe knew Kestner only as a lover, and had never seen him jealous. Goethe would only write what he had experienced. His experience, indeed, took another form in his mind; but it must first be there. Moreover, he had not the experience to enable him to portray Werther as the lover of a married woman; and even that Goethe could not invent.

But now, so providential was the disposition of things that even for this want relief was vouchsafed. A marriage unexpectedly took place which especially concerned Goethe. Maximiliane Laroche, who was only seventeen years old, became, through the mediation of good friends in whose eyes favorable outward circumstances were the chief consideration, suddenly engaged and married to the Frankfort Brentano, still a young man, but a widower with five children. In January, 1774, the marriage was celebrated, and the youthful pair, accompanied by the bride's mother, came to Frankfort, where Goethe was charged with the burden of making the young wife, who was yet half a child, enter comfortably into the life of a strange city; indeed, into a wholly new existence. Maximiliane was accustomed to intercourse with superior men as a matter of course. Her husband was a business man in the strictest sense of the word, and besides an Italian. Goethe foresaw at once what might arise, and what in very deed happened. Brentano became jealous to such a degree that Goethe, who had been influenced by no other feeling than that of the purest benevolence, made an end of the trouble by withdrawing, notwithstanding that Madame Laroche besought him not to give up visiting her daughter. But before this had happened, even in the beginning of the intercourse and before the jealousy of the man had exhibited itself, Goethe had foreseen that it must come; and the second part of Werther stood complete before his soul.

The *dénoûment* of the plot was found. Upon Kestner's tolerant and absolutely trusting nature was grafted that of the suspicious Italian spouse of Maximiliane; and from this union came the insufferable Albert of the romance, who afterward caused Kestner so much grief, which Goethe then sought in vain to allay. Goethe describes these circumstances in the most delicate manner. He saw himself implicated in Maximiliane's house in family relations in which his heart had really no share. While his natural kind-heartedness would not allow him to break off with them, he at the same time sought an outlet for his feelings, and finished his romance; and in April, 1774, was able to speak of it in his letters as a complete work, the reading of which he promised his friends

LECTURE VIII.

"WERTHER."

IN a letter from Goethe to Lavater, dated April 26, 1774, we read: "I will try to send you a manuscript, which will not be printed immediately. You will sympathize greatly with the sorrows of the dear boy I have described. We were near each other six years without being drawn very close together, but now I have lent to his story my own feelings, making a strange whole." Goethe therefore regarded the romance as follows: The memory of the unfortunate boy Jerusalem, with whose fate he feels so much sympathy, is to be rescued from oblivion, and his friends are informed beforehand that the incidents related are not Goethe's personal experience. But how far were Lotte and her husband in the secret? Had they a suspicion of what was before them? Here we meet with a curious thing. Goethe cannot find it in his heart to be silent about his work to those with whom he is in uninterrupted confidential communication, but expresses himself in such terms that they cannot possibly understand what he means. If Goethe ever needed any consolation on Lotte's account, in the year 1773 when he began his romance he had certainly ceased to mourn her loss. Both she and Kestner, through their removal to Hanover, had become to him half-mythical beings. It has often been charged against Goethe that the proverb, "Out of sight, out of mind," fitted him only too well. He openly confesses that those with whom he did not live in actual propinquity scarcely existed for him. This indeed did not apply to persons especially dear to his heart, as his correspondence sufficiently testifies. Yet, to have his friends live vividly in his imagination, he needed an actual sight of their surroundings. If a background of landscape was wanting, the outlines of the people began to grow misty. Lotte Buff in Wetzlar in the "Deutsches Haus," or in the streets of the city, always surrounded in her walks by the well-known horizon, was quite another being to Goethe from Lotte Kestner in Hanover, a North German city with which he was unacquainted. Separated from her home, her father, her brothers and sisters, Lotte lost more and more the power to draw Goethe's thoughts to herself. He found ever less and less to confide to her and Kestner in his letters. They were happy, and did not need him. What stirred his emotions was now confided to other correspondents, to new friends to whom he was indebted for fresh experiences. Lotte had become historic to him.

But now the working on the romance renews the old feeling: it is amazing how the dry leaves and stiff, hard blossoms of the summer of 1772 come to life again in his fantasy. In a letter of March, 1774, he writes to the Kestners that their letters had indeed remained unanswered, but that his thoughts had been busier than ever with Lotte. "I shall soon have it [the romance] printed for you he says; it is good, my dearest." In the same measure in which the growing work compelled him, as it were, to renew his acquaintance with Lotte as a young maiden, and to mount once more by slow steps the entire scale of his feelings for her, she rises before him more beautiful and enchanting than perhaps he had ever seen her in reality; and he naturally transfers all these imaginary charms to Lotte Kestner, whom he must always think of as the young maiden he left in Wetzlar. But now the real Lotte puts Goethe's imagination to the severest test: she expects a child. In the mean time, the Lotte of the romance was already so strongly thrown on the canvas that the living reality could not change those ideal outlines. It was far more difficult to overcome another trouble. Lotte's picture in the romance was too manifestly a likeness. Goethe had made the persons and events too realistically exact. The public at that time had little other excitement than that derived from new books and fresh family scandals; and here the two were united. Goethe was aware beforehand what would be the result. He was resolved not to be misled by these fears; but his friendship for the Kestners seemed to demand that he should not proceed without at least giving them a hint of what was before them. This he does in the most peculiar manner.

In May, 1774, Lotte's first son was born, who from over-scrupulousness was not even to bear the name of Wolfgang. Goethe was seeking a publisher for "Werther," which, if tradition be correct, had been refused by a Leipsic bookseller. He writes to Kestner: "Kiss for me the boy and the immortal Lotte; say to her that I cannot imagine her in childbed: it is simply impossible. I see her always as I left her; neither do I know you as a married man or in any other relation than the old one. And now I have utilized a chance to follow out and patch up other people's passions, at which I beg you not to take offence. I pray you let this enclosed chit-chat rest until you have heard something further: time will explain all." It was scarcely possible to express anything more mysteriously, and Kestner could only wait for time to reveal its meaning. In the next letter, dated the 11th of May, we find another allusion: "Adieu, you people whom I hold so dear! (so dear that I had to lend and adapt the fulness of my own love to the dream-picture of the misfortune of our friend.) The parenthesis is to remain sealed until further notice." This parenthesis was even less comprehensible than the former. And now for a long time nothing follows; but at last on the 16th of June a letter ends with the words: "Adieu, dear Lotte! I shall soon send you a friend who much resembles me; and I hope you will receive him well. His name is 'Werther;' and he is and was what he shall tell you himself." Goethe with this seems to have unburdened his conscience, and believed he had done enough. The following letters contain nothing more about his work. Three months later, on the 23d of September, he sends Lotte the completed book. She is to show it to no one. At the Leipsic fair it is to be offered to the public. "I wish," he writes, "each of you to read it alone,—you alone, and Kestner alone,— and then each of you write me a few words." Goethe seems so convinced that both of them will find heavenly enjoyment in the book, that he quite ignores the possibility that it may be otherwise. We have not Kestner's letter to Goethe, in which his feelings and his wife's on the first reading of the book are expressed; only a part of the rough-draft of a letter has been found, couched in the most unvarnished language. Goethe's reply to it, alas! lacks a date; so that we cannot know whether he wrote immediately, or after a lapse of time. The storm came upon him not unexpectedly. He begs to be forgiven, but not very earnestly. No sound of the enormous European applause had, indeed, at that time reached him; but he is filled with a consciousness of the power of his work, compared with which Kestner's resentment is of little account. And it is remarkable how soon this feeling predominates with the Kestners also. However much they may feel themselves injured or aggrieved, they are even more sensible that he has shown them an honor far exceeding their deserts. Kestner, indeed, might seem to have a right to feel wounded by the intolerable part Albert plays in the romance; but, on the other hand, it was manifest that at the time Jerusalem shot himself, and also when Goethe saw Lotte for the last time, she was still unmarried. This with all desirable clearness proved Albert's character in the romance to be a fiction, notwithstanding the fact that Kestner lent Jerusalem the pistols with which the poor wretch shot himself. And, more than all this, the Lotte who is raised above all idealized beings in the romance was now in very truth his wife. In Lotte Goethe had atoned for any injustice to Kestner: what he was deprived of himself was restored to him in his wife; for although Lotte Kestner had fair hair and blue eyes, while the Lotte of the romance had black, still there could be no doubt that Kestner's wife and Werther's Lotte were one and the same person.

Kestner had a friend, to whom from time to time he unburdened his soul. To him he now poured out his whole heart. We see that all the Hanover gossip had broken out over the young married pair, — a beautiful woman, a stranger and a South German, for whose sake a young Brunswick man had shot himself; and the most renowned poet of Germany who has told the story in all its details. With such an inextricable mixture of truth and fiction a statement of how things really were seems almost impossible. They must just let the storm pass by: enough if only the most intimate friends can be made to understand clearly the relation which existed. Moreover, it was a powerful antidote for this grievance that

Lotte soon appeared surrounded with such a halo that Kestner, the fortunate man who in the first place had won Lotte, and in the second now possessed her, could take a right royal share of this glory to himself. He writes of Goethe to a friend, and treats the whole subject with the most delicate consideration; indeed, he seems most anxious that nothing should reach Goethe's ears which might sound in the least like complaint on their part.

How do we view Goethe's conduct?

An author who insinuates himself into the confidence of a family in order to obtain material for literature degrades his profession. A poet, on the contrary, who is urged forward by the unconscious inspiration of genius, cannot allow external considerations to repress what wells up in his fancy because it may happen to coincide with actual events. Here, however, two objections occur: first, what are the distinctive characteristics of such a poet?—and here feeling alone can decide; secondly, governed as we are at present by the idea that high and low should be measured by the same standard, is it not very difficult for us to admit of any exceptions? Here, however, it is we who make the exceptions and not the poet, who seems to offend against the law. Were we as we should be, then all human relations might be exposed without reserve. Any misunderstandings, any suspicions would be impossible: the pure would be pure to all, and the spurious would be rejected by all. How spotless are the hands with which Shakspeare unfolds the most frightful crimes before us! A true poet goes through the world like a child, who knows of no secrets, and with innocent lips repeats the most horrible things, never suspecting with what he is dealing. What decides our question is the conviction we have as to what the poet intended. In the Lotte of his romance Goethe has given us an ideal creation whose beauty alone elevates his work above all reproach. In Albert he describes a character whose disagreeable qualities owe their origin solely to the æsthetic demand for artistic contrast; but there is absolutely nothing to show that he meant it for Kestner. How true this is was proved afterward, when Goethe, out of regard for Kestner, sought to modify Albert's character, but gained nothing with all his softening of single features. We know what was intended in the person of Werther. These three beings, owing to a singular combination of events, were created, perfected, and matured in Goethe's soul, and finally, as if by force, thrust into the light.

I should not have needed to follow the course of things which were the outward incentives to the romance, if the knowledge of these details had not been so essential to an ultimate moral decision in regard to it. If Goethe had not undertaken the work with a pure conscience, plain innocent people like the Kestners would never have spoken of him behind his back with such high esteem. In Kestner's letters, for instance, in which he gives his friend some account of the real relation on which the romance was founded, we find the remark, before quoted, that Goethe in truth behaved much more magnanimously than the romance would lead us to believe. The outward satisfaction of his vanity, to which I have alluded, would never have been able to take the sting out of the wound in such a straightforward, honest heart as Kestner's, if the poison had once entered it.

In fact the gossip soon died out. The public cared little for Albert, and all the interest centred in Werther. With most convincing reality the unhappy man stands before their eyes, surveying the misery of this temporal world of which he is still a part; who like Hamlet is too much in the sun; to whom no opportunity offers for a great deed until he makes himself the object of it; and who, maddened by a hopeless passion, feels growing within him an insane propensity to criticise himself even to the finest fibres of his nature, until at last he can endure it no longer. Whither could Werther have flown? Every young man at that time who turned his thoughts in upon himself acknowledged something Wertherian in his own nature. He saw the history of his innermost feelings written by a stranger, who knew them better than himself. And this was not alone the experience among the Germans; but, wherever the romance forced its way, it awakened the same emotions. How was it that Werther and Lotte, two radical German natures, were understood by French, Italian, and English as if they were of Celtic, Roman, or Norman-Saxon origin? It is known that Napoleon when a young man had read "Werther," and probably knew no other of Goethe's works; so that it must have been on this account alone that he asked to have Goethe presented to him, as the greatest German poet, when he hurried triumphantly through Germany.

I have proposed these questions, because their answer will direct our attention to an element contained in the romance, and in the characters figuring in it, which until now has been too much overlooked. Thus far, I have only considered Goethe's personal relations as possible sources of the romance. I have tried to explain the sort of persons it was necessary Goethe should come in contact with, to shape in his imagination Werther, Lotte, and Albert. No doubt these persons were indispensable, but it needed co-operation from another direction to cause them to take root in his imagination; or, to express it more clearly, these persons only blended with something which already existed in Goethe's soul. Werther may present ever so clearly Goethe's ideas and the fate of Jerusalem, still the combination of the two would not have been sufficient to create Werther. Even before Goethe went to Wetzlar, before he knew Lotte and Kestner, and Maximiliane and Brentano and Jerusalem, there already lay outlined in his soul the poetic possibility of Werther: not as Goethe's creation, but as that of another poet, from whose dove-cot he had stolen a brood of young birds to send out into the world as his own. And this leads us, beyond the limits of personal experience, to the universal literary experience of modern nations.

It was essential to a full understanding of "Götz von Berlichingen," to examine cursorily the history of the drama. In treating of the novel we must pursue the same method, with only this difference, that we are not obliged to trouble ourselves with antiquity; since the novel is a modern production, consequent on the invention of the art of printing. It is essential to the idea of the novel that it is to be printed, widely circulated, and read by many people at the same time, though by each for himself.

To comprehend fully an artistic work we must have in view two parties, — the artist who produces and offers the work, and the nation who receives and enjoys it. A drama would be inconceivable, if we should speak only of the poet and the actors, omitting the public gathered together for mutual enjoyment, who on the spot bestow praise or censure. We have seen in "Götz" of what decided importance the nature of the theatre public in Germany was to the German stage, and how it led to the creation of dramas merely intended for reading; while in France and other countries where the public was different, nothing of the kind is to be observed. Now as the reading-drama is to the stage-drama, so is the novel to the national epic. The novel arose in Europe, when a series of external circumstances had made the reception and enjoyment of the national epic on the part of the people an impossibility, while yet the need remained for mutual enjoyment in narrative fictions. All nations require food for their imagination; like children, the people must have their fables. We like to be told marvellous tales in which every one can sympathize. Not only do we wish to hear them for our own part, but we like to feel that others are hearing them as well. Not the mere fact that Homer was a great poet, and that it was a joy to listen to his songs, accounted for his influence over the Greeks; but it was quite as much due to the fact that he was equally at home in every part of his fatherland, and that the people came together in great masses the better and more fully to be entertained by his poems.

The national epic, which had ruled the antique world in the so-called Middle Ages, disappeared when an easier and safer way for the people's simultaneous enjoyment of a poem was made by the art of printing. The fundamental distinction between the national epic and the novel lies in the different way in which these ideal creations, otherwise essentially the same, are presented to the public. To the enjoyment of the national epic it was essential that the people should assemble at certain places and definite times in order to participate in it. This was not essential for the novel. Neither poet nor public are here necessarily visible, nor do they know each other. In some place, which nobody needs to know, is seated the poet, whom nobody needs to see or hear. In solitude he prepares his work, while his public spreads over an enormous circle around him, each one alone and invisible alike to poet and companion, with his eyes riveted on the printed page, drinking in the thoughts and images it contains. To make the novel possible there must be a poet to write it, booksellers to circulate it, and people to read it. When these conditions are fulfilled, the national epic exists only for those who cannot read, and becomes the entertainment of beggars and peasants, or forms the material for the fables among dairy-maids and in children's nurseries.

This quiet intellectual enjoyment — always accompanied, however, by the feeling that many others were reading the same book, at the same time — first appeared among modern nations in Italy, then in Spain and France, and later in England and Germany. This order corresponds to the succession of the brilliant eras of romantic literature in the different countries. In respect to Italy, the novel did not develop there as one would have naturally expected. We observed the same in regard to the drama in Italy. At the time when romance-literature became an important element in the book-trade of Europe, the prostrate political condition of Italy had reduced literature there to a mere plaything. All earnest feeling expressed itself in music, for the novel had not power enough to overthrow the form of the national epic. Ariosto and Tasso were novel writers, whose works however did not get beyond the form of the old epic. Spain was a wholly different soil. There poems were not recited, but read. In stillness and alone men pored over their romances, as Cervantes represents Don Quixote brooding over his books. An incredible rage for reading, and an equally strong conviction that all they read was true, prevailed in the sixteenth century among the people of Spain. I am indebted for these observations to the work of the American Ticknor, who has written the best history of

Spanish literature. This faith is especially necessary, if narrative-literature is to flourish. To the Spanish romance-literature succeeded the French. When Goethe appeared, the literary life of Spain had long been exhausted, while that of the French was tending towards its decline. In England, on the contrary, it was in its full glory. What has been said of the drama might in regard to England be said of the novel. In the handling of the material the two literary forms now move on in the same direction. I need, therefore, only repeat in a few words what has been already said of their development.

About the middle of the last century novels of English family-life began to fill a leading position in European literature. We saw what a sensation Goldsmith's "Vicar of Wakefield" made, when it was read aloud by Herder to the students of Strasburg, after having read it three times to himself. The English novel not only reached Germany in the direct way, but through France also. Diderot had helped us to appreciate the sterling form of the English drama; but, to affect our romance-literature, came a mightier than he, — Rousseau.

The English had simpler aims than the French authors. They delineated noble characters to challenge imitation; bad ones to repel and disgust; humorous ones to entertain and amuse. The most prominent of the English novel writers of that time was Richardson. Gellert called the British Richardson (" der britte Richardson ") the greatest benefactor of mankind. In his verses "To Innocence," written in Leipsic, Goethe says, " More rare and ideal than Byron and Pamela," — these two being the hero and heroine of Richardson's novel " Pamela," which had appeared in 1780. No higher conception existed at that time of a virtuous pair. In his epistle to Frederika Oeser in 1768 Goethe reproves the Leipsic maidens, —

"Who will not one of them submit
To be Sir Charles' devoted slave;
And, blindlings still, will not admit
All the Dictator's teachings brave.
But sneer and jeer, and run away,
And hear no more he has to say."

"Sir Charles Grandison," published in 1753, was Richardson's most celebrated romance. The hero is a huge compendium of noble qualities, in whose possible existence every one firmly believed. My Uncle Jacob used to tell me of having, as a child, seen his mother absorbed in reading "Sir Charles Grandison." And such reading was no trifling matter; it required much time and thought. These romances came like great events into our life, which at that time had little to do with political agitations. The translations spread in every direction among us. The marvellously broad and plain treatment of universally-useful and well-understood moral problems made a thorough knowledge of these romances almost a duty as well as an enjoyment. There seemed to be no more agreeable way of appropriating to oneself a life experience of the noblest kind than this convenient and most innocent one. Romances of this kind proved the best form in which to comprise all that might be conducive to genuine moral training. They came in as a supplement when the sermon from the pulpit had not fulfilled its task; and for this reason a great number of the romance writers belonged to the clerical profession.

Farther the English and Germans did not go: the French must usurp the novel, as they had the drama, before it could attain its rank and become a vehicle for the discussion of social problems. In 1760 Rousseau's "Nouvelle Héloïse" appeared, and in 1762 his "Émile," — two didactic romances which caused a tremendous excitement in Europe. The English romances had entertained and interested men; Rousseau seized and convulsed them: the publication of these two works is the most important event in the history of modern literature. Enchanting debates over virtue and innocence are introduced into the midst of the corrupt French world. Paris was not the chief scene of the events described, nor was it indeed a Parisian who described them. It was provincial French life colored with unusual intensity and filled with sensuous vigor: people were beside themselves. Rousseau rose as a great moral prophet and reformer. The romance acquired, through him, new and unsuspected honors. Richardson had written entertaining books for women, in which the tendency to a pulpit tone and the broad illustrations calculated for moderate understandings were conspicuous features. Rousseau raises inevitable problems, treats of questions which men and philosophers acknowledge to be the most important of the age, and solves them by the most radical discussions, yet as easily as if he were at play. Not the critical intellect which may err, but the sensitive heart which is always perfectly sure of itself, is constituted judge over the question of the moral order of the world. Nobody was found to rebel against these things. It is marvellous how clearly we see all this to-day. As poems, Rousseau's two works can no longer be enjoyed. They contain an almost mechanical series of letters and debates, in which the questions of the age are passionately discussed. The characters are not real, not artistically finished creations, but are everywhere simply tools to serve a purpose. But at the time nobody perceived this. The world admired St. Preux and Julie as glorious representatives of the ideas which stirred the age, and they believed in them as they had in Richardson's creations. Their highest wish was to feel as these souls felt and to see the world as they saw it. The air which Goethe breathed was filled with Rousseau's spirit; and we have only to compare Werther and Lotte with St. Preux and Julie to be convinced that without the latter the former would never have been created.

Werther's distinguishing characteristic, which even before the unhappy passion for Lotte seized him had marked him as the spoil of fate, was the place he gave himself outside of humanity. Werther is an alien not from mankind, but from corrupt human relations. He knows how to read the most delicate emotions of every heart, but reads them only to pass by with a shake of the head. The idea of labor, as we now understand it, is unknown to him; he eats and drinks, dresses like a gentleman, and criticises. The world is too miserable to suggest to a mind like his any other occupation. Floating high in the air above churches and palaces, he contemplates, with the disconsolate look of an eagle, all that happens beneath. The worthiest conceivable employment for the highly educated at that time was to be discontented with everything, and to find sufficient reason for this discontent; to take offence at all human regulations, without making the slightest attempt to oppose or alter them. St. Preux loves the daughter of a man whose pride in his pedigree cannot conceive the possibility of such an alliance, and out of this impossibility grows the tragic fate of all the characters. I would remind you how Werther came in contact with these class prejudices. In the beginning of the story Werther accidentally finds himself in an evening party of nobles, who without any ill feeling toward him do not treat him as one of themselves, which obliges him to leave the company. Some centuries earlier these distinctions were much more sharply defined in Europe; but no one thought of such a thing even then as looking at them from the sentimental point of view. The lowest servant in the castle loves the Princess. "What!" cries the old king, "the groom would marry my daughter? Kick him out!" "Ha, ha!" cries the groom, as he picks up his bones, outside the castle, "does the King think this is to end the matter?" He goes away, conquers a kingdom, presents himself once more with his prize, and the nuptials are celebrated. So things went in the old fairy tales and poetry up to the time of Rousseau. Impossibilities are accepted; but the true hero fights his way through all obstacles, and at last Heaven intervenes by a miracle. In the English romance the lord finally marries the poor maiden from among the people, as in the fashionable novel of to-day he is made to marry the governess. Every hero who is poor, or in an inferior position in the English novels, if things end happily, has unexpectedly bestowed upon him an inheritance which raises him at once among the peers of the realm. In England this gives the greatest satisfaction: intellectual merit, and at last solid gold and position added thereto. The English have never at any period allowed sentimentality to invade this field. Rousseau, on the contrary, whose own history is known, formed the new hero of romance in his own image, who in order to be happy would have needed a newly-arranged and wholly different world. Tossed about in the wildest despair; losing himself deeper and deeper in unsolvable problems, while pronouncing at the same time the clearest, truest, and most startling opinions concerning things in all directions; evincing the keenest discrimination, always separating the kernel from the shell (without indeed caring to enjoy it); and, lastly, possessing for the expression of all this mental agony a language worthy the highest admiration, — such was Rousseau's St. Preux, long before Werther was thought of.

The heroes of the "Nouvelle Héloïse" and of Goethe's romance, if their silhouettes could be placed side by side, would be found to coincide line to line. If St. Preux and Werther had met in life, they would have regarded each other with the terror with which one meets his double. St. Preux placed in Werther's circumstances would have met them in the same way, and would have been equally incapable of taking the initiative in any situation however insignificant. The motive power in both is dependent upon what the world does, or what those about them do; and, left to themselves, they are utterly incapable of taking a step either forward or backward. As soon as it is clear to us with what logical consistency everything in Werther's nature and fate is the result of this chief peculiarity, up to the moment when suicide becomes the natural and artistic close of his career, we must confess to ourselves that what Goethe added from his own character and Jerusalem's personality appear only like the accidents of costume and situation. The earliest representative of this character is Hamlet; in another way Molière sought to embody the same in his Misanthrope; then appeared Rousseau's St. Preux, and finally Goethe's Werther. In Werther his predecessors are united. We shall see how in Faust at last this struggle is ended and finds its reconcilement.

It is because Goethe was the greater poet that his romance ranks above Rousseau's "Nouvelle Héloïse" and contemporary English romances. His genius invested Werther with that imperishable element which is lacking in Rousseau's St. Preux, who long since became faded and lifeless. Goethe was neither philosopher nor moralist. "The Sorrows of Werther" had no special aim. The English poets wished to improve morals; Rousseau would have liked to reform all mankind: for both the romance was only a means. But Goethe contemplated nothing of the kind. He neither intends to recommend suicide, as was thought at first, nor to scare men away from it, as he himself later seems to assert. Goethe only wished to disburden his imagination of what it had itself created, and which tormented and goaded him on to give it visible form and shape. He longed to give utterance to what else must break his heart. His work is a poem, and nothing else; hence its powerful effect and the reason why it still lives. In " Götz " and " Werther," the German people had for the first time a drama and a novel which thrilled them with their intrinsic power.

Modern literary history affords but few examples of such phenomena. Corneille's " Cid " had as great an effect in France one hundred and fifty years earlier, and perhaps Cervantes' " Don Quixote " in Spain. Both Dante and Shakspeare only gradually forced their way. Of Homer's poems we know nothing concerning the first centuries of their existence; nor yet whether Æschylus and Sophocles in Athens produced an immediate effect with their masterly works. Rousseau alone, with his " Nouvelle Héloise," had caused a sensation in Paris, which in its extent even exceeded that of Goethe's " Werther." The curious feature in Rousseau's romance is that the love-letters are as much a bit of real life as is Lotte in Goethe's story. Rousseau, when he wrote his poem, loved a woman who also loved him, but from whom he separated out of regard for a friend whom they were both unwilling to disappoint or to betray. On this account, also, it seemed to Goethe as if a special providence had thrown Rousseau's romance into his hands; and he felt compelled to adhere to his model. This was so clearly perceived at the time, that in a copy of " Werther" which Goethe had lent to a friend he found written, when returned to him, in an unknown hand, the words: "Tais-toi, pauvre Jean-Jacques, ils ne te comprendront pas." This proves that not only Goethe himself, but his readers, were under Rousseau's powerful influence. When Goethe and Kestner met for the first time and questioned each other regarding their fundamental ideas, and whatever else people of twenty years of age or thereabout are accustomed to discuss, Rousseau was immediately the subject of their conversation. How deeply Goethe was imbued with Rousseau is shown by one of the most beautiful scenes in "Faust." It is where Faust, alone in Gretchen's chamber, examines with rapture everything belonging to her, because it all seems permeated with her presence. This scene corresponds with that in "La Nouvelle Héloise," where St. Preux, waiting for his beloved Julie in her own maiden bower, goes into ecstasies over all her little surroundings. (How far Faust's experimental philosophy was suggested by Rousseau's life it is not in place here to discuss.)

But not alone for the conception of the characters in "Werther" was Goethe indebted to Rousseau. He is, in fact, in quite as great a measure dependent upon him for the coloring. In "Werther" is first revealed his homage to Nature in all her different aspects, which was truly among Goethe's intuitions, but which had never found expression until he began to write "Werther."

There has never lived a greater literary landscape-painter than Goethe. But if we examine his works with this idea in mind, we see with astonishment that it is not a purely natural gift,— a something which from the beginning flows on in its own way without needing direction from others, — for it is only from the Götz and Werther period that we find these passionate descriptions of Nature. This he retained to the very last; and in his later days watched the mist, the clouds, the varied aspects of earth and heaven, and felt himself in harmony with it all. This, too, is to be attributed to Rousseau. Rousseau first represented men as in ever constant dependence upon the elementary powers. According to him we are subject to the influences of the sun, the night, and the character of the landscape. His romances are full of descriptions of Nature, which he knows how so to inform with life that it seems a living, breathing reality; and here he found in Goethe a pupil who far excelled his master. "The Sorrows of Werther" contain such a wealth of natural imagery that if at any time the ethical part of the romance should be lost, — that is to say should become incomprehensible, — this part alone would suffice to inspire continued admiration for the work. It is true that Rousseau alone should not be mentioned here: Herder's writings, and an acquaintance with Ossian and Homer, led Goethe just as directly to Nature, and gave him words to express what he wished to describe. But Herder must have derived his own inspiration largely from Rousseau, and without Rousseau Herder and Goethe would never have penetrated so deeply into the spirit of Ossian and Homer. Homer and Ossian were Goethe's favorite reading at the time he was working upon "Werther." Dante was as much unknown to him at that time as Italy herself. He was even less acquainted with Wolfram von Eschenbach, who, in my opinion, among the Germans is the finest delineator of Nature, and who certainly produces the greatest effects with the least material.

Goethe's awakening to the beauty of Nature may almost be said to have been sudden. It is remarkable what a difference there is in the language and ideas in his letters, from the first moment that he came under the influence of Herder. The delicately complicated

Wielandish sentences which were formed according to French syntax change into abrupt turns of speech imitating the colloquial style; the adjectives become full of meaning and amplify the nouns, sometimes in an intentionally startling manner; the verbs have a fresh spirit infused into them by union with new copulas, and everywhere we see the endeavor to build up the sentences in architectural fashion, and by euphony of inflection to strengthen the rhythm of thought, — a striving which finally led him to the direct imitation of the Pindaric Odes. Goethe's critiques and his essay on Erwin von Steinbach — and, better even than this essay, a letter written at this time — reveal strikingly this suddenly-awakened talent for seeing and describing Nature. It is to a friend; is dated Saarbrück, June 27, 1771, and contains a bit of landscape painting in the new style, which is among the most beautiful things which ever fell from Goethe's pen: nothing earlier approaches it, and nothing later goes beyond it. But now we must leave Rousseau, and pass on to what is original with Goethe in the romance.

I have connected Lotte as a poetical creation with St. Preux's beloved Julie; but the priority of Rousseau reaches only so far, that he has made an unhappy pair the principal characters in his fiction, — and Goethe has followed his example, just as Bernardin de Saint-Pierre did in his "Paul and Virginia": the imitation reaches no further. Lotte has nothing in common with Julie, with the single exception that like Julie she is perfectly natural; that is to say, she does not act from enforced rules, but follows the dictates of her heart.

Werther's Lotte is Goethe's most renowned creation, and entirely his own. He has so felicitously given the type of true womanhood that every maiden can believe herself a Lotte; and, at the same time, has so individualized her that each must confess that she could never reach this ideal. So much nature, health, and goodness no other possessed. All Europe was inspired, and sought with eagerness to catch a glimpse of the original of this enchanting vision, with which neither Pamela nor Rousseau's Julie could be compared. Lotte remained the queen among Goethe's friends, as well as among his poetic creations. Lotte's family understood this; and even her grandchildren have borne themselves as if they stood in a spiritual relation to Goethe which they deemed quite equal to any temporal one.

Up to the time of Lotte's accession to the throne, Klopstock's Fanny had been the highest ideal of womanhood in Germany. Heyne in Göttingen writes to Herder: "Greet your Fanny, which means greet your affianced bride,— on whom I bestow, in the name of Fanny, the highest æsthetic distinction." But from this time no name supersedes Lotte's.

After the appearance of "Werther," young girls named Lotte refused to be called so any longer, feeling themselves unworthy to bear the name. Lotte had a wholly different nature from Fanny's. In Lotte there was not the slightest admixture of sentimentality, nor the faintest rustle of angels' wings, which in Klopstock's ideal women was always heard. Lotte has no trace of that aristocratic distinction which is an inherent peculiarity in Jean Paul's ideal court ladies, and also in some of Goethe's heroines of a later date. Lotte is the simplest and most lovely German maiden, of whom nothing special is to be said. She enjoys dancing, she loves poetry, she *can be* enthusiastic; but she only needs to hear the slightest noise in the house, and she leaps down from the heavens into her wonted sphere and is nothing but a housewife.

Housewife she was even as a young girl, for she must fill a mother's place to a flock of younger brothers and sisters. This it was which attracted all hearts to her; for the most every-day maiden could take Lotte as her ideal, without feeling that she soared too high above her.

This feature in the romance disarmed those who would fain lay stress on the pernicious tendencies of "Werther." Lotte made up for everything. The same forms of household life which Goethe had depicted with such historic fidelity in "Götz," he now presents to us in a modern guise; and a purer, truer, more attractive picture is not to be imagined. This is also one of Dürer's charms,—that in his "Life of Mary," and his other innumerable pictures of the Madonna, we find continual illustrations of German home life. And this it is which gives to Luther's teachings such power,—the very thing which the Romish church most severely reproved in him,—that he possessed a family, and that wife and children stood around him when he closed his eyes in death.

Goldsmith's "Vicar of Wakefield," on the other hand, fails in this very respect. In it the household only affords a field upon which experiments in domesticity are tried; as, in Rousseau's story, Julie's happy marriage later with Von Wolmar is not made the climax of the book. Both of these fictions are injured by their didactic aim. Goethe never proposed anything of the sort. Like Dürer, he contents himself with representing what he sees before him, and leaves it to those into whose hands the work may fall to draw from it the moral. In "Götz von Berlichingen," how deeply symbolic the feature that the child of Götz and Elizabeth—both heirs of an old giant race—grows up to be an effeminate fellow, whose greatest delight is to stay at home and listen to the fairy tales of his aunt, thereby proving himself in every way to be exactly the opposite of his father and mother. We might say, with little exaggeration, that the whole future of Germany is contained in this. But Goethe just lets it pass before our fancy, without pointing his finger at it. This absence of intention gives the works of great artists a similarity to the creations of Nature, who does not print on the leaves of her roses and lilies any special admonition to enjoy and admire them, but contents herself with allowing them to grow and blossom.

The years in which "Werther" was written were with Goethe years of the highest productive power. We readily believe him when he says that, if it had been desired, he could have shaken out of his sleeve a whole series of dramas like "Götz." At that time "Clavigo" and "Stella" and "Claudine of Villa Bella" in their first form, and a quantity of his most beautiful songs and ballads, were written. I do not follow up these things minutely, because it would only oblige me to repeat in other forms what I have already said.

"Egmont," also, was begun at this time, not to speak of "Faust," which was already in condition to be read to some of his friends. All these works were included in the years 1774-75. People and work crowded upon Goethe in such a confused mass that it is impossible to follow things exactly. Those who have most carefully collected and arranged the material must candidly acknowledge that double and treble the amount of information would not be sufficient to enable us to do this. The attempt to give some idea of the men who surrounded him may be more successful.

Goethe was certainly at this time the most stupendous phenomenon which had appeared in the German literary world. Klopstock, Wieland, Lessing, and Herder were much older, and their general aims plainly understood.

Goethe was a wholly fresh power. His depth seemed unfathomable, his imagination inexhaustible, while between his person and his works such a harmony obtained that one was not to be understood without the other. One had to live with him, to sit days and nights talking with him, in order to comprehend him. All distinguished men who came to Frankfort sought to make his acquaintance. We have knowledge from many sources of such meetings. Goethe is constantly described as a rare phenomenon; as a genius who rises conspicuously above the rest of mankind, and from whom everything is to be expected. The fame which Goethe enjoyed after the appearance of "Werther" was the greatest the world ever showered upon him. The wild and wanton happiness of these days he never tasted again. His name was in everybody's mouth. Edition after edition of the work followed in quick succession, — criticism, sequels, dramatizations, translations. Werther's dress, — blue coat and yellow breeches, — which Jerusalem wore in accordance with the South-German fashion, became the uniform of the young people. Thus attired Goethe entered society in Weimar; and whoever, for any reason, was unable to supply himself with a like costume at court received a present of a suit from the Duke. In Wetzlar, step by step, the walks of the wretched Jerusalem were hunted out, who never while on earth had a suspicion he could become such an object of interest. And Goethe's own favorite paths and resting-places were also frequented. The well before the Wilsbacher Thor, where he set the pail on the head of the servant girl, is called "Werther's Well." Garbenheim acquired such historic interest that some officers of a Russian regiment, passing through it in 1814, were tempted to bear away a stone urn as a relic. Goethe's favorite haunt was marked by a pyramid of white marble, and in 1849 the grounds about it were newly laid out.

This romance of Goethe's is itself to-day a memorial of times gone by, and which without it would scarce be thought of. The literature which called it forth is no longer read; at least, no longer in the spirit of those days. Who would regard the "Vicar of Wakefield" to-day as a sensational romance? The people who had a share in the story of "Werther" are forgotten, and even the language in which it was written differs essentially from the style of to-day. Only the intellectual power which radiates from the book sustains its interest; but this is enough to insure its immortality. There will come ages in whose sight one or two centuries now gone by will seem hardly more distant than the present time, — just as to-day we couple Dante and Petrarch, Corneille and Voltaire together, forgetting that a whole century lies between them. Dante's poem had to pass through generations who found its language little to their taste; they thought it too primitive and unpolished, — and yet one generation after another has admired and interpreted it from new points of view, until now Dante stands as it were beyond the ages, unequalled and alone. He is no longer compared with others, but others with him. To us to-day the language of "Werther" seems in many respects old-fashioned. We believe we write a more vigorous, inspiring, and better style. But the time is coming when our present days, to the retrospective glance, will seem as unfamiliar and strange as Goethe's youthful days to us. Then only, when all comparison ceases, will it be seen clearly, as in the hour when "Werther" first appeared, what a youthful vigor informs the language with which Goethe surprised the world in his early manhood; while the dead formulas in which we are now compelled to express our best thoughts, and the provincialisms by which we attempt to infuse some life into our writings will be rejected as valueless in the scientific analysis of the future. Nothing is written to-day to compare with Goethe's prose, as it burst upon the German people in "Werther."

LECTURE IX.

LAVATER.

THE men with whom we now see Goethe associating, as we gather from his own description and numerous letters written by others at this time, form a varied and brilliant company, comprising men of all ranks in life. We wholly forget that if Goethe did not still live most of these people would form part of that shadowy throng who have no pretension to any share of earthly immortality. If we search among Goethe's acquaintances who apart from him would be known to-day, or who on account of their own merits hold a conspicuous place in history, only a few are to be found. Lavater is to be named first, and after him Jacobi.

Both of them sought like Herder to overpower Goethe; but there was this difference, that, instead of drawing him along with them, they very soon submitted to his influence, and allowed him to affect their subsequent career. They clung to Goethe, and Jacobi was successful in frustrating all Goethe's attempts to free himself. A rupture occurred between them; but by means of the slight thread of attachment which remained Jacobi gradually restored the friendly relation. On the contrary, Lavater was wholly thrust aside; and, indeed, because his nature contained more dangerous elements.

These conflicts belong among the most important

events in Goethe's further development. They form the close of what is described in "Dichtung und Wahrheit" as his youth. They are the flower of the book, if considered as an historical work of art. Lavater and Jacobi are here described with a masterly skill, which so far as my literary knowledge goes has never been excelled. They live before our eyes; they betray themselves naturally; not at once, but by fits and starts as it were, just as life and experience teach us to find men out. Goethe again and again calls them up; they do not present themselves to us at one glance, like books we read all through in a single day, but rather like the *feuilleton* fragments in a newspaper, where we may skip many numbers, but somewhere accidentally will find the beginning and the end of our story. The art of constructing characters out of what seem to be only fragments, but so that after the work is done not the slightest gap remains, Goethe possessed in the highest degree. Here we perceive how nearly related poetry and historic narration may be.

Goethe gives Shakspeare the credit of allowing us to look into the very souls of his characters as into glass clocks. In this is contained great praise, but limited; at least I find something in this remark of Goethe's which it is possible he did not have in mind when he made the comparison. Shakspeare's creations are like clocks in some respects. We see often only too minutely the moving wheels and springs instead of the free circulation of the blood. A tendency exists to-day to depreciate Shakspeare; and it would be sad indeed if this attempt should have even a transient success: but the parallel between Shakspeare and Goethe is a theme in the discussion of which Goethe for the most part, chiefly owing to his own over-modest avowal, is placed on too low a pedestal. Goethe's characters are beings from another sphere than Shakspeare's. Goethe also lets us look into their souls, but not as if they were clocks, but rather plants of glass, whose vascular system is so transparent that we can see the sap running up and down in them. Just as transparent are Goethe's Lavater and Jacobi. As in the spring, when we watch the trees and see how leaf follows leaf, and blossom blossom, — when in closest harmony with Nature we seem to be initiated into her plans, and the promises she makes are visibly though modestly realized, — so in " Dichtung und Wahrheit " we watch the development of Goethe and his friends.

Lavater's correspondence at that time with Goethe is found, in an unabridged form, in " The Young Goethe." Hirzel also collected the letters from Goethe's parents to Lavater, and had them printed Jan. 4, 1866, on Jacob Grimm's birthday, for private distribution.

Lavater was according to Goethe " a unique, distinguished individual, such as had not been seen before and would not be seen again." This was his judgment of him in later years. We will add to this a passage quoted from one of his letters, as the result of his immediate observation. The 7th of September, 1779, he writes: " It is with Lavater as with the Rhine-fall, you think you have never seen him as you see him now; he is the very flower of humanity, the best of the best." We must add, however, that after a short acquaintance with Lavater Goethe, in seeking to concentrate his opinion of the whole man in some ideal form, made him the Mahomet of his tragedy; representing Mahomet as having entered upon his mission in good faith, and compelled, for the sake of his followers, later to lie and deceive. The most remarkable feature in Goethe's enthusiasm for Lavater was, that he understood from the very beginning of their acquaintance the leading motives which governed the man, but allowed himself to be overcome by his immense personal magnetism.

Goethe in Lavater, again, met a man older than himself. Lavater was born in Zürich in 1741, son of a physician. He was a dreamy child, early inclined to the reading of the Bible, to meditation and prayer, — a puzzle to those who had the care of him. Religion was at that time the institution conspicuous in all the affairs of daily life, and nearer to the hearts of the people, who had not been disturbed by the criticism which to-day places so much stress on having established, as is believed, the historical value of the Gospels. Lavater had a natural bias towards the ministry. The leading trait of his nature showed itself very early, which was in a most decided manner, but with exact calculation of all the consequences, to take an active part in public affairs. He was only nineteen years old when he anonymously addressed to the administration a most stinging letter, complaining of the reprehensible manner in which Governor Grevel executed the duties of his office, — for which letter he was apprehended and brought to trial. Lavater soon found that, in order to attain any effectual influence, it was indispensable to have some recognition in foreign countries. In 1763 he set out on his first great theological tour through Germany, formed many connections, returned home with some renown, and began directly to write his principal work, " Glimpses into Eternity," which appeared between 1768 and 1773. This soon became a standard work, and gave Lavater a sure position. Again we see Rousseau's spirit, or in other words the spirit of the age, finding fresh expression in an energetic man. The question was as to the reconstruction of human nature; and Lavater in our eyes differs very little from Rousseau, although the latter came into the field as philosopher and atheist, while the former hoped to gain everything by means of prayer.

Lavater was now made only a deacon in Zürich, but he gained steadily in power by the gift which enabled him to read the characters of men, and from their outward aspect and behavior to draw conclusions as to their mental constitution. It is well known that physicians, policemen, and in fact all officials who, aided by a certain show of authority, are brought into daily intercourse with the general public, soon acquire a facility in reading the kind of persons with whom they may have to deal even before they open their mouths. The practised custom-house officer does not look at the trunk, but at its possessor, to decide whether it contains anything taxable. Lavater, as the son of a physician, had perhaps been familiar with the study of physiognomy from his youth up. To enlarge his position in Zürich, he felt under the necessity of making another literary effort; but it must be something great, something in accordance with the spirit of the times, and something absolutely new: this was the incentive to his extensive work called "Physiognomical Fragments to promote the Knowledge and Love of Mankind." The title reveals at once what is to be expected, — only fragments, not the intention to give a carefully worked-out and complete system. And not only was science to be promoted, but charity as well. Philanthropy at that time was the great word. The philanthropists stood foremost everywhere: the philanthropist upon the throne was the ideal of the age. Every one, high and low, should feel called upon not only to read Lavater's book, but to contribute to the work. Everywhere Lavater sends requests for portraits, which he offers to read and interpret.

Coldly criticising this undertaking to-day, we must declare Lavater a hundred years ahead of his time; for even now, when the art of puffing has been brought to the highest perfection, it would be impossible to get up anything more brilliant and effective. And for this work Goethe suffered himself to be dragged in as joint editor. He finally undertook the charge of the publishing; and thus made himself, in a measure, responsible for the whole thing. How much he actually contributed to the work must be ascertained by further and more minute researches: there are only a few passages here and there in poetry as well as in prose which are unmistakably his. The "Physiognomical Fragments" are in four full-sized quarto volumes. The imposing leather-bound tomes, usually to be found adorning old libraries, attest the reverence with which the work was received at the time. It appeared between 1775 and 1778, was hailed with extraordinary expectation and excited extraordinary satisfaction. The cool criticisms of some scholars who saw through the swindle were rejected as envious attempts at disparagement. Besides the dedication of the separate volumes to the most philanthropic German princes, a quantity of engravings and etchings — part of them good — adorned the book. In this way, the best portrait of Goethe's father has come down to posterity.

The fundamental idea of the book is that the character of the soul is expressed in the whole outward frame, but more especially mirrored in the face. And therefore the form of man must be regarded as an harmonious work of art, produced by the hand of the master-artist Nature. The doctrine of this harmony was at that time familiar to everybody; and Diderot's attempts to make art more naturalistic were founded on it. From a single finger Diderot undertook to demonstrate whether the whole man was straight or deformed. Instead of finding or even seeking laws, instead of ascertaining how far observation might be trusted here, they brought forward with a show of exact investigation the most fantastic hypotheses, and believed the brilliant conceits of men of genius were to be accepted as proofs. From the portrait of a boy, which one was not sure was at all like the original, they believed they could decipher the moral capacity and future career of the child. Lavater always deceives himself: either he evolves from the picture before him the character of an individual already known to him, and then goes boldly on into the smallest personal details; or he does not know his people, and indulges in mere commonplaces. That a brilliant man of great experience, like Lavater, should be able to utter many sagacious and at the same time amusing things is not to be denied; and as little, that many of his observations are striking and really fine. To prove how indispensable the outward appearance of a man is to any decision as to his mental nature, I will here speak of something concerning Lavater himself.

Goethe hints, as before of Merck, that one must have known Lavater to be able to comprehend him. Something like a substitute for his personal appearance was offered me in Lavater's bust by Dannecker, which I first saw in Stuttgart, the artist's home, where they have awarded to the works of this great sculptor — whose worth and dignity seem not to have been recognized in his native city — a small annex, as a place of honor in the museum. It is generally acknowledged that the bust of Schiller by Dannecker, in the library at Weimar, is one of the finest ever wrought out in Germany.

That a bust may be used as historic material, it is not necessary that it should represent exactly how the man looked in the hour when the artist portrayed him. But the sculptor must be able to give the whole presence of the man as a conception of his own, quite independent of his appearance on certain days and hours: Dannecker could do this. His bust of Lavater granted me what I had sought in vain in other ways; namely, an impression of his personal appearance as if he were living before me. Lavater's dreamy, impressionable, unsettled kind of mind was evidently united to a very real and strong individuality, which showed itself in his aggressive nature, his ever wakeful diplomatic subtlety, his inexhaustible bodily vigor, and the irresistible magnetism of his presence. The man must have been made of watch-springs, thin as paper but hard as steel. Dannecker has shown in a masterly way in this head of Lavater the powerfully strong conformation of bones and skull, with the finest play of the muscles. We feel what eloquence once belonged to these lips; how frank and peaceful this brow could seem, and yet how obstinately it held fast and concealed its innermost thoughts. This bust gives us far more than we could have derived from any sculpture or drawing which aimed at producing nothing but a so-called faithful likeness; for, if we are to find the features of a face eloquent, we must as it were see them in motion. I wish here to make myself perfectly intelligible.

In the museum in Berlin is found a picture by Jan van der Meer,—a peasant's house, with a tree before it, through whose shade the sun is allowed to play on the white wall. The artist has felt that the peculiar charm of this scene consists in the gentle undulations of light and shade; but who can paint the wind or the soft waving of the leafy branches? Nevertheless it is done here, and one would swear that he actually saw the flitting shadow and the dancing sunlight! We think we see what the artist intended us to see; and in the same way the sculptor may express in marble the motion of a figure.

Lavater, in his interpretation of his portraits, meddles with the private affairs of the men whose character and fate he believes himself able to read in their features. His friends come out of this ordeal paragons of excellence, especially when he describes simple natures from the middle or lower classes. A masterpiece in another direction is his characterization of Goethe, which against Goethe's will and behind his back was added to the book, with two portraits of him. Lavater, with consummate cunning, lavishes upon Goethe eulogies which in an indirect way lead us to divine that we have before our eyes the most extraordinary man of the century, although, as we are expressly informed, in the most unsatisfactory and inadequate representations. The portrait which Lavater wished to have of Goethe for his book seems to have afforded the first opportunity for a personal meeting. Goethe had criticised the "Glimpses into Eternity" in the Frankfort "Anzeiger," without a correspondence arising between them; but now, when the profile of the author of "Götz von Berlichingen" was needed, Goethe heard of it and offered not only to send his own but the portraits of others as well, for Lavater's work. The first contribution followed in April, 1774, and the second, with the profile of the Fräulein von Klettenberg, in the month of May. Goethe already assumes Lavater's oracular tone, which they henceforth maintain towards each other, and which is the first sign of Lavater's influence over Goethe.

Lavater had blended his simple Zürich dialect with a seemingly naïve and careless phraseology, making a jargon the advantages of which struck Goethe at once. It was possible in the most simple-hearted manner to say things out bluntly, or merely to hint at them, or to be silent about them: at a bound to be in the midst of a train of thought, and as quickly out of it again. The charm of dialect as a literary form lies in this union of delicately shaded thought with a seemingly unwieldy expression. Klaus Groth lends to the rough-sounding uncouth phrases of the *platt deutsch*, which in truth are incapable of rendering modern thought accurately, the capacity to express the tenderest lyrical conceptions, — as if, in Schleswig-Holstein, precious garden flowers grew like weeds in all the paths, and the peasant children wreathed them into crowns.

Lavater's apparently natural sentences, which sound like mere interjections, seemed at that time to be the language of the truest, most upright, and most unsophisticated of men. The stanch republican Swiss, with their unpretending honesty, had come into fashion as historic models in Lavater's time. Each Swiss cow gave the purest cream, for it had the flavor of freedom and Alpine air! Freedom began very much at that time "to dwell on the mountains." In the simple-hearted tone of his countrymen (who were perfect tyrants over each other) Lavater knew how to infuse the most elevated thoughts into the souls of his hearers by a kind of sorcery. In the June of 1774 Lavater's travelling wagon stopped in the hirschgraben before Goethe's house. They met for the first time. "Art thou he?" ("Bischt's?") "I am he!" ("Bin's!"), — and they fell on each other's necks. The first surprise over, they began a conversation forthwith in which the deepest questions were passionately discussed. All Frankfort had with Goethe expected the man whose presence promised infinite joy and blessing. Lavater understood the machinery by which to make these journeys effective: he was announced beforehand, and the public knew everywhere when and how he would arrive.

In his account of this visit, Goethe gives the first comprehensive description of Lavater. He says:—

"The rest of us, when we wish to talk about matters relating to the mind and heart, are accustomed to withdraw from the crowd, indeed from society, because, with the various ways of thinking and the different degrees of education, it is difficult to be really understood even by a few. But Lavater was differently minded. He loved to extend his influence far and wide, and only felt at home among the crowd, for whose edification and entertainment he possessed peculiar talents, owing to his rare gift of reading faces. He had such extraordinary power of discernment that he quickly discovered in the face of each person the mood of mind he might be in; and if added to this there was a candid confession, or a frank question, he was able from his wealth of inward and outward experience to answer in a manner which was appropriate to each and satisfied everybody. The perfect mildness of his eye, the constant sweetness of his lips, even the naïve Swiss dialect sounding through his *hoch deutsch*, as well as many other distinguishing traits, combined to inspire all with whom he talked with the most delightful sense of repose. Indeed, his sunken chest and stooping form rather helped to counterbalance his immense superiority to all the rest of the company. Against arrogance and conceit he knew how to hold his own quietly and skilfully; for, while seeming to evade, he all at once held forth a great idea (which his narrow-minded antagonist would never have thought of) like a diamond shield, and knew how to temper so agreeably the light which rayed from it that even such men felt themselves, at least while in his presence, convinced and instructed."

I have only given here some sentences culled from Goethe's lengthy description. While his characterization of Merck reminds us of the style of Tacitus, the tenderer and more circumstantial manner in which he paints Lavater reminds us of Cicero's full-toned periods.

This was his first over-powering impression of the personality of a man about whom fourteen years later he writes to Herder:—

"I do homage to my good genius — which means, I thank my guardian angel — who has saved me from meeting the prophet either by the way or in Weimar. The world is wide: let him live in it. We know beforehand the trail such vermin follow; like magic rods, their noses are drawn towards all power, rank, money, influence, or talent."

And finally in his old age, in conversation with Eckermann, he dismisses Lavater with the laconic remark, "He lied to himself and others."

That Goethe from the beginning well knew Lavater's weak side we discover, as I have already observed, from his making him the hero of his "Mahomet." Loeper thinks Goethe had conceived the tragedy much earlier, and that Lavater only came in later as a welcome representative of his idea of Mahomet. This would correspond to the way in which, as we see, Goethe's imagination usually worked. Goethe also, in the midst of the tumult into which Lavater's appearance threw him, made an unconscious criticism of the man, which contains at once the prediction of what his innermost motives would lead to, and the best apology for his nature. But if Goethe himself was at once able to estimate Lavater correctly, — probably assisted by Merck, who here, as everywhere, sustained his character as Mephistopheles, — all the rest of the Frankfort world were completely under the spell of the prophet. Goethe's mother was chief among his adorers: we have a touching letter from her, written to him after he had left Frankfort. "Nothing remains to me," she writes, "but the tears with which I weep your departure!" Goethe, however, accompanies Lavater as he continues his journey. He says:—

LAVATER AND BASEDOW COMPARED. 179

"So many topics had been started between us that I felt the greatest longing to continue our conversations; therefore I resolved, if he would go to Ems, to accompany him, that on the way, shut up in the carriage and separated from the world, we might freely discuss the subjects nearest to our hearts. Lovely summer weather attended us; Lavater was gay and fascinating. In spite of a religious and moral turn of mind, he was no wise pedantic, and did not remain insensible to the excitements and cheerful incidents which stirred the minds of others. He was sympathetic, witty, and genial, and liked the same in others, always restrained within the limits prescribed by refined feeling. If any one ventured beyond this, he would tap him on the shoulder, and with a playful 'Be good!' recall the offender to a sense of propriety. In Ems I saw him at once surrounded by all kinds of people, and returned to Frankfort, where some little matter of business demanded my attention which I could no longer neglect."

Goethe now brings upon the stage a curious colleague of Lavater, who was at the same time his direct opposite, by whom he was led a second time to Ems, when the real journey begins.

"Basedow arrives in Frankfort, another apostle of education. A more decided contrast could not be found than between these two men. If Lavater's features were open and frank as the day, Basedow's were introspective and closely knit together. Lavater's eyes were clear, serene, and devout, with broad lids and gently-arching eyebrows of the softest brown: Basedow's were deep-set, and peeped forth sharp, black, and small from under bristling eyebrows. Basedow's rough, fierce voice, his abrupt assertions, a kind of scornful laugh, capricious changes of the conversation, and in fact whatever else characterized him was exactly the opposite of all the qualities to which Lavater had accustomed us."

Observe with what art Goethe, after having first given us a general sketch of Lavater, now fills out his picture quite accidentally, and, as if he were only treating of Basedow, gives us another portrait of Lavater, in which he shows his marvellous ability to make language paint exactly what was floating before his mind: no one has ever been able to describe like Goethe, — none before him, and none after him.

With regard to Basedow's theory of education, I refer you to "Dichtung und Wahrheit." These theories are of importance to-day, as contributions to the ceaseless efforts of the people of Europe to reconstruct society on a basis more worthy of humanity, — a labor which seemed on the point of success, when the French revolution, like a frightful fever, came in and completely changed the course of things. Goethe is induced by Basedow to repeat the journey to Ems.

"I persuaded my father and friends to relieve me of the necessary business, and once more left Frankfort accompanied by Basedow. But what a difference, when I remembered what a grace had emanated from Lavater! Dainty as he was, he knew how to make all his surroundings dainty, and through fear of annoying him one became like a maiden at his side. Basedow was much too deeply buried in himself to consider his outward man. He smoked uninterruptedly the worst tobacco, which was extremely disagreeable, — the more so that the moment his pipe went out he lighted it again with some abominable tinder which poisoned the air horribly. I called this preparation the 'Basedowschen Stinkschwamm,' and threatened to have it introduced as a new species into natural history, which amused him greatly."

Goethe now further describes with what rapture he met Lavater again, and the experience he had with his two friends during some weeks in Ems and its vicinity.

We realize how fresh and hopeful intellectual life was in Germany at that time. In the middle of July they left Ems together; and now begins the well-known journey, with regard to which we have, besides Goethe's account of it, Lavater's own diary published by Hirzel.

This time they went by ship from Ems down the Lahn to the Rhine. Lavater noted briefly but constantly everything that happened, as if he were framing telegrams to be despatched several times a day. This excursion by water seems to have transported the travellers into a higher state of existence. Opposite Lahneck, Goethe wrote these lines:—

"High upon the tower old
The spirit of the warrior bold
Stands, and from the turret high
Bids God-speed the passer-by."

How life-like these verses become, when we think that Goethe himself was in the ship and that the lines came fresh from his soul!

We read farther in Lavater's pencilling:—

" We are passing Lahnstein. To the right the small town of ——. Went on shore. Basedow hurried ahead, went into a house where dinner was going on, fell upon it, and ate pork and beans with the people. All followed. Bustle, life, and fun! Again on board. Chapel. Passed a ruined castle. Goethe on fellows in castles. Now from the Lahn into the Rhine. Goethe read. We passed Horcheim. Fortress and valley of Ehrenbreitstein. Floating bridge between valley and Coblentz. Left boat and dined."

In " Dichtung und Wahrheit " we find an account of the sensation their appearance created in Coblentz,— the curious crowd which surrounded them; the discussions at the hotel tables; Goethe's exuberant spirits; Lavater's discreet intermediation. As we read of this in Goethe's calm narration, which was not composed until many years later, it does not sound half so fresh as Lavater's short sentences noted down at the moment. I know of few memoranda which impress the fancy with such a sense of reality as this diary of Lavater's. Strangely enough, it seems as if not he, but Goethe, must have been the author of it; yet we must remember that it was Goethe who adopted Lavater's style of writing, although to-day the reverse would appear to have been more natural.

Wednesday, July 20, 1774, the diary continues: —

"Morning, after six o'clock, on ship-board, under wet awnings; before Schmoll [Schmoll was one of the party] and close to Goethe a romantic figure, with a half-faded love-knot of flowers stuck in his gray hat, who devours his sandwich like a wolf, and behind his brown silk neck-tie and gray capote-collar is looking about all the while to see how much breakfast there is left."

Goethe always forms the centre. As it was in Strasburg, so it was everywhere. His person is always the one best worthy of description: we see how he impressed Lavater and the others. An immense vital power radiated from him. He was too modest, however, to be conscious of it, yet soon feels oppressed and uncomfortable by the side of Lavater and Basedow, and has had enough of their company. He does not wish any longer to be dragged about as a satellite of these great planets. He readily agreed to Lavater's separating from him for a time at Cologne.

The meeting with Fritz Jacobi was now at hand. Goethe had tried often to find a friend after his own heart, and now it seemed as if his wish were to be fulfilled. While he had come so near to Lavater, there had always been something which estranged them, and which no amount of mutual admiration could remove. Goethe met Lavater again on his return journey, when the united labor on the " Physiognomical Fragments " was planned; yet he was always on his guard against the great man, while to Jacobi, for the first and last time in his life, he wholly surrendered himself.

LECTURE X.

FRITZ JACOBI. — SPINOZA.

FRIEDRICH and George Jacobi were esteemed authors when Goethe made their acquaintance. George the elder was, as the expression is, a "much valued" poet, who wrote Frenchified Anacreontics, and was a favorite contributor to journals which were the organ for poetical productions of moderate worth. Every educated nation produces a certain quantity of second-class literary writers, who associate together, and, sustained by a cheerful complacency, often lead a very happy existence. The most conspicuous among the German poets of this stamp at the time of which we are speaking was Gleim. The others flocked around him, were entertained at his house, and not infrequently taxed his purse. Of the two brothers Jacobi, the younger Friedrich Heinrich, generally called Fritz Jacobi, is alone of importance to us. Born in 1743, he was thirty-one years of age when he met Goethe, who was then twenty-five years old.

Fritz Jacobi had come to Frankfort-on-the-Main when he was very young, and had there, as well as subsequently in a wider field, received a mercantile training. His religious tendencies, and a strong desire to educate himself scientifically, exposed him to many jokes, which however never disconcerted him. After having won a large circle of acquaintances, he returned to Düsseldorf to take charge of his father's business. By degrees, however, this became perfectly unendurable to him, and he obtained a place in the Exchequer of the Elector, — Düsseldorf at that time belonging to the Palatinate; and when Goethe came to Düsseldorf he found Jacobi, as counsellor of the Elector, holding a very important position. Through Wieland Jacobi had come to know Sophie Laroche, through whom again his wife and sisters, who were also superior people, had made the acquaintance of Goethe's sister Cornelia, whom they had visited in Frankfort. Goethe had maintained a correspondence for a long time with these ladies, and an acquaintance with the brother naturally followed.

After the death of Jacobi's wife, his sister Helen became his confidential secretary, and was often a medium between him and Goethe. Goethe characterized her at that time as single-hearted. Jacobi's wife, who was saved by an early death from sharing the troubled moods of his later years, must have been as beautiful as she was charming. Goethe says of her: "Free from any trace of sentimentality, she has good sense with a lively way of expressing herself; a glorious Netherlander, who without the sensual expression, yet in her strong healthy nature reminds one of the women of Rubens." Goethe here, while he seems only to describe this one woman, reveals the secret of all the women painted by that great artist. Jacobi has also represented his wife in his romance of "Allwill." Her character is the best thing in the book: the letters he attributes to her in this book are fascinating, and plainly her own letters were in his mind as models. Still, her character only comes out strongly when we add to this what Goethe has said of her.

She was living at the time of which we are speaking, in

the prime of life, surrounded by her children. Jacobi in summer left his house in the city and removed to Pempelfort. At present this same house and garden belong to the Artists' Union, "Malkasten," through which happy circumstance it retains its old ideal renown.

The cathedral, with the well-known crane, then stood a hopeless ruin, for it was not until more than thirty years later that the brothers Boisserée, who must be regarded as the second founders of it, began the rebuilding. But the city still stood, filled with venerable churches, halls, and houses, whose destruction took place in the times of the French. Among them, but undisturbed, with a garden belonging to it, was the house of the celebrated Banker Jabach, who had already been dead a century; and in it, on the spot where it was painted, the best picture, by his friend Lebrun, who has represented Jabach in the midst of his family circle. Goethe wished this picture to have a place in some public collection, and to-day it is to be found in the Berlin museum. Silent and deserted, like the old rooms, this picture presided over the well-kept domestic utensils of the last century, a monument of past times and of the reverence of the present. This house became to Goethe a symbol which filled his mind with vivid pictures of days of former greatness. While in his description of it he gave full play to these impressions, he gained the right tone in which to introduce the narration of what awaited him in Düsseldorf.

With regard to Goethe's and Jacobi's intercourse we remark, that their correspondence has been published by Max Jacobi. Zöppritz has edited two volumes of Jacobi's posthumous papers. Schöll, in his letters and treatises, has however given us the best idea of the friendship between them. Goethe was happy in Pempelfort. Separated from friends, family, and home, he would for once appear only what he had made himself — a self-sustained, self-conscious author. He introduced himself in this character to Jacobi, and was so received by him. Jacobi wholly disregards the difference in age, but at the same time he does not treat Goethe as the exotic young genius who has no equal: he feels himself of some importance also. They had each of them an overwhelming desire to be once fully understood. They surrendered themselves one to the other, as two lakes, between which the dam has given way, mingle their floods, while the fishes swim hither and thither. Goethe tells us how one evening, after they had talked until a late hour and then parted in order to sleep, they once more sought each other, and standing at the window continued the conversation deep into the night, while the moonlight quivered on the throbbing breast of the Rhine. This was on the return journey when Jacobi accompanied his friend. At the time Goethe was writing " Dichtung und Wahrheit," and sent to Jacobi for material, the latter mentioned this moonlight-talk, and bade him try to recall it to his recollection. "When we separated," — I quote the words of " Dichtung und Wahrheit," — " we separated with the feeling of an eternal union."

Goethe had already had experience enough to know that it is always a dangerous experiment to surrender oneself wholly to the influence of another. He had seen on the Rhine journey how Lavater had been tempted to use his spiritual — yes, his clerical — power for a worldly purpose. He discerned that what he had at first supposed to be pure nature was only the finest kind of acting, which by degrees became a second nature in Lavater. Goethe was compelled to recognize this all the more that he already saw the necessity of assuming a certain manner himself in his intercourse with men. He however assumed this manner not for the purpose of gaining anything, but simply to protect himself and to keep himself free. In Jacobi he now met with a nature whose entire purity and absence of anything like premeditation delighted him, and whose wealth of intellectual resources corresponded to his demands. Here is his first letter after they parted: —

"I dream that I see you, dear Fritz, have your letter, and hover about you. You have felt what a delight it is to me to be the object of your love. Oh, it is glorious that each believes he receives more from the other than he gives! Oh love, love! the poverty of riches! And what power it creates in me, — or, in other words, allows to stream in upon me, — when I welcome in another what is wanting in myself, and can give to him in addition what I have! Believe me, we could be dumb to each other from now on, and in after times when we met again, it would be as if we had moved on together steadily hand in hand. We should be united over things which we had not discussed."

Goethe never wrote again in this strain. What could have dissolved such a friendship? In one respect only Goethe had not been able immediately to judge his new friend. He could not know how much of Jacobi's personality was based on his own ideas, and how much was derived from others.

Jacobi had a marked influence on his century, was respected by the best people even to his old age, and has left behind a name whose fame still lingers. With such men, especially if they have been fruitful writers, it is not difficult to take in at a glance their whole career, and to find out the peculiar emphasis of their character. There was great receptiveness in Jacobi's nature: he was in too large a measure dependent on the sentiments which friends and books supplied to him, and mistook enthusiastic reproduction for inspired production. Goethe had taken with him his yet unpublished "Werther," and either read it to Jacobi or told him about it. Jacobi, inflamed by the feeling, reproduced Goethe's fiction in two works of his own; one of which called "Allwill's Collection of Letters" appeared even before "Werther" itself. Allwill is meant for Goethe. As early as the autumn of 1774 the first of these letters came out in the "German Mercury;" for this romance, like "Werther," was also in the form of letters. Jacobi describes a simple family (his own), into which suddenly a fiery young genius enters. Later, when the end of the book was published, the character of the hero was found to be essentially changed from what it was in the opening chapters. Julian Schmidt first pointed out that this change was coincident with Jacobi's later feeling, which through Goethe's own fault certainly had been cooled in a cruel way. Allwill's letters are so very much in Goethe's style that Lavater imagined Goethe to be the author of them; for, while Goethe had adopted Lavater's style of writing, Jacobi in this new style had imitated Goethe's. And here we see very clearly the difference between nature and exaggeration. Goethe takes naturally what suits him; but Jacobi rushes forward in conscious imitation of Goethe, and seeks to outdo him. Jacobi's letters, composed in the first moment of giddy excitement, sound to us to-day empty, odious, and vapid; while Goethe's inspired bursts of passion, rather gushing to be sure, are still natural and full of meaning.

Still more striking is the imitation in Jacobi's second work, the romance of "Woldemar," which appeared five years later when Goethe was already in Weimar. This is such an odd, insipid production that the reader of to-day could scarcely get beyond the first pages. Goethe's Werther sees the impossibility of entering into any natural relations with the wife of his friend whom he loves, and destroys himself. His fate has something comprehensible and logical in it: he should have flown earlier, but this we see with him is beyond his power. Jacobi's lovers, on the other hand, provoke their fate in the most cold-blooded manner. He presents to us an excellent young man, eminent for knowledge and refinement, the lover of a maiden equally superior, — Woldemar and Henriette. There exists no cogent reason why they should not be married; for that Henriette is not beautiful, and that Woldemar's old father is opposed to the union are secondary things, not taken into consideration. But they do not marry, because they love each other so very much that they feel an earthly tie would be out of harmony with their pure spiritual affinity. In pursuance of these views Woldemar marries Henriette's friend, Allwine, who in good time gives promise of a child. Jacobi has described this second relation in the purest and most charming colors. At the same time the spiritual marriage with Henriette continues: but the impossibility of such a tie, whose very nature is incomprehensible to them, grows ever more and more apparent; and the romance closes abruptly with a passionate conversation between Woldemar and Henriette, in which they do not understand each other, and which lets us see in perspective the destruction of all the characters concerned.

It is true, as Wilhelm Scherer first discovered, that Jacobi's own experience furnished the material which is here presented to us in romantic guise, and has enabled us to understand how he came to conceive such a plot; but this does not mitigate the intolerable impression the book makes.

"Woldemar" was, however, received with enthusiasm, and Jacobi reckoned surely upon Goethe's approval of it,

HOW HE RECEIVES JACOBI'S "WOLDEMAR."

when awful things reached his ears from Weimar. It was said that the book, in the beautiful cover in which it had been sent to Goethe, had been nailed by him to a tree in Ettersburg, as we nail some evil bird to the gable of a barn, and had been jeered at! This was gossiped about all over Germany. And still another outrage had been perpetrated upon the book, such as Voltaire alone was supposed to be capable of committing. Goethe had, with some slight alterations, so changed the meaning of the last few pages that the devil comes and bears off Woldemar! Now Jacobi writes an affecting letter: so and so you have done to me, he says, and then he quotes passages from Goethe's letters, in which Goethe avows before God and in the face of Providence that Jacobi is beyond all others his heart's friend. Goethe was so crest-fallen that he dared not make any reply to this letter. He charged a third person to say to Jacobi that the thing was not so badly intended, that he would write himself; but no letter was written. Goethe once quoted the axiom of Bernhard of Weimar, "that one should never make apologies." This was in keeping with his nature. He often reproached himself when alone for what he had done or had omitted to do; but, among all his letters, I know of only two or three in which he openly confesses any such thing. Four years after these events happened, however, he wrote to Jacobi, acknowledging the wrong he had done and begging to be forgiven. He says in the letter: "As we become older and the world more contracted to us, we think often with pain of the days when for mere pastime we trifled with our friends; when in wanton merriment we were unconscious of the wounds inflicted, or did not exert ourselves to heal them." Jacobi answered immediately. Goethe sent him his "Iphigenia," and they never again had any serious falling out with each other.

With Jacobi's years increased his tendency towards the supernatural. In his special department he was passionate and controversial. He sends his polemical writings to Goethe, who often expresses very sharply to him his disapprobation of them. Even in the earliest years of their friendship Goethe had frequently taken occasion openly to lament the printing of such things; but in spite of these harsh reproofs and disagreements they remained friends. Jacobi had a wonderful way of bearing all this opposition from Goethe, and they were always conscious of cherishing the best intentions toward one another. We see later that when Jacobi's son comes to Goethe he is received by him like a member of his family. Goethe first confided to him his " Hermann and Dorothea," in the year 1796; and so this friendship was carried on from father to son. Hence, later, the editing of the letters fulfilled by the son as a sacred privilege. Properly speaking, the grandchild, the son of Max Jacobi, should have published them; but the young man died before their completion, and the work fell back upon his father.

There is something beautiful in the authentic accounts, which by degrees find their way to the light, of the families with whom Goethe stood in the tenderest relations. Everywhere are disclosed the purest and most elevated sympathies, even where an entirely harmonious tone is wanting; and an interest in spiritual problems forms the basis of the intercourse.

On his first meeting with Jacobi, Goethe talked of the man whose writings had a more powerful effect upon him than all the philosophy which Herder, Lavater, or Jacobi offered him,— Spinoza. The violent opposition to Spinoza in which Jacobi stood all his life explains why they fell upon this subject immediately, Goethe having become acquainted with his theories much earlier. Jacobi's fame rested in part upon the position he held toward Spinoza. A controversy which he had with Lessing in the latter years of that poet's life also makes him of importance to-day to many who otherwise would scarcely have known of him. Jacobi exerted himself to the utmost to contend against what he denominated "Spinozism." And here we must mention the deeper reason why Goethe at this time discussed Spinoza. Spinoza's philosophy possessed everything which Goethe must have missed later in Jacobi's philosophy. Indeed, the acquaintance with Spinoza forms an important epoch in Goethe's development.

In considering Goethe's entire life, we remark two facts which I will call fundamental facts in his life.

The first was that, so far as we know, he never experienced anything which wholly took him out of himself, and that even when he appears most passionately excited he still retains the power to criticise himself. With him, therefore, events and his subsequent reflections upon them must always be carefully distinguished. When Goethe writes to Frau von Stein, separated from her and alone, his feelings are more intense than when near her; not until he reflects upon it does his passion burst forth in all its intensity. So, too, his relation to Lotte becomes comprehensible only when we see how his passion exhibits itself in the hours when he is absent from her.

The second was that Goethe does not mention any living man, or any contemporary book, that fully meets the wants of his nature; no man who could excite in him the feeling, "Such I would like to have been!" and no book over which he might have thought, "This is what I would have written, but it is better than I could have written it." He was enthusiastic about Herder only as a learner, and after the first intoxication was over returned to a consciousness of his own position. And so he soon recovered from his infatuation about Lavater and Jacobi, and no one came after them by whom he allowed himself to be deluded as he had been by these three men. As soon as he had gained some measure of experience in life, he always knew beforehand that in time all these brilliant meteors would cease to dazzle him, and that he should once more be sustained by his own independent judgment.

In contemplating all the influences which tended to develop Goethe we find that there were only four men who had a lasting effect upon him, who as it were lived in his soul never to be displaced,—Homer, Shakspeare, Raphael, and Spinoza. These men were to him representatives of the four mighty elements from whose workings our European culture, or the mental conditions within which we live and labor, arose and is still arising.

It is impossible to trace all the sources of human culture. We do not know the origin of language; we do not know whence art came; we do not know how political life first grew up. Even if we limit ourselves to Europe, we do not know from whence came the European man as ruler of our continent,—that is to say, when and how the emigrator or the native-born aborigine raised himself to be the specific bearer of the culture which, as an ancient inheritance, we are laboring ourselves to enrich. We have only conjectures of later origin, which lead one of these questions in a definite direction in which an answer possibly may lie. We have only hypotheses with regard to our primary condition. The great emigrations from Asia which brought to us the noble scions to be engrafted on our wild stock, and who figure now as prehistoric peoples, rest only upon an hypothesis of the philologist. The Greeks believed that they had grown out of the rocky soil of their native land. Tacitus coolly concludes that this must also have been the case with the

Germans, since it is inconceivable that foreign settlers should have chosen such an inhospitable soil. But even if we do not question these emigrations, which by degrees caused Celts, Germans, and Sclaves to come from the East through one, two, or three thousand years to crowd in upon us here; even if we accept what appears beyond doubt to be the fact, that the Jews once were concentred in Palestine, a firmly established people, and did not live scattered like exiles, which is the only way we can conceive of them to-day, — yet as we study history practically all these conjectures fall away, and we draw our conclusions only from what we positively know. It is not possible to separate the European nations from the territory they inhabit to-day; or, in relation to their interests, to treat of them separately and alone. Greeks, Romans, Germans, Semitic, Celtic, and Sclavonic races form a community irrevocably bound to its clod of earth; each, however, exhibiting the unchangeable national peculiarities which arose from the character of their original fatherland. This community seems to have been from the beginning what we see it to-day, which as a whole produces what constitutes our present intellectual life, and ever has produced it so far as we have any knowledge of it. The preservation and progress of this is given to our children as a sacred legacy; and we quietly let the matter drop with regard to the future, even if we can imagine a future in which all the things of to-day, to the very last echo of fabulous recollection, shall have died away.

Among the elemental races the Greeks, Germans, Romans, and Semites are specially to be considered. We learn in the different periods of history how they loved and hated each other; how they disowned and then again courted each other; were united and then rent asunder. We observe at times what heroic attempts they made to isolate themselves; but they do not succeed, and the conviction that they are essential to each other ever finally becomes the ruling one.

I will not say that the four men whom I have mentioned are in themselves the most distinguished representatives of these four elemental peoples, or that they have produced none mightier; for with Homer we should mention Phidias and Plato; by the side of Raphael, Michael Angelo and Dante; with Shakspeare, Luther; and with Spinoza, the men of the Old and New Testaments: but in Goethe's mind Homer, Shakspeare, Raphael, and Spinoza occupied the first place. In the degree in which he became acquainted with them the feeling of a common humanity sprang up in him, as distinct from all that was merely national; and he was indebted to them for an introduction to the historic views on which his own mental growth depended.

Homer and Shakspeare were first known to him. It was in Strasburg and Frankfort that the might of these kings among men became revealed to him; and now Spinoza was added to them. Goethe's attitude towards Homer and Shakspeare is easier to comprehend than towards Spinoza, because the first two exercise over us to-day the old power; and all attempts to deprive Homer of his individuality, or to depreciate Shakspeare, do not affect it. Spinoza, on the contrary, is less known, and from various causes stands, at present, much farther removed from us.

And here a digression is necessary, in order to lay clearly before you Goethe's point of view. Goethe had grown up in a religious family, and in full knowledge of what the Christian faith rests on. He who to-day can repeat the Lord's prayer, the ten commandments, the creed, and some hymns without hesitation, and who knows something about the books of the Old and New Testaments and the history of the Church, believes himself well instructed in religious matters. But in the last century it was quite different. The comprehension of the Christianity of the former century, as an historical fact, becomes again of importance now that our whole spiritual development seems colored by its religious tendency. Whatever our own personal belief may be, we must at any rate make ourselves familiar with the whole course of religious development in Germany. Everybody in the last century was well versed in the Bible, and thoroughly schooled in the differences of the creeds and sects even to the subtleties, which are now-a-days familiar to the professional theologian alone. As at present every one is acquainted with what concerns the army, and every family knows all the necessary facts about its organization, its duties, promotions, etc., as well as where the different regiments are stationed, and who the commanders are in the prominent places, because every family is in some way or other connected with the army,— so at that time men were at home in all matters appertaining to the Church, and knew the names and relative importance of the leading ministers. In science, poetry, and theology alone was free discussion or agitation allowed, as has been already said. Who would really catch the flavor of this state of things should read the romance of the (during his life) renowned Berlin bookseller Nicolai, —" Sebaldus Nothanker." The four volumes contain nothing but a series of rows between the hero — who is a philosophic, liberal, open-hearted country preacher — and Fate, in the shape of some bigoted old theological wrestlers. Without an acquaintance with these circumstances it is impossible to have an idea of the fights into which Lessing was constantly drawn, or to comprehend the power of

Herder, who as a free-thinking theologian had made himself master of all the subjects that were in fermentation about him. Goethe had been, even as a child, initiated in these matters, through his connection with the Moravian Fräulein von Klettenberg. And again in Strasburg he made use of an introduction he had taken with him to a family inclined to this faith. Goethe was therefore perfectly familiar with the Bible. The active part he took in the religious discussions of the day, as shown by a number of his essays on the leading topics and his intimate friendship with the prophet Lavater, was natural. Goethe's earliest poem is a bombastic song on the "Descent of Christ into Hell," which is in the ranting style of the preachers of the last century; but nevertheless we observe that while he was perfectly at home on religious subjects they never completely absorbed him, nor turned him aside from ideas which came from other sources.

Herder and Lavater were to him the two great streams whose unsteady current bore onward the ecclesiastical life of the time. Herder started from an historical point. Through his tendencies to the universal he attempted to utilize Hebrew and Greek literature, under whose conjoined influence the early Church was formed. He recognized in the Christian idea the mightiest lever which had ever been applied to lift the sinking spiritual life of European nations. Herder gives us in magnificent and even to-day thrilling language an historical confirmation, drawn from universal literature, to the fact of the revolution by which Paganism fell before a new regenerating power which had come into the world, and a description of how this power was diffused and obtained the mastery. Hence came Herder's extraordinary respect for Christianity. But it was only respect. Herder was a scholar. Later in life, when influenced by his work as a minister, his convictions became somewhat changed; but they always rested on a scientific basis.

Lavater started from a practical point. He had found out by experience that the ethical contents of the Bible were sufficient to meet all human wants; that remedy for every defect was therein to be found; and that faith leads farther than knowledge. And he lived all this out in his own way: he appeared as a prophet, but did not make converts in the true sense of the word, — rather sought to win sympathetic disciples, and to attach them to himself by means of the smoothest diplomacy.

Neither of the two men could offer Goethe anything. He did not need the religion which either Herder or Lavater held to be the best: he would only know how the solitary man, limited to himself, stands towards transcendent realities. He could better have learned this from Jung Stilling; but Stilling who lived and moved in wholly Christian ideas, and who was the only Pietist in whom Goethe really believed, was of such a peculiar nature that one could learn nothing from him. In order to have done so, one must have been just like him.

We all come in contact with the great question of religious need, — even those among us who are affected by the prevailing scepticism, or who have been educated in such indifference to the Church as to consider such things almost foreign to them. This, however, is only in appearance, for a negative relation is yet a relation. What is here in question? The question is not how to find out the form and the contents of religious creeds, or how the clergy are best treated and ranked for the good of the people, or what the relation is between Church and State, or how we understand the history of the Church or judge the critical exegesis of the Gospels; but the question is how to ascertain, without any concealment from ourselves of our deepest spiritual wants, what relation we bear to things which lie beyond this earthly life and human experience. This question arises in each of us, troubles us, and will not be thrust aside; and each takes his answer from any source that can satisfy him. Whether we are again to meet the departed, and how and where; whether we shall be able to recall the past, and what our new existence will be; and whether in this new existence there will be yet further development, — of these things every one would have some idea: if it be only to answer "No" to these questions, he would have some reason for this "No!" Now the religious training which Goethe had received at home, and the Christianity of Herder and Lavater gave him nothing which he could make available for his individual needs. He cherished and expressed only two convictions: first, that there is a personal God, who in all that concerns the history of mankind has an overruling power and aim; second, that there is a personal immortality. These two articles of faith Goethe accepted, without giving or desiring proof; for he found them built into the very groundwork of his nature. Beyond these, nothing further. He rejected all details. All supernaturalism, demanding more than these two ideas, was powerless over him. But he required, what every man should require, a theory for the moral organization of humanity, and would have this verified by the surest possible proof.

We are certain that we are all, whether high or low, members of one fraternity. We feel that this association is no merely accidental or mechanical one, but that within it a great intellectual work is going on, which, pressing forward to a common aim, constitutes its cohesive and impelling power. This aim we call the "Just," the "Good," the "Beautiful," the "Highest Ideal," —

"God." All history seems the effort of the world to attain and realize this final highest Good. But how are we to know it? And before we answer this question we ask, "How do we know anything?" The man who has never put to himself these questions, and who has never made the attempt to answer them, stands on a very low plane. But to find an answer here is not possible without much practice of the thinking powers, and therefore we study philosophy. For this reason the study of philosophy is something that has been recognized in all ages as of the highest interest.

Goethe, in the degree that he towered above other men, was the more keenly alive to the study of these earnest problems; and now as he looked about for a master, no philosopher satisfied him like Spinoza. We see Goethe during his long life testing many philosophical systems, and coming in personal contact with many philosophers; but Spinoza's system is the only one to which he adheres, and which he never criticises. He says modestly that he did not know what he picked out of Spinoza's "Ethics;" but the book attracted him, and contained secrets which were useful to him.

Let us now see how Spinoza's book was written.

Baruch, or (the name being translated into Latin) Benedictus, Spinoza was born in Amsterdam in 1632. He belonged to a Jewish-Portuguese family. From Portugal, where the Jews were treated in a most inhuman manner, one of the greatest emigrations started. The Jewish colony arrived by ship in Holland, and there, while retaining a constitution of their own, occupied a distinguished position in the body-politic. If we look at Rembrandt's pictures and etchings of Biblical events, we shall see that the persons represented from the Old and New Testaments wear a very peculiar costume, — the men in long kaftans and fur-trimmed garments, and the women with very curious ornaments. This was the costume of the Portuguese Jews living in Holland, which Rembrandt found artistically appropriate, and which is in such striking contrast to the garments in which the Italian artists of the classic age draped the same figures.

Spinoza carried his dissent from the religion of his people so far, that he was first cast out of the synagogue and then out of the Jewish community. Gutzkow has made such a banishment the subject of his "Uriel Acosta," and gives us an idea of what passions here came into play. Spinoza went to a Holland physician of whom he learned Greek and Latin. He had a love affair with the daughter of this man, which, however, did not end in a union. I may as well add at once that he never married. He was a lonely being, rejected by his own people. An attempt was even made, on the part of the Jewish community in Amsterdam, to assassinate him; but he escaped. He threw himself wholly into his philosophical studies; but at the suggestion of his teacher Descartes he learned to cut optical glasses, by which he gained an independent livelihood. This occupation brought him in contact with the most distinguished naturalists of his time.

The Jews in Amsterdam finally succeeded in exiling Spinoza, and from this time he lived either in Leyden or at the Hague, in such absolute retirement that often for many weeks together he never left his house. One of his friends — and there were many who clung to him with passionate devotion — wished to make him a present of a considerable sum of money; but Spinoza refused it, calling his friend's attention to the fact that he had a brother to whom the money was due. Another wished to give him an allowance of five hundred guilders yearly, but

Spinoza would only accept three hundred, just what was absolutely necessary to sustain life. His patrimony he gave to his sister. A call to Heidelberg, where as professor of philosophy he would have been free to teach what he liked, he declined for the sake of continuing his work in his independent way at the Hague. And there he died of consumption at about forty-five years of age.

Spinoza published in his lifetime an exposition of the philosophy of Descartes, which is not of so much importance as the great works published after his death,— "Ethics," and the "Political Treatise." Next to the latter his letters are most valuable. We see how favorable Spinoza's peculiar position was for scientific study. He was without family and perfectly alone. He had renounced his nation; there was no State to which he owed allegiance, or which he must in any way regard, for in Holland at that time one might think, say, and print what he liked. Spinoza, moreover, possessed that excellent gift of the Hebrew mind which enables one to take up things objectively. He did not allow himself to be led astray by any considerations which were outside of the subject before him. A man so prepared devotes all his thoughts and all his labor to a calm, unselfish contemplation of the human world which with all its whirl of passions and interests is moving about him. And the book in which he demonstrated his results was undertaken with the settled purpose that it should not be printed until after the death of the author. Under the name of "Ethics" he works out the following: "A theory of mutual intercourse in which each man is considered as part of a whole." Spinoza has included within a few simple formulas the whole monstrous complication of feelings and motives created and engendered by human intercourse. Throughout we find nothing personal in the book; nothing in the remotest degree that looks like an anecdote; not the slightest attempt to convert the reader by any other means than mathematical demonstration, or to dictate to him "Do that, it is good!" or "Do not do that, it is bad!" Indeed it is a book written in a language which one can hardly call a language. In order to be rigidly exact, Spinoza has used the dead Latin of the scholars of his time as mechanically as possible. With the pointedness of a business man, he makes use of such words and phrases as guarantee that no mistakes shall arise; there are no provincialisms, no fascinating sentences, no comparisons, no pleasing reminder in the reading of the good Latin authors, but the barest statements follow one upon another in the barest syntax. Spinoza therefore appropriately chose the title, *Ethica ordine mathematico demonstrata*, — " Theory of the Moral Relations of Men presented in Mathematical Order."

And this book was not only to remain unpublished until after his death, but even then it was to appear anonymously. Spinoza says: "The name of the author upon the titlepage influences the readers: this must not be allowed; no one is to know that I am the author of this book. It shall lie before the eyes of men as if it had been the product of humanity."

There is a book by Desor, translated by Carl Vogt, which relates the efforts of a company of learned men to fathom the locomotion of the glacier. A number of people betake themselves to the spot. They are sure of only two facts: first, that glaciers move; and, second, that how they move they do not know. They begin to study the matter as one would a book written in an unknown tongue. Slowly and laboriously they find the right method of observation, and at last the secret is discovered how the huge mass of ice moves forward. In the same way Spinoza took the moral progress of mankind for the subject of his investigations, and without resorting to historical evidence trusted simply to what he had before his eyes and ears. He brings an endless number of symptoms into distinct groups ; gives to each group its name; then proceeds to find the relations between them, and thus finally gains the clew to how the united stream of humanity is flowing, and whither it flows. He is only an explorer, nothing else. He has no favorite personal ideas, no national prejudices, no aims of any kind whatever, but the single intention to state the matter as it is; and in conclusion the one result arrived at is that the " Good " is something real and positive, and that the " Evil " is nothing real, but only negation of the " Good." This book, which from the moment of its publication until now has had the greatest effect, satisfied a want in Goethe's nature by its manner of interpreting all things, — a want which nowhere else had found relief.

Goethe's Faust speaks of the *beiden seelen* which dwelt within his breast. This twofold spiritual existence Goethe had been able best to observe in himself. There was in his nature a mixture of blindness with the keenest perspicacity, which apart from each other worked out their various results side by side within him. He says of himself that he first wrote, rushing unconsciously on, and only knew what he had done when he saw it on paper. Added to this was the necessity of expressing himself in parables. He was once phrenologically examined by Dr. Gall, who introduced phrenology and by his personal experiments spread it far and wide in Germany; and Gall declared that Goethe's most conspicuous trait was to express himself in tropes. He could not convert his thoughts into exact words, and availed himself of poetic imagery to suggest what he wished to say. To state it emphatically, Goethe gave up trying to understand himself. In his old age, speaking of himself to Chancellor Müller, he said: "What one actually is he must find out from others." Goethe shows himself on one side a poet; a somnambulist who is not conscious while he writes what flows from his pen; a dreamer who does not understand himself, and is in his own eyes a half-fictitious creature, — is vacillating, confused, and passionate; will enjoy the goods of this world, will surrender himself to the vague instincts of his nature, and remove from his path all obstacles which threaten to hinder it. But on the other side, in opposition to this, stands his unmerciful objectivity and clearness of apprehension. A demon whispers to him instantly where the weak side is in men and things. He practises the subtlest criticism, anatomizes men, — others as well as himself, — and will not allow the least embellishment of his results. So we see him as naturalist, statesman, historian. He is decided, keen, cold. Now he will not be tempted by the pleasures of this world, but insists that renunciation is commanded. This is his great word. With an unrelenting severity, toward himself first of all, he seeks to fulfil his duty.

The result of all this is that we see Goethe always either one or the other; never both together, never the two orbits running into one another. Either he writes poetry, or he views almost indifferently what he has written, not quite knowing what to do with it; either like a deluded child he gives himself wholly and confidingly to men, or he advances to meet them sternly like a man hardened by experience. These alternations in him never ended. He always meets men with fresh curiosity, and loves them while new, but repulses them unmercifully when the hour for criticism arrives; for the conscious-

PECULIARITY OF HIS RELIGIOUS BELIEF. 207

ness of the folly outgrown irritates him, and in general when he begins to criticise nothing satisfies him.

Goethe's double nature found in Spinoza's philosophy its only adequate interpretation. In general, those who surrender themselves to a philosopher demand of him not only what belongs to the cold intellect, but that he shall include in his system the things which, beyond the reach of dry explanation, reveal themselves only to the vision of the prophetic soul; for what does not here admit of proof is then accepted on the personal responsibility of the philosopher. Precisely this last neither Goethe nor Spinoza would permit. The things which lie beyond comprehension and proof Goethe did not desire to have extended to him by strange hands. The distinction which Spinoza held fast, that when he spoke of God he meant God only in so far as human reason was able to comprehend him, and surrendered blindly to theology everything beyond that, corresponded to Goethe's deepest convictions. The God of whom he was conscious was not the God whom he sought to interpret. Like Spinoza, he considered philosophy and theology wholly distinct elements, as unlike one another as land and water. On the one man stands or moves with firm tread, while over the other he is driven at the mercy of the winds and waves. Lessing also felt this, and clung to Spinoza's theory with his inmost soul. Jacobi, on the other hand, who in reality began in philosophy where Goethe stopped, groped about among the mysteries of supernaturalism, and sought to make Spinoza's solemn awe before things which do not come within the region of the understanding a reason for suspecting him of atheism. This was the point where Goethe and Jacobi separated. Goethe's faith in God and immortality had nothing at all to do with his philosophy. This faith had grown up in him and belonged to him; he wanted no proof of it, and in general allowed no discussion of the subject. Only in rare moments would he speak of it, when he felt assured that he was fully understood by his friends. Jacobi loved openly to discuss these things; and this fundamental difference in their natures gave occasion for argument between them, even to their last days. Jacobi fostered the curious mistake that if only the right lever could be applied, Goethe would be brought over to his dogmatical philosophy, while Goethe always repudiated him with the like firmness. Goethe has had many opponents who could not understand him in this respect, and who have called him the "great Heathen." He has occasionally called himself a heathen, but never an atheist or an unbeliever.

After Jacobi, Goethe never found an intimate friend to whom he so wholly surrendered himself; and after Spinoza he made fresh acquaintance only with Raphael, as if even in the kingdom of the dead there was no other who might command his absolute devotion: under the name of Raphael, however, I understand not Raphael alone, but his epoch, and Rome with all her treasures. Yet before this last great acquaintance was to be vouchsafed him, Goethe needed a series of years marked by the severest toil.

One thing more concerning Spinoza.

Goethe's description in "Dichtung und Wahrheit" of the beginning of his acquaintance with Spinoza's works is unique of its kind. We see that Spinoza is revealed to him only by degrees. A dim feeling of kinship attracts him ever anew to Spinoza's book, which he reads at first hardly knowing that he is learning anything from it. In this account is an experience valuable to all men. How many who have found themselves, as it seemed by accident, attracted to some great soul have followed in its orbit with just such an indistinct consciousness of dependence, and only as they came nearer and nearer to him realized what they sought in him! How many have become acquainted with Goethe himself in this way, having taken his works into their hands at first only because a feeling of affinity inclined them to the perusal!

LECTURE XI.

LILLI SCHOENEMANN.

AS it is inconsistent with our plan to speak of anything which did not immediately influence Goethe's development, it seems like a digression if I mention, *honoris causa*, specially the visit which he received in the autumn of 1774. Klopstock passed through Frankfort. He was going at the invitation of the Margrave of Baden to pass at least a year at his court, where he refused permanently to reside. There were in those times of " philanthropic enlightenment " a number of small princes in Germany to whom intercourse with such men seemed a vital necessity.

It is curious that Klopstock, whom Goethe from his childhood regarded with extraordinary veneration, seems to have had no effect upon him either as a writer or a poet. We can nowhere trace Klopstock's influence. Even the odes in which, after the Strasburg time, he liked to pour forth his feelings, suggest Pindar rather than Klopstock. The one thing in the tragedy of "Mahomet," which can be called truly Klopstockian, is so much of an exception that it only confirms what has been said. If we did not know its origin, we should scarcely ascribe it to Goethe. The impressions of his childhood seem to have implanted in him a kind of historical reverence, which made his manner towards Klopstock very different from what might be almost called the saucy unconcern with which he often met such venerable dignitaries. In his old age Goethe once used the expression, "We silly boys of 1772," alluding to the reckless indifference with which he and his companions opposed the prejudices of their time in every direction. They passed over rough-shod what did not suit them, and proclaimed their opinions openly; but Klopstock was an exception with Goethe.

When Lotte and Werther, at that eventful ball, stood together at the window and looked out into the night, only one word was exchanged between them, — *Klopstock*. All that could be expressed of the sublime was exhausted in that one word.

Klopstock was Prime Archangel in the Hierarchy of German poetry. His "Messiah" placed him, in the eyes of his contemporaries, as much above Homer as Voltaire with his "Henriade" was placed by himself and his nation. The last five cantos of the "Messiah," which Goethe and his sister read by stealth when children and became so wildly enthusiastic over, had just been published; and the "Odes" appeared while Goethe was studying in Strasburg. Klopstock was only fifty-one years of age, but had already given to his fame its last and highest consecration. His German was the noblest, the freest, the richest; and great thoughts were allowed expression among us only in the language which he had created.

Klopstock was an imposing presence; not only was he the friend and confidant of princes, but in his own appearance there was something regal. Thus we see Cardinal Bembo in the sixteenth century, as a learned theologian, raising himself to be a prince among princes. Goethe, when he talked with Eckermann about Klopstock, said he had looked up to him as to a revered uncle. Later, in the same vein, he describes him to Chancellor

Müller as somewhat stiff and stately, with an assumption of superiority. The aspiring youthful generation looked up to Klopstock, and offered him that modest reverence which later surrounded him as an atmosphere. Klopstock also had begun his career as a theologian, and to minister and care for the souls of men had become a second nature. If among the younger poets anything was not as it should be, Klopstock, asked or unasked, wrote a letter of remonstrance, which they complied with. With Goethe, however, this became the cause of a very sudden and decided rupture.

Klopstock had not struggled to gain his high position. The laurel had peacefully and luxuriantly grown about his house, almost without any effort on his part. He was always in comfortable circumstances. Lessing, a lonely being in Wolfenbüttel, and Herder, who still more neglected had run aground in Buckeburg, from whence even with humiliating conditions it was almost impossible for him to gain a professorship at Göttingen, were to Klopstock like small energetic islands in comparison with a vast continental empire. They stood alone, and maintained their policy single-handed. Klopstock, on the other hand, worked as it were aided by the machinery of a well-organized government, and as a symbolic representative of the kingdom over which he ruled; wrote his "Republic of Learned Men," — "Gelehrtenrepublik," — a mixture of romantic narration and dry reasoning, like Rousseau's "Émile," and in imitation of it.

Rousseau had not dared to make France the scene of his Ideal Kingdom, in which at the end of his "Émile" every one found peace and comfort, but chose the Greek-Asiatic Islands, which at that time were always at hand ready for such use. Klopstock, on the contrary, organized his republic, composed of the literary and educated, in Germany itself. This book contains an account of events in this already constituted republic. Presiding over this republic was the Areopagus, an assembly of the most eminent philosophers; and from them the ranks graduated downward to the masses, who formed the Corona, and were only allowed now and then to discuss a subject and to give their opinion. All Germany subscribed for this book. When it was published, Goethe wrote: "It is the greatest work of the century, and contains the only true poetry;" while Herder said: "This learned republic is composed merely of little boys, with Klopstock in their midst."

The style of the "Gelehrtenrepublik" and of his letters is monotonous and wearisome, and the metaphors in his "Odes" seem anything but natural; while the somewhat heavy swing of his graceful cadences is no longer imposing, and has lost all the charm of novelty. Still we cannot be sure that the future will not, in some degree, reverse the present judgment of them. Klopstock's pathos sprang from true feeling, and his language possesses a vitality of its own, while his position in our literary development is unassailable. Like Ennius in Roman literature, he will perhaps remain chiefly distinguished for having made the first successful attempt to bring the emphasis of the words and sentences into consonance with their meaning.

It is certain that Goethe highly revered Klopstock, but what personal relations they could have had at that time I really do not know. In those days Goethe carried his "Stella" about with him, a subject which would have been revolting to Klopstock. Even Frederick the Great, although alike indifferent to conventional morals and the young poets of Germany, felt himself moved to make known his displeasure at this work. Klopstock would not have judged it otherwise, and Goethe himself, after the enthusiasm had flown with which for a few years he clung to the poem, yielded to the universal judgment and gave to the plot another ending.

Owing to the peculiarities of this work, a few words are here required concerning it.

In order to comprehend how Goethe was led to think of such a radical change at the close of the story, — that the hero, instead of marrying *both* the women who have claims upon his heart, shoots himself, — we must bear in mind that the new construction is suggested much more naturally than would at first appear. Stella closed with a double marriage; and nothing was more natural than that Goethe should be reproached with defending bigamy. But this end was by no means the conclusion required by the development of the plot. Wherever the question is whether a man shall be allowed to marry more than one woman, as among the Mormons, it is understood to rest on the pleasure of the man, who decides whether he wants more than one wife. But in Goethe's "Stella" the question concerns two women, both of whom believe they have a right to the man to whom, at different times, each has wholly belonged. Not only to the surprise of the spectators but of the hero himself, who had never dreamed of the like, he is reminded in the most critical moment of the Count of Gleichen and his two wives; whereupon he instantly follows his example. The piece closes with rapture at having found this way out of the dilemma, and no time is afforded the spectators to look farther into the future. What Goethe valued in this work was the contrast in the character of the two women, who, with all their vehemence and passion, appear before us to-day in imperishable colors. Ulrich's, and after him Scherer's, investigations have shown us what circumstances led Goethe to deal with this curious problem.

The renown which Goethe won by the publication of "Werther," which at this time had just appeared, — a renown which lasted fresh many years, — indicated to him the path he should follow. He was proud and in the wildest spirits. Such sweet wine as the autumn of 1774 mellowed for him Fate never again offered to his lips! And, as if to crown this joy, the one treasure in life which had been denied him was to be granted him, — love for a beautiful young girl, who returns his love, and whom he is willing to make his wife: and now all the elements seem to exist which for a well-to-do citizen constitute the happiness of a lifetime. We have seen how each new love-affair has shown Goethe in a wider horizon. When he first loved Gretchen, or in Leipsic the good and pretty maidens captivated him, a bar-room formed the background of his stage. In Strasburg the scene is somewhat enlarged: here we have a village with rural perspective. Wetzlar offers the Deutsches Haus, with all the life of the little town and its surrounding landscape, as the scene of action. But with Lilli the piece is, as we might say, acted on a great opera-stage brilliantly lighted. She belonged to one of the distinguished Frankfort families. Receptions, masquerades, excursions by sea and land occur, and many important personages figure in the play. Instead of a one-act performance with few *dramatis personæ*, we have here a comedy in five acts, which, after violent struggles for and against, reaches its long-deferred conclusion.

Goethe was certainly at that time one of the most desirable matches in Frankfort. He was not only young and handsome, but famous. He had the overflowing fountain of youthful power which no one can resist; he was just the being for a young girl of sixteen to fall in love with! What he was at this time gives the key to one of his poetical creations, which else would be somewhat inexplicable to us, and which now in its turn throws a light on Goethe himself.

Rugantino or, as he is called in the first edition, Crugantino, in the drama written at this time of "Claudine von Villa Bella," is a vagabond; that is to say, he is the son of respectable parents, but (in the style of the Spanish novels) spends his time on the highways and among the hills with gay companions who sustain him in the wildest adventures, until love entices him back to a quiet, respectable existence, — a milder kind of Don Juan: certainly at that time Mozart's opera had not been put on the stage. Cervantes, however, had long been among Goethe's favorite authors; and, later, he took the same theme for his "Wilhelm Meister."

Goethe, the ideal vagabond, now meets his Claudine; and the experiment almost succeeds, as it did with Crugantino.

Goethe charmingly relates how the summer of 1774 passed in Frankfort; his journey with Lavater interrupted only for a while the gay social life which had drawn together a great number of young people. The special persons whom Goethe mentions, or who are spoken of by others as belonging to this circle, have been followed up by the Goethe investigators, and many details about them have been brought to light. Düntzer and Loeper give us knowledge of them. By one of this circle Goethe was incited to write "Clavigo."

In the course of this summer Goethe became better acquainted with Lilli. He had met her earlier as a good, open-hearted, fresh young girl who gave him her confidence. When, at the beginning of 1775, in the midst of the brilliant society of Frankfort, he saw Lilli

HE FALLS IN LOVE WITH LILLI.

again, she had all the presence of a lady. Besides Goethe's own account in "Dichtung und Wahrheit" of his experience with Lilli, we have a series of a very peculiar kind of letters written at that time to the Countess Augusta Stolberg, who was personally unknown to him, but whom nevertheless he addresses as "du" and "Gustchen." His imitation of Lavater's style is nowhere so apparent, and they are written in such a curious style as to distinguish them from all his other letters. In January he had first seen Lilli again. In February he writes to the Countess, —

"If you can picture to yourself, my dear, a Goethe who in gold-laced coat (and forsooth from head to foot in the same ornamental attire), under a blaze of chandeliers and candelabra, surrounded by all kinds of people, is chained to the card-table by a pair of beautiful eyes; who in a round of gayeties is driven from receptions to concerts, and from there to balls, and with all the interest of the frivolous courts a pretty little blonde, — you have before you the, at present, Carnival Goethe, who lately blundered out to you some stupid sentimentalisms," etc.

We see what a dangerous little blonde she was, — no flower growing in the woods like Frederika, nor blossoming in the window of a retired country house like Lotte, but one in a magnificent garden, amid artificial fountains, unfolding itself to the admiring gaze of all; and, though none may pluck it, we must marvel at its beauty and rejoice in its fragrance.

Mark now how Goethe repeats in verse these thoughts in the letter : —

> "Wherefore so resistlessly dost draw me
> Into scenes so bright?
> Had I not enough to soothe and charm me
> In the lonely night?

" Homely in my little room secluded,
  While the moon's bright beams
In a shimmering light fell softly on me,
  As I lay in dreams:

" Dreaming through the golden hours of rapture
  Soothed my heart to rest,
As I felt thy image sweetly living
  Deep within my breast.

" Can it be I sit at yonder table,
  Gay with cards and lights,
Forced to meet intolerable people,
  Because 'tis *she* invites?

" Alas! the gentle bloom of spring no longer
  Cheereth my poor heart:
There is only spring and love and Nature,
  Angel, where thou art!"

" To this, then," Goethe says to the beloved one, "you have brought me, that I find the hated amusements of society more alluring than Nature herself."

But he has no right to complain. He might have known it all beforehand. Lilli had openly and candidly talked about herself. She had grown up in the enjoyment of every social advantage, had been indulged in pleasures of all kinds, and made no secret of the fact that she neither could nor would do without them in the future. We call her without the slightest hesitation a little coquette. But she had been perfectly open about it: it delighted her to have adorers. Goethe describes this in the most delicate way: " She made no secret of her little weaknesses, and could not deny that she had a certain gift to attract people to her, together with an inclination to drop them again as lightly."

But it was one thing to hear a young girl prattle of

such things in an afternoon ramble through the woods and meadows, and another to experience the truth of them in practice on oneself. Lilli met Goethe again as a fashionable lady, who was admired and received the admiration gracefully, and who treated everybody, especially Goethe, after a way of her own.

Without doubt she had informed herself in the mean time with regard to many things which Goethe at his confessionals certainly had not confided to her with equal plainness, and had found out what a dangerous customer he was. Of all these things she made a note. A young girl of sixteen has not much conscience in such matters. Lilli makes her adorer jealous, keeps him on tenter-hooks, then smooths him down again only to exasperate him afresh; in short she takes the right way to fasten him irrevocably to her, — and this continues three months, until an engagement is the result.

Lilli had conquered. But scarcely was the game won when the tables were turned. We remember how it was with Frederika. The moment Goethe divined that he had conquered a heart, an involuntary perception sprang up in him that the summit was reached, and that henceforth the path lay downward. The same thing happened here, as Goethe himself describes, — his growing passion, his happiness, and then the awakening from the intoxication. As soon as he was officially announced a bridegroom, his thoughts centred about the one idea of setting himself free again. He sees how seriously his mother is preparing to receive Lilli as a daughter: a fright takes possession of him. In April the engagement takes place, and in May he announces to Herder that it is all over. But he deceives himself this time, for the affair could not be dismissed so easily. It is now Lilli's turn to suffer, and to try to win her lover back. But I intend to touch only the main features, and dare not attempt to give even a sketch of this exquisite love-story, which with all its charming details is told in "Dichtung und Wahrheit." Goethe's description is not to be excelled, and we would not lose one word of it.

It is something pitiful to see how the poor girl conquered at last forgets her little artifices, and only tries to please him whom she loves. But with all her cleverness she does not understand the power against which she is contending. Goethe's demoniac impulse to free himself from all bonds, even the dearest, led him to rend and break these which had been so tenderly woven and so firmly joined.

From Goethe's letters to the Countess Stolberg we see how fully the matter absorbed him. To this friend whom he had never seen he could pour out his heart as freely as if he were talking to himself. We feel that by writing to some one he hopes to be relieved of what oppresses him. It is curious to observe how he refers again and again to the changes in the weather and the seasons, as if they were an indispensable accompaniment. Something of this kind we have remarked before. "Werther" is full of it; but here he emphasizes all these externals as if they were quite an essential part of the story. Goethe's account of this engagement, and his moods before and after make us feel as if we were watching one of the organic processes of Nature, where the changes are as beautiful as they are necessary; and when the separation at last takes place, it seems as inevitable as the coming of autumn and winter, which must shake from the trees the leaves which the spring and summer had brought forth and nurtured.

At first we pity Goethe, then in a greater degree Lilli, and at last we pity both equally. We see what a strong

A JOURNEY TO SWITZERLAND.

feeling draws them to one another and holds them together. Nevertheless they both feel that they must separate, but cannot find the right words. In serene moments, when everything that is beautiful and lovable in them is manifest, they feel with rapture what they possess in each other; and at such times no thought of separation has any power over them.

In May Goethe makes the first attempt to release himself. He undertakes a journey into Switzerland, with Italy in the background. The two young Counts of Stolberg, brothers of Augusta, model pupils of Klopstock, had appeared in Frankfort and been hospitably entertained by Goethe. Later he became estranged from them, and speaks of them in a tone of irony which is not usual with him. He describes their enthusiastic natures, their thirst for freedom, and how they drank to the death of the tyrant with clinking of glasses of course, without having any particular tyrant in mind; how the old Rath Goethe looks on uneasily, and the mother, even more disturbed, cannot comprehend how they can drink so merrily to the death of any man. The scene which follows has been often related: how the Frau Rath goes into the cellar where the big wine casks were peacefully resting side by side, draws from the most excellent vintage and returns to the party, and as she fills their glasses says: "This is the best tyrant's blood to shed and make an end of." To this visit she was indebted for the name of "Frau Aja," by which she was henceforth known in the convivial meetings of literary men throughout Germany, and of which she herself was not a little proud.

With these two Stolbergs Goethe set out on his journey; but before they reached Carlsruhe the younger one had given proof of his eccentric nature. He had been in love with an English lady, and the recollection of her caused periodical fits of madness. The Count of Haugwitz, who was also of the party, attempted to quiet the young man at these times; while Goethe was of the opinion that it was better to let him exhaust his fury. In Carlsruhe, we are told in "Dichtung und Wahrheit," they met Klopstock, who exercised his usual moral authority over his adoring pupils in a most becoming manner; while Dr. Hennes, to whom we are indebted for the last published accounts of the Stolbergs, proves that at that time Klopstock had long been in Hamburg. Here we will leave the two counts, who are of no further importance in the study of Goethe's life. They have become famous enough in their way; but as poets, with the exception of the place of honor they occupy in literary history, they are almost forgotten. In my opinion they possessed a language much purer, richer, and more beautiful than others around them whose works are not so entirely forgotten. The translation of "Æschylus" by Stolberg is the best that we have; and Voss would never have been able to construct such noble verses, breathing as they do the very spirit of the Greek tragedians.

Goethe's journey was no flight over the map as to-day. He advanced by comfortable stages from city to city, visited his married sister, and called on many friends. He explained himself fully to his sister Cornelia, who advised him to break his engagement. One aim of this journey was to have a conference with Lavater, the first volume of whose book he had some time since begun to publish, and of which his supplementary work as editor was the best part. Goethe at this time had perfect faith in these things. Augusta Stolberg sends him her silhouette, and he reads her soul in it, as he in his enthusiastic interpretation tells her. In Zürich Goethe staid in the "Schwert," which house is still standing. He who is familiar with the description of this journey cannot sail over the lake or look upon the mountains without being reminded of Goethe, who, thinking of Lilli, composed these verses:

> "Eyes, my eyes, what weighs you down?
> Golden dreams return again!"

We feel how in his loneliness Lilli appears to him more charming than ever; and, while he believes himself free, his longing for her becomes more and more intense. His journey now leads him over the mountains to the lake of Lucerne. In mist and rain he climbs the Rhigi, drives along the shore we many of us know so well, and up toward the St. Gothard with the firm resolution to go down into Italy. But now comes a turn in affairs: his things are packed and ready for the moment of departure, when it occurs to him that it is Lilli's birthday, and a little golden heart she had given him, which he wears round his neck on a bit of ribbon, catches his eye. He kisses it. An unconquerable longing overpowers him. He orders his people to wheel about with the luggage, and goes straight back to Frankfort. He tells us that it was at this time that the poem sprang up in his mind, beginning: —

> "Angedenken der verklungnen Freude
> Das ich immer noch am Halse trage
> Hältst Du länger als das Seelenband uns beide?
> Verlängerst Du der Liebe Tage?

> "Flieh' ich, Lilli, vor dir? Muss noch an deinem Bande
> Durch fremde Lande,
> Durch ferne Thäler und Wälder wallen?
> Ach! Lilli's Herz konnte sobald nicht
> Von meinem Herzen fallen.

> "Wie der Vogel, der den Faden bricht
> Und zum Walde kehrt,
> Er schleppt des Gefängnisses Schmach

> Noch ein Stückchen des Fadens nach;
> Er ist der alte freigeborne Vogel nicht,
> Er hat schon jemand angehört."

Goethe himself gives this time as the date of these verses; competent critics, however, put it later, and believe they were written when Goethe, forever separated from Lilli, thought of her in Thuringia and gave his longing words. I myself am of this opinion, and that Goethe's memory is at fault. So little could even a man like Goethe, who faithfully recorded all his experiences, give an exact account of the past; for there is no reason to suppose that any literary motive tempted him to change the time of the little poem.

Before the end of July Goethe was at home again. Lilli was away visiting some relatives in Offenbach. His feeling for her awoke in all its freshness. His letters at this time tell us how happy he felt to be allowed to return to the all too delightful bondage. A letter to Lavater, written in the middle of August, brings the figure of the beautiful maiden before us. "Yesterday we rode out, Lilli, D'Orville, and I. You should have seen the angel in her riding-dress, on horseback." Lilli was not merely beautiful; she was versatile, she was charming, she was— I pray you do not misunderstand the word—elegant. And so was Goethe. He paid great attention to his appearance, and dressed expensively. He spent more money at this time than he gained by his writings or than his father allowed him; and we see him accepting money as a loan from his good friends Jacobi, Frau Laroche, and others. As he had himself a taste for dress, he knew how to value in others the harmonious effect produced by fine personal appearance, and Lilli, who moved in society with the ease and grace of a high-born lady, certainly lost nothing in his eyes through this attraction. And yet at the end of the letter, in the most unexpected way, he asks Lavater if he will be so kind as to point out to him the things he wishes him to see in Italy. We find the thought of this journey still lingering in a corner of his soul.

Things did not long continue as they were. The inevitable change came. A series of misunderstandings arose, for which Goethe and Lilli were not alone to blame. There were members of the family who for various reasons did not approve of the marriage. Goethe does not tell us all in "Dichtung und Wahrheit," but in the conversation with Sulpice Boisserée, forty years later, he is more explicit. We know to-day that Lilli's mother was opposed to it.

Certainly Lilli did not wish to be the deserted one, neither could she resolve to be the first to withdraw. Goethe says that she once actually proposed to him that they should turn their backs upon all these hindrances and obstacles and fly to America, there to live entirely for each other. But of this Goethe could not approve, and it would seem as if the thought with Lilli was only, as Bancroft says, "like a cloud passing over a garden." The manner of their separation at last gives almost a prosaic end to the affair.

In Frankfort the yearly fair was the great event: a crowd of acquaintances poured in from all sides, and in the families fun and feasting reigned. On this occasion Lilli accepted the tender devotions of many young and old family friends and relations to an extent which Goethe found unendurable. He remonstrated earnestly; and they separated, without, it would seem, shedding too many tears over it.

After this rupture, Goethe felt more than ever that Frankfort was not the place for him. The city was, as the Bible says, swept and garnished for him: he must and would get away. The wish nearest to his heart was to see Italy; but, as if directed by Fate, circumstances intervened which led him in a wholly different direction.

Shortly after Klopstock's departure the two Weimar princes, — Carl August the elder, with his tutor Count Gorz, and Constantine the younger, — with Knebel, formerly a Prussian officer, appeared at Goethe's house. They remained only a few days, but between them and Goethe there arose an immediate understanding and attachment. Knebel especially — a man of thirty years of age, whom Goethe when he first entered his room in the twilight took to be Jacobi — became Goethe's friend. His enthusiastic, pliant nature was as great an advantage to him in his youth as it was a disadvantage in his old age. When the princes went to Mentz he remained behind with Goethe, with whom he hoped soon to follow the others. In Mentz the intercourse with the princes was renewed, and on the journey into Switzerland Goethe met them again in Carlsruhe. Carl August had in the mean time become the betrothed of the Princess Louise of Hesse Darmstadt. Goethe now came into more intimate relations with the princes and began a correspondence with Knebel, by means of which a constant and lively communication with Weimar was maintained. On Sept. 3, 1775, Carl August assumed the reins of government in the place of his mother, the widowed Duchess Amalia, and repaired to Carlsruhe, where his marriage was solemnized. Upon the journey there and back he saw Goethe again; and when with his young wife, in the middle of October, he spent a day in Frankfort, a visit to Weimar was planned. One of the chamberlains, who was to come after from Carlsruhe, should bring Goethe on with him in the carriage. Day and hour were decided on, and Goethe instantly set about making all the necessary preparations for leaving Frankfort.

But now the whole thing seemed in doubt: the carriage did not come; day after day he waited for it in vain; nor did any letters appear to explain this extraordinary delay. It looked as if they had changed their minds, and considered the easiest way to get rid of the Frankfort lawyer was quietly to give him the slip. Goethe, who had had no experience of the uncertain favor of princes, judged the matter not so badly as his father. The truth was that the old gentleman did not wish his son to go away from Frankfort, and seems to have had a presentiment, since the marriage with Lilli was no longer thought of, that if he once went away he would never come back again. Kestner had before this attempted to engage Goethe in some foreign service. This time it really seemed as if the old gentleman had judged rightly. Goethe promptly decides to go to Italy, and starts October 30. Now he writes to no one, not even to Augusta Stolberg, but confides everything to his diary. The few pages which describe his journey to Heidelberg are more beautiful than any letters could have been. In Heidelberg, however, in the night, he suddenly hears a postilion blow his horn under his window. A courier has been sent after him from Frankfort. Goethe once more turns his back on Italy, and on the 7th of November, 1775, he arrives in Weimar.

On the evening before his departure, as he was strolling for the last time through the dark streets of Frankfort, he came to Lilli's house. The sitting-room was on the ground floor; he looked in and saw through the dropped curtains Lilli go to the piano, saw lights brought to her, and then heard her sing his own song, "Wherefore so resistlessly dost draw me?" Goethe says he had to summon all his self-control to resist the temptation to rush in upon her.

This clinging of his heart to a being whose own heart seems to have come very little into play is somewhat striking. Lilli's strongest trait, if we go to the root of the matter, is found in a certain wilful energy which made her refuse to set Goethe free: nothing deeper than this. She had none of Frederika's tenderness of nature, which made the separation almost a death-blow; none of Lotte's impressionableness of soul: she was fresh, vivacious, and had rather a cool understanding of the world; nevertheless, her promise once given, she was capable of a matter-of-fact, respectable loyalty which looked almost like genuine affection. Exactly this contrast explains the whole relation. Lilli's resistance, her perfectly self-sustained demeanor, piqued and charmed Goethe. Although it seemed as if *he* left her, he had to confess to himself that in reality it was she who had left him. And this must have justified him finally in the step he had taken.

But he did not so soon forget her. That poem to the golden heart, if indeed it was written in Thuringia instead of Switzerland, assures us of this. Another poem which he sent to Lilli from Weimar, at the beginning of the next year, with the newly published "Stella," speaks still more clearly: —

> "In the sweet vale, on snow-crowned height,
> Thy image still is near,
> And pencilled on the clouds in light
> The form my heart holds dear!
> And love in vain would fly from love,
> Where heart is drawn to heart,
> And ties by Nature's cunning wove
> No time or distance part."

He has paid the most beautiful tribute to Lilli's ever-occurring image in his mind in the "Night Song of the Ranger," written in January, —

"In the field I wander still and gloomy."

Now only as memory reproduces her is he conscious what he had in her, and what she might have been to him. Lilli's childlike nature is the excuse in his mind for the easy way in which she gave him up. It is possible that Goethe resolved to remain in Weimar only after the last prospect of a reconciliation with Lilli had disappeared.

In a lovely way Fate took this matter in charge; and, long years after the events had passed away which troubled Goethe's heart so much, we see Lilli appearing to him and giving to their love a kind of consecration.

Three years after her separation from Goethe, Lilli married Baron von Türckheim, an Alsatian; and, when Goethe passed through Strasburg in 1779, he saw her with her first child, and never saw her afterward. When the French revolution broke out the Türckheims fled, and in the year 1794–95 reached Erlangen, where Lilli became intimate with a young Countess Egloffstein, a Weimarian, who, although acquainted with Goethe, had no idea that there was a Lilli, and that Frau von Türckheim was that Lilli. But one day Lilli related the story of her life, and confessed, in a most touching manner, Goethe's influence over her. She said that she owed to him her moral and spiritual existence; that, in fact, she looked upon him as the creator of it; and that throughout their entire intimacy he had considered her alone in the most touching manner, and had managed everything so delicately that she had come out of the affair without blemish on her fair name. With an *abandon* which proved her earnest desire to have Goethe feel her gratitude, though late, Lilli made this confession not for the Countess Egloffstein alone, but to beg her to repeat it all, in her name, to Goethe. This the countess nevertheless omitted to do.

She excused herself on the ground that, being a young, shy woman, she had not the courage to speak to Goethe of such things; and later, when she met him again in his old age, said, as a sort of apology, that her deafness hindered her from having any conversation with him. Many years after she resolved to write to him. The letter is dated 1830, when Goethe was eighty years of age. He was occupied at the very time in writing the close of "Dichtung und Wahrheit," which on Lotte's account he had long hesitated to finish. He replied to her: —

"Only with a few words, my honored friend, can I express my profound gratitude. I pressed your dear letter with emotion to my lips. I do not know how to say more. But at the appropriate hour may some such refreshing words be vouchsafed to you as a blessed reward."

The countess describes Frau von Türckheim as of slight figure, with a gentle, melancholy expression.

Lilli's children, when they visited Weimar, were received by Goethe in the friendliest way. When in 1815 he related to Boisserée, as they travelled from Heidelberg to Carlsruhe, his love affair with Lilli, he hoped at that time to see Frau von Türckheim again in Carlsruhe. But he found her not.

LECTURE XII.

WEIMAR.—ANNA AMALIA.—VON FRITSCH.—WIELAND.

WHEN Goethe left for Weimar he resigned his home forever. The Frankfort lawyer was a thing of the past. Upon his decision, some months later, to enter the Saxon state-service, several letters were written to his father, asking *pro forma* for his consent; but whatever answer he might have received he would never have gone back to his old life. We see it is decided from the beginning that he is to remain in Weimar, although the form is adhered to of speaking of it only as a visit. Goethe subsequently writes his mother a very sensible letter, as if all was settled and clear, in which he explains the advantages of his new situation, and asks her conscientiously what would have been the result if he had chosen to stay in Frankfort. It appears that with the help of the mother Goethe's father was brought to understand the case, and was content to have his son, " since the Duke could not do without him," Councillor of the Legation in Weimar, with a salary of twelve hundred thalers a year.

Goethe was twenty-six years old when he went to Weimar. At this stage in the development of a man a change usually takes place; the desire to learn, to receive, to form attachments, to subordinate oneself, passes over into the necessity to impart, to teach, to command. Goethe possesses now, what he has so long coveted, a position in which he is thrown wholly upon his own resources. The past vanishes like a dream, and his life rests on a new foundation.

When Goethe exchanged Frankfort for Weimar, the difference was much greater to him than to a European now-a-days who seeks a home in America. Distances at the present time are almost illusory, while then the smallest trip was called a journey. Goethe was a South German, or rather a Southwest German; the Rhine was his native stream, and wherever he had wandered all the waters flowed toward the Rhine. His Leipsic episode is hardly to be counted, for not a single thread spun there held. The life of the Rhinelanders is a brisk, stirring, out-of-door life. The land is rich and luxuriant. If a year comes which does not bring an extraordinary harvest, it is counted among the bad years. Rich independent nobles, rich merchants, rich country-people gave the tone to the whole region.

Middle Germany and Thuringia, on the contrary, were poorer: men lived at home and practised economy. They had not cellars full of their own wines: they drank beer. To be frugal was respectable; and government officers living in a quiet, modest way gave the tone to society, and the years were counted good which were not positively bad.

In the last century the ship-bearing waters of the Rhine lands had a wholly different value, as a means of traffic, from that of the present time. Frankfort was the centre of a constant stream of people passing to and fro; while Weimar was a poor little out-of-the-way town, overshadowed by the greatness of her neighbor Erfurt. The Frankfort houses were palaces compared with the little Weimar dwellings. Goethe was accustomed to the bustle

of a great city, to hurrying crowds and lively traffic : in
Weimar he found the streets almost deserted, and the few
passers-by loitering dreamily along. The pitiable impression which the city made at that time in the midst of bare
surroundings, with its walls and ditches and recently-
burned-down old castle, is spoken of more than once. It
was not the Weimar of to-day, charmingly blending town
and country, with its parks and gardens and villas stretching out toward the distant horizon.

But with these externals was associated a far more
important internal difference.

In Frankfort Goethe was the son of one of the first
families. He did not indeed belong to a patrician house ;
but if his father was sometimes made to feel a difference
in rank, in the case of Goethe the son it was wholly
forgotten. Young Goethe was a veritable prince among
the young people, — elegant, foremost in all that was
going on, a lawyer whose opinion had already a certain
weight and an acknowledged literary power. While
restless, and constantly striving for progress and development, he was firmly established in advantageous
circumstances which were thoroughly understood by
him, and with which he was qualified to deal. But in
Weimar he found himself transferred to an uncertain
position, which it depended upon him to define and establish, he was in the midst of haughty nobles, accustomed
to intercourse only with those of their own station, and
from whom the citizens themselves on their side, without
hatred but with decision, held themselves aloof. To the
Bourgeois Club in Weimar no noble was allowed admittance. This peculiar position and tone among the Thuringian nobility was the more sharply maintained, as
their poverty obliged them to depend upon the Court and
Government service for their support.

Goethe — whose intercourse henceforth was to be only among these nobles, who had to tolerate him as a genius and as the confidant of the Duke, although they did not count him as one of themselves — was placed in anything but an easy position. "Among the friends of my youth there was no nobleman," he himself tells us. Now he was placed in the midst of them as friend, counsellor, minister, and educator of a sovereign not yet twenty years old. He was unacquainted with Weimar relations. He had passed through no previous training which would enable him to take the lead in practical affairs; still less did he know how to obey, — and both were henceforth his task. On the other hand, the light-heartedness of youth came to his aid, and prevented him from taking alarm at difficulties of which he had had no experience. An extraordinary self-reliance encouraged him. He was confident that he was able to carry through whatever he undertook; while after all, in a certain sense, he looked down on all these petty doings, and knew he could at any moment break up his tent again and go to Italy, or wherever he chose. He possessed the unlimited confidence of the Duke, and as an old Darmstadter he was especially near to the Duchess, who like himself had been transplanted from South Germany to Thuringia. Goethe was from the beginning established in the closest intercourse with the Duke's household, and soon became indispensable in the family councils. These relations were sealed by the favor of the Duke's mother. This lady was the soul of Weimar life, a most distinguished princess, the niece of Frederick the Great.

For the history of the Duchess-dowager, as well as for all relating to the entrance of Goethe into Weimar, we have an excellent work in the little book by the Baron von Beaulieu-Marconnay, — "Anna Amalia, Carl August, and the Minister von Fritsch,"—which appeared in 1874. Fritsch was the minister upon whom everything in the State had devolved until the Duke became of age, and who had to be kept in office by some means or other when, owing to Goethe's advent, he wished to resign. Fritsch was a stern disciplinarian, who had long been in office; and it did not please him to have to submit to a new, passionate, eighteen-year-old sovereign, and to share his power at the same time with a foreign literary adventurer, who would continually stand between him and his master. The contents of this book of Von Beaulieu's is a detailed account of how they succeeded in keeping Fritsch in office. Beaulieu himself, an old diplomat, knew exactly what to select from the records, and has given us a description so carefully worked out that it may be called a model of simplicity and clearness. A supplement to this book contains a sketch of the youth of the Duchess Anna Amalia, by the Countess Julie Egloffstein.

Amalia's husband, the father of Carl August,—Ernst August Constantin,—was an orphan, educated in Gotha under the guardianship of the House of Gotha. The Countess hints that the intention existed in Gotha to ruin the prince in order to obtain his inheritance. He was sickly, and this was made a pretext for not allowing the Weimar people to come near him. He was not permitted to leave his chamber, was deprived of the necessary exercise, and given a kind of court fool for a companion. However, through this man the prince contrived secretly to put himself in communication with the Weimar Government; and by them all the necessary steps were quietly taken in Vienna to have the majority of the prince declared on his eighteenth birthday. In the same secret way his marriage with the Princess of

Braunschweig was arranged. Not until all these preparations were satisfactorily completed was the matter made public. The prince, freed from his Gotha prison, was declared of age in 1755, and in 1756 was united in marriage to the seventeen-year-old Anna Amalia. The next year Carl August was born, and the year after Ernst August died. Anna Amalia, not twenty years of age, and again to become a mother, was left by the testament of her husband sole guardian of her children and declared regent of the dukedom. This was in 1758. (Let us here remember that the Seven Years' War was going on between 1758 and 1763.) The Duchess was a niece of Frederick the Great. At first there seemed to be no one on whom she could rely, but she was resolved to execute the duties of her office, and was successful.

One cannot sufficiently admire the penetration shown by Anna Amalia in choosing the men she needed, the tact with which she used them, and the successful way in which she steered her little ship in the midst of the contending powers of Dresden, Vienna, and Berlin.

At the same time she had to educate her two sons, the moulding of whose characters was no easy task. The younger, Prince Constantin, does not here come under our notice: he had the weaker nature, and perplexed his teachers rather than offered any real difficulties in his training. Carl August was made of much sterner stuff. There was something intractable in him, a certain savagery sometimes called rudeness by those about him, excited and sustained by a powerful *physique*, though held in check by the noblest qualities of mind and heart. But for Goethe's friendship he would never have stood before the world in such a strong light, nor should we have known so much about the formation of his character. But now we follow his development in connec tion with Goethe's, and both men bear well this close inspection.

We see from Beaulieu's representation how very soon this strong nature felt that it was born to rule, and with what energy the mother often had to oppose the wilfulness of the son. Many conflicts were necessary on both sides before the Duchess, who had been accustomed to hold the reins, and her son, who early wished to seize them, had each found their right position. At last he was of age, which put an end to this ambiguous situation, a good marriage crowned the whole, and the Duchess withdrew into private life. This woman was the first in Weimar to recognize what a fortunate thing it was that the Duke had chosen to attach Goethe personally to himself. She immediately became Goethe's champion, and his remaining in Weimar may be chiefly attributed to her.

The Duchess Amalia had the advantage of uniting to a manly coolness and decision in business matters a wonderful ease and grace in social intercourse. She was good-natured, cherished the best intentions, heartily enjoyed life, and manifested a true benevolence, which when not combined with weakness wins men instantly, and is recognized by infallible signs, since it is impossible to feign this warmth of heart. She was finely educated, and a fit companion for learned men and artists. She drew, wrote some music, loved the theatre, and sought unconstrained and genial society: in fine, she was still young. The Duchess was only thirty-six years old when it seemed as if she was expected to retire from the stage and live in seclusion, like one whose life-task was ended. But she was in full possession of all her powers, and very soon it proved that there was still something left for her to do.

There are many and excellent portraits of the Duchess. She had a lively, expressive face. Her eyes reminded one of Frederick the Great's, whom she much resembled in later years, as we discover from a bust of her taken at that time. Frederick's eyes were once compared to two piercing lights, and the same might be said of Amalia's. How Goethe's eyes kindled and flamed has been often enough described. When two such natures met, they could not fail to appreciate one another. Goethe was the right man for his place at Weimar.

Let us now see what extraordinary advantages Goethe brought with him, on his part, to create in the Duchess this instant decision in his favor. Goethe was a novelty in Weimar. No memory of the discords which had disturbed the Regency of the Duchess were in any way connected with him. Goethe was young; and, if a prince of eighteen was to be influenced by a friend, that friend must also be young. He had a breadth of intellectual horizon, which could not fail to impress Carl August; for not only was Goethe fully imbued with all the new ideas of his time, but saw far beyond them. Withal he was healthy, untroubled, and as fond of life's pleasures as the Duke himself. Could a person have been found better calculated to act as a presence upon Carl August, and to lead him without his being conscious of it?

If the Duchess saw this with her natural tact, she was confirmed in her opinion by one who possessed her confidence, and whom in all literary matters she regarded as authority, — Wieland.

Goethe found Wieland in Weimar. He had long held a distinguished position in Germany as poet and writer, and had been called to Weimar four years earlier, where he was now permanently established. Goethe took him also by storm.

In the history of German literature Wieland may properly claim much space; he has exercised great influence, and if he is to-day little read, he was nevertheless in his day one of the mightiest and most fruitful of writers. Klopstock, Lessing, Herder, and Wieland were the four literary sovereigns in Germany. That Goethe in the beginning had rebelled against him was but natural, and equally so that Wieland should have taken offence at it. The more complete and the more surprising, therefore, was the conquest Goethe made of Wieland when they met in Weimar; and the more the wonder that Wieland should so unreservedly have acknowledged Goethe's superiority.

We know all about Wieland. A great quantity of elaborate letters exist from him and about him, and, more than all, his nature had no dark crannies in it. He was good-natured, vain, sensitive, and needed a considerable amount of barefaced admiration : we know at once what to think of him; one-half of the printed papers lying before us would be enough to tell the whole story. Wieland was editor of the " German Mercury," — the favorite magazine of the people, which was conducted by him with a full consciousness of this fact and in a way to meet their demands. He had the gift to please the public, and, while he appeared to lead the people, secretly and in the cleverest manner to conform to the ruling taste. He lacked independence, but was a very active man, and had so much tact that he seemed adapted to all situations; and, more than this, he knew how to make himself comfortable in all.

This German poet also was the son of a clergyman. Wieland was born in Biberach, in 1733; was considerably older than Goethe, although not really an old man, when they first met. When he was only twelve years of age he had composed presentable verses (as Voltaire had done in his time), and had been early thrust into the world. From the school in Klosterbergen, near Magdeburg, he came when sixteen years old to Erfurt, and from there a year and a half later returned to his home on the Rhine, being already at work on a great didactic poem called "Die Natur der Dinge." At this time occurred his love affair with Sophie Gutermann (later Frau von Laroche). He next went to Tübingen to study law, but devoted himself exclusively to literature, and before his twentieth year published his first work, in which he had made Klopstock his model. Wieland was always an imitator, and had no conception of anything else. He next goes to Bodmer in Zürich, and makes himself the prophet of his "Noachide," the genuine offspring of Klopstock's "Messiah," which in turn gave him the inspiration necessary for an epic, glorifying Frederick the Great, called "Cyrus." On this and other things he worked while tutor in Zürich. Scherer has attempted to disentangle his relations there with almost a dozen women who figure under allegorical names in his poems. In Bern, where he was again tutor, he composed a tragedy in 1760, and accepted a permanent position in his native town of Biberach as director of the chancery. Two years later Sophie, who in the mean time had married Herr von Laroche, appeared in his neighborhood, and together with her husband received in the friendliest way her old lover, who was now entering a new phase of life. He catches the fashionable tone, surrenders himself to the influence of French and English literature, and on this new basis displays an uncommon activity. His most meritorious work is the translation of Shakspeare, which had come out long before Goethe's time, between 1762 and 1766. The year that Goethe returned home from Leipsic and prepared himself for Strasburg, Wieland went to Erfurt, as Primarius Professor of Philosophy and Councillor of the Elector of Mentz.

Erfurt, which first became Prussian in 1802, had been from time immemorial one of the chief seats of intellectual life in Germany. The Erfurt University was founded in 1400. Luther studied there as an Augustine monk. In the times of the Reformation and throughout the Thirty Years' War Erfurt had maintained her position as a free city, and up to the middle of the seventeenth century, when she fell under the Elector of Mentz. Ten years before the arrival of Wieland the Erfurt Academy of Science had been founded. The Erfurt library was renowned. Weimar gravitated intellectually toward Erfurt, until in later years Jena took its place.

In Erfurt, Wieland now offered his tribute to Rousseau. Wieland's specialty was the regeneration of princes. The title of the book in which he laid down his theories was the "Golden Mirror; or the Queen of Scheschian." He pictures an ideal State according to his own notions, which he plants in Asia. Asia toward the middle of the last century was the Arcadia of book-makers. Persia was the usual theatre; but if virtue in man was to be described as wholly credible, the scene had to be removed to China. The Chinese were the great, just, placid nation in whose character everything excellent was to be found as a matter of course. What Wieland suggests in this book for the education of princes is called "Chinese wisdom." The book contains an epitome of the leading thoughts which might be of use to a prince who desired to benefit his people. Considering that the young Emperor Joseph, inspired with these very ideas, had just ascended the throne, it had been no useless literary work. The book made a sensation. Heyne writes to Herder: "Have you the 'Golden Mirror'? Does not the Wieland genius develop itself to advantage, and run in the groove we would like to have it? To be sure, most of the thoughts, perhaps all, are *en second;* but the dress in which they are invested, even if they themselves are borrowed, has yet a character of its own it seems to me." Herder, on the other hand, writes to Caroline Flachsland that he is looking forward with great delight to reading Wieland's " Golden Mirror;" but after he has read it he says: " Properly speaking, it is only a college lecture for fine lords on politics and government, though interspersed with beautiful scenes."

If we would know with what a sovereign glance Goethe regarded these things, we must read his criticism of the book in the " Frankfort Anzeiger." He begins with the construction of the whole man, Wieland; points out three stages in his development, and follows him to the working out of this book — at that time his last work — with a calm assurance that excites our admiration. Goethe acknowledges the utility of the book, but does not hesitate to show what models he has had before him; and we are allowed to observe how little practical value he really attaches to such a work. " How much to be honored is the man," says Goethe, with light irony, " who, with Wieland's great knowledge of the world, yet believes so much in influence, and has no worse an opinion of his fellow citizens and the course of things ! "

It was to be expected that such a book would attract the attention of Amalia; the more so, that the political wisdom in it was put into the mouth of a woman. Wieland was invited the next winter to a masked ball at Weimar. The Duchess begs his advice with regard to the principles in which her sons shall be educated, and he imparts them to her in a long, elegantly-composed, sentimental letter. A careful delineation of the character of the prince is given, for whom only one thing is necessary, that "he should be made an enlightened ruler." The further somewhat long-winded correspondence between Wieland and the Duchess cannot be judged according to the standard of to-day, but we see again with what conscientiousness men sought to raise themselves above old prejudices, and to gain what was understood as enlightenment.

Wieland was not comfortable in Erfurt: the professors there did not appreciate him. He needed something that was to be found in Weimar rather than Erfurt. Thither he transferred his residence in 1772, where he started the "German Mercury," and by stories, poems, and other literary productions increased in every way his reputation. His fulsome flatteries, his adulation of the public, his literary bad manners now found full opportunity for display, and gave Goethe and his friends a distaste for him which broke out openly in the satirical pamphlet, "Gods, Heroes, and Wieland!" It is not necessary to follow up these matters, for they amounted to nothing. Frau Laroche, Jacobi, and others again and again smoothed things between them. Wieland put up with a good deal; and Goethe before going to Weimar wrote to him, whereupon Wieland immediately signified that he had experienced a radical change in his feelings towards him. But the grand effect was reserved for their personal meeting. Wieland fell down in admiration, and began to write like Jacobi in "Lavater-Goethean style," which before this he had sneered at in the "Mercury."

Once together in Weimar, Goethe on his part did not fail in admiration. Wieland completed the poem which alone among all his works lives to-day, according to Goethe's prediction, who, after reading it, declared that it would be admired so long as the German language existed, — the romantic epic of "Oberon." In the graceful tone which had its origin among the Italians in the sixteenth century, and whose irony was imitated by the French until it broadened into wanton mockery, Wieland relates the adventures of Huon, who is sent by Charlemagne to Babylon, and commanded to bring back several impossible and unattainable things. In imitation of the Italian rhythm later poets have been more successful, — that is to say, more correct, — but no one, after Wieland, added to it the grace and playfulness of the French. Goethe's enthusiasm is indeed conceivable.

The ecstasy into which Wieland had fallen we find soon spreading throughout Weimar society, as Goethe, author of "Götz" and "Werther," appeared among them, it was said, for a visit. He was hailed as the Adam of a regenerated spiritual world, for which people in Weimar and elsewhere ardently longed. The first winter was before them, in which the youthful Court, with festivities of all kinds, was to make its début; a round of entertainments, very innocent in themselves, but wholly filling the heads of men by day and by night, were to be carried on. In proportion, however, as men came to realize that Goethe's presence among them was more than a visit, angry feelings sprang up among those too old to be amused by such things; who knew full well that sobriety of counsels and a thorough knowledge of affairs were essential to government, and with what effort they had created the existing state of things, laboriously saving by pennies the money now so lavishly flung away. They knew the day must come when their help would be needed again. We have to consider things in this light to comprehend the opposition of Herr von Fritsch, or to appreciate the masterly management of Goethe, who was able, amid these circumstances, to retain this deeply wounded man in the service of the Duke and the country. Herr von Beaulieu leads us step by step through these transactions until we come to know Goethe as a skilful diplomatist, to see the Duke yielding in a dignified, truly princely manner, and to observe with a kind of satisfaction that when nobody knows where to turn, Anna Amalia steps in and finds the right word which finally persuades Fritsch to remain. The letters in which these matters are negotiated are in the highest degree interesting. All four characters stand forth unreservedly, and in the conflict between them each makes clear to the other of what stuff he is made. And when Fritsch at last gains sufficient confidence to consent to remain and work in union with Goethe, he offers the most flattering tribute not only to Goethe himself, but acknowledges to the Duke and his mother at the same time that they have not made a mistake in the choice of their new friend.

This concession in a man who was moved by no outward considerations, and who conscientiously took counsel only with himself, will be of yet further use to us in judging Goethe and the Duke.

In the same May, 1776, in which these things were talked of, Klopstock's famous letter came about the scandalous doings in Weimar, of which monstrous reports had reached him in Hamburg. Goethe was now, in Klopstock's eyes, a man who allured a young and virtuous prince, expected to promote the welfare of his people, into ways of wickedness and vice. We must consider what earnest things were going on in Weimar, in order to understand fully how Goethe came to answer the revered Hamburg uncle in a manner which sounds so disrespectful. For, with all the severity contained in Klopstock's letter, there is yet transparent through it all his real anxiety for the moral well-being of the Duke and

Goethe, two young people of the greatest promise, and with whom it was really quite proper that he should remonstrate. Goethe repels Klopstock's interference coldly, or we may say roughly, but at the same time gives the necessary explanations, if not quite directly. The Stolberg brothers were at the root of all this trouble. The Weimar princes had offered them the place of chamberlain, and the plans were settled, when reports reached Klopstock's ears of debaucheries in Weimar, how they drank brandy out of beer-glasses, and the Duke and Goethe had their mistresses in common, etc.; and he vetoed instantly the whole arrangement and wrote the letter.

Goethe now appeals again to his trusted friend Gustchen. His long letter to her contains a statement of entire days spent in Weimar, with what thoughts he arises in the morning, where he goes, what he does, thinks, and feels: just as he used to write to her about Lilli. This letter gives a glance into Weimar life, and like a sunbeam lights up the whole scene, showing a simple, rural, quiet life, in the midst of much heat, perplexity, and unrest. We must add that one of the Stolbergs declared in the most decided way that, even if he gave up going to Weimar, he believed the wide-spread rumors about Goethe and the Duke were scandals.

But it is not through this letter alone that we learn how things went on at the Court in Weimar. With Goethe's entrance into his new home began the new and all-absorbing friendship which led to communications year by year, and almost day by day, of all he thought and did, which may be considered unique of their kind.

LECTURE XIII.

FRAU VON STEIN.

"DICHTUNG und Wahrheit" closes with Goethe's arrival in Weimar. His autobiography was continued in summarized reports of each year, whose form differs greatly from that adhered to in " Dichtung und Wahrheit." They are rather, as one may say, indexes of men, events, and deeds.

Yet we are not wanting in material for the further description of these years; on the contrary, documents of every kind are constantly coming to light increasing our information about them: but the loss of the old tone in Goethe's own narration remains irreparable, since nothing can compensate for the want of that element which he himself, as distinguished from truth, designates as fiction. The myth of every man's life is formed in his own recollection. Only before the inward-turned look do our experiences round themselves off into distinct groups, each having its own definite outline and coloring. The relation of these groups to one another cannot be stated by strangers; and therefore we can go no further with the confidence we have hitherto felt, since Goethe ceases from this time connectedly to disclose the secrets of his life.

With the acceptance of his new position in Weimar begins the epoch of the Ten Years which closes with the journey to Italy, and of which the distinguishing feature is the unexpected change wrought in Goethe as a literary man.

We have seen how Goethe, from year to year, approached nearer to his ideal, which was to free himself from the duties of common life and to live only for poetry; but now, at the very outset of his life in Weimar, we find a change in his principles and in his habits which fills us with amazement. Goethe breaks off abruptly from his unremitting literary labor. He gives up the old circle of Frankfort, Darmstadt, and Rhenish friends,— the primitive public for which he had written,— stands aloof from them, both as poet and critic, and enters upon his new life by renouncing all poetical and literary work. The glory of belonging to the young poets who were the hope of Germany no longer allures him.

If you look in "Hirzel's Catalogue" for what Goethe published in poetry or prose, between the years 1776 and 1786, you will find the yearly column becoming ever smaller. He is wholly engrossed, during the first ten years, with his official duties, and devotes his best powers to the fulfilment of all the obligations he has taken upon himself. This he does with a steadfastness which we admire the more, in that we perceive how soon he begins to realize the monstrous burden of these tasks and their fruitlessness.

This, in general, is the substance of that epoch concerning the particulars of which we are accurately informed, as to the earlier part, by Schöll and Düntzer; as to the latter, by Burkhardt and Keil, who tell us what Goethe did and did not do from day to day. We have the most intimate knowledge of things, the connection of which certainly no one in his time would have believed could be ascertained after so many years with such hair-splitting exactness; and yet all these records do not make up for the one glimpse into the peculiar relation of events which Goethe in many cases wished to conceal, and which no amount of criticism can now bring to light. Hence it is that, although we have such abundant information, we miss with each fresh addition only the more painfully the cunning hand of the master himself, who no longer fits together the building-stones of his life as he has hitherto done to form a distinct edifice. The farther the man advances in life the more distracted are his days! To Goethe himself the vicissitudes through which he was passing must have seemed ever less coherent, and the goal for which he was striving ever more enigmatical. He felt, indeed, that apart from outward considerations, which compelled him to be silent, only our youthful days transform themselves into fiction, or at least that later days are less adapted to such transformations.

Let us now try, so far as possible, to combine the particulars into a concrete whole. The Ten Years of which I have just spoken are not a critic's arbitrary division. Goethe himself speaks of them as a whole; while he also calls them his Second Literary epoch. These years have so much in common with each other, and stand in such marked contrast to all that preceded as well as followed them, that it seems necessary to speak of them as a special period.

Most distinctly Goethe appears before us, during their continuance, in his connection with Frau von Stein, who so wholly chained him to herself that it almost seemed as if this woman held him as firmly as Calypso held Ulysses. Goethe's love for Frau von Stein has become of the more importance as, since the publication of their correspondence, — that is to say, of the letters which Goethe wrote to her (for hers to him are said to have been burned), — the question what relation they bore to one another has been renewed, and has especially of late been discussed with vehemence, indeed almost with malignity.

Goethe's love affairs prior to his life in Weimar were all marked by one peculiarity, which was that he himself had given to the beloved ones the power to enchant him. It is an Oriental legend that the touch of a maiden's hand causes the trees to bloom. Goethe meets a simple, lovely creature: his heart, by chance in need of a goddess, feels the whole fire of his own nature reflected from the face of this maiden, whose eyes, beautiful though they are, could never possess, apart from Goethe, such luminous power. And each time the same natural process is repeated: after a brief period of blossoming there comes a pause; the blossoms do not expand, but droop gently, then fade, and all is over. Nothing remains but the painful question, How could such a thing befall one? It was the same even with Lilli; and that she was a little wiser than Lotte, Frederika, and others whom I have not named made no material change. But in Frau von Stein Goethe encountered for the first time a nature that possessed its own fire.

Goethe's letters to Frau von Stein, from 1776 to 1826, have been published in three volumes by A. Schöll, to whom we are indebted for the best accounts of this time. From the Stein family papers Düntzer compiled a biography of "Charlotte von Stein, Goethe's Friend," in two volumes. In the strife regarding the nature of her relation to Goethe, Julian Schmidt, Düntzer, Stahr, Keil, and Edmund Höfer have taken part. This contest still goes on. It is not my intention to enter into it, nor to discuss the statements of these contending parties, but simply to express my own opinion.

The letters of Goethe to Charlotte von Stein form one of the most beautiful and touching memorials in all literature. They will be read and commented on so long as the present German language shall be understood. Not only from these letters, but from a remarkable wealth of material of every kind, we are perfectly informed as to Frau von Stein's character, as well as concerning her intercourse and that of her widely spread family with Goethe.

From all these documents, I think it impossible to characterize Frau von Stein's relation to Goethe otherwise than as a devoted friendship of the noblest kind; if it was not, then we must assume an amount of lying, self-deception, obliviousness, and effrontery on the part of Frau von Stein, and an amount of coolness, coarseness, and (we repeat) effrontery on Goethe's part, to which their natural capacities were wholly inadequate. In order to maintain the unnecessary hypothesis that Frau von Stein was Goethe's mistress, we must arbitrarily impute to them qualities of which the rest of their lives furnish no evidence.

We know, indeed, how liable we are to be deceived. One has only to read the reports of recent lawsuits to discover how men reveal themselves when all veils are unsparingly torn away, how incorrect men often are in their judgment of those nearest to them, and indeed how almost impossible it is, through the mass of testimony, to decide positively what truth and what falsehood there are in a character. I will, therefore, in no wise assert that my belief regarding the nature of the connection between Frau von Stein and Goethe admits of proof in a legal sense: I will only speak of my conception of it.

It is through personal experience alone that we are able to estimate human relations. Every year adds to our store of knowledge and judgment with regard to all that human life brings with it. When we hear that a man, having first murdered his wife and children, calmly goes into the tavern, we do not indignantly exclaim: "I will never believe such an insult to humanity until I am absolutely forced to do so;" but we confess to ourselves that such things, alas! have happened often enough, though experience in such matters is mainly confined to police-officers; yet a certain knowledge of the world, obtained as a rule through the newspapers, teaches us that such things do occur.

Opposed, however, to these overt crimes, of which as spectators we very rarely have direct knowledge, there are cases which would be better described as disorders, and concerning which our judgment is formed not from the newspapers, but from our personal experience. For instance, if the relation between a married woman and her admirer is spoken of, everybody has some idea in regard to it, but the judgment is restrained; not everything said is instantly accepted as true, nor is everything denied,— the matter is allowed to rest until one can come in contact with the people who are definitely informed about it; one does not immediately declare it to be adulterous. But even if this were admissible from a legal standpoint, still in the case before us we have to deal with wholly peculiar circumstances, and we know, as a fact, how subtle social distinctions are.

No one, in judging Frau von Stein's relation to Goethe would dream of saying that we must make the frightful choice of deciding whether it was an innocent or a criminal relation. The case is treated more superficially.

And therefore why should we, on the one hand, take the position of champion to clear this woman from a ruinous charge when no one wishes to ruin her, or on the other hand why should we, without ceremony and only on the ground of possibility, assume Frau von Stein to have been guilty of such conduct as no one could bear to have his mother charged with? Are we to attribute the legal axiom *quisque praesumitur bonus* to a chance benevolence of Roman lawyers, who were certainly not benevolent, or did it well up out of genuine human experience? Is there anything in Frau von Stein and Goethe which compels us to suppose an intercourse which would be hideous in view of Goethe's close relation to the husband of his friend and to their children? Do such things, save in the conception of French sensation novelists, happen every day?

Has any one ever encountered in his own experience, or heard from others, of circumstances like the following: A young man enters a family in which he soon assumes toward the wife the position and all the rights of a husband; the husband, universally esteemed as an honorable man, pretends not to know anything of it, or really does not know anything of it; the children become deeply attached to this friend of the mother; a friendship springs up openly under the eyes of a sharp-sighted little town, while such a veil is drawn over its essential feature, and preserved, that no one, even had he been willing, dares say anything ill of the lady in question; and when in after years an estrangement takes the place of the old intimacy, so that once again everybody talks of it, even then not the faintest suspicion is whispered against her! This is now said to have been possible. After almost a hundred years, on the authority of some incomplete published letters, a preposterous relation is said to have existed, which relation is not supposed to need any facts to verify it! It seems to me that this should not be permitted, not so much for Goethe and Frau von Stein's sake, as in the interests of historical methods. I am not here to take up the gauntlet. The people are long since dead, and such matters are no concern of mine.

To us neither Goethe nor Frau von Stein are of so much consequence as the integrity of scientific investigations. We are often obliged, in the study of conspicuous men, to wade through a pool of immorality for the sake of what they achieved, and to hold fast to their writings while trying to forget the rest; but why artificially make a swamp, when a dry, clean path lies before us?

Making such use of our material as its nature allows, what are the facts by which to judge Goethe and Frau von Stein?

We see a woman of somewhat cool temperament, who from her youth has been accustomed to render an exact account to herself of her life. She is married and the mother of many children. She lives in no way separated from her husband, whom she indeed has never passionately loved, but who treats her well, and with whom she has lived, and still lives, in entire harmony. With this woman Goethe becomes acquainted. An enthusiastic admiration for her seizes him, which extends to her whole family, not excluding her husband. From this moment Goethe makes the interests of this family in every respect his own. One of these children he educates, takes him into his own house for a time, remains through life his highly revered friend; and the child develops into a sagacious, energetic, and by no means insignificant man, whose friendship is not changed in any degree, even after Goethe has ceased to see his mother: nothing could be more respectful than the letters in which Fritz von Stein to the very last maintains his intercourse with Goethe. No disagreement ever arose between the husband of Frau von Stein and Goethe. Never has the honorable character of Herr von Stein been doubted. Last of all, it may be mentioned that the old confidence was replaced by a genuine mutual esteem in later days, when Goethe renewed his friendship for Frau von Stein.

Let us now see how this intercourse was judged in Weimar. The severest thing said of Frau von Stein was that, amid such hopeless prospects, she was willing for long years to monopolize the thoughts and feelings of a man much younger than herself.

It is known that Schiller, before his friendship with Goethe began, was his passionate opponent. Schiller confesses that he was jealous of Goethe, and that it would have pleased him to discover weaknesses in his mighty rival, — not to make them conspicuous, but as an apology to himself for his own dislike. Schiller came to Weimar when Goethe was in Italy. He mentions, in his account of life in Weimar, that Frau von Stein received the most letters from Goethe at this time; but he says also, quite incidentally as one repeats such gossip, that no one was able to cast the slightest reproach upon this lady in relation to Goethe. And yet at that time every sort of gossip was rife in Weimar!

This, however, is not my final reason for holding the opinion I do of this relation: there are yet stronger proofs.

We can trace through the whole of Goethe's life the impulse to confess. He entered into no relation that is not somewhere symbolized in his writings. If the intercourse between Goethe and Frau von Stein had ever been clandestine, we should certainly find a confession of it somewhere in his works. Considering Goethe's intimate relations with the son and husband of Frau von Stein, what monstrous conflicts must have gone on in the solitude of his own soul, if he were her secret lover and she in later years his publicly forsaken mistress! But nowhere in his writings do we find an attempt to portray anything of the sort, or even symbolically to lead us to infer it.

And now, finally, let us put Frau von Stein upon trial. This lady had literary gifts. When her friendship with Goethe was rudely severed, she was filled with an indescribably bitter feeling. What could she lay hold of by which to recover herself, and how could she give vent to her feelings? She had been taught by Goethe to transform real experiences into poetry. She composes a drama, in which in hateful colors she paints the change that in her opinion has taken place in Goethe, and which she regards as the cause of his estrangement. She never withholds this work, but shows it to many people. We have a letter of Schiller's about it, in which he highly commends it.

But what subject did she choose? Dido! She represents herself as Dido; if not, indeed, as *the* Dido forsaken by Æneas, still as the woman whose name we can never hear without instantly thinking of Æneas, and how and why she was by him forsaken. Would any one believe such indelicacy possible? A deserted mistress, who, instead of at least being silent, parades herself before her family and friends as Dido, — and such friends as the Duchess Louisa, Schiller's wife, and other women of like character! They read the drama, accept it, and retain for the author of it, in their intercourse and in their hearts, their early love, reverence, and esteem.

Life brings with it many surprises; but if we are to believe things of this sort, except on the most convincing proof, I know not why the like may not be imputed to our own wives, mothers, and daughters.

This is all I have to say on this great controversy. Let me proceed to depict the friendship as if such things had never been said.

Goethe's letters to Frau von Stein consist of a series of

almost innumerable billets. I know no other correspondence which mirrors so instantaneously the slightest modulations of a heart. Poems are interspersed. If he or she leaves Weimar, the notes become letters or diaries. Like a deep unbroken melody, ten years of Goethe's life flow on in the same strain. So constantly is he by day and by night hovering about this woman, that it seems as if he neither thought nor did anything which was not contained in these letters. We overlook the fact that weeks often intervene between the letters, the whole having the appearance of poetic continuity. Whatever he experiences assumes the form of a communication to Frau von Stein.

In the beginning there reigns in his heart, and perhaps in hers also, an indistinct feeling that they might possibly be united. This was in the first years, when he was supremely happy. A vague expectation lifts him above the deprivations of the moment. But by degrees the impossibility dawns upon him. It then requires some years for Goethe to bring the suspicion that he must resign her forever to a certainty; and only when these struggles are over, and the matter firmly decided between them, does their intimacy assume a natural form, which from its very simplicity is no longer comprehensible to those who do not know how to interpret such things. And here I can fall back on my own experience. I have watched such attachments run on amid severe trials for long years, and seen them dissolve at last without leaving any trace of unpleasant remembrance.

I sought to describe the young maidens whom Goethe loved. It was no difficult task: they stand like perfect pictures before our eyes. Goethe has, with the touch of an artist, given us such accurate impressions that we may distinguish in his portraits the *coup-de-brosse* of each. We see in Frederika and the parsonage a hasty sketch in water-colors; Lotte is like a soft pastel picture; while Lilli is like a work of Watteau's, bold and spirited. These figures look steadily at us, as it were, from their golden rococo frames; but Frau von Stein stands in strong contrast to all of them. No picture of her do we find on which fancy dwells. Intellect is chiefly conspicuous here. While in Strasburg, and shortly before any thought of Weimar had occurred to Goethe, some one gave him for Lavater's work a silhouette of Frau von Stein. This mere outline made a great impression upon him, and, without knowing anything more of her than the one who brought the silhouette could tell him, he proceeded to interpret the lines of the face, and brought out a whole list of superior qualities, all tending to prove rare mental development. When he finally met her, what did he find? A mother, among her children; a beautiful woman, but with none of the bloom of maidenhood; no timid, wistful being, whose experience is all before her, but a woman acquainted with life.

Goethe was enchanted with the vivacity with which she seized things and held them fast; with her natural self-possession and distinguished appearance. From the first days in Weimar, Frau von Stein became his intimate friend. Goethe came laden with what seemed to him an intolerable burden of recollections. He met a mild, resigned, judicious woman, to whom he felt that his whole life was known. He becomes calm and quiet in her presence: her voice soothes the agitation of his heart. He attaches himself to her, and she permits it, as the most natural thing in the world. And he tells her immediately what she is to him, and finds an expression for this in a poem which contains the following line: —

"Oh, thou wast in times outlived my sister or my wife."

These verses are among the first which he wrote to her. He assumes that already, in ages past, he had enjoyed a life with her. Then they were not separated as now: their life to-day is only a memory of those days.

> "Thou didst know each motive of my being,
> Feel each subtle nerve ring out reply;
> Glance of thine could read without the seeing
> Deeps almost unknown to human eye.
>
> "By thy quiet touch the flood was breasted
> Of the wild blood rushing through my veins;
> In thine angel arms my soul was rested
> Safe from storm and flood and winter's rains.
>
> "Magic-like above the waves of sadness
> Thou didst hold him with thy laughter sweet:
> Can aught blessed equal the fond gladness
> When he flung him grateful at thy feet?
>
> "Felt his heart upon thy bosom swelling,
> Felt the heaven's light shining from thy face,
> Every restless sense within him quelling,
> Taming the hot desires in their race!
>
> "And of all this only one remembrance
> Floats and hovers round the uncertain heart—"[1]

. . . .

At first he alone seems to grieve for the loss of what was perhaps his in times past; but now he discovers that Frau von Stein has never been happy. Her existence hitherto has been aimless, insipid, accidental. She had been married young, in a kind of business-like fashion. She is passionate without ever having come in contact with passion. She is in need of consolation quite as much as Goethe, and she also feels what might have been. Not alone is her presence indispensable to him,

[1] Translated by A. F. (Boston).

but his to her. Yet so firmly is her position established among her children and at the side of her husband, that neither she nor Goethe could ever think of setting these circumstances at defiance.

Still, ideas forbidden will necessarily intrude upon both. An uncertainty takes possession of them which is at times almost unbearable. At last relief comes in a free mutual outpouring of their hearts. The moment is almost discernible when Goethe compels himself to see in Frau von Stein forever only a sister. Now he becomes more quiet, and the intercourse begins which indeed, as was to be foreseen, could only continue in this form for a limited time; but these years were enchanting to both of them, and we live them over again with them. The little incidents in the course of this episode form a series of most captivating pictures which nestle in our imagination. Not merely do we hear of what concerns their inward life, but owing to Goethe's passion for describing what he saw and experienced we are taken at once into the midst of their mutual affairs, and comprehend men and things as if we had witnessed all with them. We know Goethe's little garden-house in the park as well as our own home, as if we had ourselves spent a part of our youth there, and had seen it by day and by night, in sunshine and moonlight, and knew from our own experience how rain and wind, heat and cold, alternated there; how the grapevines, for which Goethe had the grafts sent from his own home, entwined their tendrils about the windows, and the tender shoots of the young trees he had planted in the garden gradually developed into great boughs. We see Goethe going in and out, sleeping at night enveloped in his cloak in the open air, and waking at intervals to watch the stars above him. Even to-day the small house in the garden stands an instant reminder of those first Weimar days. That house, too, is still unchanged (if I was rightly informed by those who showed it me) in which Frau von Stein herself dwelt. The great orange-trees still stand in tubs during the summer-time under the windows, although somewhat faded and hoary. Only the Ilm, which flows through the park close by, has the youthful freshness of those days. This rivulet, which Goethe has immortalized, winds among the now tall trees which he helped the Duke to plant a hundred years ago. All these mighty avenues of trees were at that time young stock, for which he and the Duke chose the places, and all these walks were laid out by their hands.

But Goethe has not only made the city and the park a memorial, but all Thuringia is forever glorified through his letters to Frau von Stein. As Frederika stands in the midst of Alsace, and Lotte of the Wetterau, so Frau von Stein stands before our eyes in the midst of Thuringia. All the beautiful points in this region are idealized in our minds through Goethe's description of them to Frau von Stein. From what spot do we not find notes and letters addressed to her! — and it is always exactly stated where he is. In these letters the Thuringian forest and the whole country — which in its modest beauty, together with Hesse, is the finest type of a true German landscape — lie before our view. In the luxuriance of summer, in autumn, in winter, and in the freshness of spring Goethe describes his new home. With confidence we expect to hear of the watching and waiting for the hour when Nature awakes from her wintry sleep, and each spring this is followed up as if it had never been spring before. On foot and alone, rambling through the woods on horseback or in a carriage with the Duke, at the chase, upon journeys of inspection, or on visits to the little courts and country seats, — from all and everywhere Goethe, in the midst of the wealth surrounding him, turns his glance toward his beloved friend. She constantly draws him back to Weimar. The days seem lost to him in which he is away from her. She and her family are his first care. As he thought of Lotte in the "Deutsches Haus" in the circle of her dear ones, so he cannot think of Frau von Stein except as mother and housewife. Sometimes he addresses her in his letters by the honorable title of "Hausfrau." We grow familiar with all these relations. We sympathize with the vicissitudes of these people, and all their little incidents become events. It is impossible here even to indicate all these things, or to speak of Belvedere, Wilhelmsthal, the Wartburg, Kochberg, the country-seat of Frau von Stein, and other valleys, mountains, and castles.

And not these alone; the intercourse with Frau von Stein shows us what Goethe worked upon,—what he read, wrote, drew, and read aloud. He dictates to Frau von Stein; he carries her all his poems, piece by piece, as they arise. Together they make themselves acquainted with all the new literary productions. Day by day, he stores up, like a beaver, an infinite amount of intellectual matter for her. Life offered at that time nothing else. Men were not persecuted with daily papers, and even events happening quite in the neighborhood were only drop by drop and slowly circulated. We may take Goethe's letters to Frau von Stein as proof of how gently the clouds moved in the political heavens at that time. An atmosphere of indescribable and beneficent peace pervades this book. We see how the stormless character of these years is calculated to foster and mature an intellectual culture which in the gale of to-day has long since become impossible.

Sparingly and slowly the new appears and is harmoniously blended with what has been already gained.

Noiselessly one day follows another. In quiet contemplation of past times and provision for the future, life, step by step, is measured with a conscientiousness which is not allowed to-day.

On the 9th of April, 1781, Goethe writes to Lavater: "The coming weeks of spring are ever to me blissful; every morning I am greeted by a new bud or flower. The still, pure, ever-recurring, sorrowless growth of plants often consoles me for the miseries of men and their moral and physical evils." One would believe himself listening to a philosophic gardener who all his life had found his sole companions among his flowers.

To how few is granted to-day this restful intercourse with Nature, unless they are people upon whom life imposes no other tasks! Goethe was capable at every turn of giving his whole nature to whatever moved him.

And now, in conclusion: in this atmosphere and with the sympathy of Frau von Stein we see the poems grow slowly which are the gain of these Ten Years, and which are the grandest poetical works German literature possesses. Of these the most distinguished are "Iphigenia," "Tasso," "Egmont," and "Wilhelm Meister."

I will speak of them when I lecture on Italy, where Goethe gave to them a definite form.

LECTURE XIV.

CARL AUGUST AND GOETHE IN THE TEN YEARS.

GOETHE and Carl August's friendship was indissolubly cemented by the fact that Goethe was essential to the Duke.

Between the two men there was difference in years, in social position, and in gifts of mind. Both were aware that Goethe was the stronger and the leading power. The Duke never attempted to alter this relation. All Goethe's letters to the Duke, even while he adhered most strictly to the forms prescribed by court etiquette, are written as if looking down from a superior position; and all the letters of the Duke, though he sometimes tries to have the reverse appear, are written from below to one above him. On the other hand, from the first meeting it was clearly understood that the Duke had a right as prince to claim a certain homage; and Goethe never failed to render this. The *esprit de suite*, which Richelieu missed in the great Corneille, has often been misinterpreted in Goethe. The address with which he stepped into the second rank beside his "most gracious sovereign" has been thought to signify that he really yielded in abject submission to the spell of princely grandeur. But Goethe and the Duke knew full well it was only a form, and also why this form must be observed. Both felt that they gave to one another what nobody else could give to either of them, — the Duke, that he would never have a truer, more unprejudiced counsellor; and Goethe, that under no other circumstances could he find such satisfactory use for his noblest powers. *We Germans* are all born "Marquis Posas." The German is never satisfied until he has found the place in which, while preserving his independence of mind, he can serve those whom he recognizes as having legitimate claims on his service. Something is always wanting to us until we have secured this. Even Frederick the Great could not live without it, but represented himself as the first servant of his people, and endured from Voltaire the severest reproofs, simply because Voltaire was the only man whose mental power he acknowledged as greater than his own, and with whom it was indispensable to him to be in connection. With Goethe and the Duke the subordination was mutual, and herein lay the indissolubleness of their friendship.

In this sense Goethe's relation to the Duke was one of the purest and most profitable. Never did an ignoble suspicion force itself between them. Never was a serious attempt made to break up their intercourse. Even on the occasion late in life of the famous quarrel about the dog on the stage (where, however, the question was not merely about the dog), when Goethe resigned his office and went to Jena, the correspondence between them was not given up, and the appearance steadily maintained that nothing had happened; whereupon, of course, the breach was soon repaired. Until their latest breath the friendship of these men continued, and I know not where one could have placed Goethe's coffin but by the side of the Duke's.

We have before us " The Correspondence of the Grand Duke Carl August of Sachsen-Weimar-Eisenach with Goethe, from the year 1775 to 1828," in two volumes. We must not expect to find here a regular correspondence; there are only the occasional notes and letters of many years, which from their quantity assume something like an appearance of connection. It is said, however, that there are many gaps. Since Goethe and the Duke were most of the time together, of course the matters of chief importance were not discussed by letter. About Goethe in his official capacity Schöll has written excellently well. An infinite amount of documents is before us! In order to appreciate the extent of his influence a thorough revision of these papers would be necessary, which nobody to-day feels called upon to make, even if capable of so doing. In general, it may be stated that from 1776 to 1828 nothing of importance happened in Weimar without Goethe's previous knowledge or co-operation. In detail, so far as we have followed his part in these affairs, it must be admitted that Goethe never treated any business matter as a secondary consideration: he entered into even insignificant concerns with the most minute care, devoted to them unwearying attention, and labored for the welfare of the country in all directions. There is no case on record in which, after Goethe's advice had been followed, things turned out badly.

Under the circumstances danger was to be apprehended from two causes: first, because this kind of work was not specially suited to Goethe's nature and capacities, and sooner or later, therefore, it must become unendurable to him; and second, in practical questions of government and finance, and in matters which concerned the welfare of the country, the Duke frequently refused to follow Goethe's better judgment. As soon as Goethe perceived that his labor was fruitless, the feeling that his position was unendurable must have gained the upper hand; and this was the course things took, but in a way neither to destroy the work of the Ten Years, nor to make the relation established on the new basis appear anywise inferior to the former one.

In these Ten Years Goethe had guided his friend in such a manner that the lives of both took the direction most natural to them. He gives ample scope to the youthful inclinations of Carl August, but never loses him out of his sight, and is constantly at his side as his good genius. While he with youthful heart shares in the exuberant spirits of the Duke, he does not forget for a moment what he owes to himself and to him. We have from year to year assertions in letters and diaries which manifest the almost pedantic manner in which Goethe strove to fulfil his duty. The most trying points, indeed, he dared not confide even to his diary. We see how the hardness, or rather obduracy, of the Duke and his dislike to restraint of any kind sometimes brought Goethe to the verge of despair. Moreover, he became tired of forever mediating between Carl August and the Duchess, who (to use an exhaustive phrase) did not understand each other; so that Goethe was made the confidant on both sides.

Of these things Goethe might not, *could* not, speak to any one: only once in a while he gives vent to his feelings to Frau von Stein and a few other trusted friends. When we compare the passages in his letters in reference to these things, we find from year to year the same sighs and ejaculations, alternating with expressions of inward satisfaction, as an indication that he had settled this or that matter with the Duke. But from the beginning we see shining through all the clouds the sincere attachment which always characterized their friendship. Goethe understood clearly his relation to the Duke. He reviews and superintends the condition of things in the most careful way, like a merchant who always has the state of his property in clear figures in his books. Once, when he felt that the friendship needed a thorough freshening up, he tempted the Duke to go on a journey into Switzerland. This was in the winter of 1779 and 1780, and attended with most beneficial results. Goethe wished for a space to be alone with Carl August, separated from the Court, surrounded by the grandest and most elevated phenomena of Nature, in the enjoyment of which high and low meet as equals. In presence of simple realities the peculiarities of the Duke came out clearly. A consciousness of superfluous strength tempts him constantly to do too much; so that when after having with fatigue and difficulty gained the top of a mountain, without aim or necessity and at the risk of greater danger, he still desires a farther adventure. Goethe calls it the Duke's fashion " to lard the fat." " This put me so much out of humor several times," he writes, " that I dreamt last night I had a quarrel with him and left him, and that I cheated the people he sent after me in all sorts of ways. But when I see how to each the thorn in the flesh is given which he has to bear, it all passes away again. He has truly good powers of observation, sympathy, and curiosity, and often puts me to the blush by his perseverance and eagerness to see and learn something where I myself am often absent-minded or indifferent."

Let us add to this judgment what Goethe much later said to Eckermann, after he, the older man, had lost his friend by death : " He was interested in everything that was in any way important, in whatever department it might be; he was always progressive and sought to introduce into his own country every new and good invention or institution of the time. If anything proved unsuccessful, nothing more was said of it. I often considered how I would excuse this or that failure to him; but he ignored every miscarriage in the gayest way, and went on freshly to something new. This was the peculiar greatness in his nature,—indeed born in him; not the result of education."

Goethe himself possessed the same power of dropping defects out of sight,—in this respect being a genuine scholar of Spinoza,—considering them mere negations and not as anything that ever existed. In this way he treated the faults of the Duke, and clung only to the sterling qualities he found in him. The good effects of the Swiss journey were visible in better order and more consistency, besides other things which he prized equally: soon enough, however, all fell back into the old ruts. Goethe perceives this with pain, but adheres to his duties nevertheless with unshaken fidelity. Among his shorter poems, one contains such a comprehensive and beautiful sketch of the Duke's character that I must give it space here. It describes a night they passed in the chase upon the mountains. They camp out in the open air. Goethe, sitting at the fire, keeps watch at the side of the sleeping Duke, when a kind of vision of his whole situation rises before him. He gives us the picture of himself, the party, and Carl August,—each figure plainly recognizable, and yet the whole wrapt in that weird, fantastic light through which, in his state of half-dreaming, half-waking, he saw men and the world about him that night:—

> "Near the rude hut the fire burns low,
> I watch the men glide to and fro,
> Each having something still to seek:
> They whisper low and would not break
> His sleep, lulled by the distant flow
> Of waterfall. Just here the valley closes,
> And while the royal youth reposes,
> The chasm tempts me near its verge to stray,
> And from the group unseen I steal away."[1]

[1] I have hastily translated the opening scene: the reader may prefer to do the remainder for himself.

Now Goethe first perceives himself in the dream: —

> "Sei mir gegrüsst, der hier in später Nacht
> Gedankenvoll an dieser Schwelle wacht!
> Was sitzest du entfernt von jenen Freuden?
> Du scheinst mir auf was Wichtiges bedacht.
> Was ist's, dass du in Sinnen dich verlierest,
> Und nicht einmal dein kleines Feuer schürest?

> "O frage nicht! Denn ich bin nicht bereit,
> Des Fremden Neugier leicht zu stillen;
> Sogar verbitt' ich deinen guten Willen;
> Hier ist zu schweigen und zu leiden Zeit.
> Ich bin dir nicht im Stande selbst zu sagen,
> Woher ich sei, wer mich hierher gesandt;
> Von fremden Zonen bin ich her verschlagen
> Und durch die Freundschaft festgebannt."

In retrospect he continues to himself: —

> "Wer kennt sich selbst? Wer weiss, was er vermag?
> Hat nie der Muthige Verwegnes unternommen?
> Und was du thust, sagt erst der andre Tag:
> War es zum Schaden oder Frommen?
> Liess nicht Prometheus selbst die reine Himmelsgluth
> Auf frischen Thon vergötternd niederfliessen?
> Und konnt er mehr als irdisch Blut
> Durch die belebten Adern giessen?
> Ich brachte reines Feuer vom Altar,
> Was ich entzündet, ist nicht reine Flamme,
> Der Sturm vermehrt die Gluth und die Gefahr,
> Ich schwanke nicht, indem ich mich verdamme.

> "Und wenn ich unklug Muth und Freiheit sang
> Und Redlichkeit und Freiheit sonder Zwang,
> Stolz auf sich selbst und herzliches Behagen,
> Erwarb ich mir der Menschen schöne Gunst;
> Doch ach, ein Gott versagte mir die Kunst,
> Die arme Kunst, mich künstlich zu betragen.
> Nun sitz ich hier, zugleich gehoben und gedrückt,
> Unschuldig und gestraft, unschuldig und beglückt.'

Now he apostrophizes himself, as if his monologue could be overheard: —

> "Doch rede sacht! denn unter diesem Dach
> Ruht all mein Wohl und all mein Ungemach:
> Ein edles Herz, vom Wege der Natur
> Durch enges Schicksal abgeleitet,
> Das, ahnungsvoll, nun auf der rechten Spur,
> Bald mit sich selbst und bald mit Zauberschatten streitet;
> Und was ihm das Geschick durch die Geburt geschenkt,
> Mit Müh' und Schweiss erst zu erringen denkt.
> Kein liebevolles Wort kann seinen Geist enthüllen
> Und kein Gesang die hohen Wogen stillen."

The headstrong, refractory nature of the Duke: —

> "Wer kann der Raupe, die am Zweige kriecht,
> Von ihrem künft'gen Futter sprechen?
> Und wer der Puppe, die am Boden liegt,
> Die zarte Schale helfen durchzubrechen?
> Es kommt die Zeit, sie drängt sich selber los
> Und eilt auf Fittigen der Rose in den Schoos.

> "Gewiss, ihm geben auch die Jahre
> Die rechte Richtung seiner Kraft.
> Noch ist bei tiefer Neigung für das Wahre
> Ihm Irrthum eine Leidenschaft.
> Der Vorwitz lockt ihn in die Weite,
> Kein Fels ist ihm zu schroff, kein Steg zu schmal,
> Der Unfall lauert an der Seite
> Und stürzt ihn in den Arm der Qual.
> Dann treibt die schmerzlich überspannte Regung
> Gewaltsam ihn bald da, bald dort hinaus,
> Und von unmuthiger Bewegung
> Ruht er unmuthig wieder aus.

> "Und düster wild an heitern Tagen,
> Unbändig, ohne froh zu sein,
> Schläft er, an Leib und Seel verwundet und zerschlagen,
> Auf einem harten Lager ein:
> Indessen ich hier still und athmend kaum

> Die Augen zu den freien Sternen kehre,
> Und halb erwacht und halb im schweren Traum,
> Mich kaum des schweren Traums erwehre.
> Verschwinde Traum!"

Wonderful effect! Suddenly all becomes indeed a dream. He now speaks calmly to the Duke, who awakes, little suspecting what nightly visions Goethe has seen. All is bathed in sunshine. He gives to him cheerful advice, best hopes for the future, and closes with congratulations: —

> —"Nein! streue klug wie reich, mit männlich stäter Hand,
> Den Segen aus auf ein geackert Land;
> Dann lass es ruh'n: die Ernte wird erscheinen
> Und Dich beglücken und die Deinen."

And this was written after Goethe had persevered in Weimar seven years, often enough despairing of the Duke, but ever captivated afresh by the magnanimity of his nature. These verses breathe a love and devotion which Carl August appreciated better than any one, and which, as I said, was the real tie that held Goethe steadily in Weimar and at the side of the Duke.

The times when Goethe had completely identified himself with all the Weimar circumstances, such as we have in mind and of which we involuntarily think when Goethe and Weimar are talked of, are however those of his old age. In the first ten years things were very different. The opposition Fritsch showed to him was not limited to one instance. It was necessary that Goethe should be raised to the position of a noble. In this connection we must call to mind how the matter was looked upon in Germany previous to 1780. Goethe says of the distinction between nobles and commoners: "In Germany, only the nobleman is able to obtain a general, and if I may say personal, education. A commoner may render service to his country, may acquire the necessary amount of intellectual culture; but he will never have any personal influence to speak of, do what he will." This was written in 1782. No reason existed for withholding from Goethe the privileges of nobility, which would make his position in Weimar easier to him, and which could be given him without trouble. About this Goethe said very haughtily that it had not made the least impression on him; for, as a Frankfort patrician's son, he had always considered himself as belonging to the nobility. In 1782 he received his diploma from Vienna. After having been made Privy Councillor in 1779, he was now in 1782 chosen President of the Chamber. We must not here think of Goethe as the modest, shrinking poet who does not quite know his place, but rather as the rigorous official well conscious of his high employment, and who, if it were necessary, could show his rough side as well as the Duke.

Goethe was a strong, broad-shouldered man, to whom heat and cold made little difference, who could ride the day long in the saddle and spend all night in the woods or at a "kneip," without its having any particular effect upon him. At sleighing parties, balls, the chase, or at fires, he was one of those who held out longest. He took the foremost place whenever he thought it was his right. In masked processions he was seen on horseback, in magnificent old German costume; and after he was more than sixty years old he appeared as a Knight Templar at a Fancy Ball, and astonished everybody by his commanding beauty. He rode out bravely to the fray at Valmy, where the balls at the renowned cannonade fell thick about him, watched the symptoms of the "white feather" steal over him, and afterwards described all minutely. Such a *physique* was necessary in order to master the iron will of the Duke, and to hold his place close beside him. Goethe had the inexhaustible vitality necessary for his office.

But now that we have studied Goethe and Weimar, Goethe and Frau von Stein, Goethe and the Duke, what of Goethe in himself alone?

"Wilhelm Meister" has already been mentioned. In this romance Goethe has written out the experiences of his first Weimar life. Apparently it is the history of a rich merchant's son, who, born with the desire for that all-inclusive personal culture which Goethe looked upon as the privilege of the nobles alone, ventures into aristocratic circles, is petted and appreciated by them, so far as he gives them the benefit of his literary and dramatic genius, but is by no means received as their equal. Goethe was one of the most zealous members of the Duke's amateur theatre. He appeared as Alceste in his "Mitschuldigen," as Belcour in the "West Indian," and in many other characters. It is known that on such occasions, for the most part, the rehearsals are considered more interesting than the actual performance. Every one who has once had the experience finds that nothing brings people together so agreeably and in such familiar contact as theatrical rehearsals by amateurs. All is permitted, and the maddest freaks seem natural and warranted by the occasion. These complications furnished the material for his romance. Wilhelm Meister rushes on from one episode to another until he reaches his aim, and is really allowed to enter aristocratic circles. This is Goethe's history; and through a transparent veil we see his own experience turned to account. Hence the diary form of the romance, and the slow stages of its growth. In Frankfort he wrote a short story which formed the beginning; and the fiction grew steadily through almost twenty years, until it became the comprehensive work we now have.

In later confessions about this romance, Goethe gives hints as to what his situation was in the beginning at Weimar. "The Meister," he says to Chancellor Müller, "betrays the horrible loneliness in which I found myself, with my aspirations constantly directed toward the universal." Here we have the point at which Goethe felt himself destitute and estranged even from Frau von Stein and the Duke.

Truly Weimar swarmed with men whose mental activity was not to be denied. Each man was at that time sitting beside the stream of new ideas with his line out, hoping to bring some big fish to land. There was Knebel for instance, who up to his later years seemed like a man destined to strike out an original career; but, if we read what he has printed, we find he is also one of those who without Goethe would have been mere shadows. And thus, accurately weighed, do they all collapse around him, and cease to have any individual significance: therefore, as we take in the whole scene, we come to feel the bitter truth in Goethe's assertion. And yet his good fortune, very soon after his arrival, led to Weimar the only man from whom he could learn, — the only one with whom in these years a helpful, sympathetic friendship of like to like bound him. This was again Herder. Goethe's first effort in Weimar was to make a place there for Herder, who with his wife was moping in Bückeburg; and he did not rest until all hindrances were removed that stood in the way of it.

Herder, after making himself one of the most renowned authors in Germany, had by degrees fallen aside from the march of general progress. His works are the fruit of great theological learning, and addressed to a very limited public. At first, he went on in the same way in Weimar. Goethe was too absorbed in his own new circumstances to seek Herder, and it was only gradually that he was drawn to him. In the measure in which the feeling, whose depth no outsider could estimate, arose in them both of a common need, did they truly comprehend each other. The former difference in age, experience, and knowledge was blotted out. Goethe was more quiet; Herder had become somewhat softened, — the transactions with regard to the Göttingen professorship, from which the call to Weimar saved him, having humbled his pride. A friendship grew up, on Goethe's side assuming the tone of conciliating patronage, which Herder's stormy, unequal temper too often rendered necessary; while Herder, as Schiller in a conversation later with him asserted, came to feel for Goethe an idolatrous veneration. Herder realized that in Goethe's presence he, as it were, returned to life. The result of these years was his grand work, "Ideas of the Philosophy of the History of Mankind," — perhaps the basis of our present conception of history. To be sure, Montesquieu and his successors had struck the key-note, but never was a universal history written of such compass, drawn so directly from the common nature of the nations concerned, and from such an elevated point of view. And in the progress of this work Goethe was the confidant. From all we know of his intercourse with Herder through these years we see that Goethe was more free with him than with any one else, and allowed his roaming thoughts the most untrammelled flight in all directions. Herder's wife, not yet irritated by her jealousy of Herder's supposed rivals in Goethe's affection, made for him at this time a second home, and next to Frau von Stein's. Indeed, it is said that he preferred to read his productions to her. At any rate, Herder's wife and Frau von Stein were the first to hear the poems he wrote in these days. The romance of "Wilhelm Meister" he read to them chapter by chapter, and his plays scene by scene.

But with these people the list is exhausted. Wieland's opinion soon enough ceased to be especially worthy of consideration. In literary matters he was a comfortable authority, which one could yield to or not as they chose; but, on the whole, he had his own person too much in mind to care much about others. Frau von Stein, the Duke, Herder and his wife, and perhaps Knebel, made the extent of Goethe's intercourse. These at the first performance of "Iphigenia" he calls "his public." I would willingly speak here of Corona Schroeter, the play-actress and singer, of whom it is asserted that she stood nearer to Goethe than even Frau von Stein herself, and his lately published diaries make it clear that he divided his time in a considerable measure between the two; yet the records of Corona Schroeter are so fragmentary and contradictory, really amounting to so little, that as yet her position relative to Goethe cannot be clearly defined. I would here emphasize the following remark, that, because we know so much of Goethe's life from letters and other sources, we must not imagine we know all. Goethe formed many connections whose nature is unknown to us. There are names of many maidens for whom he had a special affection; there are many characters in his poems which are plainly drawn from life, and for which the originals are missing. We do not know, in the Frankfort epoch, who Clärchen was in "Egmont," or who Marianne or Mignon or Philina was in "Wilhelm Meister." Goethe says "the first Weimar days were perplexed by multifarious love affairs." About all these we know so little that we cannot even guess at them. It is possible that Corona Schroeter suggested Philina rather than Iphigenia; but who can decide the matter, and what is the use of speculating about it?

It remains for us to speak of the reasons why Goethe at the end of the Ten Years suddenly disappeared from Germany, came to light again in Rome, remained there almost two years, and after his return to Weimar established a new existence for himself under wholly changed conditions.

Goethe had entered Weimar as minister and at the same time educator of an inexperienced young prince, whose character now, however, began to develop more and more from day to day. In the degree in which Goethe attained the aim set before him his own position became the more precarious. As Prime Minister, sooner or later all important cases fell into his hands; while at the same time the increased sagacity and active participation of the Duke deprived him more and more of all independence. Having everything in his hands, he was allowed to decide upon nothing. Here we see the reason why, even within the Ten Years, Goethe begged for some relief from his duties. Wherever the Duke entered he drew back; step by step he yielded the ground, which thus imperceptibly changed masters. There was nothing in this which could cause offence; on the contrary, he had striven to bring about this very result. The Duke should more and more become the actual regent; and that he succeeded by degrees in giving the reins wholly into his hands was a triumph for Goethe. But this change must not be affected in such a way that he should lose ground in Weimar, for Goethe loved it as his second home. The proper means must be found which would enable him to remain without being the costly fifth wheel in the coach. At last, when things were ripe, and the great change could be initiated, it was so happily managed by him that without the slightest injury to his friendship for the Duke all matters were newly adjusted between them. There is not a doubt in my mind that when Goethe departed in the autumn of 1786 for Italy (without letting even Frau von Stein know of his intention), the reason for and the result of this absence, as well as the mode of his return, had all been thoroughly talked over with the Duke. In the schedule made by Goethe of the possible events of his life, of which Goedeke has printed only the headings, we read for the year 1785: "Examination of my circumstances;" "What is wanting;" "Journey to Italy planned;" "Superstition." By "superstition" Goethe refers to the conviction he had that the proposed journey would be a failure if he allowed any one to know of it beforehand; but the Duke was in concert with the whole thing. Before Goethe went to Carlsbad, from whence, after the course of treatment was ended, he started secretly on his birthday for Italy while he was positively expected back in Weimar, the Duke had given him two hundred thalers extra pay, and had made him a present of a considerable addition for the journey. It seems to me that Goethe accepted this with the implied understanding that he was going out of office, and should henceforth have his place on the retired list.

The letters which he addressed to the Duke from Italy may almost be said to have been written for show, so that the archives might prove that his retirement from office had taken place in the prescribed, conventional way. I look upon this act of Goethe as a kind of acknowledgment that the Duke was now of age. They had addressed each other familiarly like boys; but now all this was solemnly buried: henceforth the Duke, even in private intercourse, becomes "my most gracious sovereign," and Goethe his "most humble servant." What earlier had been a relief from empty formalities became, with years, a kind of childish nonsense, while adhering to the established forms allowed them a far greater independence in their intercourse. Goethe proposed to go to Italy for a short time, then to visit his mother in Frankfort, and from there to return as a free man and friend of the Duke, to enter into a self-chosen sphere of business activity which, while giving him an opportunity to exert an influence by word and deed, should at the same time insure to him the necessary leisure for his own pursuits.

If in looking at the Ten Years we keep this idea in mind, that the crisis was not sudden nor unexpected, we see how very naturally the change came about, and how, in the proportion that his active share in state affairs diminished, Goethe's literary work began to reassume the prominent place. Until the beginning of the year 1780 he had, with Spartan self-command, held his Pegasus bound in the stall. He writes to Kestner in this year that " book-making is subordinate to life."

"Yet I allow myself, after the example of the great king who devoted some hours each day to the flute, to practise occasionally the talent which is peculiarly mine. Much lies written in my desk, — almost double what I have printed. I have plans enough, but for their execution and completion lack the necessary leisure and concentration of mind. I have prepared different things for our present amateur theatre, — coined indeed in a conventional manner."

In September of the same year he writes to Frau von Stein : —

" *O thou sweet poetry!* I often exclaim, and commend the happy Marcus Antoninus, who thanks the gods that he never meddled with poetry and eloquence. I deprive these fountains and cascades as much as possible of their water, and reserve it for the mills and purposes of irrigation, but before I am aware of it a bad genius draws the stopper, and all bursts forth and splashes. And when I think I am trotting along on my old Klepper on my round of duty, all at once the hack under me becomes a glorious-winged creature, which, with irresistible impulse, bears me away with him."

And again, on the last day of the same year, 1780, to Frau von Stein: —

"I pity my Tasso: he lies upon the desk and looks at me in such a friendly way! But how to help him? I must bake my wheat into commissary bread."

This he says after having been four years in Weimar; but with the coming of 1780 a total change is gradually perceptible. At first, he seeks to unite duty and pleasure by writing history. In this year he works on a Life of Bernhardt of Weimar, and studies for it in the archives, but leaves it unfinished because he cannot combine the parts into artistic unity. In the October of 1780 he begins earnestly to write the "Tasso;" March, 1781, the first two acts are finished, and in 1782 science and poetry without any excuse decidedly take the precedence. He writes, in the August of 1782, to Frau von Stein: —

"This morning I finished the chapter in 'Wilhelm Meister' of which I dictated to you the beginning. It gave me a happy hour. I believe I am a born writer; for it gives me purer joy than ever when I write something satisfactory to my own ideas."

This sounds quite different already, and less like self-reproof. After this, four years elapsed before he really broke away and left for Italy; but we hear no longer of any voluntary abstinence from poetical labor. In his correspondence we see the old literary things and his scientific pursuits crowding into the foreground. Even though to all appearance his official activity takes an ever wider range, the study of natural history and astrological and microscopic researches engross him at least quite as much; while he makes good progress with "Wilhelm Meister," and prepares the first complete edition of his works. In the year 1785 these literary matters take such a prominent place that very little else is talked of by him. At this time, as we see, the quiet preparation for a great change was in full progress. And when from Rome Goethe finally announces to the Duke, as the latest discovery, that he has found himself an artist again in Italy, this "finding again" as artist, and we may add as scholar, had been already accomplished before he left Weimar; for Goethe had long given to these the chief place, and the officer of state held only second rank.

A very advantageous position eminently suited to his character, and such perhaps as was never again offered to any mortal, was in reserve for Goethe in case of his return to Weimar. And if during his absence envy and jealousy found fault with his plan, his personal influence, when he again appeared at Weimar, worked so powerfully that everything took the happy course which by the Duke and himself had been hoped for and prophesied.

LECTURE XV.

THE GERMAN AND THE ROMAN IPHIGENIA.

WE have seen that for "Götz von Berlichingen" Shakspeare was the standard. In this work, as Goethe said himself, he offered his tribute to Shakspeare. We next find him in "Clavigo" imitating the prosaic form of the "bürgerlich Rührstück," which was very like the common sensational drama of modern times. But now, when Goethe had begun to rely on himself, it would have been quite natural for him to create a form of his own in which to embody his further productions. So it was with Lessing, who, after imitating various styles, gave us, in "Nathan the Wise," a new and original work of art. Moreover, Goethe, in Weimar, now came practically in contact with stage life. It is true, castle and theatre had been burned down; and it was not possible in the first years to have a resident *troupe* of actors in the city: but the court party themselves, as has been already remarked, made good this loss through their own efforts; and Goethe took part in all this earnestly from the outset. He acted himself on the stage, and wrote for it; indeed, it was here that he had first the direct intention of writing anything for the boards. No fairer opportunity could have been afforded him to test practically the convictions he had arrived at theoretically.

If any such expectations had been entertained, however, they were disappointed. Goethe, as poet and writer, had abdicated his throne. He unhesitatingly resigns the elevated stand-point already won, where he had appeared to the Germans, yes, to the European public, as a man who justified the grandest hopes, and from this moment produces only a number of small plays. He begins his "Iphigenia" it is true, — not with the intention of rivalling the ancients, or with any very grand aim before him, but simply to please the narrow circle of the Weimar court with a drama; and, since the subject accidentally admitted of it, to prove to the Duke, who had been educated in a reverence for the French classics, that the same kind of plays could be produced in the German language. "Iphigenia" was a step backwards.

Let us now see out of what elements this poem was developed.

When, in the discussion of "Götz," the genesis of the modern theatre was considered, I had in mind only the spoken, and not the sung, drama. The spoken drama we have seen was cultivated only in Spain, France, and England: Italy remained in the background. Here the opera took the first rank; and its form, in the course of the seventeenth and eighteenth centuries, was brought to such perfection in France and England, as well as in Germany, that the Italian opera soon rivalled the native spoken drama.

The opera differs entirely from the drama in its origin. The drama arose as the product of the common life of the people: the opera flourished only at the courts as a pastime for an exclusive aristocratic circle. The drama sought more and more to represent national characters and events: the opera adhered to the traditionary classic phantoms which in Italy, France, and England — in short, everywhere where operas were performed — displayed to the audience the same feelings, and were best rendered in the Italian language.

The drama kept pace with the entire progress of the century in literature and culture, while the opera remains as it was in the beginning, — a hot-house plant, to which it matters not what the outside climate may be, — an imported, artificially sustained creation.

When in the fifteenth and sixteenth centuries the modern theatre sprang up in Italy, the distinction was at once made between comedy and tragedy, according to the antique models. The comedies based upon Plautus and Terence sought to maintain the conversational tone; while the plays based on an imitation of the Greek tragedies consisted of solemn declamation, alternating with ballet and choruses. Here it was only necessary to transform the monologues into *arias*, and to raise the dialogues to *duettos*, and you had an opera. In this form the opera was steadily maintained. The music changed, composers following one another; each rose to a higher eminence than the last: but the outward form of the opera remained unchanged, because the music always made the same demands on the text; the composer required a readily understood plot, — leaving history and politics in the background, — simple ideal characters, as well as plausible motives founded only on the logic of the heart and the passions. The plot must like some great stream, with an ever-broadening, increasing strength of current, bear the hearer away with it. These *librettos*, which it was not difficult to prepare, early took a permanent literary form. The acts must have very few scenes, the plot be perfectly simple, and the *dramatis personæ* find the proper opportunities to manifest extreme passion. It was not necessary that the verses should be equal in length, nor rhymed, nor especially good. Nevertheless, there have been poets who, in this simple unfinished form, so wholly inferior, have yet contrived to produce something original. Metastasio's opera texts in the last century were so renowned for the beauty and sweetness of their language that they were played on the Italian stage without music, as spoken dramas. This form of the spoken opera text Goethe chose for his "Iphigenia." He calls it the " French form ; " for the French also had distinguished *libretto* poets, among whom Quinault took the first rank. By an accident, as it were, this form seemed to have slipped into Goethe's hands.

After Handel, who had died in 1759, Gluck took the first rank among opera composers. In Vienna and Italy Gluck had had unrivalled success; and later, when he turned to Paris, his " Iphigenia in Aulis " produced there the greatest possible excitement. The text to this was written by Rollet after Racine's tragedy. This opera appeared a year before Goethe went to Weimar.

Gluck, born in 1714, was at that time an elderly man ; he had no children and lived with his young niece, whom he tenderly loved, and lost in April, 1776. It was at that time the custom, in a far greater degree than now, to honor the dead in memorial verses. Gluck wished, as a tribute to this young maiden, to compose a *cantata* and applied to Wieland for the text. Wieland's answer to this request we have, dated July 14, 1776. He says:

" I myself am not able to send anything worthy, and the only person who can do it, beside Klopstock, is Goethe, and to him I went, and showed him your letter: the following day I found him possessed with a great idea that he was working upon. I saw it taking form, and looked forward with the greatest delight to a successful consummation however difficult the task had seemed to me ; for what is impossible to Goethe? I saw that he brooded over it with love : only a little quiet, a few lonely days, and what he had permitted me to see in his soul I felt would be put upon paper. But fate denies this comfort to him and to you. His present situation is full of unrest, his attention more and more drawn to other things; and now that he has accepted a place in the privy council, conferred upon him by the unlimited confidence and special affection of the Duke, I fear that almost all hope is passed of the immediate accomplishment of the work begun for you. He himself, however, has given up neither the intention nor the hope. I know that he from time to time revolves it seriously; but in this state of things, and while he is not master of a single day, what promise can be held out? I had expected to send you the whole or at least part of the piece Goethe has dedicated to the memory of your lovely niece. Goethe hopes this himself, and has put me off with promises from time to time, and as I know this glorious creature, it seems to me it must yet be achieved."

From Goethe's correspondence at the same time we see how much this *cantata* was in his thoughts; but nothing is said of its contents, nor is it even mentioned later. I believe, however, we may assume that this *cantata* in honor of Gluck's niece was the origin of his " Iphigenia." Through a curious calculation this is made plausible. Long years after this time Goethe once dictated to his secretary Riemer, as an inscription upon a fly-leaf on which was found one of his poems, the following: " Schwalbenstein, near Ilmenau, *sereno die, quieta mente,* — I wrote, after having hesitated three years about it, the fourth act of ' Iphigenia ' in one day." From a letter to Frau von Stein we learn that Goethe wrote the fourth act of " Iphigenia " at Schwalbenstein, March 18, 1779. If we now reckon backward three years we come to March, 1776; and the request for the *cantata* came in April, 1776, — one or two months, more or less, matters not here. That Goethe, who had been deeply impressed by Gluck's "Iphigenia in Aulis," should have chosen Iphigenia as the theme for the obsequies of a young girl was a thought as natural as it was beautiful. It is possible indeed that Gluck, who was informed about the matter, finding later that nothing could be obtained from Goethe, composed the music to Guinard de la Touche's "Iphigenia," first performed in 1772, and made into a regular *libretto* by one Mr. Guillard (not Guichard).

Why did Goethe suddenly drop this *cantata* after having carried it on to a certain point, and which he had begun with so much enthusiasm? I suspect not merely for the reasons given by Wieland, but because the material under his hands changed into a poem, the subject of which was Frau von Stein.

Goethe had sought from the beginning a poetic symbol for his relation with Frau von Stein, and, as we see, believed he had found it in the beautiful phrase,—

" Oh, thou wast in times outlived my sister or my wife!"

This was the form the theme took in his soul. He sought to embody it in this sense in the short comedy of the brother and sister,—" Die Geschwister." A brother and sister lived together, and cherished a passion for each other without being aware of it; an accident discovers to the maiden that she is not his sister, and the tragic element resolves itself into the purest happiness. In order fully to appreciate this touching little piece, which is written in prose, it is necessary to see it well acted.

But Goethe's relation to Frau von Stein admitted of still higher possibilities. At the time his imagination seized upon Iphigenia as material for a poem, perhaps he did not immediately perceive how dear this form was to his heart. As soon as he realizes it the work flags ; for now it needs a wholly different handling. In Iphigenia could be represented what peace the sisterly friendship of the beloved Frau had given his heart. Their mutual intercourse could be raised to a height on which it was permissible to say everything. Orestes, tortured by the Furies (I remind you of the curse of Cain which made Goethe so restless), is delivered by the mere presence of Iphigenia: the moment when Orestes recovers himself in the presence of his sister and friend forms, as Goethe himself emphatically said, "the axis of the piece." In this new sense he began the mental work; but it was three years longer before the poem was so far matured that it could be written down for the first time, and the fourth and fifth acts be joined to the first three, which were started much earlier.

The mere relationship of Orestes to Iphigenia offered no climax for the action, because the dividing and opposing elements were wanting, which together with the element of union constitute material for a plot. By degrees only could real experiences supply these to the poet; for gradually, though steadily, the burden increased which his new relations laid upon Goethe. In the character of Thoas he personified them. I will not go so far as to say that Thoas is Carl August, but that part of the Duke's individuality helped to form the character is certain. Let us consider all we know of the character of the Duke, and inquire whether Thoas does not contain every feature, and whether we find any qualities which differ from his? Goethe was bound to this character by the sacred ties of duty and gratitude. The foreboding of a separation arises in him, while at the same time reverence and gratitude hold him back; only ideally shall this parting take place. Goethe intimated once, when the piece was read aloud at court, that the Duke probably had understood what was meant by the farewell with which the tragedy closes, and what Thoas signified. It is impossible to read in the last scene of the last act the thrilling petition for freedom, without detecting in Iphigenia Goethe's soul supplicating for enfranchisement from unendurable conditions.

We often see Goethe work thus. The primary thought of the poem arises in him, then comes a long pause, and then the real construction of it begins; therefore Goethe dates the work of "Iphigenia" not earlier than the beginning of 1779, when he for the first time seriously took it in hand, because he wished to have it performed on a special occasion.

In February, 1779, we find mention of the progress of the poem. On the 14th of February we have a notice in the diary, " Began this morning to dictate 'Iphigenia.'" If we had only this note, we might infer that Goethe really began the piece on this day; but a letter to Frau von Stein the same day tells us what is meant by this "dictating." He writes to her:—

" I have brooded the whole day over 'Iphigenia,' until my head is perfectly confused, although, as the best preparation for the work, I slept last night ten hours. In the midst of all this distraction, and with only one foot in the stirrup of the poet's Hippogriff, it will be very difficult to produce anything that is not clad in shining rags. Good-night, dearest; I have ordered music to soothe my soul and set the spirits free."

We see by this that it was not the first unfolding of the idea of the drama, but the working it out, which he referred to on this day. Goethe, as it were, tried to set at rest the different versions of the drama contending in his mind, by dictating the words aloud to himself, and thus making the living language the judge. He hoped in this way to work the elements of his poem into a more clearly defined form.

We must go still further here and speak of the difficulty which chiefly urged Goethe to make this dictation the means of gaining for his work a form which he then hoped was final. In the Frankfort days Goethe had formed his own language,— a mixture of the South-German dialects which here and there he had heard, and had himself spoken, together with reminiscences of the Folk-songs, and of the German of the sixteenth and seventeenth centuries, as well as some Greek and Shakspearian touches, and, added to all, Lavater's method, which imprinted a distinguishing stamp upon it. The prose in which Goethe composed " Werther " shows his use of this new idiom, and also the conscious, careful, thorough way in which he had wrought it out.

During the first and second years in Weimar this tone is still the prevailing one; and he carries on his correspondence in the accustomed style and way. " Stella " is printed at this time, and he continues to write his short poems in the same manner as hitherto. These poems of immortal beauty, and inspired with a melody of thoughts and words such as has only been attained in a few of the old Greek lyrics, did much to convince Goethe's friends at that time that he was indeed a great poet. They are of the nature of Folk-songs, and seem intended to be sung. He repeated them willingly when asked. We often hear of his reciting to his friends " The King of Thule." He was not reserved, and read or repeated from memory what pleased him at the moment.

But now gradually his literary intercourse with his western friends ceases, and soon the romances and ballads cease as well. The influence of his new home makes itself felt, where the people read more than they talk. Goethe sees that he needs other resources than those hitherto at his command. His new public do not understand him, and his new thoughts require another dress. The defiant tone of his prose in the Frankfort days was in keeping with his youth, when the more talent a man has the more radically he is accustomed to think; but now his altered position demands dignity and stateliness. The thoughts which were in his soul could no longer be dashed off without regard to what people might say of them, but required veiling and silent circumspection. Even in 1776 Goethe was no longer the "splendid boy," as the Stolbergs caressingly spoke of him: such terms were no longer admissible. Goethe begins to adopt the phraseology of the North-German syntax,—a language more written than spoken; and the effort to write no longer as the people speak is manifest, but to teach the people how to speak the language best suited to the expression of feeling and the statement of facts. Only the beginnings of these endeavors are visible, but we realize that they exist. These attempts and vacillations account for the hesitation which prevents Goethe from acknowledging his works as finished, even after having written them over many times. Hence the slow progress of his works. He feels himself a homeless wanderer in literature: he will form his own language, but finds no living germ in his surroundings which might be used for this purpose; and nothing remains for him but to rely entirely on his own resources. The sound of his own words shall tell him whether they render exactly his feeling and thought; and he begins to dictate a kind of desperate measure to save himself from the chaos which forced him in Italy to seize upon wholly new means, and to create, instead of the accidental natural sound, the harmony of conscious art pursued according to principles.

It is worthy of notice how, on resuming the work on "Iphigenia," he called in the aid of music. It seems to be no mere accident which led him to work with its assistance. A week after he first spoke of it we find it mentioned again, in connection with " Iphigenia." On the 22d of February he says in a letter to Frau von Stein: "My soul by the delicious tones is gradually freed from the shackles of deeds and protocols. A quartette in the green room. I am sitting here, calling the distant forms gently to me. One scene must be floated off to-day, therefore I shall hardly come. Good-night."

This resorting to the musical element seems almost to prove that " Iphigenia" was first suggested by the Gluck cantata; but it also shows that dictation was not sufficient to create that rhythm in Goethe's soul which he needed in order to find a new language for fresh thoughts and ideas. In his " Götz " the women spoke a hearty, home-bred dialect: they were Germans, who carried on the intercourse with their own country people in their own language. To Iphigenia, on the contrary, — a royal princess, who thousands of years ago lived in communion with gods and goddesses, — such downright homely speech would have been wholly unbecoming. The mythical surroundings required the purest expression of feeling, quite free from all local coloring. The experiences of actual life here offered Goethe nothing. He must adhere to the models in which the same things had already been accomplished. The mere syntactic harmony of the French language and the euphonism of the Italian suddenly became more attractive to him than anything the German language could offer; and, in order to raise himself wholly above the region of every-day experiences, he sought to create a new poetic language by writing under the inspiration of music.

Willingly would one here believe that the quartette referred to was music from Gluck's "Iphigenia in Tauris," and see in the "distant forms" the figures of the tragedy as they once dwelt in his soul, though they had long since, as it were, taken flight again. In later days Goethe made use of the same expression in the opening of "Faust": "Again ye come, ye hovering forms." It is assumed that Gluck's "Iphigenia in Tauris" influenced Goethe's work; nevertheless, it is well to bear in mind, in this connection, that the opera appeared for the first time in Paris on the 18th of May, 1779, while, as we see, Goethe had already begun to write his tragedy in January, 1779. In 1780 the score of the opera was published; in 1781 it was given for the first time in Vienna, and in 1795 in Berlin.

Goethe was so very much engrossed in this work in February, that during a journey in the service of the Duke, upon which few quiet moments were permitted him, he still managed to write on it. In a letter to Frau von Stein dated March 1, from a little miserable Thuringian town in which he was trying to raise recruits, he says: "I have finished my grabbing up of men; I have eaten my dinner and talked of old times: my drama comes on." Again from Dornburg the next day: "You can say to Knebel that the piece is getting into shape and beginning to have members. To-morrow I am busy with the enlisting; after that I will lock myself up in the old castle, and for some days puzzle out my characters. Now I live with the men of this world; eat, drink, and sometimes joke with them, but nevertheless scarcely perceive them, for my deeper life holds undisturbed its course."

This inward communion with the forms of his imagination Goethe calls "talking with spirits." The 5th of March he writes to Knebel: "I must confess to you that as a vagabond poet I am almost fagged out; and if I had not had several beautiful days in the quiet, lovely Dornburger castle, the egg must have rotted half-hatched."

FIRST PERFORMANCE OF "IPHIGENIA." 295

In this strain he continues: "*Recruits* and *Iphigenia*." From Apolda he writes: "Here the drama will not get on at all. The king of Tauris shall speak as if there were no hungry stocking-weavers in Apolda." On the 4th of March he announces his return to Weimar, without having, as he had confidently hoped, finished the drama; goes again into the mountain and writes on the 18th of March, as has been before mentioned: "Alone upon the Schwalbenstein, the fourth act." The 1st of April we find: "Rehearsals of 'Iphigenia' and management of all belonging thereto." At last on the 6th of April, 1779, the first performance takes place. Goethe played Orestes; Knebel, Thoas; Prince Constantin, Pylades; Corona Schroeter, Iphigenia. At the second performance, the Duke himself took the part of Pylades. A court lady, Fräulein von Göchhausen, reports to Goethe's mother that her son's dress, as well as that of Pylades, was Greek, and says she had never seen him look so handsome. How the whole representation went off, after all, we do not exactly know. To-day we are accustomed to historical costume on the stage: then it was something quite new. In the last century even classic pieces were acted in a kind of picturesque conventional costume of the time, in which wigs, knee-breeches, high-heeled shoes, and long stockings were not to be dispensed with. In 1770, for the first time, an attempt was made to bring national costumes upon the stage.

Goethe was not by any means satisfied with this first form of "Iphigenia;" he called it from the beginning only a sketch, where the question was what colors to put on. The representation was the chief consideration with him. Even for a fresh performance in the following year it was entirely rewritten. Stahr first published the oldest edition of it, and Düntzer printed the three oldest forms of

"Iphigenia" together. Goethe cannot let it alone; he takes the manuscript with him on all his journeys, or when in Weimar it is constantly on the road between his house and Frau von Stein's. Wieland, Herder, Knebel, and Frau von Stein continually give advice with regard to it, and there is no word used in it which is not tested and turned hither and thither. Goethe did not think of printing it, but gives away written copies of it. Knebel on one of his journeys reads "Iphigenia" aloud in many places, and arouses enthusiasm. Kestner has a copy sent him in 1783. Single scenes even find their way *per nefas* into a magazine. The Duke also kept up his interest in it. In August, 1785, Goethe read the piece again aloud to him. "The Duke felt somewhat oddly disturbed about it," he writes to Frau von Stein, perhaps because at that time — although she was not aware of it — the separation which was imminent between Goethe and the Duke had been talked over anew. Iphigenia is Goethe's child of pain. She was the confidant of his most secret feelings. She is unceasingly spoken of in his letters and notes; and all this work of ten years was, after all, only preparatory, and wholly sacrificed to the new "Iphigenia" which arose in Italy.

Another aim of Goethe in this journey had been to gain leisure for the supervision of the already-mentioned edition of his works. Hitherto there had only been an unauthorized collection of them, published by the Berlin bookseller Himburg in four volumes, the proceeds of which had gone into his own pocket. Now Goethe had arranged with Göschen to print the first legitimate edition of his collected works. It was the intention at first to include "Iphigenia" in this edition, in the form it had in 1786 before Goethe's departure. Goethe conferred about this matter with Wieland and Herder; he sat with them, as he writes, in judgment on "Iphigenia," but finally took the manuscript with him to Carlsbad, in order, as he said, to devote a few more days to it; from there, he disappeared as we know into Italy, and the few days were lengthened into many.

In one of the very first letters from Italy the work is spoken of. He describes the passage across the Brenner.[1] Düntzer has called attention to this letter, as having undergone a change; if so, it was to its advantage. Goethe added to the letter, in preparing it for publication, all the longing for Italy which he felt at this time, and in this way gave to it the right tone as an introduction to his Italian experiences; but all concerning "Iphigenia" remained unchanged in it. He was alone in his carriage; and from the great package which contained his writings he took out the manuscript of the drama. "The day is long," he writes, "and reflection undisturbed, while the glorious images of the world about me do not by any means banish poetic thoughts, but rather attract them."

How true is this remark! Herein lies the inspiration of the mountains, that the levelling work of man shrinks into insignificance, while the simple, grand, destroying and creating forces of Nature retain their visible power. One is prepared for grand results, and knows from the outset that there is no contending against them; while in the plain one believes again and again to have so skilfully dammed the rivers that after the late flood no other can ever occur. Goethe's description of the Alps, the moonlight night, when driven by restlessness he went alone in the little carriage over the pass; then the descent into Italy, and the wholly different kind of scenery there, — is painted with all the resources of his descriptive art. Be-

[1] A mountain in the Tyrol.

ing always at work upon "Iphigenia," a reflection of the thoughts in his poem shines upon the path he travels. He seems to have had nothing else in his soul. "Iphigenia" must take the place of the absent friend to whom most of his letters from Italy were written. Formerly, I interpreted the leaving Weimar like the Swiss journey in which he made an attempt to free himself from Lilli, and thought Goethe was governed by a desire to place himself in a different position towards Frau von Stein; but I believe that in this I was mistaken, and that the element of separation came in only later. In his last letter to her, before leaving Carlsbad, were the significant words:—

"In any case I must stay a week longer; but then all will end quietly, and the ripe fruit fall off. Then shall I live with thee in a free world, in happy retirement, and without name or position feel more at home on this earth from which we sprung."

Iphigenia was the representative of the beloved woman, the form in which she accompanied him.

"On the Gardasee, as the strong south wind drove the waves from the shore, where I was as much alone at least as my heroine on the strand at Tauris, I wrote the first lines of the new rendering, which I afterward continued to work on in Verona, Vicenza, Padua, but most industriously in Vienna."

This is said in that letter of the "Italian Journey" in which he gives a general account of the work. From Verona he writes on the 16th of September:—

"I feel tired and overworked, for I have had my pen in hand the whole day. I must copy the entire drama."

A week later from Vicenza, towards the end of September, he writes:—

"I am copying 'Iphigenia,' which takes me many hours; yet it gives me, among this strange people and surrounded by new objects, a certain identity, and is a recollection of home."

Now for Venice! His progress in the work keeps pace with the journey. We know the verse in Goethe's poem to Lida: —

> "Afar from thee,
> The din and hurry of the busiest days
> Seem only a translucent veil,
> Through which I see thy form as in the clouds
> Forever near."

So through all the phases of this new and unaccustomed life the image of Iphigenia was ever before his soul. This continues for a whole month in Venice, until the middle of October, when he proceeds to Rome.

Goethe was now convinced that he was doing the final work on the drama; and yet when he left Venice "Iphigenia," though so many times rewritten and copied, was as unfinished as before, and must still farther accompany him. Why, indeed?

While in Venice Goethe was overwhelmed with the following thought, which as regards this play was a wholly strange one. Sitting in the theatre at San Crisostomo, he begins suddenly to consider how he should perform his "Iphigenia" with this *troupe* and before this public. On the same day he writes: "I have not been able to produce one verse for my 'Iphigenia,'" — yet this very day he had hoped to finish the work.

He leaves Venice without sending the manuscript home. The city had been still too near the boundaries of Germany; he does not wholly cut himself off from Weimar, until, travelling in the direction of Bologna, he enters the heart of Italy. The past grows more indistinct: Iphigenia alone remains true to him, as if she were the only thing he had saved out of the great shipwreck. In a wholly new form, however, she now comes suddenly before his mind. Tauris also is lost in the mist, and another landscape discloses itself. Iphigenia is at Delphi. Seated in the carriage which brings him to Bologna, he is surprised by finding his imagination filled with new thoughts and pictures. Electra is now to be introduced. "There is a recognition in the fifth act," he writes to Frau von Stein, "over which I have wept like a child."

Yet this too passes away from his soul like a dream, but only later to arise again. A fresh experience awaits him in Bologna.

Of a picture which represents Saint Agatha, he writes:

"The artist has given her the health and strength of maidenhood without any coarseness. I have noted the picture well, and as she stands before my imagination shall read to her my 'Iphigenia,' and not permit my heroine to say anything which this saint might not utter."

With this the fate of the piece was decided. Again it was plain that all the recent work upon it had been only preliminary steps. Before the Bologna picture Goethe realized that Frau von Stein was no longer the only inspiration of his poem; that other forms beside hers, with potent influence, had begun to assert their mastery over him. Goethe's thoughts had hitherto been too much at home in Germany: the nearer he came to Rome, the clearer it became to him why he had not been able to finish his work. In the theatre of San Crisostomo the idea dawned upon him, in relation to his drama, that beside that amateur theatre at Weimar, and beside those who played upon its boards, a classic stage of noble kind for which he had written before the Weimar time might yet have claims on his work; and before that picture in Bologna, that the figure of his heroine must be drawn with other lines than those in which the image of his friend was engraven on his soul. The grandest work on the drama had only now become possible. Disengaged from the earth to which it had hitherto clung, it had been transplanted into classic soil that it might be fully unfolded. Nowhere but in Rome could that have happened.

LECTURE XVI.

ROME.

ON the 1st of November, 1786, Goethe writes for the first time from Rome to Frau von Stein (even she had not been permitted to know beforehand the aim of his journey). The letter begins: " I have at last reached the metropolis of the world."

What does Goethe here call "the world," and what does he mean by "the metropolis"?

In these words we are made conscious that Goethe, from our point of view, already belongs to a past world. As Homer was the first great phenomenon of the European world in contradistinction to the Asiatic, within whose boundaries the earliest chapter in the history of mankind was unrolled, so Goethe may be considered as the last great phenomenon of this European world; since, through the coming in of steam and electricity which annihilate distance, all the five parts of the earth are now consolidated into one common basis for the further development of humanity. It no longer suffices for the study of the current politics of the hour to consult the map of Europe, — they must be studied from the globe.

It is only since we have realized that the past is set aside, and things by new paths strive after new aims, that we have been in a position to consider what I may call European history as a fact accomplished, of whose beginning and end we can speak.

We know how America was discovered and colonized; how the German races went over and settled in the North, and the Romanic in the South. They planted themselves firmly on the sea-coasts, and it was only by degrees that their small stray settlements expanded into countries. The contests of the Germans and Romans which stirred all Europe were participated in by their respective colonists in America; but ever broadened their lands, ever deeper penetrated the settlers into the western wilderness, ever greater became the mass of indigenous people, until we see individual countries and peoples arise, forming in less than four hundred years independent nationalities, whose politics were free from European relations, and to whom the European himself now goes over as a stranger.

So there were times, I conclude, when Europe and Africa lay beside Asia as the great unknown continents of the West; times when the earliest colonists of the Nile valley came over from Asia, bringing with them that oldest of old Egyptian art which distinguishes the first thousand years of this people, and which after the reign of Hyksos was lost never again to be attained. After this, in indefinite periods of time, the progenitors of the later Greeks, coming from Asia Minor, pressed forward over the isles to the Greek peninsula; while more to the north by the inland route Celtic, Germanic, and Sclavic races spread over the broad plains of Central Europe.

We know neither when nor how this happened. We know not whether democratic masses, or stray cavaliers roaming in search of adventure, or confederate families of nobles preceded with their followers. We know not if Celts and Germans brought, as ancient feuds from their old manors, the material for the eternal war which has raged in the Rhine valley since historic time. We know not in what order things developed themselves, — whether the ancient pre-historic inhabitants, whose highly valued skulls are so keenly cross-examined to-day, were exterminated or made slaves, or whether a mutual understanding was arrived at, and whether and how mixed races arose. We know not how long a time these Asiatic settlers on European soil needed before they felt themselves to be denizens of a part of the world which was to have its own independent life separate from that of Asia. To create this feeling, it was essential that in the eyes of the Celts, Germans, Sclaves, and Greeks the people and their home should become indivisible factors; that the Germans should not be able to identify themselves without their woods and swamps, and that if transferred to any other zone, even to their original Asiatic home, they would degenerate.

The oldest historical epoch in European history is the Greek. But this was only visibly unrolled upon European soil. The eyes of the Greeks were turned back to Asia, and they felt that as inhabitants of the extreme West they were still a part of their old native land. Xerxes only wished to recover an apostate province; and to Æschylus himself, while he celebrates the victory of the Greeks over the Persians, Asia is still the old mother. Alexander the Great hoped to conquer Persia: what did he care for Europe? This identification of Greece with Asia characterizes so strongly the first European era that it distinguishes at once the difference between the sway of the Greeks and of the Romans.

With Rome European history properly begins, and with Rome it ends. Only from the moment when Rome becomes conspicuous do we comprehend men and things; only from this time are we able to apply the standards which are in use to-day. Everything Greek, even in the periods of most authentic history, wears a somewhat fabulous aspect. Even where the records before us are cut in bronze and stone, the prefatory words should stand, "Once upon a time there was." We willingly believe the things, but cease to apprehend them when the story halts. We seem to hear only tales of vague wanderings and adventures. Alcibiades is the veriest prince in the Fairy Tale compared with Cæsar, who, with so much that is black in him, yet stands before us in such a clear white light. The Greeks were even in practical affairs visionaries, and apparently governed by whims. It is often impossible to draw the line between gods and men. A faint echo of an earlier primitive conception of creation seems to float before us, awakening the same strange feeling we have when looking at the remains of animals and vestiges of palm-trees under which they roved, which have been exhumed from the German mountains and caverns: we hold them in our hands and cannot doubt their genuineness, but lay them aside as something that after all has no connection with our native land. This unfamiliar element in the Greek character we never overcome. It is said that, as the last token of negro descent in those who have become otherwise perfectly white, the moon in the finger-nail of the quadroons of America remains dark; this tiny spot on the body betrays the original African home, where man stood on a somewhat lower plane. In the same way Homer and Plato, Aristotle and Thucydides, or Phidias and Pindar, may seem ever so near akin to us; yet there is always a little moon on the finger-nail reminding us of the ichor, the blood of the gods, of which the one last drop was infused into the veins of the Greeks. But this fabulous element was wholly wanting in the Romans. They bear no trace of mythical descent, and are recognized from the first moment as politicians, jurists, soldiers, magistrates, and merchants. Their virtues and their vices lie open to us without poetical varnish. They needed neither poet nor artist; and no real poet or artist was found, of his own free will, among them. By these Romans for three thousand years the drama of European history was played, whose last act had just reached its closing verses when Goethe entered Rome,—without a suspicion indeed how soon after his time the great spectacle would be ended and the lights extinguished. But just to have heard even these last verses on the spot was enough for Goethe!

The history of Rome is our world-history. Between the already ancient States which had sprung up in Italy in the earliest European-Egyptian epoch some new and energetic people of unknown origin planted themselves, selecting for their home an unapproachable spot. This happened three or four hundred years before the time of Alexander the Great. Over half a thousand years this Rome needed in order to come to its full power. In the unhealthy swamps of the Tiber banks these first settlers sought a home, where nobody disputed their possession, but from the beginning showed themselves impelled by the same stern principles to which they adhered to the last,—bloody power without, bloody order within. What we observe as the characteristic of Roman history (which means the European) is, that the inhabitants of this town absorbed into it everything within their reach; until, in the course of a thousand years after its foundation, all the nations of the world, who could be seen or clutched from this centre, were converted either into participators in its greatness or subjects of its power.

Rome was not at its foundation the principal city of a people, but a place guarded by walls, an abode of homeless men whose origin became speedily effaced upon Roman soil; and it never quite lost this character. So long as

Rome continued to exist, it attracted to itself all the strong foreign element it could make serviceable. From an ever-increasing circumference everything streamed toward it, and every newcomer was drawn within the pale of its political interests. In the degree in which men were needed, it was made easier to the stranger to become a Roman citizen; until we finally see, as the world sovereignty of the Romans becomes a fact, not merely an individual nation on its own territory, but a monstrous mass of civil and military officials, recognizing only the single interest of Rome, and above whom, controlling both elements, was a common jurisdiction uniting them all under the name of Roman citizens. Only in matters appertaining to the public service was the Roman language and religion necessary; beyond this every Roman might think and speak as he chose, and pray to whom he would. Every form of worship was to be found in Rome, — Etruscan, Greek, Egyptian, Jewish, and all with equal license. This is the history of the first thousand years of Rome and Europe.

The annals of the second millennium contain the history of the decline of this power, but at the same time of the rise of a new and again European Roman sovereignty, growing up on the same spot, out of the ruins of the former, indeed almost before this had fallen into ruins, and proceeding on the same principles, while its power was extended over a much wider circumference. Rome, after having through many centuries maintained its high position as the seat of the all-mighty Imperial power, had finally been drained of the last drop of the vital sap with which it had so long steadily renewed its strength. The people who unsubdued, or excluded as useless material, were settled round the borders of the Empire, now began like vultures to hang about the expiring body, which was soon, as they felt, to become their prey. These people were thrilled with a presentiment that sooner or later the boundaries of the Holy Roman Empire would be open to them. They pressed forward more and more impetuously; and ever more frequently must the Romans, instead of conquering, consent to treat with them. But so natural was authority to the Romans, so inborn their qualification to be masters, that, after their self-begotten strength had long been exhausted, they recruited their army upon the ranks of these invaders, and fighting them with their own people created a new power out of their very weakness. With an ever-increasing dexterity the Roman policy organized the hostility of the barbarians toward one another for the protection of Rome. But, during the century in which cunning took the place of power, the army, which almost wholly consisted of Germans, rose to be a political power, with an organization of its own ; and thus by a natural transition the Germans became ever more and more powerful, until in the revolution of centuries a German Empire was established in Rome in place of the old Empire. Here, however, only one factor had been changed, — the German element had assumed a Roman form. Rome remained the capital of the world. The old harshness and bloody, unrelenting severity continued to exist. The ruling principle, to draw all energetic men into Rome and make them Romans, was carried out as before, and with the same result; only instead of a juridical community whose fountain-head was the law as developed in Rome, by degrees another community sprang up, based on the dogmas of the Church as formalized in Rome. It is marvellous with what persistency the old idea repeats itself; so that we see in the saddest times, when Rome was demoralized, nearly destroyed, and void of inhabitants, it yet possessed, through the faith in the mission of the city, such a vitality as to give to its ruins the same attractive power as had belonged to its earlier grandeur. Rome remains the centre of the world, the head of the world, the wonder of the world, the golden Imperial Rome, — *aureæ arces Romæ!* Who enters it is beguiled into resigning freedom and country; and what ancient Rome never achieved, — the entire subjugation of the Germanic lands (England and Scandinavia included), — is now accomplished by the Roman bishops who convert these countries into provinces of the Roman Church. The fallen palaces of the emperors and temples of the gods rise anew as palaces and churches of popes; and over the *débris* of the ruined streets new streets are laid out, and this power commanding in the old place finally succeeds in accomplishing the unheard of. Confronting the newly added German provinces, birthplace of the emperors now reigning in Rome, it consolidates the scattered inhabitants of the old Roman Empire into a veritable nation, — the Romanic, — overthrows the dominion of the new Germanic emperors, delivers the papacy wholly into Roman hands, and thus accomplishes in the fullest sense what had been begun by the old robbers in the swamps of the Tiber. This last revolution is the substance of the third millennium of Roman history; but with this all possibility of the further historical greatness of Rome ended. This millennium was its most brilliant one. Do not let us be deceived by the history of republican Rome, or of imperial antique Rome: modern papal Rome has been far greater.

The Rome of the first and second thousand years produced no art or poetry of its own. The wild agglomerate of people had not changed the soil on which they lived. Greek artists and scholars, even though numbered at that time among the inhabitants of a Roman province, filled Rome with Grecian art; but no specific Roman work of art was ever achieved, nor even a genuine Roman book, with the exception of the *Corpus Juris* and the writings of the Apostolic Fathers. All the Roman authors and poets, from Plautus to Pliny, only repeated Greek sayings in Latin forms. But in the times when the second millennium of the city was passing into the third, — which, regarded from a one-sided political point of view, seemed the time of its deepest decay, — the Italians, Spaniards, and French began so completely to identify themselves with the soil on which they dwelt as to form separate independent nations, — unitedly the Romanic nations, — who, each in its own language revealed individual creative power. But here also was required the slow growth of centuries, although the progress was visible throughout. While the Greek-speaking part of Europe separated from Rome, again attached itself to Asia, and, mentally unproductive, was lying, as it is to-day, a great vegetating mass between Europe and Asia (although signs of something like an awakening more and more appear), Europe developed a creative life, and Dante is to be regarded as the first genius of this Romanic world, — to which he is what Homer was to the Greek world. From Dante's time the intellectual life of Europe gains ever greater reinforcements, and in and about Rome (Rome being always the main point) art and science flourish to a degree which exceeds all ever attained under the old Empire. Italy, Spain, and France rival each other in the production of masterpieces; the defection of Germany, England, and the Netherlands does not lessen its ascendancy; and not until the life of this fresh Romanic spring has passed into its autumn and winter does it begin to change and decline. We of to-day are witnesses to its downfall. Passing over the Romanic world, which to the Germanic races is no longer *the* world, but only one province in the great realm of humanity, we have made America and Asia the immense stage on which to carry out the further destiny of mankind. The Romanians with Rome are left to themselves. Their power is not quite destroyed, but other powers hold the balance. Rome, as a city, exists to-day only because it happens to be there. As in Venice we have long been accustomed to look upon the receptacle of the big government machine there, though whole and freshly varnished, as nothing better than a money-making institution for custodians and hired servants, so we find Rome changed under our eyes into a colossal show-place, to which the people repair from all quarters of the globe. Crowded hotels and empty palaces are the principal features. What never before has been witnessed in the course of human history is taking place there to-day. At the visible close of an epoch of three thousand years, its magnificent impressive edifices are being transformed into mere historical decorations.

Goethe had also foreseen this. All that to the generation contemporary with his declining years was incomprehensible in him grew out of his clearly expressed expectation of revolutions in the latter half of our century, involving changes in comparison with which the political attempts of his own time appeared to him worthless and insignificant. But in 1786, in Rome, he witnessed the last days of the third millennium without a suspicion at that time that this glory must so soon come to an end. Not the slightest tremor among the people announced the approach of the French revolution. The struggle of the American colonists with England was like some Quixotic adventure seen from afar. Europe was as quiet as if it had the repose of centuries yet before it.

Gilded as with the splendors of an eternal sunset, the city lay before Goethe which to Raphael, Michael Angelo, and an endless series of great men had become a second home, and which was to be the same to him.

Rome still ruled without any visible decline of its power. The French, German, and Italian clergy were each in their own countries in full possession of their accumulated estates and revenues, whose *per cent* went on to Rome. Rome was the centre of educated Europe. The refractory Protestants of North Germany, the English and Scandinavians, felt this power just as much as the Romanic nations. From his youth the longing for Italy had lived in Goethe's soul. Three times he had started to go there, and at last the desire grew so intense as to make him wretched: he felt like one recovering from some terrible illness after he had become acquainted with Rome. Goethe's prosaic, pedantic father had had his heart thawed in Italy, and for the only time in his life felt himself inspired. He, therefore, in his time insisted on sending Goethe to Rome, also in the hope of dissuading him from Weimar. Herder's finest historical essays are those in which he portrays the civilizing power of the Roman Church; Lessing was grounded upon antiquity and the Renaissance; and Winckelmann, born and educated far in the Protestant North, submitted to the formulas of the Roman Church in order to get to Rome. Rome and Italy were full of Germans, who sought and found there what no other place could offer them. Well might Goethe write to Frau von Stein: "Yes; I have at last reached the metropolis of the world."

Goethe was surrounded by a wealth of historical reminiscences, which this city unfolded before him as in a dream. The fate of its people passed before his eyes in an endless succession of pictures. Even to-day, Rome awakens such dreams in the minds of all capable of being so stirred. What a sensation, now that the dust and rubbish of a thousand years are cleared away, to feel once more the old well-worn pavement of the Forum under one's feet, over which have passed so many German chiefs, emperors, and slaves, either as conquerors or conquered!

But only dreams could at that time excite Goethe. The past alone stood before his view; the present did not seem to him great enough to create anything worthy to be looked upon as a continuation of these achievements of former times. He did not dream of the revolution so close at hand, nor yet of the conflicts of to-day: at that time the outcast Jesuits flying in every direction found a protector in Frederick the Great. The world of which Rome was the metropolis in Goethe's eyes was a Europe striving toward the development of the highest civilization, whose people, free from envy, lived together in peaceful relations. There was no freer or better place for artists or for literary work conceivable than Rome at that time. The palaces of the cardinals were places of resort for the learned and gifted, no matter whence they came; while the city was filled with a stream of distinguished people coming and going from all quarters of the globe. One should not read only Goethe's letters to gain a true conception of this; Goethe revised his "Italian Journey" in later years, when a freer air had long blown over Germany itself. One should read Winckelmann's letters to Berendis, if the difference is to be appreciated which at that time existed between Rome and Germany,—the capacity to enjoy and let others enjoy, which at that time seemed to exist nowhere but on this one spot of earth; the affluence of life, without one faint note of that artificially created agitation which from Italy to-day vibrates on our ears. One could think and speak aloud what one thought.

Everything was allowed, with perhaps the single exception, according to Cardinal Albani, of erecting a pulpit in the Piazza di Spagna for the preaching of Antichrist. No hail-storm for a hundred years had broken the windows of the enormous dome of this mental hot-house. The third millennium of the city seemed lengthening out to a never-ending period of peaceful sovereignty, — Rome, a world-university for mature men of all nations; a motley crowd in which many languages were spoken, all subordinate to the Italian; where every newcomer was welcomed, and where, untrammelled by names or titles or outward distinctions of any kind, each pursued his own way and was valued only for himself. Goethe was thirty-seven years old. He called Rome his second Academic Franchise.

It was indeed to him like exchanging the narrow confined life of a school-boy for the free breath of a more expanded existence. Goethe had until now only gone from one paltry provincial town to another. He had neither been in Paris, London, nor Vienna. Dresden and Berlin were the largest places he had visited, and these only as a flying traveller. Leipsic, Frankfort, Cologne, and Strasburg were narrow old burgher towns, shut in by walls and ditches; while Berlin only drew from him the comment that "the bigger the world the nastier the farce." Goethe had indeed here and there come in contact with the ruling powers of the world, but he had seen next to nothing of the actual universe of men and things previous to his arrival in Rome. Whatever Goethe had seen earlier he had been able to picture to himself beforehand; but this Roman life came to him as something utterly new and foreign. An unlimited field for mental development opened before him; added to which, things most worthy to be known lay piled in vast masses at his feet and all around him. Instead of single miserable casts from the antique, to get a sight of which he had often been obliged to travel, he was now transported into the midst of the wealth of the yet unpillaged villas and palaces of the Vatican, with Raphael and Michael Angelo in close proximity, as the noblest refreshment after his studies, for his own work continued to be of undisputed importance; added to this a free, agreeable, social intercourse, and no master over him as at home, who might command him at any hour. All this must be taken into account in order to understand the rapture with which life in Rome inspired Goethe. Truly, for the first time in this world he was wholly his own master. He was not filled with the artificial enthusiasm, the empty, affected intoxication, created by an over-excited æsthetic sensibility, which so many travellers of the present day, guide-book in hand, think it to be their duty as educated people to experience; but in him it was the natural delight of a man who, after long repression, feels himself for the first time in his proper element. At last he could abandon himself to his impulse to go into the universal, with all it implied.

To see the simplicity and genuineness of this feeling reflected as in a mirror, we have only to recall Winckelmann, who had a similar experience in Rome. With heavenly satisfaction Winckelmann had, thirty years earlier than Goethe, made himself at home in Rome. His letters express much more forcibly than Goethe's this exhilaration at finding himself in this land of freedom. All Goethe's letters, even the most confidential, have a certain form and stateliness, owing to his consciousness that they would be circulated; and in the working over and preparing them to be printed he was still further affected by consideration for his readers. Winckelmann, as an obscure writer, poured out his whole heart to obscure friends, and his letters have been printed just as they flowed from his pen.

We must bear in mind that Goethe's "Italian Journey" was not published until 1817. He has made a selection from his letters, put together parts of different letters, and given to the whole the harmony of style which distinguishes his later writings. In a letter from Rome before his journey to Naples, where an eruption of Vesuvius was expected, we read now: "May kindly Nature give us a stream of lava! I am full of impatience to have a personal experience of these great things." In the original letter it stood thus: "Only one stream of lava, and I'll ask for nothing more!" The last is certainly more natural, and expresses the same thought. This book has been supposed to be a guide-book in which the traveller might find definite information, and as such has been found fault with for being incomplete and unreliable. But only the thoughtless can so misunderstand it; and as for the correcting and revising of it, this has certainly given to the book the harmonious tone and artistic finish which will preserve it as a living work for hundreds of years. It bears the same relation to the original letters that "Dichtung und Wahrheit" had to his actual experience. All the letters which have not been tampered with, even if they seem to affect us more deeply still, do not disclose to us the higher import of the journey, which in their present rendering constantly breaks forth.

Goethe's later edition of Winckelmann's letters, together with the biographical notes which he places over them in their proper order, — thereby inventing a wholly new plan for a biography, — is his tribute of gratitude for all that Winckelmann was to him in Rome. Winckelmann had been the first to speak in Germany of national Greek art in such a manner as to rouse the public, and in the midst of the paltry affected art of their own age to give them a conception of Greek beauty. Curiously enough, all the enthusiasm for historical art which Winckelmann, Lessing, Herder, and later Goethe himself created grew up without a sight of the actual works, which one would naturally suppose must have come first. The German public caught the inspiration from the words, and supplied the sight of the works from their imagination, as if indeed these could be dispensed with.

At the house of the painter Oeser in Leipsic Goethe first heard of Winckelmann (who was Oeser's intimate friend), and he afterward felt his assassination to be a terrible blow; but only in Rome did he fully comprehend the value of this man's work. It is certain that without Goethe's book upon Winckelmann he would not stand before us in such a strong light, nor should we see so clearly with what pains and with what success he made himself master of ancient art, while at the same time he was in perfect sympathy with his own age.

We must, however, limit ourselves to what is pertinent to our theme. Winckelmann's Life has been written by Justi; and while Goethe, from personal sympathy with all that Winckelmann accomplished, dwells upon him personally, Justi, in filling out this single portrait, has given us a picture of the whole period, thereby furnishing a brilliant background to Goethe's work.

We need not follow Goethe through the complicated maze of his Italian life, but satisfy ourselves with noting the general direction of his progress. Very soon after the first storm of surprise had abated, Goethe, to whom it was natural to go systematically about everything he undertook, found it necessary to make a plan for his proceedings. He would embrace everything, and leave out nothing. But all could not be done at one stroke; and, more than all, he must bring everything into accordance with the time he had at his command, while he was obliged to go on with the task of preparing the collected edition of his works for publication. Added to this was his old desire to cultivate his own hand and eye as an artist; and, lastly, the absolute necessity of being surrounded by a host of intellectual men. We learn from his " Italian Journey " how easy it was for him to gratify all these demands; how he devotes himself to everything, and nevertheless does justice to each in particular. With such interpretation, there is no better guide for a long stay in Italy than this book. It shows us that without a certain amount of solid daily work to convince us that even in the midst of these immense works of art we are still chiefly dependent on our own efforts, that without a certain calmness and steadiness to set against the first rush of impressions, and without the sympathetic co-operation of congenial friends, we cannot expect to win the highest results from such a journey. Goethe likes to apply to himself the simile of the diver, who for a while remains invisible under the water and then emerges again. I will, therefore, once make use of the figure. Goethe dives under in this new element, really learns to swim in it, fights with the waves and billows around him and advances slowly, but is borne onward by his own strong arms; while the traveller of to-day in search of improvement is hurried over the waters by paid rowers, and sitting high and dry imagines he has had a great experience if by chance a wave dashes over the edge of the boat into his face.

Yet one thing I will add. This Rome of Goethe's, even in its outward aspect, no longer exists. I myself may say that I have witnessed the very last glimmer of the evening glow in which Goethe saw Rome. It is twenty years since I entered the Porta del Popolo, after a long drive, every step of which had brought me nearer and nearer to Rome, and saw the priests and monks living and laboring still with full authority who to-day, as poor *figurantes* dismissed from the service of a burned-down theatre, still struggle about in their old costumes.

And now even the last shadows of this old life have vanished. There are no longer any cities which, as cities, have anything individual about them; even Rome has lost this character of city *par excellence*. To-day one enters as through a gap a breach in the walls, and in a wholly new part of the city, to find himself in a railway station surrounded by newly-built elegant houses, which might just as well belong to Berlin, Vienna, or any other modern city. From there one hunts up " old Rome " as a curiosity lying apart. Formerly we were taken directly into the heart of the old city, and saw ourselves surrounded and enclosed by it. No power can ever recall this sensation; for the conditions are radically changed among which men now dwell upon the earth. Every place is rummaged over in Rome to-day; and the antique subterranean city is laid bare and exhibited for a fee to the curious crowd, while the palaces either secretly or openly offer their art-treasures and their furniture for sale. One goes about in the midst of this colossal chaffering, and sees at the same time the official buildings of the new kingdom rising up bald, large, and tasteless, planned by some unknown architect, without one critical eye deigning to look at them or to feel hurt by their disproportion. The old city is metamorphosed; and Rome has become a plain modern collection of dwelling-houses, like other cities. The works of Raphael and Michael Angelo, the galleries of the Vatican, the historical reminiscences, will never lose their power. Who wanders upon the ruins of the Palatinate, now covered with a garden of laurel and roses, letting the warm sun play about him there, while letters from home tell of cold and snow, and then gazes upon the mountains far away on the rim of the distant horizon, whose outlines from time immemorial have been the same as to-day; who in sunlight and moonlight hears the rippling murmur of the Roman fountains, — who can fail to enjoy all this; who ever forget it?

But the soul of this vast organism has fled!

The Jesuits, who in fancied omnipotence move about to-day, have nothing in common with the priests of the Gregories, nor with the cardinals of the sixteenth century, nor yet with the abbés of the eighteenth. Who would now become acquainted with Greek art goes to Greece itself, where in Olympia works are being exhumed which give a better idea of the artistic power of the Greeks than all that is contained in Italian museums; and who will become acquainted with the life peculiar to each nation goes to the principal cities where to-day the ruling powers of the people are manifest.

Unless we keep clearly before us this great contrast, we cannot understand either Goethe's enthusiasm or the influence which Rome had upon him.

LECTURE XVII.

THE END OF "IPHIGENIA." — "TASSO." — CHRISTIANE. — "ROMAN ELEGIES."

WHEN Goethe had finished the last work on "Iphigenia" in Rome, it was a matter of course that the piece should be read aloud: all his works are written as if intended for the single aim of being read to friends, and Goethe had very soon drawn a social circle around him there. At first, indeed, he had concealed his name; he wished to be wholly alone: but by degrees a number of persons had gathered about him in Rome whom he influenced. This last was a peculiar feature in his intercourse with people. He needed to be surrounded by a society in which he was the leading spirit; and whoever resisted his elevating influence must resign all intercourse with him.

As a matter of course, too, a woman was the soul of this circle. Goethe had here found the painter Angelica Kaufmann, to whom this *rôle* was allotted. Angelica Kaufmann, after many sad experiences, had finally gained a distinguished position. She was esteemed as an historical painter, and was also renowned and courted as a portrait-painter. She made much money, and with her old Italian husband entertained in her own house; for which, as is well known, very little money is required in Rome, the only essential being a suitable room and personal charms: eating and drinking each one provides for himself. With her Goethe found the comfort of a home. She took many pictures of him at this time which are known, and also painted a scene from his "Iphigenia," which Goethe speaks of in terms of praise.

Angelica was surely not in her lifetime valued either as much as Rafael Mengs — who, as the German hero among the painters of the last century, was placed by Winckelmann and others on the same level with Raphael — or as Battoni, who was Mengs's Italian rival of highest renown. As a woman, she held a modest position; yet her works, though less strong in drawing and modelling, are to-day more interesting and have a more intrinsic vitality than those of either Mengs or Battoni. As a woman, it was to her advantage that the whole tone of painting in her time was rather feminine and delicate, and suited to pastel rendering; for the time had not arrived when manly genius was forced to raise exhausted art on to a higher plane. We to-day recognize instantly Angelica's works; we feel how purely she looked at Nature, and how chaste was her manner of representing it. Who could now obtain one of her works would seize it without hesitation, hang it in a good place, and surely rejoice in its possession every time he passed before it.

At Angelica's, the reading of the at last finished "Iphigenia" took place. The poem had been looked forward to with eagerness, and the flower of the German colony assembled to hear the distinguished poet himself read his work.

Goethe was now to have a wholly new and unlooked-for experience: the public received coldly this work of whose inspiring effect long years of experience had made him perfectly sure. Goethe tells of this himself. People had expected something different. Goethe's fame as Germany's first poet rested on his "Götz," or even more on his "Werther," which was at that time still at its full height of popularity. Men looked for something passionate, world-storming, revolutionary, and, above all, for something "German;" instead of this, Goethe offers them a Greek fable, in smooth antique verse, with subdued feeling, a longing for seclusion and repose, a uniform tone of sublimity, and a meaning in the work which must have been an enigma to his new Roman friends. How should they know who was meant by Thoas, and where by Tauris? Moreover, what had surprised Germany in "Iphigenia" was to be encountered at every step in Rome; and here people did not want the spirit of ancient Greece, but craved what was not to be had in Rome. Fresh German air they longed to breathe again, and to be transported to their distant Fatherland. This disappointment Goethe felt all the more keenly, because soon voices from Germany also reached him, — voices of friends who without his inspiring presence did not know how to interpret the printed piece in its new form; it was much dearer to them in its old familiar shape. The knowledge that he did not fulfil the expectations entertained was from this time such a frequent experience with him that it almost formed the rule. But he never allowed himself to be unsettled in his opinions by it, but accustomed himself to see his works laid aside for years before men began to understand them; and he never questioned for an instant the correctness of the new principles he had adopted in Rome.

It is something grand to see the modesty with which from this time he allows himself to be found fault with as "smooth and cold." He feels that he has ceased to create for the present moment, disregards his limited public and the blame of the day, and works for the nation and for the recognition of the century.

We have curious statements with regard to the reception which "Iphigenia" met in his own home. I will speak only of a single one here which shows Goethe's character at the same time in a wholly new light.

He had taken with him from Frankfort to Weimar a young man to fill the place of secretary and servant, named Philip Seidel. We are indebted for the first particular information concerning this person to Burkhardt, who published Seidel's correspondence with Goethe. Seidel's letters to his Frankfort friends, in which he tells of the first Weimar times, have also been printed. These letters show a relation between master and servant which of its kind is perfectly unique.

Seidel was called a "stereotyped edition" of Goethe. His letters show how far imitation can be carried. He made himself a perfect Werther. It is delicious to hear him describing the aristocratic society of Weimar as if he looked down upon it from a height. Desponding, benevolent, he believes fully in his better understanding of all things, and gives his dogmatic opinions without the slightest question of their absolute correctness. While he copied Goethe's poems, or wrote them down according to his dictation, he assumed the air of being joint author of them. Finally, he started out himself as a writer.

Seidel slept in the same room with Goethe. At night, after Goethe had returned from court, both lying in bed, they took a review of the world and of God's providence. While Goethe had learned to qualify his opinions of things, Seidel maintained Werther's old radical views.

November 23, 1775, at 11 o'clock at night, Seidel writes to his friend Wolf, in Frankfort (not three weeks after Goethe's first arrival in Weimar) : —

HIS SECRETARY PHILIP SEIDEL.

"In this blessed situation I must write to thee, good brother, for here I am copying a romance of which my master is the author. I am in a perfectly enchanting place, and will write to you about it, although much pressed for time, being in a hurry to finish this book. I have everything,— work enough, money enough, and plenty to eat and drink; only — only — no love, — no soul to whom I can disclose myself. They are an idle, stiff, luxurious people here, — insufferable to me. Their highest merit is that they read books, by which, however, they contrive to make themselves still more intolerable. You wish me to tell you something about the court; but I cannot much, because I have little to do with it, and it does not specially interest me. But this I must say to you, — it is a delight to my soul to see the princely family. One cannot enough admire the grand ease of the widowed Duchess and the fresh, good expression of the Duke. And you should hear when the people speak of them, how they extol them, — their 'God be thanked,' and 'God preserve them,' uttered with weeping eyes, — it is really touching!

"Nov. 17, at the masquerade. This I liked; there was a variety of pleasing nonsense. But hear! this night we had no sleep; the following we went to bed at quarter past twelve: sleeping, three in a room, we fell into talk from one thing to another down to the very devil. Imagine the tremendous leap from love-stories to the island of Corsica, where we remained in the hottest hand-to-hand skirmish until toward four o'clock in the morning. The question about which we disputed with as much vehemence as learning was this: Whether a people is not happier *free* than under the control of a sovereign master? for I had said, 'The Corsicans are truly unfortunate.' 'No,' he replied, 'a blessing has been vouchsafed to them and their posterity; they are becoming refined, civilized, and instructed in art and learning, instead of remaining rough and wild as they were.' 'Sir,' I rejoined, 'I should say *to the devil* with all these refinements and improvements at the expense of freedom, which alone gives real happiness. The Corsicans could not have been wild, except the inhabitants of the mountain regions; else they would never have had such a love of liberty and never have evinced such bravery. They were happy; they were comfortable in the satisfaction of every want, because they made themselves no unnecessary wants. Now their needs increase daily, and cannot be gratified; for none of us can eat, drink, dress himself, go into company or not as he likes, etc. They had all they desired, because they did not desire much; and that much they had in freedom.'"

Seidel was the only person in Weimar who had known of Goethe's Italian journey. He was left behind as his agent, to open his letters, take charge of his money, etc. To the great Seidel Goethe now sends his new "Iphigenia." Seidel impudently writes him how dissatisfied he is with it; and we hear how Goethe answers him, *the first poet in Germany, a man forty years of age, to a subaltern secretary six years younger than himself!* The middle of May, 1787, he writes to him from Naples: —

"Your letter of March 7 reached me yesterday as I was leaving the ship, and your true words were heartily welcome to me. The journey through Sicily has been happily accomplished, and will remain to me an indestructible treasure the rest of my life. What you say of my 'Iphigenia' is, alas! in a certain sense true. When I, for the sake of art and my vocation, was forced to write it all over, I saw beforehand that the best passages must lose if the worst and medium ones were to be improved. You point out two scenes which have manifestly lost; but when it is printed, read it again calmly, and you will realize what the whole has gained."

A humanity, a genuine humility, breathes through these words, which reveals Goethe's heart as it was.

But one thing is said in this letter which, after all that has become known, amazes us. Goethe continues: —

"Yet the principal trouble with the drama is, that I have had so little time to devote to it. The first sketch I wrote in the midst of picking up recruits, and I went on with it while making my Italian tour. If I had had time to elaborate the piece, you would not have had cause to regret a *line* in it."

We see, then, that, after all, Goethe considered "Iphigenia" as a hasty work, which might have been made quite different.

It seems that Seidel, even after these explanations, retained his preference for the earlier form of the piece. Goethe writes him again in October, 1787: —

"You shall have an 'Iphigenia' in prose as well, if it gives you pleasure. The artist can only labor and strive. Applause is like love returned, — only to be *desired*, never to be *extorted*."

In the same modest way Goethe defends "Claudine of Villabella," whose prose form had been changed into iambics in Italy, against the like censures from Philip Seidel. He always placed the greatest value on honest criticism, let it come from whom it might.

Goethe, however, never touched "Iphigenia" again after it was once printed in the form under discussion; in less than a year, he was as much estranged from the work as if it had never been his own. As his love for Frau von Stein cooled, his interest in the work cooled also. He confesses openly to Schiller, some ten years after the Roman remodelling, that he no longer feels any sympathy with the piece, and treats it as indifferently as if it had been the production of a stranger; so that Schiller is obliged to take it under his protection. "Iphigenia" is to be brought upon the stage and some alterations are necessary. Schiller undertakes them, as Goethe cannot be induced to touch it. Even as early as 1792, when Goethe met Jacobi on the Rhine, and was asked to read something aloud, he refused " Iphigenia," which they proposed to lay before him. He said that the prevailing tone of tenderness in the poem had grown uncongenial to him. He spoke of it to Schiller as the " Grecianized Play," and said sarcastically that Iphigenia was " devilish humane." It is curious that when Goethe in his old age spoke to Eckermann of " Iphigenia," he said he had never seen a truly good representation of it ; and I believe that very few persons now-a-days can say they have ever been so fortunate as to see it well rendered on the stage. It is seldom acted. At present when we hear " Iphigenia " spoken of as a stage performance we think of Gluck's opera.

If the work of " Iphigenia " signalizes Goethe's going to Italy, another of his poems symbolizes his leaving it. " Tasso " is the fruit of his longing to return to Italy. Goethe sought by writing " Tasso " to benumb his feelings on the way home from Rome, and finished it in Weimar, when the sight of the old unchanged circumstances seemed to him unendurable. In the Boboli gardens in Florence, where he stopped only a short time, he worked on it, and also devoted to it every leisure hour in Weimar after his arrival. Tasso must take Iphigenia's place, wholly, as the confidant of his soul. It is Goethe's ripest and most perfect tragedy. " Tasso " was written when he was in his full vigor and in the prime of his manhood.

" Iphigenia " was like some young fir-tree which, transplanted into Italy, changed into a pine. In " Tasso " only the core remained German. Two acts written in poetic prose Goethe had taken with him to Rome, which in conception, plan, and development, while having something similar to the ones at present existing, yet had a soft and nebulous coloring which they soon lost when, in accordance with his new ideas, the form became of more importance, and he put it into verse. " Tasso " sprang up afresh from the old root, tender and stròng, like a glistening laurel-tree which had never tasted any but the sun of Italy.

Greek feeling, Roman culture, and German sensibility combined in him to form a new modern element, which we may well call " Goethean " in the most pregnant sense. " Tasso " shows Goethe's style in its highest perfection. These iambics taught Schiller to write iambics, and furnished Schlegel with the language with which he made Shakspeare as it were a German poet. Without " Tasso " our poetic diction would never have attained its present perfection. The first idea of the work perhaps dates as far back as Goethe's earliest period as a writer. At the time he was with Jacobi in Düsseldorf he read a romance picturing Tasso's insanity. It may be that, without a thought of committing it to paper, the idea of a drama then arose in his mind, as that of " Iphigenia " did in connection with the *cantata* in honor of Gluck's niece. It was necessary for Goethe to have repeated experiences before his first idea took the form of a settled plot. To those who would follow the growth of " Tasso " we offer the following :

Among Goethe's Strasburg companions Lenz was conspicuous as one of the most talented. Single verses in his poems are strikingly beautiful. Goethe seems to have valued him almost more than any of the others. After a confused and wasted life he died insane in Russia. Not long after Goethe was established in Weimar, Lenz appeared there as *Genie*,[1] and as such was received. He

---

[1] It is difficult to find an English equivalent for this. The German term " Kraftgenies " was assumed by the literary youth of the period, who

was eccentric in dress, manners, and pretensions. Goethe knew how to restrain him within the bounds of decorum, and make him appear to the best advantage; but Lenz, who ascribed his kindly acceptance by the people to his own merit, may through this mistake have been tempted into a positive act of folly.

At any rate, one day the cup overflowed. Lenz did some crazy thing, of what kind we are not told, and people agreed in calling him a jackass. I suppose this term, used by a circle of Shakspeare admirers, may have been an allusion to "Midsummer Night's Dream," where Bottom, changed into an ass, makes love to Titania. I believe this piece of stupidity (*Eselei* as the Germans call it) suggested the fatal scene in "Tasso." Tasso, beside himself at the signs of favor received from a distinguished lady, who cares more for his mind than his person, and who has no conception how far her condescension may mislead a genius, draws her violently to his heart, and ruins himself by the act.

However, this is mere conjecture! The pre-Italian version of "Tasso" is lost to us. Goethe had begun the "Tasso" six years before he went to Rome. He wrote it "to relieve himself," as he told Eckermann, calling Tasso at the same time "an enhanced Werther." In another place he calls Tasso one of those creatures of the imagination to whom we could impute all our own follies and then name him "Tasso."

But Antonio also is Goethe, as he has likewise said. In the antagonism of these two characters, who unrelentingly repulse each other, Goethe represents the irreconcilableness of the two parts in which he was condemned to appear during the Ten Years. Tasso is Goethe in

thought themselves above all conventionalities, and affected a boisterous extravagant style in language, dress, and manners.

his innermost nature and tendency. In Lenz he saw his caricature, and in the decisive scene of the piece — for which, as I suspect, Lenz gave the motive — Goethe paints what might have happened if he had allowed himself to be carried away as Lenz was, without, figuratively speaking, leaving his own kingdom open for retreat. Antonio, on the other hand, is what Goethe felt he must become if he, as a statesman, allowed himself to be enticed in a one-sided direction, — at best a man like Fritsch! And here we see right clearly what is meant by "symbolic poetry." Goethe represents in "Tasso" the thoughts day by day rehearsed in his soul, while the incidents of the piece bear no reference to the real events of his life. It is impossible to cull out of the figures in "Tasso" a single living character. They are wholly original beings, — all of them created to personify ideas and duties; and precisely because these characters were spontaneous creations with Goethe they are so much the more genuine. With them Goethe has produced a new world, which he informs with the thoughts which animate his soul; while if he had written a piece filled with the persons of the Duke, Duchess, Von Fritsch, Frau von Stein, Lenz, himself, etc., introducing word for word the things which had actually been uttered, compared with "Tasso" it would have been only a perishable puppet-show, suited to throw some lover of the so-called literal facts into ecstasies, but in reality not possessing a glimmer of the absolute truth which beams upon us from the "Tasso."

While glorifying Ferrara, Goethe has lavished on Weimar indirectly the most exquisite praise imaginable, and such as could never have been bestowed in a direct manner. So might Weimar have been, and he represents it as if it were so! The actual Ferrara has also through this poem gained a wholly undeserved renown; but out of a deserted princely residence of the second rank a new shoot of the old Pericles Athenian life has arisen. Strangers to-day wander about in the tiresome streets of Ferrara, which probably were not a bit more interesting in the sixteenth century, sniffing the old walls for the sake of the past. In the same way Goethe has re-created the person of Tasso himself; and of a poet who to German taste is insipid, and whose works to-day only a few succeed in reading through, notwithstanding their splendid cadences, he has made a heroic figure, a genius to whom one ascribes the most glorious possibilities. And this Ferrara of Goethe's imagination, its princely family, its court, with its court poet, are portrayed with such convincing reality that the facts weigh as nothing in comparison with it. All this fictitious splendor has been grafted upon history, and so interwoven with it that the sharpest critical shears will never be able to sever it again. Study as we will, Goethe's Ferrara remains for us a picture of the flower of Italian life in the sixteenth century; and, as he represents the sentiments and manners of the people, a soft splendor radiates from the pages, which we seek in vain to dispel by a perusal of the actual documents of the time.

And yet we must assert, in face of any facts to the contrary, that Goethe's view was correct. There existed in the Italy of the Cinquecento a spirit which could be personified as it has been in "Tasso." We need only read the condition of things in Germany then: in contrast to the dismal wilderness all other nations presented, Italy was like a well-cultivated sunny garden, where golden fruit peacefully ripened on the espaliers; only the souls of men did not lie so open to the light as they appear to us to have done in "Tasso."

In the construction of the acts, in the carrying out of the scenes, and in the expression of the ideas this work is perfect and unrivalled. Every word is a thought. But, as I have said already, this drama also was not written for the stage.

We have seen how Goethe on his entrance into Weimar gave up that ideal stage which he had in his mind when writing "Götz." "Iphigenia" truly was written expressly for the boards, and it was chiefly for this reason that it did not gain a higher form. But the new "Iphigenia" which was written in Rome returned to that old ideal stage, and in a yet higher degree "Tasso" belonged to it and to no other. This piece contains nothing which could give the managers a chance to show their skill. It scarcely offers rôles for actors. The characters are too finely wrought out: they play them best who mar them least. Only slowly could be understood in Germany what Goethe had intended and what he had accomplished in this work. It took years to mature the thought that it was within the limits of possibility to make it an acting-play. For if the actors could be found, where could they find a public? Leopold Stolberg wrote to Jacobi: "What do you say to Goethe's 'Tasso'? The tone displeases me eminently. Why does he give the petty, proud, ostentatious Antonio such superiority over the pupil of the Muses and Graces?" "Single passages are excellent," he adds. The same kind of criticism, leaving out of sight altogether the higher meaning of the poem, Goethe had to accept as the common judgment. But Goethe was not to be misled. He was now in every respect a man, and knew what he had to do. It was clear to him that in the future no critic could teach him anything, for that he alone knew what direction he ought to keep.

"Tasso" is the grateful tribute which Goethe dedicated to Italy. Yet he did not rest satisfied with this. To Rome herself he raised another memorial,—the

"Roman Elegies," on which he worked in Weimar at the same time. Of these we will now speak.

We have seen Goethe become a legitimate member of the aristocracy. He knew how to value the qualities which distinguish this society from any below it, and did not neglect also to make them his own. So understood, Goethe was in the best sense a *parvenu*. He gives himself this title quite openly. Nevertheless, we have seen that he was so much led to seek it either because he was charmed with its novelty, or because in a practical sense he could make it useful to him. How modest and genuinely humble Goethe yet continued to be is shown in his treatment of Philip Seidel, and in his intercourse with the poor Krafft,—a miserable youth, the scape-goat of Fate, whom he comforts with touching kind-heartedness, supports, and bears patiently even with his distrust. To the externals of his high position he never ascribed greater value than they deserved. He considered them in the light of relays in his life-journey. He knew how to make a display of his nobility, of his titles "Minister" or "Eccellenza," if it would shorten his way to his object; but as poet, and in his friendly relations, he always remained unconscious and unpretending.

Goethe demanded truth at any price. The labels must show in clear characters what the contents of the jars were. His poems contain the highest and most elevated thoughts which have ever found expression in the German language, while at the same time it never occurred to him to disown what is inherent in human nature. Goethe shrinks from nothing. He sees everything, and calls everything by its right name; and there are few things to which he did not, once at least, find an opportunity to give that right name. What stirred him was put into words. There are verses written by him which indeed were not intended for others, but which have at last come to light (the Paralipomena to the "Faust"), in which things most earthy and filthy are spoken of with a plainness and assurance, as having the same right to be poetically and precisely symbolized as what is held to be finest and most sublime. Goethe knew the double nature of man, and never denied that he spoke from his own experience. He was rather cold than passionate: his nature may have been like his sister's. He was never dissipated. His works do not contain one single passage which could be called lewd. But Goethe was human; and, to pass from a general view of his life to details where the demands of his nature came in collision with what he regarded as mere external conventions, he as genuine democrat at heart never doubted on which side to place himself. On his return to Weimar Goethe needed the presence of a woman in his home. He had in thought so wholly freed himself from the outward restraint of Weimar life, that it would have been impossible for him to take to himself a wife out of one of the aristocratic Weimar families; and his existence there, so far as his inmost life was concerned, seemed to him to have ended. Frau von Stein had plucked the flower which such a union might have offered for herself. Goethe asked now only health, freshness, youth, and devotion, added to genuine mother-wit; and for the rest it was all the same in what sphere of life he found it. Therefore he did not hesitate, when in a lower grade in society he met a beautiful maiden who possessed all these requirements, to take her to himself.

This is Goethe's relation to Christiane, or, as his old friends emphatically called her, "Mam'selle Vulpius," — from the beginning a marriage, the one circumstance deducted that no church ceremony took place, and never looked upon by Goethe in any other light. He very soon took Christiane, together with her mother and sister, into his house, and lived with them as with his legitimate family. Christiane and her children were his wife and his children to anybody who might inquire after them.

Nor in Weimar did any one really take this ill in Goethe. All the reproaches were attached to the qualities of the woman, whose appearance was said to be "vulgar," — which meant that her education and manner of thinking had never so far raised her as to enable her to satisfy the demands which good society makes on those esteemed worthy to be one of its members.

But how are *we* to regard this person who from now on — almost thirty years — was an inseparable appendage of Goethe, and had a significant influence upon him?

We often ignore people whose existence we cannot deny, though we heartily wish they did not exist: we bury them in thought, and seem no longer to see them. But a being that stood so near to Goethe, and had such an effect on his works, compels us to form an opinion of her. It truly would not become us to take advantage of the great amount of faults of which she has been accused, and to accept the accusations as sufficient evidence on which to base a judgment. "A kind of cook," Christiane was said to have been, "who later gave herself up to drinking," and by whom Goethe must to the very last have often been placed in awkward situations. But why, instead of repeating the prevailing notions in Weimar society, should we not rather hold fast to what Goethe saw in Christiane and had in her, — a maiden, whom he "passionately loved," as he avowed to Herder (using these very words); who was his pupil and confidant in his investigations of the metamorphoses of plants; the mother of his son, on whom he hung with his whole heart; the woman who directed his household, whom he missed sadly when she was away from him, and whose death brought him to despair.

Never has anything been said against the life of this maiden before she belonged to Goethe. He himself spoke of her to Frau von Stein as "a poor creature;" but he never let her suffer for it. He wrote letters to her when they were separated, which were preserved by Christiane as her greatest treasure. They are now said to be burned. Goethe's mother called her in her letters from the beginning "her dear daughter," and was on pleasant terms with her when Goethe took her to Frankfort. After the death of his mother, when he sent her to Frankfort again to be the representative for his claims on the estate, she behaved so generously that the relatives could not complain. We have a letter, lately published, owing to this circumstance, which does full justice to Goethe's wife, and from which we learn what Christiane thought of the way in which the world had treated her. The expression "vulgar," after all, seems only to have been called forth by the unpolished bluntness she showed on all occasions; for she never displayed any selfishness, and she never flung back the malicious criticisms of which she was the victim, — which, in an historical sense, is considered as the special mark of vulgarity. As soon as social contrasts cease, her vulgarity no more exists; and it is inconceivable that Goethe could have endured any one near him whose character fundamentally would not bear the test. When, after the battle of Jena, the French plundered Weimar, Christiane had the courage to press through the marauders to the French officers and obtain for Goethe a *sauve-garde*. Everywhere that we see this woman in action, we see her acting courageously, energetically, and with circumspection. It is well known that, after the battle of Jena, Goethe married her.

Goethe composed a beautiful memorial to his wife and Rome at the same time in the "Roman Elegies," where the heroine, surely to his imagination, corresponded to Christiane.

Goethe's soul was full of Roman pictures when he met Christiane in Weimar. Her appearance may have had something Roman in it to him at that time. That she had the stout, somewhat undersized, figure and development which distinguishes Roman women we see from the portrait that remains of her. The Roman women have a proud carriage, as if they all descended from the old emperors, and encounter life bravely. Goethe, in his "Elegies," makes Christiane as genuine a Roman as ever appeared in the Carnival or upon the Piazza Navona.

In coming to Weimar from Frankfort, Goethe had felt the unconstrained tone of Thuringian society to be a relief. Frau von Stein represented the *animus* of this new life. But in Rome he met with something which exceeded even the most refined society of Weimar, — perfect freedom, — only held in check by the mighty weight of history with which Rome burdens every one encompassed by its walls. He purposely avoided aristocratic society in Rome, saying, truly, " he had had that at home." Before the past which surrounds us in Rome all distinctions of rank disappear. Here one understands how clerical and secular nobles could rise so high out of the very lowest ranks. Wherever else this happens, some trace of early surroundings remain. Not so in Rome. Goethe there learned that it is the highest conception of freedom for a man to be able to give to a maiden, of whatever rank, a position at his side; and on his return to Weimar he made use of this freedom. Who has ever been in Rome counts himself in imagination henceforth in the list of its inhabitants. Who must leave Rome, like Wilhelm Müller in his Roman letter, writes a *rivederci*, and never *addio*. When very old, standing with Chancellor Müller before the great map of Rome which hung in his room, Goethe touched with his finger the Ponto Molle, and said: "I must confess that since I drove over it for the last time I have never known a really happy day." He never ceased to cherish the refreshing idea of once again and then forever returning to Rome. When he took Christiane into his home, it seemed to him as if he still lived in Rome; and he shut himself into his house with her as he might have done there, without its occurring to any one to spy over his garden hedge. Goethe, haunted by thoughts of Roman freedom, believed he could do without the world in Weimar as in Italy; was at any rate resolved to keep people at a distance as he had done there. He ventured quietly to continue in Weimar his wonted free life; and, if it was not done wholly without injury to himself, we must confess that he had his way.

Goethe says in his "Elegies" that the Triumvirs of love inspired him, — Catullus, Tibullus, and Propertius. He forgets in this place the poor Johannes Secundus, to whom perhaps he was no less indebted. Nothing modern has ever been written so antique as Goethe's "Elegies." He is once betrayed into a half-joke over himself: it seems to him as if his soul had in the time of Hadrian lived in a Roman. We imagine that in course of transmigration one of the three Roman poets has again appeared on earth, — that in Weimar he tunes his lyre anew; and though everything is changed around him, intoxicated with the joy of his strange life he puts the old accustomed wine to his lips, which during two thousand years has every year been pressed out as in the primal days; and the ancient spirit of pure delight in being stands before us, newly risen from the tombs.

Goethe has made Christiane a Roman maiden, who pours out the wine in an Italian *vigna*, and himself the one who among all the guests is dearest to her. With everything which adorned Italian life in his recollection Goethe has surrounded this maiden, and has wrought what was at first his and her secret into the most beautiful idyl. How he first met her unknown in the dark, how she secretly came to him, how they understood each other without the world's suspecting it, — all this Weimar experience has been transferred to Rome. With the fragrance of Italy he has draped her figure. The " Roman Elegies " are the first fruit which the Italian sun ripened later in his soul on German soil.

If we would wholly appreciate " Tasso," we must think of this obscure and lowly-born one as the foster-sister of the princesses in " Tasso." Goethe, in imagination, was not only at home among the intricacies of the society which moved upon the heights of life, but understood likewise and depicted in a masterly manner the different experiences of a heart which, belonging to a wholly different sphere, was yet drawn in sympathy to his own. We see Goethe as ardent here as there: he is refined and reverent. The " Roman Elegies " and " Tasso " sprang up together, and may not be considered separately. They are the complement one to the other, as indivisible parts of the same harvest, — in " Tasso," historic inspiration; in the " Elegies," enjoyment of the present.

Christiane, the little wife, died in 1816. In some verses on her loss, we feel that the necessity of relieving his oppressed heart called them forth. They show that she was a part of him, and how inconsolably he longed for her. " All the use I can now make of my life is to weep her loss," he said. Since now this lies clearly before us ; since nothing betrays that Goethe through Christiane's influence was ever taken out of his intellectual life, or that she was in any way a detriment to his work ; since he, as Louise Seidler testifies, looked upon her presence as something indispensable to his welfare, — I do not know why we should speculate as to whether his marriage with any other woman would have proved happier for him.

Considered from our distance to-day, there is something humorous in the fact that our most aristocratic poet — aristocratic in every sense of the word — appears as the husband of a rollicking, buxom " Hausfrau," and brother-in-law to that Vulpius from whose fancy sprang the famous robber-chief Rinaldo Rinaldini ; but it does not injure his memory. Robinson, Goethe's old adorer, who, after studying in Jena in 1802, returned every ten years to Germany, mentions Christiane in his first visit there : —

"During my calls on Goethe I saw the companion at his table, the mother of his children, and, as is generally known, afterward his wife. She had an agreeable face, and a hearty tone in conversation. Her manner was unaffected and without formality. Curious things were in circulation about her submissive demeanor and the freedom of her intercourse with Goethe when young, but as I saw her all these eccentricities had long passed away."

As with all well-educated Englishmen, one has with Robinson the feeling of his absolute sincerity.

" Eccentricities " is a very innocent word, and truly the correct one. Without doubt Christiane often gave the Weimar ladies occasion to observe how little she cared for etiquette; but Goethe's character, humanly considered, loses as little by this back-ground as Socrates loses in our eyes by his marriage with Xantippe. I do not think it necessary that we should be obliged to honor in Goethe's wife such a nature as that of Tasso's Leonora.

After so cursorily reviewing what happened on his return from the Italian journey, in the next lecture we will revert once more to Rome.

LECTURE XVIII.

ROME. — SICILY. — NAPLES. — PHILIPP HACKERT. — SECOND SOJOURN IN ROME. — RETURN TO WEIMAR. — SCHILLER.

I RECAPITULATE: Goethe went in the autumn of 1786 to Italy, and returned in the summer of 1788. In the beginning of November, 1786, he had arrived in Rome; in March, 1787, in Naples; in April had gone to Sicily, returning in May to Naples. In June he is again in Rome, and leaves it finally, after almost a year's stay there, to hurry back to Weimar.

The letters from Sicily are the most perfect in the "Italian Journey." The reader's curiosity is here at its height, because he brings less of his own personal criticism to bear upon it. This excursion stands out from the rest as an episode. Goethe himself is wholly in the background. We have before us only the glorious roads he travelled over and the places he visited. Here he found fewer opportunities to weave in his own thoughts, for he had never been so completely under the sway of outward things. He is simply a traveller who starts off early each morning, goes to bed tired at night, and in the interim is a keen observer, whose thoughts rarely turn homeward.

Naples stirs him to the most brilliant descriptions. I doubt if any account, by anybody or in any language, can compare with the one in Goethe's letters of the journey up Vesuvius; but Naples itself soon forms only the background to his own distinguished personality. Goethe becomes acquainted in Naples with the painter Hackert, who, in great favor with the King and Queen, lived in the Royal Castle, and he subsequently wrote the story of Hackert's life as a pendant to that of Winckelmann. The Castles of Capodimonte and Caserta, which are at present wholly deserted, made receptacles for collections or converted into public institutions, were at that time just in process of erection. Hackert, one of the good *genii loci*, soon formed with Goethe an intimate friendship.

Goethe praises Hackert's landscapes, — not extravagantly, but he speaks of them as deserving attention in a high degree. To-day one is accustomed to dismiss them with a shrug of the shoulders. But those who judge them in this way have seen very few of Hackert's landscapes; or, if so, they were mere faded water-color paintings. One such landscape (and a view of Rome into the bargain) we see hanging framed in the Berlin "Cabinet of Engravings." The *gauche* colors have assumed the milky verdigris tone into which such productions often turn in course of time. My own opinion for a long time rested on the impression these pictures had made, and until, in other places, I fell by chance upon a greater number of his works, which induced a much more favorable verdict. A delicacy in the handling, a genuine eye for Nature, and an absence of all seeking after meritricious effects struck me in these works, united with a perception of the lines in the landscape which made Goethe's preference for the master quite comprehensible. In the landscape paintings of our days we are so much accustomed to find truth to Nature aimed at by strong effects of color roughly blotched in, that a picture of a wide landscape, depending for its effect on a carefully drawn imitation of the outlines, makes scarcely any impression on us. Here lies Hackert's forte; and this is what was, at that time, specially demanded.

Goethe's "Italian Journey" contains so many descriptions of landscape that a few words on this subject must be said.

The representation of an unpeopled bit of Nature as seen by the eye from any convenient point is, as a finished work of art, a wholly modern production. To the ancients the landscape was only a background for human action. The meaning of solitude in itself was not known to them. They could only think of inanimate Nature by personifying it, and just as they expressed Darkness by adding the figure of Night to the rest of the figures in a composition, they could have represented Solitude only by bringing the godlike inhabitants of trees and fountains into the foreground.

The modern landscape, in its present sense, was unknown even to the Renaissance, and is an outgrowth of the seventeenth century. The glorious representations of land and water which Titian and Giorgione have given are never without human accessories, — as if to show who ruled over all this beauty, and without whom all this landscape would be quite unnecessary. In the seventeenth century first arose, among men who saw themselves both politically and religiously bound by what seemed indissoluble chains, a longing after a place where this fearful tyranny would be powerless; and only the solitude where never foot of man had trod offered this refuge. At that time began the *cultus* of Nature as an impersonal divinity, the healer of all ills; the longing after unexplored distances; the seeking for undiscovered islands, where man, led only by the pure impulses of his heart, might live united with a few congenial spirits whose laws of existence were the laws of Nature. They began to regard the landscape as a portrait of this same Nature: the law by which the trees grow, the law by which the rocks are decomposed, the undulations of the sea as well as the far-stretching land, should express in lines the spirit of the Mother Earth and bring us nearer to it. In this sense the landscapes of the last century are to be apprehended. Goethe had taken a young artist with him to Sicily, who, with fine hard-lead pencil, sketched for him the outline of the mountains and the lines of the sea on the coast.

We see Hackert in his drawings and paintings following the same aim. As if he were the owner of the land who looks at his property with a practised eye, neither overvaluing nor undervaluing anything, he draws most accurately the rising and falling of the faintest wave-lines in the far perspective which he so enjoyed depicting. With loving sympathy he paints each tree and bush, and follows the course of the streams. The less a work of art depends upon effective coloring, so much the more strongly does it work upon the imagination of the beholder; and I do not doubt that the time will come when these paintings, which to-day seem so pale and uninteresting, will again be valued, and Hackert will take his deserved position.

Goethe has, as was his way, introduced into Hackert's biography everything that could tend to explain the individual career of this artist. He has raised an historical monument, not only to him, but also to Hackert's patron, King Ferdinand of Naples, whose simple, innocent, kindly manner he describes admirably, and to Queen Caroline (daughter of Maria-Theresa) whose straightforward good-nature he places in the most beautiful light. This is all the more interesting to us as it pictures the condition of the Kingdom of the two Sicilies before the storm of the French Revolution had reached there, and previous to the reign of Murat, which was followed by the series of wretched years of tyranny which paralyzed them, and reduced them to the mere nonentities they are to-day; for Naples itself is at present a city like any other, rapidly increasing in modern elegance and comfort, and one of the chief points of attraction to curious travellers who crowd its hotels.

The most important portion of Goethe's visit to Italy, however, was his second sojourn in Rome. Now, for the first time in his life, he establishes himself voluntarily in a place with the thought that he would like to remain there forever. He had neither gone into exile, as when he first left Frankfort; nor was he lured by a prince, as when he went to Weimar, — but he settles himself in Rome because the city itself captivates him. He feels perfectly at home in it. He takes a comfortable dwelling; loses all the earlier hurry, the feeling that he must press forward, that he must concentrate himself; and lives quietly and at his ease, without a thought for the morrow. And here again, in the account of his Italian life, Goethe is the principal feature, and Rome around him only the landscape. Goethe's life in Rome, from 1787 to 1788, is depicted in his letters with a power of illustration which far exceeds that in " Dichtung und Wahrheit." The letter-form makes it all the more real. He does not propose any historic painting, but seems to lay before us his book of sketches that we may look them through. Goethe has an eye for everything, and, added to this, the wonderful gift of being happy everywhere. He travels like a prince visiting his new domains, who feels himself to be master wherever he comes.

The house in which he lived in Rome is indicated to-day by a marble tablet, — " Here dwelt Goethe," etc., — placed there by order of the municipal authorities.

To Gnoli belongs the merit of having suggested this, and of having found the house, which previously had been only known to have been somewhere on the Corso, opposite the Palazzo Rondanini. Goethe tells us that he looked from his window into a garden where lemon-trees standing in tubs were cared for by an old secular priest. The name of this old man, as well as that of the family with whom he dwelt, has been ascertained: the house has been divided and somewhat differently arranged from what it was formerly. A bit of his life, however, we get in a water-color by Tischbein, who at that time belonged to the Goethean circle in Rome. He has given us a back view of Goethe as he stands in his shirt-sleeves looking out of his window.

As another memorial of Goethe's stay in Rome stands a palm-tree in Villa Malta, which was transplanted there; while the Botanical Gardens in Padua (as Paul Hertz says) are also in possession of a "palma di Goethe," the same which attracted Goethe's fancy so greatly that he had a number of branches cut off, which he revered, even years after, as fetiches. Lastly, an inn is famous connected with the Marcellus Theatre, which, according to the inscription, was visited by Goethe (without doubt to drink a better wine than was offered me the last time I was there). The latest personal reminiscences of Goethe in Rome are related by the old landscape-painter Koch, whom many persons now living have known.

If Rome is no longer the Rome it was a hundred years ago, there are memorials enough of its former life to give us at least an idea of it. The modernizing is limited to certain parts of the town, and in Rome proper the old Italian economy prevails to a much greater degree than in Naples or Florence. The many families, and especially among the higher nobles, who have throughout maintained their loyalty to the Papal government, have helped greatly to preserve the outward appearance of the city. We find in the heart of Rome very few either new or restored buildings. As one descends the Scala di Spagna, he looks upon the *piazza* beneath just as it was centuries ago, — the stores of the merchants excepted, — and in the Villa Ludovisi or the Pamphili Doria very little has been changed. The palaces still form the capital letters in the old stereotyped confusion of houses, and the dungeon-like basements meet us everywhere as odd relics of former times. Travellers still go to the old taverns when they would drink good wine; and the nearer one comes to the Vatican, the more the modern aspect of things disappears, — in the Trastevere, indeed, we seem thrown back some hundreds of years. These dark palaces with their histories have become like living beings, who out of the empty windows look down upon the life of to-day as upon an insignificant masquerade which might be swept from the boards. I never passed the Palazzo Farnese, begun by San-Gallo and finished by Michael Angelo, without having this feeling. The building stands there with aristocratic self-consciousness as if mocking the centuries, and in invisible letters seems inscribed thereon: " A hundred years, and again a hundred years, shall I stand here as to-day, and look down upon the mortal men whose lives are only a span like thine." The more one comes to know these streets and court-yards, relics of so many centuries, which now close to one another stand a mass of decay, the stronger grows within one the curious feeling with which we go about, borne as it were beyond all historic computation, as if there were nothing more important to be done in the world than to look at all this obsolete glory and magnificence, and philosophize over past greatness.

And in face of all this grand and imperishable material a man's life may glide away unawares amid these eternal ruins, only in daily intercourse with the unceasing stream of travellers who come to Rome with more or less decided aims; but surely once, earlier or later, will he be impressed with the solemn meaning of Destiny, which has here left such traces of its revolution.

Not merely for Goethe, therefore, was it appropriate to speak of his "second academic life" when he would describe his experience and enjoyment in Rome. Every one who can live long enough in Rome to study the remains of the past there, and at the same time to enjoy the present, will feel applicable to himself to-day, in a certain sense, Goethe's words.

Never had Goethe belonged so wholly to himself. He became so accustomed to living just as he pleased that it seemed to him his normal state. Immediately after his return from Naples he gives expression to this:—

"Of new thoughts and ideas I have enough. Being left to myself I find my youth again, even to its trifles; and then the dignity and sublimity of my surroundings bear me as high and far as my ripest years can reach. My eye is wonderfully cultivated, and my hand shall not remain behind. There is only one Rome in the world; and I feel here like a fish in the water, and swim to the surface as a cannon ball in quicksilver, which would sink to the bottom in any other fluid."

This was the freedom which Winckelmann would never be deprived of again, and for the sake of which he refused all the advantageous offers he received from Germany. We read of the rapture of Frenchmen who after a long absence tread once more the beloved pavement of the streets of Paris; but what is that compared with the feeling with which one is inspired in Rome? The colossal weight of history makes the individual humble. As we speak softly in the presence of the dead, although they no longer hear anything, so our thoughts are subdued in Rome, because the past approaches so near to us and is so overpowering ; and yet one nowhere realizes so truly as in Rome the imperishableness of human greatness, for Raphael and Michael Angelo seem as if still living, and only withdrawn into a solitude from which the world is not good enough to tempt them to come forth again. Nowhere do we seem to trace with our own eyes the footprints of the great men themselves as in Rome.; and nowhere is it so imperatively demanded of us to occupy ourselves with them. In Naples and Florence the tumult of the day drowns such thoughts : one must isolate himself who would be absorbed by them. In Pisa or in Sienna, on the contrary, where everything is old, we feel oppressed, and say instantly we shall remain only a few days. But in Rome we breathe easily the breath of the past: it awakens no oppressive feeling of sadness, but, like the apostles at the sarcophagus of Mary, we seem to see fresh roses and living green springing from out the tombs, and we accustom ourselves, as Goethe says, to converse with spirits.

But now, in the midst of this transcendent life, something stirs within him, stronger than anything which could chain him to Rome, — *home-sickness.* Homeward! Weimar, which he believed he had shaken off as an uncomfortable dream, begins to assume to him another aspect; for was not all that he knew and loved still there ? " This egotistical life," he writes to the Duke, " makes men cold and overbearing."

Home presented itself to Goethe in a new form. Weimar had for a time been lost to sight; but suddenly it emerges again. What had grown old and distasteful to him takes on a fresh lustre; his friends, whom he had left widely dissevered, unite to form a circle which is expecting him; he feels that what he would find in Weimar, his little house and garden, is, after all, his nest from which he had flown. As Dante says, "Il disiato nido," to which like the doves he would return. He had left behind the Duke, Frau von Stein, Herder, Knebel, and many other *minorum gentium* who were dear to him because he knew them.

This Weimar rises again before his view.

There is only one thing which truly unites men : it is the consciousness that they have known each other. An old rascal who knew my mother is dearer to me than many an honest man who did not know her. Goethe recalls the fate of many a person at home in which he took a special interest. The thought seizes him that all his present experience is not for himself, but only for his Weimar friends. For them he collects and acquires. He can enjoy nothing alone, nothing in Italy, without inviting the invisible distant circle to share the enjoyment with him. One day the feeling overpowers him, and he makes up his mind. Away to Weimar!

Goethe gives a wonderful description of how sorrow for the loss of Rome and a longing for home were equally strong within him; how, from the moment he decided to depart, Rome lay behind him, and he really was no longer there. He pictures the last night, how he wandered about the Coliseum in the moonlight. He quotes Ovid's thrilling verses in which, on going into banishment, he takes leave of Rome. In Germany, later, the tears start into his eyes when he repeats them : this was when he compared Weimar with Tomi. He tells us what arrangements he makes to work on "Tasso" during his journey. And now he takes wing for home.

THE RETURN TO WEIMAR. 353

The whole of April Goethe had enjoyed in Rome; but, before the end of June, he was again in Weimar. He had been gone almost two years. So much was accomplished! What now? Although his yearning to return home had been so very great, yet all he could feel on crossing again the longed-for threshold was, "Once more crept under shelter in the North," re-entered the old prison, away from Rome! For what did he find? All the longed-for persons together indeed, but with still less sympathy with each other than before, and every one of them two years older. There was, first of all, Frau von Stein. When they became acquainted, he was twenty-six and she thirty-five; now he was almost forty, and she nearly fifty. There had been no disagreement between them; their correspondence had been lively: but yet both felt that the Ten Years belonged to memory as something done with. Goethe had accustomed himself, while at a distance from her, to work out his daily thoughts in his own breast. The first period of his relation to his old friend had come to an end, and was now a matter of history. Should he once more begin to share all his ideas with her, and to work with her? Had he wished to make the attempt, he would have been deceiving himself; but he did not even wish it.

Goethe found the Duke a wholly self-sustained man and sovereign. Carl August had reached the age when we do not look upon any man as absolutely essential to us. For these two, also, their former life had become a thing of the past. They had wished it to be so, and it was so: all had been foreseen. On the other hand, something came in which had not been foreseen. Carl August so far took advantage of the past as to continue to treat Goethe with a certain cordial familiarity to which Goethe could not respond. By so doing, the Duke had a color on his palette which did not stand at Goethe's command; and the consequence was that Goethe clung the more inviolably to all the forms of respect. He could not be tempted in any way to break through them. The Duke knew how to contrive inducements enough, but Goethe withstood them all. Nevertheless, empty and uninteresting must this play appear to him which, man against man, was henceforth day by day to be continued, and which could lead to nothing in the future. All it amounted to for Goethe was that he behaved in every case as judiciously as possible, and said to himself that no guarantee was given for the future. How correctly he judged was fully confirmed by the incidents of later years.

In both these cases Goethe had lost. In his relation to Herder only was there a gain.

Herder's character to those who stood nearest to him was an enigma; and he had either blind partisans or so-called friends who shook their heads. There was a want of harmony in his nature. Jacobi writes in 1788: "Unfortunately Nature has not mixed the elements in him happily. *Vultu mutabilis albus et ater.* Whatever he takes up is sure to burst and disgust him at once. There was hardly ever a man who made others feel so uncomfortable." The expression "burst" was probably suggested by a comparison of Goethe's in earlier days, where he speaks of "Herder's everlasting blowing of soap-bubbles."

But Herder knew himself very well, — knew how insufferable he could become to himself and to others. In the year 1769, before coming to Germany, he had written about himself: "My spring steals, unenjoyed, away. My fruits were too early ripe and untimely." Still more unfavorably he judges himself in a letter to his betrothed in the following year. Herder's correspondence shows wherein the trouble lay. His great devotion to others was outdone by a still greater egotism. He was capable of doing much for his friends, but never in such a way as to forget himself at the same time; and, amid his greatest joy at the achievements of others, something like a feeling of jealousy always persecuted him, as if he himself ought to have been the originator of the thought or work.

No one understood Herder so well as Goethe, who spoke of him after his death quite impartially and in the most beautiful manner. "With illness," Goethe says, "his malevolent spirit of contradiction and critical tone increased, until it dulled his inestimable capacity for loving, and overclouded his singular lovableness. No one approached him without rejoicing in his benignity, nor left him without being wounded by him." Extraordinary meaning is contained in these few words.

The words "capacity for loving" seem specially invented for him, and "lovableness," the attraction Herder had for every one; but the closing antithesis is, at the same time, the hardest thing which could have been said. If we would judge Herder dispassionately, we must examine those of his letters which afforded the least opportunity for any kind of æsthetic effect. These are, in my opinion, to be found in his early correspondence with the bookseller Hartknoch, a very honest man who sincerely revered Herder. They convince us that Herder had a very uncertain temper. He often gives vent to his ill humor to this simple, friendly man of business. Just so had he treated Goethe himself when, working on "Götz," he awaited with so much confidence Herder's infallible judgment. We must indeed take into consideration that a man like Herder might be allowed to bring a certain intentional pressure to bear upon a young upstart, who so visibly was preparing to grow over his head; but what makes Herder's conduct so hateful to us is his settled purpose to do so, contrasted with Goethe's frank, unsuspicious heart.

Herder had never perhaps been more favorably disposed towards Goethe than in 1788. Goethe's "Iphigenia" had met with only a problematical success; while Herder's "Ideen" had been a grand, bold stroke, which made Goethe himself again, in a certain sense, his scholar. In Goethe's judgment, Herder never produced anything better than this book. Herder felt once more that he was something to Goethe, and nothing chains men so closely to one another as such a consciousness. The benefits I bestow, not those I receive, bind me.

Goethe had felt in Rome the need of a grander conception of history. Herder now, for the second time, opened his eyes, as he had done before in Strasburg. Goethe was indebted to Herder for not finding Weimar quite unendurable after Rome; and it was owing to Herder that Goethe's intention to return to Italy was not carried out.

But all this is only secondary to the things of which we are now to speak. Goethe found on his return to Germany that not only had the old become older, but that he had something new to encounter.

In Italy first broke out his sovereign contempt for the German public, which he never lost again. The cool reception of "Iphigenia" was to him a token that he was forgotten; and he returned this forgetting in full measure. But the real cause of it dawned upon him only when he came to see with his own eyes what had happened. A new generation of authors had arisen. Goethe had ceased to belong to the younger generation, on whom the hopes of the people rested with fond expectation.

It was in the year 1788. In France the pulse of the people was already feverish. In Germany, also, men were less inclined than ever in literary matters to give themselves up to the enjoyment of pure beauty refined by the study of the antique. They had never attached any special value to the form: the subject-matter must surprise, inspire, intoxicate. Young writers had appeared who satisfied these demands. One among them, the most distinguished, is so great that we can pass over all the others; and this author was living in Weimar when Goethe returned, — Schiller.

If any one had anxiously awaited Goethe's arrival, it was Schiller; if any one was conscious of Goethe's whole power, it was Schiller; and if there had ever been a time in Goethe's life less appropriate than another for his meeting with a man like Schiller, it was at the moment of his return from Italy: and therefore we shall see what the result was when this meeting could no longer be avoided.

It is not here my intention to give a biography of Schiller, any more than it has been to give one of Goethe himself. I only say — though I consider even this superfluous — that Schiller, born in 1759, was ten years younger than Goethe. He was a Würtemberger, a Swabian, a South-German; while Goethe might be called a North-German. Schiller's father held a small office under the Government. He himself speaks of his youth as having been "dreary" and "joyless." We need not trouble ourselves here with the tenor of his early days; for they form no prologue, as with Goethe, to his later history; it would be better altogether if we knew nothing about them. Neither did Schiller's outward experiences form the elements of his poems, as with Goethe. Schiller might have trod wholly other paths, and he would yet have handled his material in the same way; and if he had not had the same material he would have chosen other, which in his hands would have had the same captivating effect. Concerning Schiller's works, the question subsequently will not be so much with regard to their special contents, as whether his health was sufficient to enable him to carry out his plans. The one real event in Schiller's life was his meeting with Goethe.

No one of Schiller's works had an individual history, like all of Goethe's. I have compared "Iphigenia" to a fir-tree which was metamorphosed into a pine; and it would be easy to find for each of Goethe's pieces, even to his smallest poems, a botanical simile, — fragrant lindens in "Werther," oak-trees rustling in "Götz," and so forth. In Schiller these differences are lost: a tree is a tree to him all the same whether it has round or involuted leaves. Instead of speaking of the fragrance of the firs or lindens, he brings in more general conceptions; he knows shady, wide-spreading, firm, deeply-rooted, cloud-piercing, lightning-shivered trees, but enlarges on no other distinctions. He removes us to such a distance that botanical details disappear, and we see only great masses before us. It is the impression of the scene as a whole which remains; and such is the effect of his works. It is comparatively indifferent to him what the solitary reader who approaches his work closely, with refined perceptions, may think of it: he wishes to thrill masses of readers, and the individual interests him only so far as he is a part of them. Schiller would inspire a whole nation with a power which unites and an enthusiasm which elevates them: his public shall be counted by thousands. Goethe was always satisfied to have a few friends who understood him; and it was indifferent to him who afterwards shared in the enjoyment. One might apply to Goethe the illustration he himself makes use of in "Wilhelm Meister," — " He went out to seek

SCHILLER AND GOETHE COMPARED. 359

his father's asses, and found a kingdom." All Goethe's works arose in this way,— their extraordinary popularity came unexpectedly; and where it seemed as if he had reckoned upon it, as in " Werther," the anticipation has more the character of a childlike, joyous impatience than a man's sober calculations based on a clear knowledge of his public. When, on the other hand, Schiller won kingdoms, he had had them clearly in his eye from the outset. Read his correspondence with Cotta: he is always full of enormous undertakings, many volumes, contributors, great advertisements, vast profits, and a distinct plan, with estimates beforehand of all the chances. Schiller was a poet and man of letters in the sense of Voltaire. He sees that he needs a faction; he coins his gold, not into medals, like Goethe, but into ready money which is thrown upon the market by millions.

In Goethe's poems we feel with every lightest breath from whence it comes; we are fanned by the air of the south and the strong sea-breeze which blows over the Greek Sea to " Iphigenia; " we catch the fragrance of the laurel hedges and the orange groves of Ferrara; we inhale pure draughts of the Rhine-valley air as we read Goethe's letters about the Strasburg Cathedral. In Schiller we feel only the dynamic power of the storm, all the same whether the wind comes from the north or the south. Goethe's poems were occasional: his fruits ripened in proportion to the sun that shone on them. Schiller had no time to wait for that: he built a hot-house to protect his fruit-trees in rough weather, that there might be no interruption in their growth, and heated it up when the sun did not shine.

Schiller demanded freedom. He forced his sickly body: the spirit should have complete control over his intellectual working-power. With him was no hesitation, no patient waiting till the hand of Fate beckoned him on, none of the somnambulism of Goethe: he tore off recklessly the fetters which bound him to real life. Hence in youth his wild conduct, — debts, flight, the notion of being ill-treated and hunted down by barbarous Fate; the restless search for human sympathy; the clinging to the first persons who offer him friendship. Goethe's antechamber was always full of people: he needed only to beckon, and they burst through the doors to greet him; if he felt lonely, it was only a question of satisfying the higher claims he made in his intercourse with men. Schiller, on the other hand, was bitterly destitute and forsaken; he looks down the long streets in which there is no one who troubles himself about him; he offers his hat to Fortune, and accepts gratefully the poorest coins she drops into it. In Dresden there was one Councillor Körner, with his wife and sister, — good, honest, educated, enthusiastic people: they feel impelled to write to Schiller. How eagerly we see him snatch at this! how thirstily he puts the proffered wine to his lips! A sincere friendship springs up, and the people who had very little to spare lend him money.

This was not the way to win Goethe. Long before he had arrived at Schiller's time of life, he knew all the wines in the cellar of mankind, and tasted carefully ere he drank. Goethe might go comfortably from one place to another, while Schiller was shoved by Fate from spot to spot. He flies from the service of a tyrannical prince; does not find a new home in Mannheim; goes into the country, where he is hospitably received; on to Leipsic, Dresden, everywhere pursued by debts, and reaches Weimar finally, with nothing but an empty title conferred upon him by the Duke, just to try if he can maintain himself there. Always the same old story: work from day to day, in order to live; oppressed by debt, conscious of having made his poor, cramped family more wretched by his desertion; tired out and discouraged in the vain attempt to find men such as he had dreamed of.

Only one thing sustains him, — the consciousness of a mighty power of achievement. It became almost indifferent to Schiller at last for what he used his pen, — whether in the direction of History or Poetry; he knew that whenever he willed it he could write something which would be sure to be a success. Well might he be proud of this, and count himself among the great of the earth!

He cherished only one grand expectation, — the meeting with Goethe, whose return was looked for and talked of by every one at the time Schiller settled in Weimar. Whatever Goethe did formed the subject of first and greatest interest to the Weimar people; but no one knew when his return would be. Everybody missed him, even those who did not confess it. From Schiller's letters we learn what barren ground Weimar was after Goethe turned his back upon it. He pictures the society there, describes the distinguished people with whom he became acquainted, the houses at which he visited. Like Goethe on his first coming, Schiller also found himself in horrible loneliness, — only that his work burned under his fingers, and his money often slipped away, even to the last groschen. What more natural than the thought that all this would be changed for the better as soon as Goethe returned? We see how eagerly he looks out for news of him. He considers himself of significance enough to suppose that Goethe is stirred with some desire to meet him.

Schiller had already seen Goethe, — when, on the Swiss journey with the Duke, in the year 1779, he had touched at Stuttgard. Schiller, a charity scholar, standing among the others, saw Goethe pass by him in the stiff costume prescribed by the court. Goethe was at that time at the height of his youthful renown: he made a great impression upon Schiller. The next year, upon the birthday of his patron, "Clavigo" was performed by the pupils of the Karl-school, and Schiller played Clavigo. At that time he was twenty-one years of age, and had just finished "The Robbers." In the same year he was made surgeon of a regiment; and in the midst of the maddest life the printing of "The Robbers" was begun on borrowed money.

Schiller dreamed of no Goethean career. He never expected to become the friend of a prince or a companion of nobles: he simply wanted to write for the stage; would descend into the arena and fight his way to the great public. No quiet pressure of the hand here and there for him; but clapping, weeping, trembling on all sides, should attest his success! When Schiller ran away, the stage was his natural aim; and in becoming a stage-writer he considered himself to have taken the first step towards attaining the object of his ambition. But the illusion did not last long, and blow upon blow followed the disappointments in the life he had so eagerly adopted.

In 1785 Schiller had become acquainted with Carl August in Darmstadt, when Goethe was not with the Duke. Up to that time he had published "The Robbers," "Fiesco," and "Cabal and Love." He read aloud to the Duke the first act of "Don Carlos," and had a conversation with him; and for this the title of "Councillor of the Duke of Weimar" was awarded him.

We are not told whether this matter passed through Goethe's hands.

SCHILLER FINDS A HOME IN WEIMAR.

After this, in the April of 1785, Schiller, on his way to Leipsic, finished at Gohlis the "Don Carlos," and, as he could not support himself there, sought in September a home with his friend Körner in Dresden. From Dresden, in July, 1787, he went to Weimar, and had been there a full year before Goethe returned.

LECTURE XIX.

SCHILLER AND GOETHE. — THEIR ESTRANGEMENT.

ON the 18th of June, 1788, at ten o'clock in the evening, just as the full moon was rising, Goethe once more arrived in Weimar, — "the aristocratic Roman," as Herder said. We see how a demon put something insulting into the mouth of this man at the very moment when he most heartily revered Goethe. Herder called Goethe's letters "great dishes with broad edges and trifling contents." Herder best knew how little Goethe pretended to be "aristocratic," and just now when his longing for his friends had brought him back how very much he preferred being a Weimarian to a Roman.

Schiller was at that time in the country at Folkstädt near Rudolstadt. He had become acquainted with the Lengefelds, and for the first time, after the homelessness of his whole life, thoughts began to dawn upon him of making a home of his own. Nothing more bleak and sterile could be imagined than the circumstances by which he was surrounded at that time. The letters written to Körner at this period are the saddest and the most despairing he ever wrote. This explains the rapture he felt at the hearty fraternal reception given him by the family of Lengefeld.

A week before Goethe's arrival in Weimar, Schiller had sent Körner word from Folkstädt that Goethe was expected. "We are eager to know whether he will remain." July 3, some time after Goethe's appearance in Weimar, Schiller, still at Folkstädt, writes to Körner: "Goethe has now been in Weimar a fortnight. They find him little changed. What further will become of him no one knows." Again, three weeks later, July 27: "I have heard nothing from Weimar for some weeks; but one of these days Frau von Stein will come, who will give me an account of Goethe." This sounds quite unconcerned; but one feels how Schiller is trying to restrain himself in writing Körner: nevertheless in the postscript his excitement breaks out: "I am very curious about him — about Goethe; in truth at bottom I like him, and there are few whose mind I so reverence; perhaps he will come hither, at least as far as Kochberg, a short mile from here, where Frau von Stein has a country house." The style here betrays at every turn Schiller's feeling. "Curious" should be "burning with impatience;" curiosity indicates intense expectation, but with composure; curiosity, moreover, says that an unbiassed criticism is reserved; and lastly curiosity excludes all idea of inferiority. Further, "at bottom I like him" is as much as to say: "I vacillate in a way inexplicable to myself between like and dislike;" and when he speaks of revering Goethe's mind, it shows that any opinion of his heart, temperament, and whatever else constitutes personality is withheld. From this last sentence we see with what certainty he anticipated a meeting with him, and an eventful one; and from his putting all this into a postscript that he had tried carefully not to say a word about it to Körner, and that almost against his will it had overflowed from his pen at last.

Schiller admired Goethe; he fully appreciated both his intrinsic superiority and his immense influence over others. That a man like Goethe should come to Weimar without taking any notice of Schiller was, all things considered, inconceivable; but if it proved so, Schiller felt that he would be obliged for the sake of his own reputation to take a decided stand. Schiller was a writer who understood his trade perfectly. To bow before Goethe, to make the first advances, would not have been hard for him; but who would guarantee how Goethe would accept this? And therefore nothing remained for him but, setting aside all personal like or dislike, to make clear to himself how he was to maintain his position.

Things, however, turned out quite differently. Since nothing was heard from Goethe, Schiller secretly within himself began to capitulate. His letters to Körner show this; if Goethe had gone to Kochberg, Schiller would have had no objection to presenting himself there also. They would then have come from different sides to meet each other. But Goethe did not go to Kochberg; and truly Schiller, less than almost any one else, could suspect the reason why,—for how could he, waiting in Folkstädt, know what had occurred during his absence between Goethe and Frau von Stein?

From their first meeting, Frau von Stein had noticed the change that had come over Goethe. She did not understand it, and indeed how could it be anything but incomprehensible to her? Goethe's letters had kept up the fiction of the old intimacy; and now he was at her side cold, constrained, evasive, reserved, and disinclined to talk freely on any subject. Frau von Stein did not know that, in scarcely three weeks after his return, Christiane had already taken possession of Goethe. This relation was at first veiled in the deepest secrecy. Some poems in trochaic measure, which more than any other seems fitted to express love and longing, contain the idealized story of his clandestine intercourse with Christiane, — how he went to her, how she came to him, how he expected her! All his thoughts were given to this beautiful maiden. Finally Frau von Stein could bear the restraint no longer, and attempted by force to wring from him an explanation. But Goethe knew how to evade it. A week before Schiller's tidings to Körner that Goethe was expected in Kochberg, he had sent a note to Frau von Stein ending with the following: "I may truly say that my innermost condition does not correspond to my outward behavior." We see that Goethe realized himself how inexplicable his conduct must appear to Frau von Stein; that he not only declines to explain it, but is satisfied with writing a sentence, by way of excuse, in which he clearly enough signifies that on the matter in question he is resolved to remain silent. This was too much for Frau von Stein, and she left Weimar. Goethe certainly had no intention now to follow her to Kochberg; and, so far as Schiller was concerned, it only occasionally entered Goethe's mind that such a person was in the world. He lived in recollections of Italy, wrote on the "Tasso," confined himself in secret to Christiane, who was the confidant of his botanical studies, and sought "to live on in this way in Weimar, although it was indeed a curious task." A letter to Frau von Stein, July 22, betrays his state of mind: "May you," he concludes, "in quiet Kochberg, be contented and remarkably well." It would have been impossible for him ten years earlier to have approached his beloved friend with such a stereotyped phrase, which indeed implies the secret wish that Frau von Stein may as long as possible find herself contented and well away from Weimar. And therefore Frau von Stein had long been in Kochberg when Schiller wrote to Körner that she was expected; but Goethe did not follow her.

Schiller waits a month, and again in a letter written at the end of August Goethe is spoken of: —

"I have not yet seen Goethe, but greetings have been exchanged between us. He would have visited me on his route to Weimar had he known that I was so near. We were within an hour of one another. It is said he is not devoting himself to bnsiness affairs at all. The Duchess has gone to Italy, but Goethe remains in Weimar. I am impatient to see him."

Schiller had considered the matter so much that he stops with the simple truth contained in this last sentence.

And now, at last, this impatience was to be relieved. Goethe in the beginning of September appeared in Rudolstadt, at the house of Frau von Lengefeld, afterward Schiller's mother-in-law.

Herder's wife, Frau von Stein, and her mother Frau von Schardt were there, beside the three Lengefeld ladies, — the mother, Lottchen, later Schiller's wife, and the sister Caroline von Wolzogen, or von Beulwitz (which was her name by her first marriage at that time), who later became Schiller's biographer.

In Schiller's imagination Goethe was still the same being he had seen ten years before, for the first and only time in Stuttgart, " when he had devoured him with his eyes." September 12, he writes to Körner: —

"At last I can tell you of Goethe, about whom I know you are eager to hear. I spent nearly the whole of last Monday in his company, when he visited us, with Herder's wife, Frau von Stein, and Frau von Schardt. The first look at him disappointed the high conception I had been led to form of this attractive and handsome man. He is of middle height, with a stiff carriage and bearing. His face is not an open one; but his eyes are animated and full of expression, and his

FIRST MEETING OF SCHILLER AND GOETHE.

glance is captivating. Though there is much seriousness in his mien, it is still full of goodness and benevolence. He has a brunette complexion, and seemed to me to look older than he is, according to my calculation. His voice is extremely agreeable. He is fluent, and when in good humor, as was specially the case this day, talks willingly and with interest. We soon became acquainted, and without the least effort: indeed, the party was too large and each one too jealously intent on being near him to admit of our being much alone, or talking of anything beyond the subjects of general interest. He speaks gladly, and with passionate longing, of Italy. What he has told me has given me most striking and vivid pictures of this country and its people."

Here we see again how much the style betrays Schiller's thoughts. We feel the intention to write justly and free from prejudice, but that a feeling of deep disappointment and depression gains the mastery. Schiller had believed that something special would be the result of this meeting. Instead of that, it had passed off quite indifferently. Körner did not reply to this part of the letter, and only remarked, not without a certain satisfaction it would seem: "Goethe's meeting with you turned out much as I thought it would. Time will show whether you will yet come nearer to one another. Friendship I do not expect, but friction and mutual interest." In Goethe's letters written at this time we find no allusion to this meeting. Schiller is referred to only once, and then his name is purposely withheld.

The occasion for this reference to him, however, was not insignificant.

There had appeared at this time a new volume of Goethe's collected works, which contained "Egmont." "Egmont," begun in Frankfort, and continued from time to time in Weimar, gained a new form in Rome,—the only one in which we know it, for no portion of the earlier manuscript has ever been published. It would seem as if in the Frankfort version of it the Bürger element in the politics of the time, and the relation between Clara and Brackenburg, had stood more in the foreground. But this is mere guesswork. Whether the Regent first came into the piece in Weimar, suggested by the Duchess-dowager, and other questions, we leave here untouched: only this we know, that even Clärchen in the finished manuscript, which was sent from Rome to Weimar to be printed, found no favor, and Goethe had to defend the character.

Goethe's new volume had been sent to Schiller for criticism, and he went at the work. Not long after this first meeting with Goethe his article appeared, and like every literary production at that time made much talk.

Goethe read the criticism. He was again reminded that his day was over, and that the time had come in which, as he says himself, "the German public knew nothing more of him." A new generation had sprung up for whom Goethe's subtile heroes no longer possessed anything heroic.

Egmont may be called the tenderly-nurtured aristocratic twin brother of Götz von Berlichingen,—a man who follows implicitly the dictates of his own noble nature, which becomes the ruler of his destiny. He allows the impulses of the moment to decide for him: he is passive in the sense of passive nature. Egmont is like a luxuriant fruit-tree which has no protection against a sudden chill in spring, which freezes all its young shoots. Götz and Egmont offer themselves to Fate, and accept good or bad weather without murmuring. In this unconditional submission to the bias of their nature lies the tragic element. This moving on through life as in a dream is the ever-recurring theme in all the poems of Goethe's earlier years. His heroes are at the same time free and not free, both in the highest measure and finest manifestation. This mixture of freedom and servitude is the old eternal problem to which the thoughts of mankind have ever been directed; this mingling of *would* and *must*, for which man will never find an exhaustive formula.

Goethe felt himself to be the most excellent representative of this antagonism, and he was always personifying himself in this aspect, with the hope of finding a solution. In Götz we see the highest patriotism, demanding his submission to the laws of the country, united with an individual self-reliance which scoffs at all laws; in Tasso an almost sacred regard for the wishes of the Duke, who in the sixteenth century was looked upon as a kind of demigod, combined with the most heedless neglect of the duties imposed by his position whenever distrust arises in him or caprice turns him aside from them; in Egmont the grand self-reliance of a free Netherland nobleman, who is the representative of his people, together with the impossibility of sacrificing his individual untrammelled life or his child-like enjoyment of existence to political considerations. Egmont's tragic death must be the conclusion.

But so far as this inward conflict was concerned "Götz" had been no better understood by the public. People had recognized enthusiastically in this work a genuine picture of German nature,—the sincerity, the confiding honesty, the imperturbable good-tempered robustness of Götz, and in contrast to this the wretchedness of court life visible in all its worst results in Weislingen; added to this the life-like, spirited sketches of the women about Götz and their simple goodness as contrasted with Adelheid. So far as these same elements are found in "Egmont" they certainly were appreciated if only as reminders of "Götz," and the "Folk" scenes were declared to be most successful *genre* pictures; but here also ruled the distinction between the approbation of the few and the enthusiastic applause of the many. The unknown author of "Götz" had been greeted with acclamation as a savior in time of great literary dearth; while the known and renowned author of "Egmont" was given to understand that on certain conditions his work would be allowed to pass. For the first time this was said openly in Goethe's face, and without any varnish; and moreover in Weimar and by Schiller, and by way of welcome! Schiller's milder tone at the long-deferred meeting with Goethe possibly arose from the kind of melancholy satisfaction he felt at having already finished his harsh and independent criticism of "Egmont." It contained his programme. It was to suggest a great deal to Goethe. The leading idea in the essay was that Goethe had become historical in Germany; this further was ascertained, that younger writers were in existence who considered themselves the men of the future, and that they now — as Goethe had formerly done in the "Frankfort Anzeiger" — must take the liberty frankly to call to account the older generation and give them a piece of their mind. It is true, Goethe was certainly the most brilliant representative of this older generation, as Schiller was the authorized mouth-piece of the younger, and as such they hoped to have with Goethe the intercourse of like with like. If Goethe were a power, they on their side were not altogether powerless; if he avoided them, they would not seek him, — all were of equal importance; and if anybody was inclined to think there was any difference in rank, they did not share in this opinion.

It is not difficult to read these hints between the lines in Schiller's criticism of "Egmont." Schiller proves to Goethe with the professional knowledge of a trained author that he has failed in his treatment of Egmont. He does not spare him an historical lecture in relation to it. The actual Egmont had been a high-born, impecunious gentleman, the father of a family, who never confronted King Philip in any such way as Goethe describes him to have done. The whole weight of the hackneyed argument, as to how far it is necessary that historical heroes should correspond to the originals whose names they take, is brought to bear upon the piece, and everything concerning politics is expunged as being an utter failure. On the other hand (and this too was in the spirit of the times), high praise is bestowed on the popular element in it, and Goethe at last coolly dismissed. To be sure, Schiller awards him *magna cum laude* as the homage deserved, but with the hint that *summa cum laude* must this time be decidedly withheld.

But now that we may see Schiller exactly as he was, we must add that when this criticism was published (which was shortly after his meeting with Goethe), in the September of 1788, some one told him that Goethe had spoken in praise of it, and Schiller believed this! All the innocence and simplicity of the man is here revealed! He truly thought " Egmont " a weak production, and gave Goethe the credit of being able to see it in this light.

We have only one single allusion by Goethe to Schiller's article. Early in October he writes to the Duke that there is a criticism in the literary paper on his " Egmont," which analyzes well the political part of the work; but with regard to the poetic the critic might have left it to others to say something.

And here, too, the style betrays clearly enough what Goethe felt. If we supply what can be read between the lines, the letter to the Duke runs thus: " This political writer made by your Highness a Weimar Councillor, and living now only three doors from me, whose name I need not mention, has proved his gratitude to your Highness and to me at the same time, by passing sentence on my 'Egmont.' So far as concerns the political wisdom now prevailing in Germany, he may be right; but as regards poetry, he does not understand anything at all about it."

No fictitious letter is needed, however, to prove that this was Goethe's real opinion of Schiller at this time: he gives expression to it in other places in words not to be mistaken.

At the time of Schiller's death, some seventeen years later, — when feeling in his heart an indescribable void he repeats the circumstances of his connection with the dear friend from the beginning,— Goethe recounts how changed he had found everything in Germany on his return from Italy; how Schiller next to Heinse, whose "Ardinghello" was at that time devoured, stood as the most distinguished representative of a tendency which he condemned; how the enthusiasm which "The Robbers" excited shocked him; and how his firm intention had been either not to meet this man at all, or, if a meeting proved unavoidable, to limit the acquaintance as much as possible. Goethe was a hero in holding aloof from people, and in maintaining his reserve.

Now we see what was in store for Schiller on his return from the country late in the autumn. I have just mentioned into what an error he had been led about the reception of his criticism of "Egmont." He came back therefore with the definite expectation that his relation to Goethe must now assume a pronounced character. The old self-confidence was still strong in him. Soon, however, it dawns upon him how the matter really stands.

SCHILLER'S CALL TO JENA.

We read in his first letter to Körner: "Goethe is away on a journey of some days. It is now quite settled that he is to remain here, but in a private capacity. His chair still stands in the council indeed, but he himself has as good as withdrawn." For a fortnight Schiller writes nothing special to Körner, and in the letter of the first of December Goethe is not even mentioned. November 27, Schiller had written to Caroline von Beulwitz: " I have not yet spoken with Goethe, but one of these days I shall." Would Schiller seek him, or did he hope to meet him somewhere? Enough, neither of the two happened, and we nowhere learn why not.

In the mean time Goethe had long returned, and begins on his side and in his way to interest himself about Schiller. He should be cared for who was living in Weimar without a salary: the discussion of Schiller's call to Jena as professor came now upon the carpet.

Eichhorn had been called from there to Göttingen and had accepted, and Goethe recommended Schiller to fill his place. We have Goethe's *promemoria*, dated December 3, 1788, concerning Schiller's appointment. Goethe pursues this matter so very much as an outside interest that he wastes no words over it in his letter, written in the midst of cold and deep snow, to Herder, who was at that time in Rome. Schiller, although he had applied for the place himself, when he found things taking the desired course, had a feeling creep into his mind that he was being overreached, — or, in other words, that Goethe had hit upon an honorable way of removing him from Weimar.

However, Schiller had desired it, and nothing remained for him but to express his obligation to the " Herr Geheimrath" for the support granted ; and he calls upon Goethe to present his thanks in due form. About this visit we hear nothing in the letters, but it seems at last to have opened his eyes.

Schiller is formally announced at Goethe's house; but he hopes, nevertheless, to be received by the poet as a poet. The coadjutor of Mentz, Baron von Dalberg,— who, still governor, resided in Erfurt, an intimate friend of Schiller as well as of Goethe, not a power as a politician, but a patron of art and science, and one of the infinitely good-hearted men, — had taken steps with Goethe to open a successful approach for Schiller. Schiller writes to Caroline von Beulwitz with some certainty that in this visit to Goethe, "who indeed was rarely to be found alone," he hopes " to find some refreshment for mind and heart, and not merely to have a chance to look at Goethe." This proclaims beforehand the intention to make an assault on Goethe's heart. But in vain. Schiller finds only the Prime Minister, his official superior, who concentrates himself on the case in question, and admits nothing beyond the Jena professorship. Schiller hesitates about accepting it, and enlarges on his great deficiencies. Goethe encourages him with *docendo discitur*, and says, in the most benevolent way, that the position will contribute much to Schiller's happiness. The 15th of December he sends him the official papers, wherein Schiller is directed to prepare himself for the professor's chair. It would seem as if Schiller once again called on Goethe, " who had indeed been very kind;" but certainly this was the last visit. Even when " Don Carlos " had anew turned the thoughts of all Germany to Schiller, Goethe cared as little to know anything of the piece as of his former productions, and Schiller saw nothing further was to be expected from Goethe.

Truly pitiful is it now to observe that Schiller, as time went on, — for he did not go immediately from Weimar to

Jena,—could not bear this ill-treatment; pitiful, when we think how in later times Goethe would have given his life for one more day with Schiller. Through a peculiar combination of circumstances at this time Schiller saw himself absolutely cut off from further intercourse with Goethe.

One of those who belonged to the circle of Goethe's most intimate friends in Rome was Moritz. Moritz wrote his own life in the form of a romance, "Anton Reiser," which is still worth reading. He had succeeded in raising himself out of the most wretched circumstances. He will ever deserve praise for having written excellent German prose, and for his theory of German versification, which, as Goethe declares, rendered him the greatest service in the remodelling "Iphigenia." Moritz brought the cadence of the verse into harmony with the meaning of the words, and moulded into a theory what Klopstock had first practically introduced. He found for a language which has no quantities a theory of accentuation which established "intellectual" long and short *quantities*, and thus rendered possible an imitation of the antique metres in German, in the classic sense, and according to fixed principles. Moritz's letters from Italy, written in the Goethean epoch, form an interesting supplement to the "Italian Journey," before whose publication they were issued. Moritz, on his return from Italy, came to Weimar and stayed with Goethe in the December of 1788.

With him Schiller now became acquainted. "Moritz is powerfully impressed with Goethe's personality," he writes. "His nature has much depth; his mind labors: but he works out his ideas with the utmost possible clearness." Goethe himself, however, has told us that it was Moritz who confirmed him passionately in opinions which excited him against Schiller. It appears that Moritz drew everything out of Schiller, and reported all to Goethe in the most unfavorable light. At any rate, Moritz and Schiller met often at that time, and Goethe's character was the theme ever freshly and hotly discussed between them. There was nothing illegitimate in it; either in that Moritz himself entered into the discussions, or that he repeated them to Goethe. Indeed, so long as Moritz remained in Weimar — from December, 1788, to 1789 — this intercourse formed a kind of compensation to Schiller for actual acquaintance with Goethe; since he could, at least, talk freely about him to one who knew him intimately, — for the weight of the mere presence of Goethe brought him constantly before the minds of men as an object of contemplation. But now Moritz goes away, and even this substitute for an intercourse with Goethe is lost to Schiller. Nothing remains to him but the correspondence with Körner, in which he begins to give vent to his injured feelings in the bitterest tone.

The first of February, 1789, he writes to Körner: —

"To-day Moritz went away again. He is a profound thinker, who goes into the depths of things before bringing them to the surface. The idolatry with which he follows Goethe, which leads him so far as to canonize even his mediocre productions, and extol them at the expense of all other intellectual work, has prevented my closer intimacy with him. Otherwise he is a very noble man, with a drollery that makes his conversation entertaining.

"To be often with Goethe would make me unhappy: he never for a moment overflows even to his nearest friends, and is never to be caught unawares. I truly believe he is an egoist to an unusual degree. He possesses the talent to attract men, and, through little as well as great attentions, to make them indebted to him. Still he understands at the same time how to retain his own independence. He makes his presence beneficently felt, but only like a god, — without giving himself. This conduct seems to me consistent and systematic, and calculated to insure the highest enjoyment of self-love. But of such a character men should not make an idol. To me he is hateful in this regard, although I love his genius with my whole heart, and have an exalted idea of him. I consider him a prude. . . .

"He has aroused in me a perfectly curious mixture of hatred and love, — a feeling not unlike that which Brutus and Cassius must have had for Cæsar. I could murder his spirit, and love him again with my whole heart. It is chiefly for Goethe's sake that I wish to make my poem as perfect as possible; for I attach the greatest weight to his opinion. The 'Gods of Greece' he judged very favorably, only he found it too long, in which he may not be far from right. His mind is ripe, and his opinion, if he has any bias, rather against than in favor of me. As it is of special importance to me to hear the truth of myself, he is among all the men whom I know the one who can do me this favor. I will surround him with eavesdroppers; for I myself shall never ask him any personal questions."

We see Goethe had driven Schiller beside himself. There could have been no more severe torture devised for a man with Schiller's self-esteem than to live in such propinquity to Goethe; to hear of him constantly; to acknowledge him secretly as the greatest poet, the critic from whom there was no appeal, — and to be repulsed by him like a leper! The most stinging thing in the letter to Körner has plainly been left out. After the sentence, "I consider him a prude," we find even in Goedeke's last edition the mark of omission still placed; we suspect that what he said will not even to-day bear repetition.

Over the possible contents of this dropped-out phrase suspicion, nevertheless, need not range far: a letter in the beginning of March expresses the bitterness which filled Schiller's heart:—

"I must laugh when I reflect what I have written you of and about Goethe. I dare say you have probed my weakness, and already laughed at me in secret. But never mind: I am willing you should know me as I am. This man, this Goethe, is an impediment in my way; and he too often reminds me how cruelly I have been treated by Fate, how easily Destiny has led on his genius, and how I have had to struggle even to this minute. I cannot repair all I have lost, — after thirty one does not change; and, indeed, I could not attempt any radical transformations at the present time, since I must sacrifice four more years at least to relentless fate. But I am of good courage, and believe in a happy revolution in the future."

This, then, was the summary: an almost blighted youth; and now when the terminus had been reached where recompense for all these losses was to have been expected, — now, too, only wretched necessary work, just to win daily bread and cancel old debts! And close to him the great genius whose animating intercourse would have been able to fill this monstrous void in his life, but who coldly and indifferently passed him by! The subject of Goethe should henceforth be a closed one to Schiller.

Easter, 1789, Schiller went to Jena.

The Jena University work on the one hand, and his happy marriage with Lotte Lengefeld on the other, now absorbed him for a while. At the end of September, 1789,— a year after first meeting Goethe there, — he writes to Körner from Rudolstadt about Goethe and Herder, with whom Körner in the mean time, without Schiller, had come into close contact. A situation had been offered Körner in Weimar, and it was now Schiller's turn to prophesy the nature of the meeting which awaited him there with these two great men. Schiller writes: —

"As for you, I hope you will soon be able to value your acquaintance with Goethe and Herder for what it is really worth; but, with all your caution, you will not escape the common fate which meets every one who becomes attached to these two men."

Which means that Körner will at first be captivated, and then one day, in the most cruel manner, find himself out in the cold, abandoned to his own resources.

These and other assertions, too often repeated to make it necessary for me to quote more here, show how wide the breach was between the two poets.

Schiller's letters are of most striking importance, as showing how difficult — indeed, almost impossible — it is to judge great men rightly through their relations to one another. Let us ponder it. Five years this estrangement continued, during which time neither of the two was able to see the other in the right light. Suppose now that Schiller or Goethe, one of the two, had died during these five years, — would not these merciless judgments of Schiller, repeatedly and passionately uttered, have clung to Goethe like a stigma forever? Would they not have brought Goethe's whole moral nature in question, and shrouded him as with a hoar-frost which no breath would have been warm enough to dispel? Would any one have had the courage to assert, in face of these numerous letters of Schiller, that he was blinded, unjust, and prejudiced? Would any admirer of Goethe have stood any chance at all of being listened to, if he had suggested that had Schiller or Goethe lived they would have discovered how very much they were both deceived? Who would have been allowed to establish such an hypothesis? And yet we know to-day that each was persuaded of this at last.

It must be regarded as one of the happiest dispensations of Providence that, in spite of all that lay between them, Schiller and Goethe nevertheless were finally brought together.

LECTURE XX.

GOETHE'S SECLUSION. — THE UNION WITH SCHILLER. —
SCHILLER'S WIFE.

BY the admittance of the Vulpius family into his house, Goethe had shut himself off from the Weimar world. It is scarcely necessary to recount in what way the rupture with Frau von Stein followed. As the misunderstanding between them grew more and more trying, and the secret cause of it by degrees came to light, Goethe wrote the notorious farewell letter upon whose reception the old friend must have felt that she was dismissed. However much might be said which would mitigate certain details in this letter, the letter itself cannot be denied, nor the want of consideration manifested in it. A hard letter! A formidable historical memento for all women in like relations! Let us picture to ourselves Charlotte von Stein's situation.

For more than ten years made by Goethe the arbitress of his fate and of his intellectual achievements; with unvarying fidelity surrounded by no end of flattering proofs of his care, and above all supplied with whatever new things appeared in the literary horizon; all her best faculties developed by him; raised to be the envied participator in his mental life, — of all this she sees herself, wholly unprepared and without any apparent fault of her own, suddenly deprived, and cast down from her exalted position into a gloomy void which she could never fill by any effort of her own. Goethe had insensibly persuaded her that his attachment to her would never cease, at least as a matter of sentiment; and now, to break away from her in such a shameful way! — for she not only felt herself dethroned, but was shocked at the person she saw in her place. At the same time, Charlotte von Stein must say to herself that a Nemesis was hidden in it, — or she ought to have confessed this. She should not have accepted his fruitless homage, nor have permitted him to be so constantly near her through the years when he, otherwise, might have founded his own household. Possibly she was the chief cause why Goethe, satiated with the delicacies on the table of life which leave the heart hungry, had now taken a great loaf of wholesome brown bread under his arm, from which he could take a bite *ad libitum* and continue to cut at many a meal-time. However this may be, the decision had been made. Goethe's door was bolted, and remained so. He gives parties, where ladies are invited; but they are not introduced into his family circle, and from this time he is to the world bachelor *ad infinitum*. The man who had really the most aristocratic house in the city was no longer a desirable match at the disposition of the Weimar world. Society resents such things.

Moreover, Goethe had, by repelling Schiller, put himself out of connection with the rising literary interests. At that period a keener and more active spirit was dominant in literature; formerly there had only been cliques, now we see the beginning of factions. Goethe fancied that he had quietly passed from an active to a contemplative life, but his publishers soon perceived that the complete edition of his works was not to be a success. The collection of his poems, which Goethe now offered Germany for the first time, met, as Düntzer said, a very cold reception. The reviews did not go beyond polite recognition, and the public just accepted them without manifesting the slightest enthusiasm. This did not vex Goethe: he was fully occupied. He worked on his poems according to his own idea, and with the purpose to finish what he had begun. With "Tasso," and what beside interested him, he scarcely gave a thought to the *great* public. Even when he had written from Italy to the Duke about "Egmont," he had said: "I would now write only what men who lead, or have led, great and exciting lives may — yes, must — read." We see his circle of readers so very much limited by his own ideal, that it no longer deserves the name of "the public."

Finally, Goethe had ostensibly resigned his official duties: he appeared no longer in the Council Chamber.

Goethe established himself in Weimar anew in a private capacity. The Ten Years were added to the mythic Frankfort period, and a new account opened. Goethe's interest in public affairs is now directed to the fostering of science. There grew out of his strivings, in the *dilettante* fashion of Lavater, an earnest study of anatomy and osteology. Botany and geology had long been his favorite pursuits, and he now follows them up with the thoroughness and accuracy of a patient scholar. The history of Art, since his visit to Italy, was like a rich garden adjacent to his own house, enticing him to constant and indispensable labor. Goethe was convinced that the works of representative art are more trustworthy historical material than is offered by historical writers, who, with the best intention, are apt to produce only myths of their own creating. Likewise, his relation to philology and the history of literature took a wholly new form after he had discerned and acknowledged the essential importance of Greek and Roman culture, which he recognized as the basis of all education, and at once made himself the champion of this truth. I have before said that it seemed as if Goethe founded an invisible University in Weimar, where he filled every department himself, — rector, professor in all the Faculties, private tutor, pupil, and beadle; everything revolves about him, and he cares for everything separately.

Rarely has such comprehensive scientific work been undertaken, in such an earnest way, as was now begun by him. Only to a power like Goethe's was it possible to labor so ardently in wholly diverse directions, and to prosecute with such concentration enterprises involving such entirely different results. His freshly gained knowledge began to be productive in leading him either to take an active part in scientific investigations, or to serve the public whenever explanatory criticism was demanded. This scientific labor made his connection with Jena more and more intimate. I close this survey by giving as the sum of what he achieved during the first few years after his return from Italy, that Goethe succeeds in establishing himself as the integral member of the Weimar government, in a position at once in consonance with the essential requirements of the Duke, the interests of the country, and his personal wishes. He raises himself to the rank of Chancellor of State for the sake of its opportunity of conferring appointments, and opens to himself a vast sphere for independent personal activity, in which he could turn his energy now here, now there, as suited his inclination. And all these relations were matured as naturally and imperceptibly as apples ripen on the tree without artificial aid. Goethe feels that he is a man of forty, equips himself as suitably as possible for the coming years, and moves on with the firm step of a man who is conscious that he is fulfilling his destiny. The city of Weimar is no longer, as in the times of Frau von Stein, the only spot on earth to him, but a temporary abiding-place only, to which he returns from longer or shorter absences with the feeling that his movements are of no consequence to any one outside of his own family.

In order to make the background of this new life perfectly understood I add the following, — that from the time of his leaving Frankfort Goethe had ever, more and more, withdrawn from general society. He had gradually placed himself on the defensive, and manifested but little desire to continue his intercourse with his old friends. He picked out his associates very carefully, and allowed a certain tone of unapproachableness, not to say oddity, to become apparent in his manner. No doubt he many times coolly put the people out of doors who tried to clap him on the shoulder familiarly as in the good old days.

But this phase also passed away.

After Goethe had resigned the cordial intimacies which he had enjoyed during the Ten Years, he gave up all idea of friendship, and welcomed to his companionship only those from whom he expected furtherance in his aims. All mankind became transformed into an object deserving, in the highest degree, of study. Where there was anything to be learned, there Goethe was found. Instead of the passionate fancies or aversions of earlier days, a calm, scientific desire for every kind of knowledge made the acquisition of it equally grateful, whether derived from the printed page or through the medium of men. To this epoch of Goethe's life Emerson's words are applicable: " Enemy of him you may be, — if so, you shall teach him aught which your good-will cannot;" and therefore we see him renewing even discarded friendships with a certain cool graciousness: they belong to his great store in which no bit which is good for anything is to be allowed to become food for moths.

His friendships from this time have quite another character; and even when there is ostensible familiarity, it must not lead us to over-estimate them.

In youth, personal intimacy depends upon the influence one man's whole personality has over another's. What a man really is — his *character* — decides with whom he shall associate. I need not name single instances among Goethe's earlier attachments to prove this, for each and all confirm the truth of it. In later years, on the other hand, only specialties are valued in men, of which we take advantage for a time for a definite purpose, intentionally ignoring the sum total of the man himself. How else could we get on with people? Many of Goethe's new intimacies bear testimony to this.

With Moritz, for instance, there were certain clearly defined points which in his intercourse with this queer fellow Goethe kept ever in view, while the rest of his dark existence was ignored. In spite of this, we see Moritz in the closest relations with Goethe. In Rome Goethe sits by his sick-bed, and in Weimar takes him into his house. In the same way he treats Meyer, — the so-called "Kunst-Meyer," — who as Goethe's artistic aid-de-camp attaches himself to him, and ever after lives near him in Weimar, sometimes even in his house. But this intimacy also was limited to the province of art history. Goethe in his relation to this man and many others might be compared to a prince among his ministers, each of whom is restricted to his peculiar department. Goethe's associates — whether official, scientific, or social — from this time had each a programme prescribed which both parties were bound to carry out.

This, indeed, the so-much younger Schiller could not know, who appealed to the whole man in Goethe. He ought to have come ten years earlier, for this was one of the causes why Goethe could not be just to Schiller's claims. No wonder this change in Goethe's nature remained a mystery to Frau von Stein: formerly Goethe had given her the key to his pantry, while now he only doled out to her, as to others, the crumbs they needed. Christiane understood this, and never coveted the entrance to any apartments which Goethe preferred to keep locked against her. Even Herder could not interpret this change rightly, and from this time his friendship for Goethe slowly cooled again. Herder's wife could not bear Christiane; she defended the relation indeed, but talked of it without reserve.

The Duke alone fully understood Goethe, because he found himself in precisely the same case; for though Carl August was much younger, like all princes he had begun earlier to live. Between these two men we see the ever-enduring influence of character upon character. As genuine *grands seigneurs* they walked side by side, and the distance which separated them was exactly to their tastes. They interested themselves about each other only just so far as was consistent with keeping their affairs wholly distinct from each other; but they fully realized how useful they were one to the other. From friends Goethe and the Duke became allies. While all the world found fault with Goethe's lengthened absence in Italy, the Duke would generously have granted him even a longer furlough; and when Goethe returned, he helped him, in the same princely fashion, to create a new sphere of activity. In the beginning of 1790 he conferred upon him the supervision of all the provincial institutions for art and science. In the spring of 1790 he sent him as far as

Venice to meet the Duchess-dowager, who was then in Italy, and whom Goethe should have awaited there. This was Goethe's second Italian sojourn, at which time, in recollection of Christiane, the "Venetian Epigrams" were written. In the summer of the same year he accompanied the Duke to the Prussian manœuvres in Silesia, where, besides obtaining a knowledge of camp life, he made valuable scientific and official acquaintances, and the journey was extended as far as Galicia on account of its mines. About Goethe in Silesia we have a well-written monograph by Wentzel. In May, 1791, he became director of the Court Theatre, which had been newly established after the Belluomo *troupe* went to Göttingen for want of the necessary support in Weimar. For this theatre he furnishes a mass of dramatic material, — prologues, epilogues, interpolations, and original plays. He enters heart and soul into these new duties; decorations, costumes, rehearsals, care for the personal welfare of the actors, — all these matters are considered as if they were essentials in a large household, and to which he, the master, attended with painful conscientiousness.

In July, 1791, Goethe, with the Duchess-dowager, founded, under the name of the "Friday Receptions," the meetings at which cognizance was to be taken of all the latest ideas in science. In the summer of 1792 he follows the Duke to the French campaign. The fruit of this expedition, the description of the "campaign," is written in the most graphic style; and we hear of new acquaintances made, and of meetings with old friends. Meanwhile the rebuilding of his house is going on in Weimar. In 1793 he was at the siege of Mentz. At the end of this year the Duke leaves the Prussian service, and Weimar once more becomes the point of their mutual labors.

I forbear even to indicate the things in anything like

completeness. We may say of them what we said of
Schiller's experiences in early life, — all might have happened differently, or not at all: their value would have
been the same. But these excitements came opportunely
to an energetic nature, trying to stifle for a time the
consciousness that it lacked a special and ultimate aim
for its existence. The more common remedy for the
favored few, under such circumstances, is to divert themselves by travel. On the whole, the one thing to remember about this period — from 1790 to about 1793 — is
that it was of no special importance in Goethe's life.

Goethe had in these years what he wished and needed.
He had initiated a new life, and felt at home in it; he had
his daily tasks, enjoyed influence, consideration, and renown, and could quietly await the sequel, — if, indeed, he
gave at that time any special thought to the future. But
this existence lacked its evening glow, its supreme consecration. It seems to resolve itself into minutiæ. He
admits, with a certain cynical air, that he " has become
older," and " if he would be quite honest, he must confess
that with all his outward successes stagnation had set in."
" Egmont " and " Tasso " do not attract; and even the
beginning of " Faust " (finally printed in 1790), which
when read aloud to his friends had produced such an extraordinary effect, was allowed to pass almost unnoticed.
The " Roman Elegies " found no public, and a crowd of
other things which need not be mentioned here were
almost entirely overlooked; while the first part of the
" Theory of Colors " excited the disapprobation of the
professionals of that department by its mere title, —
" Contribution to Optics." All these were scattered
effusions of a writer whose final aims no one was able to
discover, and about whose future career there was no
further speculation. If Goethe, at the cannonade of

Valmy, had been struck by a ball, or in any other way taken from the world, his best friends would certainly have lamented his loss; but, while they must have acknowledged that he fully merited his poetical renown, they would have felt, as in the case of Lord Byron, that nothing greater than he had already written was to have been expected of him.

But such was not the will of Providence. The time had at last come when Goethe and Schiller were to look upon each other in a wholly new light. In speaking of Jacobi, I said that he and Goethe mingled like two seas. Goethe and Schiller were to unite like two rivers, to make one giant stream of mighty power. They now came together as naturally as they had before remained apart.

Schiller was settled in Jena. He was happily married, had enough to live on, devoted pupils, and worked uninterruptedly. His poetical effusions gave place to historical and æsthetic work; but respect for him as a writer grew visibly, and his ideas were always in unison with what at the time chiefly interested the world. His wife was one of the most intimate friends of Frau von Stein, and sympathized with her grief, which was kept alive by a memory of the past which consumed her and a present that preyed upon her. Goethe was regarded by this circle as a burned-out volcano, an extinguished star, the stately councillor with the double chin, an epicurean. We find his new works hardly alluded to in Schiller's letters.

So things stood, when Schiller on his wedding journey, in 1793, made the acquaintance of a man whose decisive influence on his later career is not to be mistaken, — the bookseller Cotta. The correspondence on both sides, which now lies printed before us, shows clearly the secret of Cotta's success, — a sagacity almost amounting to genius, which instantly discerned the vitality in all liter-

A NEW MAGAZINE — THE "HOURS." 393

ary undertakings; an equal cleverness, not only in finding the right people, but in holding them fast; and, so far as the matter of money was concerned, a generous patron. To-day, when conferring the title of nobility has become the common reward for commercial success, we must say that Cotta, through his grand business capacity, richly deserved his title of Baron.

With Cotta originated the idea of the Augsburg " Public Gazette." That a cool, judicious, business man like Cotta should recognize Schiller as the man who must be placed at the head of such an enterprise, with two thousand guilders at his disposal, proves that Schiller's position had indeed become a commanding one. Schiller was at this time, first and foremost, a politician. His historical writings aimed at a direct effect upon the public: he never dreamed of writing as a learned man for the learned. He could not comply with Cotta's request because of his feeble health, but arranged with Cotta for the publication of a magazine, the first number of which was to appear early in 1795, — the renowned " Hours." Every month a work of sixty-four pages. If any one would know what the change had been in Germany in twenty years, it is only necessary to compare with the " Hours " Wieland's " German Mercury," which in its day had satisfied the highest claims of the reading public.

This magazine was started in Jena under Schiller's supervision. By offering the highest prices, the most eminent minds in Germany were to be induced to become its contributors; and Kant, Jacobi, and Goethe were the first to be won. Cotta would have insisted on securing Goethe at any price, but Schiller took the matter in hand and with perfect success. Schiller's letters to Cotta give ample proof of the diplomatic skill with which he managed Goethe. He is most careful to respect Goethe's idiosyncrasies. The way in which he at last conquers him fills us with genuine admiration.

Schiller must certainly have had people who kept him informed about things; for, after the unfortunate attempt we have already recounted to draw near to Goethe, a man in Schiller's position would never have undertaken this unless he had been certain of the result. With keen discernment Schiller saw Goethe's unfavorable situation more clearly perhaps than Goethe himself, and, with the talent of a general, planned his attack and prosecuted the siege.

As the first record, we cite the letter of June 1794. Respectfully, but in business style, in the name of a company entertaining for him sentiments of the most "unbounded veneration," Goethe is invited to become one of the contributors to the "Hours." To be sure, they had offered the same "unbounded veneration" to Kant; and we find Humbolt at this time presenting his "unbounded veneration" to Körner.

There had never been an entire breach between Schiller and Goethe. In the years 1790 and 1791 there had even been a kind of intercourse between them. Goethe designs a frontispiece for one of Schiller's literary undertakings, visits Schiller in Jena, whether once or more is not quite clear, and discusses with him Kant's philosophy (but how disagreeable Schiller's manner of informing Körner of this in a letter!); finally Goethe brings "Don Carlos" upon the stage, which necessitates a certain co-operation with Schiller. From this time we find scarcely a trace of any personal meeting.

To this company who had offered Goethe their "unbounded veneration" Wilhelm von Humbolt, Fichte, and others of like distinction belonged. Goethe did not let the fourteen official days pass, but replied, on the 24th of June, in a cool, friendly, encouraging tone, consenting to join in the undertaking. He could not well have done otherwise; besides, it was a concession to the company and not to Schiller. If this is to be regarded as the first step towards their approach, it was certainly a very little one.

Goethe's closer connection with the University of Jena in his capacity of highest official authority brought manifold personal relations with it. He went over there very often. On the now smooth, excellent road between Weimar and Jena, one would never suspect that in Goethe's time even a short journey (*Reise*) like this was not free from danger to the carriage. Batsch had started a Natural-History Society in Jena, whose periodical meetings Goethe attended. Here he met Schiller. By chance they left the hall together: a conversation arose which enticed Goethe as far as Schiller's house and up the stairs. When he left, he said he hoped soon again to have a conversation with Schiller. This time it had been Goethe who was the first to set foot in his illustrious neighbor's house.

On the following day he returned to Schiller a manuscript for the "Hours" which had been submitted to him for criticism, with the added words: "Keep me in friendly remembrance, and be assured that I should often enjoy an exchange of ideas with you." One must compare these words with the very measured phrases which Goethe was at that time in the habit of using to his correspondents, in order to appreciate their cordial tone. Yes, even more than this! Goethe's whole manner had assumed something stiff, unbending, ceremonious, which struck people at once, even from the way he had of holding his head and back.

Now another meeting in Jena. They fell into an earnest conversation, and again about philosophical matters, when Schiller was at his best and Goethe was most uncomfortable. Goethe describes, with quite dramatic effect, how Schiller's systematic opposition had been so trying to him that all became doubtful again between them. Schiller had a very thin, narrow-chested figure, and carried his head somewhat bent. He smoked and took snuff, which was unendurable to Goethe, and was restless and jerky in his movements. " In spite of all this," continues Goethe, " Schiller's personal charm was irresistible and held me fast." The practical wisdom and adaptiveness which Schiller possessed in a far greater degree than Goethe captivated him. These two great natures had come near to one another, never again to be divided. To Goethe it brought back the inspiration of his youth. He had once more found, as in Jacobi and Lavater, a soul from which he could not detach himself.

What Schiller possessed over and above these two men he so well knew how to conceal that when, after his death, Goethe took a retrospective view of the growth of their friendship, he was himself unconscious of it: it was the unfathomable cunning of the Swabian, hidden, as it always is, under the mantle of geniality. Experience had taught Schiller how to deal with men. Like an expert chess-player he knew every move in the game of life. Those with whom he wished to be on good terms he knew how to avoid displeasing : I need only remind you of Kotzebue. If he wished to be rid of a man, he despatched him with *aplomb* down the staircase: I need only recall to you his letter of dismissal to August Wilhelm Schlegel. Whom he would attract he charmed with the most exquisite manner: I need only refer to his management of his mother-in-law. She was a good-natured old lady, brought up among aristocratic conventions, ennobled by birth and marriage, the mother of nobly born daughters, — one of whom was already married according to her rank; and it would never have occurred to her even in a dream that such a fate could befall her unaffianced daughter as to be borne off by a plebeian Professor Honorarius of History, whose father had begun life as a leech! The way in which Schiller entrapped and coaxed this simple lady, — simple in the best sense of the word, — until she finally almost lost her senses; how the love affair was first concealed from her, and at last such a general assault made upon her that a wiser would have had to surrender, — all this was irresistible! Schiller's letter to "ma chère mère," which won the day, is a masterpiece, and with all her pride in her noble birth the good Frau von Lengefeld was done for! Every objection she could have made was cut off beforehand. If Schiller had lived in our day, no rival would have been allowed to go ahead of him in the Imperial Diet, and few would have desired to meddle with him.

The decisive step for Schiller and Goethe was Schiller's letter of the 23d of August, 1794. This letter, long, broad, circumstantial, — written in faultless, colorless German, — should prove to Goethe that only one man among his contemporaries was capable of understanding him fully and giving public evidence of it, — Schiller.

Goethe, in his character, in his works, in his first successes, in his then in many ways misunderstood position, could, indeed, be truly valued by no one but Schiller. Goethe's whole career was spread out before him, — what he had intended to do; what he had attained; what the German people owed him; and, finally, what was understood and acknowledged by no one except Schiller.

Once more Schiller offered himself to Goethe; once more he proposed a fixed programme; once more he ranked himself as a power opposite to him, — no longer as like to like, but in plainly expressed submission to him.

And this time Goethe accepts him, and, truly, in a way that manifests his real magnanimity.

His letter is dated Aug. 27, 1794: —

"For my birthday, which occurs this week, no more agreeable gift could have come to me than your letter, in which with a most friendly hand you sum up the amount of my life, and through your sympathy encourage me to a more earnest and vigorous use of my powers.

"The highest enjoyment and actual benefit must be reciprocal; and I rejoice to have a suitable opportunity to tell you what your conversation has been to me, and how I also reckon from these days a new epoch, and am contented, without special encouragement, to go on my way, — since it seems as if, after having found each other so unexpectedly, we must now continue our pilgrimage together. I have always known how to value the honesty and very rare earnestness which shines through all you have ever written or done. I may now claim to be made acquainted by yourself with the development of your mind, especially in these latter years."

People at their age do not fall upon each other's necks, or stand together by night at the window gazing up at the stars, and with endearing terms kissing each other, but adhere to the forms which correspond to their more mature views of life. They say to one another the most inspiring things which can be put into words, and Goethe is now the first to utter the word "friendship." He gives himself. There was nothing of this kind in Schiller's letter: he had not ventured beyond the bounds of business courtesy. But it is insufferable to Goethe that he should have failed to appreciate the comprehensive mind of this man. With mortification he recalls his earlier behavior, and confesses it plainly in the tone he now strikes. He gives himself so ingenuously and without reserve, that now Schiller might have made his own terms. But we recognize Schiller's greatness in the moderation with which he follows up his success. It soon dawns upon him how falsely he too has judged Goethe. Goethe had no suspicion of the letters in which Schiller had pronounced judgment upon him in such a harsh way; but Schiller was conscious of his error, and sought so far as possible to make amends for it. The separation had been a preparatory time of trial for both.

Schiller was away on a little journey when Goethe's answer reached Jena. He gives, in his reply which follows,— August 31,— a continuance of his letter of the 23d: —

"Our acquaintance, though late, which awakens so many fair hopes, is a fresh proof of how much better it often is to let accident rule than to anticipate things by too great officiousness. However intense my desire has been to enter with you into a more intimate relation than is possible between the spirit of an author and his most attentive reader, I now perfectly understand that two persons, taking such wholly different roads as you and I, could not earlier than just at this moment have come together with advantage. But now I hope that so much of the way as may yet remain to us we shall pursue together, and with the greater gain; since travelling comrades, near the end of a long journey, always have the most to say to each other."

It is not conceivable that what Schiller wished to say could have been better or more beautifully said. Schiller was, unquestionably, the master of German prose. How delicate the reproof in the adjective " late " acquaintance, and how charmingly he at the same time exonerates Goethe from blame! How sadly prophetic for a man, still so young, the " so much of the way as may yet remain to us," and, directly after, the overflowing confidence that henceforth they are companions in arms! He next passes on to a characterization of *his* individuality as contrasted with Goethe's. These first letters of the correspondence contain revelations of character sufficient to place the two men before us in a perfectly clear light, if we knew nothing else about them. Dating from the time of these letters, the correspondence continues regularly. September 4, Goethe invites Schiller to Weimar, where he spends a fortnight in his house; and then one should read Schiller's first letter after his return to Jena, his heart still lingering in Weimar! I have called Goethe a professor. Now, at last, he has found a listener suited to his taste. Schiller, too, asked for nothing better. Never did he overstep the limits, by one line, which reverence and gratitude, and the feeling that he was receiving while he could offer nothing, placed between him and Goethe.

In speaking of the growth of this bond of friendship, there is one more element which must be taken into account, which had been at work secretly all the time, and without which, after all, these two men could hardly have found each other, since their natures were so wholly different that their union must seem a kind of miracle.

Schiller had insisted on having, in his new home, what Goethe had declined, — a wife out of one of the families of the Lower Thuringian nobles. Schiller himself was, later, ennobled; and from that time his wife belonged again to the most aristocratic Weimar society. While "Goethe's boy," as Frau von Stein called him, ran about as an illegitimate sprout, Schiller's children were blood relations of many families of "vons," who had a right to consider themselves the first in the Weimar realm. If this marriage raised Schiller a step higher in social estimation, his wife was in other respects a very valuable acquisition.

The German Frau of the old school stands to-day in something like discredit. Bashful maidens, believing in ideals and revelling in tender emotions, who on their way through the city avoid the crowd with a certain reserved demeanor, are no longer regarded as successful specimens of modern education. We require that a young lady shall have a certain aggressiveness in her nature, and be able to use her elbows in case of need, so that wicked people, not only out of respect, but from something akin to fear, may lose all desire to meddle with her. Experience, however, shows that many of these courageous young heroines make, later, very inefficient housekeepers; while the more reserved maidens overcome the difficulties attending their new and untried domestic relations with wonderful success, and maintain their position with tact and grace.

What makes a woman strong is a certain subtlety of mind, — a well-trained gift of observation. Through this she learns to know the strong and weak points in the character of those with whom she has to deal, and rules (while she appears to have no will of her own) more powerfully than those combative natures to whom in their own homes it is often of little use that they know how to strike terror into the breasts of strange people in the street.

Schiller's wife was one of those delicate natures. As Lottchen von Lengefeld she is well known through her correspondence with her lover, and later, as Lotte Schiller, most charmingly, through a recently published correspondence with an old Jena pupil of her husband's, — Fischenich. Without this woman Schiller would not have lived even the ten years which were granted him by her side. Perfectly devoted, almost without any will of her own where Schiller's wishes were concerned, we still never find her wavering in her own individual convictions; while as a widow she worthily sustained Schiller's memory, and knew how to educate their children. Her gifts were not brilliant, and her desire to gain knowledge had at times something pedantic and mechanical in it. Nevertheless, she sat at Schiller's side in judgment on Goethe's thoughts and productions, as Herder's wife did beside Herder; and Goethe paid her due homage in the position of critic. The way in which she is again and again brought forward, with all her modesty, shows how indispensable she was as a spiritual element in her circle. The style of her letters is simple and fluent, and displays the same natural gift which in her sister was so splendidly cultivated that literary histories make a point of noticing her novel "Agnes von Lilien," which was declared by the acute contemporary Jena critics to be an anonymous work of Goethe's. One sees by Lotte Schiller's letters that she is Caroline's sister.

To Lotte Schiller's earliest convictions belonged an absolute faith in Goethe, which nothing later could shake. We see with what spirit she sought, in her correspondence with Schiller, to conquer his aversion to his great rival. Schiller was inclined to acquiesce in all the views of his betrothed, — only, when she tells him of Goethe's great and good heart, he refuses to believe her. He expresses his opinion of him to Lotte in the strongest terms. She takes it calmly, and waits; but always after a time recurs to the great subject. At last she becomes wholly silent about Goethe, in order not to wound Schiller; but she never relinquishes the idea of a union between the two. This young maiden's holding so firmly to Goethe at a time when he seemed to be so completely changed that even his best friends did not know what to make of him, is glorious; and it appears in a still greater degree the emanation of an independent nature, later, when Lotte, as a married woman, became the most intimate friend of Frau von Stein, sympathized in her grief, mourned with her what she had lost, and certainly shared her aversion to Christiane, whose eternal presence in Weimar was a cause of mortification to the ladies there. Under these circumstances, Lotte must often have listened to the bitterest things said against Goethe; but it never had any influence on her own views of him. Without a doubt, therefore, when the possibility finally offered of bringing the two men together, Lotte did her best to help on matters; for though I have represented Schiller as a practised chess-player, whose desire it was to checkmate Goethe, yet the old pride was strong within him, as also the feeling that he ought to be sufficient to himself, and to make no further advances than he had made. It lies chiefly with women, after all, to separate men or to hold them together. We soon see how Schiller's wife, in her own quiet, womanly way, influences both the men, and becomes the third in the bond. Goethe takes Lotte and the children with Schiller into his heart. It is a beautiful picture, after the first steps had been taken, to see Goethe in Schiller's house, and how much at home he felt there; while Schiller's at first assumed tone of dependence upon Goethe gradually becomes a natural one.

Goethe's effort from this time was to bring his friend back to Weimar, in which, of course, he succeeded.

Their correspondence was exchanged for daily personal intercourse, and only when journeys, or, what was worse, illness, for a time separated them, did the short notes take on again the substantial character of the old correspondence.

LECTURE XXI.

GOETHE AND SCHILLER IN WEIMAR.

WHEN two men of conspicuous ability unite in a common activity, their power is not merely doubled but quadrupled. Each feels the other invisibly beside him. The formula would not be: Goethe + Schiller, but (Goethe + Schiller) + (Schiller + Goethe). To each accrues the power of the other. This is the meaning of every business company, — of the disciplined army as compared with single warriors brought together by chance; of an association as contrasted with accidental co-operative labor. " Schiller and Goethe " is a collective idea in German history. They stand beside one another in Weimar, with hands clasping the same laurel wreath. This is in keeping with the feeling of the great public (who have not all the details in mind), that the best works of Schiller and Goethe were the result of their united power, and that neither without the other would have become what he was.

But here a distinction obtains; and, if we may be allowed to be hypercritical, we must say that Rietschel in his beautiful group reverses the relation of the men to each other by the apparel in which he clothes them. Rietschel has represented Goethe in court costume; Schiller in a kind of dressing-gown, intended to denote a man who rarely left his study, and whose great broad side-pockets suggest a certain indigence. Begas has also adopted this coat for the Berlin statue ; but it is to be hoped it will never be used again.

Things were not so. Schiller, who now with restless energy began life anew, is actually the representative of the union. Schiller's delicate health was never allowed to interfere with his pursuits, and he always seemed equal to every exertion. He returns to Weimar, is raised to the rank of noble, appears at court, drives his carriage and horses, and altogether conducts his *ménage* on a very comfortable scale; while Goethe at his side appears more like the quiet companion, the unpretending private friend, who indeed sought so far as possible to bestow on Schiller all the glory resulting from the new alliance. And here I will say at once, that for Schiller this union with Goethe was the dawn of a new epoch, which gave rise to a fresh series of works, in which Goethe as fellow laborer participated ; while, on the other hand, this fellowship was only an episode for Goethe, and what he achieved during its continuance, in the way of new works, was of no special importance in his development. Goethe owed to Schiller a reawakened interest in producing through literary work an instantaneous effect upon the public. Again he wrote, as in the old Frankfort time, in sympathy with the day and the hour; but when Schiller finally departed, the great stream resumed its wonted quiet measure, and flowed on lonely as before.

Schiller and Goethe's united capital was a power against which none could contend. Their position was such to the outer world that they defied all competition. What they gave the public must be accepted with rapture, and was ever so received. What in private they were to each other was so absolutely sufficient to them both, that one who felt naturally that he had a right to be a third in the bond, was thrust out in the most cruel manner,— not certainly Wieland, who had already reached that age of harmless good nature when one takes gratefully whatever is offered, but Herder. From Schiller's friendship with Goethe dates the separation of Goethe from Herder, and a bitterness entered Herder's soul which from this time never left it again. Fate seemed always to have misplaced Herder in the most pitiful way; and that he was himself conscious of this did not a little add to his doleful condition. Armed with immense intellectual power, he never had the opportunity to give it full scope, and was finally, through his controversy with Wolf (the odious representative of an hypothesis by which archæology still suffers), involved in undignified conflicts which have injured his reputation even with posterity. To later generations who have formed acquaintance with this great man from better and more carefully revised editions of his writings, it will be an enigma why such a mighty light had such a feeble radiation. Herder reminds one of Leonardo da Vinci, who, by the side of Michael Angelo and Raphael appears as a giant, but as a giant who, after having moved some rocks which no other hand could have lifted, wasted his strength in the treadmill of daily life. But until the very last Herder retained the power to wound by his criticisms. It would not be possible to give a colder, more malicious recognition of Goethe's poetical ability than Herder gave in his sketch of German literature in the "Adrastea." This is his expression: "An exact, unsympathizing description of the visible." Every word is a cut which pierces to the bone. I confess myself to a personal special reverence for Herder, in opposition to friends who have a much cooler feeling towards him. But this diabolical power to strike and hit his best and most intimate friends frightens me. Much more harmless sounds what Knebel, who also felt himself set aside for the sake of Schiller, repeated to Herder's wife as the sarcasm current among the Jena people, that Goethe was "the most polished man of the age." Here was only the wish to say something cutting, just as Heine, thirty years later, called him the cold, gray man of art,—"kalten Kunstgrei." Goethe had silently turned away from Herder, while Schiller gave strong expression to his dislike of him. It may be that without Schiller in Weimar Goethe would not so unrelentingly have stood apart from his oldest friend and teacher.

What Schiller gained through Goethe affected all his relations. In bringing Cotta gradually into connection with Goethe he gave to the most enterprising publisher, who, domiciled in the heart of Swabia, controlled the South-German market at that time, an increase of power, for which Cotta must be eternally grateful to him; while Goethe and Schiller secured not only the wide circulation of their books and a large amount of money for them, but insured also significant salaries to all on whom they conferred the honor of being their colaborers. It would have been impossible at that time to have started a magazine in Germany which could have held its own by the side of the "Hours." Schiller and Goethe had their choice among the best minds, and at the same time did the principal part of the work themselves.

From this time, Schiller no longer needed to trouble himself to gain the good-will of strange theatre managers; the Weimar stage, under Goethe's direction, stood always at his disposition. In Goethe's house the first inspiring rehearsals of Schiller's dramas were held, and every kind of scenic effect tried and discussed between them; while Schiller prepared Goethe's pieces for the stage,—"Iphigenia," as has already been said, and "Egmont."

Schiller no longer needed to regard outside critics; Goethe's criticism was at hand from the very first conception of his dramas, and helped him vastly. Goethe assisted him to change the form of "Wallenstein" (which was the first of Schiller's dramas in this new epoch), and brought it out on the stage, every character in new brilliant satin costume; finally, by a discussion of it in Cotta's "Allgemeine Zeitung," he dictated to the German people what they were to think of the piece. How Goethe's hand from this time helped to mould all Schiller's creations the correspondence shows; and (what in fact has been already said) Goethe supplied Schiller with ideas so profusely that this union rendered all other relations unnecessary to him, — indeed, in a certain sense, cancelled them. Körner and Humboldt remain dear as ever to Schiller's heart; but as critics he could henceforth wholly dispense with them.

Goethe, on his side, found in Schiller a friend who stimulated him unceasingly to poetical and critical work, or who quietly excited Cotta to do the same thing; and by his unstinted appreciation he reinstated Goethe at once in all his old glory, so that the intervening years of coldness vanished like a dream, and his life seemed a continuance of the brilliant Frankfort epoch. Schiller and Goethe now organized public opinion in the best sense of the word, and from them emanated praise and blame in Germany; while those who were not in concert with them, and would have preferred to take the position of critics themselves, were left to smother as they could their impotent rage. This was the case with the brothers Schlegel, certainly the most talented writers of the age, one of whom, after Schiller had shown him out of the door, maintained an intercourse with Goethe (for this was another advantage of Goethe and Schiller's fraternity, that, if they liked, they could repulse people by halves); while Frederick Schlegel wholly abdicated North Germany, and, sustained by his wife, in Vienna emitted incessant streams from his poisonous volcano against Goethe. Goethe's oldest enemies in our century are to be attributed to the views of these Romanticists; his former adversaries are antiquated: the censures of the present generation are still of literary value in forming our opinions. Close beside Goethe, in Weimar itself, some of these vermin planted themselves, — Kotzebue, Merkel, and others, contriving to sting when they think they can do so with impunity, and then, as cunningly, making themselves invisible. If Goethe succeeded in evading a great man like Herder, he certainly considered this rabble rout so far beneath his notice that he let them go wholly unpunished. But, if we look into the depth of the matter, Schiller's literary policy strikes us as a very questionable thing; since there were always about him people whose good-will he did not wish to forfeit. Between him and Goethe these subjects were never discussed. The great intrigue to separate these two men, once spun by their enemies in Weimar, and based chiefly on their own mean conception of Schiller's vanity, called forth scarcely an explanatory word between the friends. Schiller and Goethe's communion rested on firmer ground. How could they dispense with one another? These two men, who lived in the interchange of the highest thoughts, felt too deeply the world-historical significance of their union to heed the trivialities of a few passing days.

Goethe had found in Schiller a friend whose endeavor it was to be introduced into all the paths which his thoughts had followed, and Schiller quickly made himself thoroughly at home in departments into which Goethe had only given him a cursory glance. Schiller united to the ardor of the pupil the ripe critical judgment of the man, who feels himself to be the equal of the master.

And now, most felicitously for them both, their friendship bore within it the possibility of an endless growth. Their natures were so radically different that the moment would never come when one would be merged in the other. The good Kunst-Meyer, after living some years in familiar intercourse with Goethe, had become so infused with Goethe's views, and Goethe with his, that neither of them could have given any opinion in matters of art with which the other was not already acquainted. Schiller and Goethe could never have so melted into one another. As two converging lines which by small intervening spaces are still prevented from uniting, they would again and again have found some reason for renewed divergence. Goethe, in his deepest soul, thought absolutely unlike Schiller. He recognized only Schiller's person, his strivings, his manly greatness. What, on the other hand, Schiller understood as poetry was no poetry at all to Goethe. Schiller's way of creating was something wholly foreign to Goethe. Schiller searched for his matter; then worked upon it long enough to get it completely into his hands, after which he composedly made his disposition of it. Now he labors on it, from day to day, as a mason erecting a palace according to a distinct plan; then follows the plastering, ornamenting, and furnishing; till, finally, with a certain splendor of novelty, the edifice is submitted to the use of the public.

This knowledge of *technique* was Schiller's power. He was a poet by profession, and recognized as valid the claims of other professional poets. Goethe certainly understood this, but not for himself. He handled the technical questions, which as regards the genesis of poetical works and their criticism are of so much value, with the greatest seriousness, but quite objectively. *Creating* poetry was to him an incomprehensible process. Whoever asked Goethe whether he should become a poet fared pretty badly. Young people gifted with the rhyming faculty have the natural faith that there is an Areopagus somewhere which, solemnly and authoritatively, can give them the license to write verses which will be a success, — which means, will be read and admired. Goethe had only one reply to make to such applicants, contained in this simile: " The genuine silk-worm needs only to eat leaves, and the silk is sure to appear. " He answered evasively, warningly, doubtfully. Schiller, on the contrary, enters into the matter cheerfully, criticises the verses sent him, and, if he likes them, advises the young people to work on diligently. He encourages them ; but at the same time says, " One must dedicate himself wholly to the poetic art if one would attain anything," and more of the like practical advice.

How could Goethe, in his intercourse with Schiller, pretend to acquiesce in all this while his nature disavowed it ? Here, having spoken of what forever prevented the lines from meeting, we must turn to the other element which constantly drew them towards each other.

Goethe had learned that without the aid of mechanical skill no perfect poetry could be achieved. Plastic art had first taught him this, and the poetical works of the Greeks confirmed it. In the fabrication of Greek verse there was much " Meistersängerei." Goethe always felt and regretted the lack of mechanical proficiency in his art. He would have liked to write, not as in a dream, but clearly conscious of what he was doing. He had, not only in the Greeks, but in Shakspeare as well, recognized the advantage contained in the fact, that as paid theatre poet a man was forced to regard the satisfaction of the public as his decisive criterion.

For himself, indeed, Goethe was unable to profit by this knowledge, — his manner remained the same. But Schiller should have the benefit of his experience. Hence it seems sometimes (read the correspondence) as if Schiller wrote his pieces as Goethe's plenipotentiary. Goethe gives the orders: Schiller carries them out. In little things Goethe springs personally to help, by adding or erasing. This working together, which proved the source of the greatest pleasure to both, never tempted them to encroach on each other's rights; for Schiller was never initiated into his friend's innermost ideas, however much Goethe persuaded him that he valued his advice. Schiller as theatre poet displays a vast, steadily productive activity, calculating one summer for a play; and on this he concentrates all his faculties. Goethe, with just as much of a regular plan, begins to publish a rare amount of accumulated material, — poetry, prose, and scientific matter. It was not so much his intention to manifest his own nature in his new works, as to mature the opinion of the public and to feel himself in direct communication with it; and this is the emphasis of his work. Both of the men furnish immense material; while Cotta stands ever at hand with an unlimited supply of paper, ready to pay enormous salaries, and sustained by a public who have unlimited capacity for receiving all that is offered them.

But now the question arises, How would things have gone on if Schiller had lived?

It seems unnecessary to ask what nobody can answer, or indeed needs to know. I have just shown in the diversity of the two natures a guarantee for the inexhaustibleness of the ever-growing, ever-expanding friendship. Some remarks concerning Goethe's past life, which he himself dropped in later years, lead us to conjecture what might have arisen.

This union never was to Goethe what it was to Schiller, — the culmination of his life, — but rather like a ten years' marriage, at the end of which one loses the beloved companion, who is long sincerely mourned, but after a time more calmly estimated. The time came when Goethe was able to discuss Schiller as freely and impartially as he did himself. But we cannot doubt that Goethe knew the nature of their friendship perfectly while Schiller was still living. Goethe possessed the gift of being able to regard contemporary things in an historical light. He says indeed, "It is impossible to show the day to the day;" but this only proves how unique was the capacity in him to do this. He saw with the eyes of the future, and judged the present as we judge things of fifty years ago. He knows as early as 1820 that there is no perception in Germany of the real value of the present. He shows himself indifferent to politics in his old age, because he foresees the storm which must break out in Germany without any intervention from himself or others. Therefore his opinions have an influence to-day, owing to their truth and correctness. With the genuine historian objects retreat, without any effort on his part, to exactly the right distance, — as the portrait-painter knows how far back or how near he must step to see a head in its true proportions. There are characters which can be represented only in simple colossal lines, and which appear to the best advantage at a great distance; while others are effective only in miniature, and must be held close to the eye. Goethe, in his intercourse with Schiller, never forgot on what a height Schiller stood; but there he watched and criticised him calmly as any other historical object.

Twenty years after Schiller's death Goethe expressed his opinion of his friend in the following manner : " Schiller, who had a genuine poetic nature, but whose mind was philosophical, accomplished much by sheer force of reasoning which in a poet should arise intuitively and spontaneously. He tempted many young people to follow in his path, although they only succeeded in so far as to imitate his language. So much for Schiller's rhetoric!" And further, when Eckermann, Goethe's last amanuensis. asked for instruction as to what he could do for himself as a poet, Goethe for once vouchsafed a species of encouragement by saying : " Concentrate your powers. If I had been wise enough to do so thirty years ago, I should have accomplished something vastly different. What an amount of time I wasted with Schiller over the 'Hours,' and the 'Muses' Almanac'! Just within the last few days, in looking over our letters, all has come vividly before me again. I cannot think of those undertakings without vexation, wherein the world abused us, and which were wholly without result for ourselves."

What does the expression mean, " Wherein the world abused us"? Had not Schiller and Goethe forced their undertakings on the world? It must be that Goethe would not speak more plainly through fear of being misunderstood by Eckermann, whose comprehension did not reach beyond certain limits. What he really meant was that Schiller had abused him. We must take the word here in its best and noblest sense. He meant to say, " If I had quietly kept on my solitary way, which was in accordance with my nature, I should have made more progress than by all my great enterprises with Schiller." When Goethe recovered self-possession and repose after Schiller's death, he looked back upon these last ten years of his life as a traveller who, having long wandered through

POSSIBLE RESULT OF THE FRIENDSHIP. 415

much toil and weariness in foreign lands, returns at last exhausted, though enriched with countless experiences, to find at home quite as much accomplished in a different way, — things having progressed quietly during his absence, carried forward by their own law of gravitation; and while he would not give up, for any price, the remembrance of his toil, he cannot help acknowledging to himself that he might have been of much more benefit to himself and others with less waste of power.

So much we may infer. At any rate, Goethe looked at things in this light if only on the one day when he talked them over with Eckermann. He regarded his co-operation with Schiller as the greatest outward event of his life, Schiller as the most remarkable person he had ever met, and his loss as the bitterest that ever befell him. He looked back on those times as a general on a victorious campaign, about which result there can be no doubt, while at the same time there might be some question as to whether it would be wise to continue such an heroic career. One would not pass his whole life hurrying from victory to victory! And therefore we ask, What would have happened if Schiller had lived longer? Would he have succeeded every year in all the future in starting a new literary undertaking, and monopolizing Goethe as his ally? We must admit its possibility, for who ever appeared before or after who engrossed Goethe as Schiller did? But how about Goethe's sense of independence? Perhaps one day he might here also have said "Enough!" and actually carried out the purpose ever lurking in the background of flying to Rome, and remaining there forever. It seems foolish to speculate thus; but what Goethe has said forces upon us these questions.

Certainly there would have been warlike times for Goethe had the first ten years in Weimar been at Schiller's side. Their friendship was not a year old when Goethe, through Schiller, became involved in an affair which he had neither foreseen, nor with his own hand would ever have undertaken,— the renowned and most notorious "Xenienkampf": to speak more clearly, the offensive alliance of Schiller and Goethe against their united literary contemporaries, for the purpose of clearing themselves by one fell stroke from an amount of uncertain relations, and of establishing the firm of Schiller and Goethe as absolutely self-supporting, against all other firms.

I might assert that not only had Schiller recognized the result of this proceeding more clearly than Goethe, but had also more decidedly wished it.

It was first announced by the issue of a number of witty, harmless headings, in the form of distichs, addressed to different persons and things in Germany that needed a gentle reproof. While they were engaged in the work, the thought struck them that a certain completeness would not be amiss; so it came to pass that no one went unscathed, and, to do no injustice, the nearest neighbors by no means came off best. At the outset no one was seriously disturbed, for the persons attacked did not rightly know whether they ought to laugh or cry. But by degrees some were too sharply hit to be able to pretend to ignore the home thrusts; and thereupon a storm of indignation broke out, followed by attempts to retaliate like with like. The result was both poets saw themselves attacked and blamed. This perhaps they had expected; but at the same time they must defend themselves, and to this they were driven. Schiller was once so much excited that he thought of applying to the police for protection against the personal insults let loose upon

Goethe and himself; for, unable to take revenge on the thing, one seeks to do so on the person.

While Goethe was of opinion that it was best to let the storm spend its force, Schiller saw only one means of salvation, which was to form a faction. This was the beginning of a school of poetry whose name even yet preserves its glory,— the so-called "Romantische Schule." At the outset it was a union of the young and rising talent of the country, which centred in Jena, and, being needed, was allowed free course,— of whom Schiller took command as their stern leader. Goethe stood in the background as highest authority.

The Romantic School undertook to defend their two leaders in the midst of these difficulties. They declared Schiller and Goethe to be beyond competition the greatest poets,— in fact all others were left out of consideration; and only they, the Romanticists, were recognized as next of kin and inheritors of the true art of poetry. Goethe's popularity was now far greater than it had ever been. Schiller's works drew Goethe's along with them. Goethe was valued as the first poet of the German nation. Crabb Robinson says in the year 1800 : " Goethe was the ideal of the literary world in Germany." Goethe acquiesced: who would not ? But scarcely was Schiller dead, when he gently disengaged himself from the whole crew.

Schiller worked from the beginning with a ruined constitution. He was ill when he first came to Thuringia,— suffering from spasms in his chest. When Goethe invited him for the first time to visit him in Weimar, Schiller accepted, explaining at the same time how carefully he was obliged to live : this letter makes us feel under what menacing and burdensome conditions Schiller created his noblest works. The grandest productions of his life were crowded into ten wretched years. He worked feverishly, hastening from one work to another, and, even before the preceding one was finished, bearing about with him new plans for a fresh undertaking. He must, as he said himself, pursue many great enterprises at the same time, going from one to another, to stimulate his working power. But one day the golden store was exhausted; there was a sudden close as with Byron, Raphael, Mozart. Had these lived slower, they might perhaps have overcome the fell disease which destroyed them; but they had lived too fast, too extravagantly, to have anything in reserve for such an emergency. Schiller wrote between 1795 and 1805 the three dramas which together constitute his "Wallenstein," — "Marie Stuart," the "Jungfrau von Orleans," the "Braut von Messina," followed by "Wilhelm Tell," and died just after beginning the "Demetrius." At the same time he wrote a quantity of small things, — minor poems, though not short ones, treatises, and essays; added to these a rare correspondence with friends, besides an extensive business correspondence; finally the editing of the "Hours" and the "Muses' Almanac," and other considerable undertakings. Schiller utilized every moment, and was obliged to resort to violent means near the end to conquer the weariness of the flesh. A sadder struggle was never fought between desire to work and breaking down. With regard to Schiller's last hours, the best and calmest account is to be gathered from the letters of the younger Voss (son of the renowned Voss), who, hastening himself to an early death, was the teacher of Schiller's children. A gentle, finely strung, thoroughly cultured nature, he loved Schiller with a childlike affection, and in his last hours lent him a helpful hand.

One always has the feeling that there was some mistake about Schiller's early death, — as if the misfortune might have been averted. We seek to blame some one for it; and, since it came so naturally and was so inevitable, we try to find at least something to complain of in the manner in which he was buried. Since here too it seems that everything was done properly and in order, people have made attempts to reproach Goethe with a lack of sympathy for Schiller. Goethe was ill himself at the moment of Schiller's death. We know exactly how he bore it when the dreadful news could no longer be concealed from him. There is nothing more affecting than to see Goethe as he stands bereft, forsaken, and saying to himself that this loneliness must forever be his; for Goethe knew life well enough to be sure that Nature, who only grants " the necessary," would not bestow on him a second time such a friend.

LECTURE XXII.

SCHILLER AND GOETHE.

IF a history of German literature were to be given, it would be absolutely necessary, in speaking of the united work of Schiller and Goethe, to speak also of the great movement in the literary world which arose with it. This was the chaos out of which the world of thought in our century was evolved. Farther back we need not go, but thus far it is necessary to go. Then began the new era in poetry, philosophy, philology, and history, which is still in progress of development, brilliantly inaugurated by the labors of the learned men of Jena, at the close of the former and the beginning of this century.

As soon as we fix our eyes upon Goethe only, however, the scene changes. We saw him before his union with Schiller a lonely man, guided on his destined way by stars whose light shone for him alone. By the side of Schiller we see him for a number of years, in the midst of the great and universal progress of the nation, occupying a leading position; but we also see that, as soon as Schiller dies, he falls back into his old seclusion. Goethe, our greatest poet and writer, had very little direct connection with the general literary work of his day. Its representatives had a certain intercourse with him; but it never amounted to systematic, continuous co-operation.

Goethe never gave to the public anything but what accident had brought to him as a gift. As poet or learned man he planned, willed, and executed but little: his labor at times, indeed, assumed the character of regular productivity, especially under Schiller's helpful presence; but it never was such, even then. As soon as he was tired of things, he left them alone. Only in matters of science did he make an exception.

And, further, although Goethe's poems between 1795 and 1805 seemed to be called forth by Schiller's help and co-operation, Goethe in truth produced them wholly by himself. Although no verse of " Iphigenia " was declared finished without Frau von Stein, Herder, and Wieland's approval, yet we must not for a moment think of it as having been written with the aid of these persons; nor can any one point to a single sentence in Goethe's works attributable to Schiller's influence. They are all alike the product of Goethe's unaided genius. Schiller's suggestions had had some effect on the final form of " Wilhelm Meister," but only so far as to induce Goethe to make outward changes in it, for the sake of which he as it were lent his pen to Schiller. Schiller might have failed, and then Goethe would have fallen back upon the advice of the earlier critics to whom he was accustomed. The result of Schiller's advice on " Wilhelm Meister " is almost to be regretted. Without him, the romance would not have been rounded off in such an absurd way, but as a fragment would have produced a far greater impression.

Goethe was busy about the " Roman Elegies " when he renewed Schiller's acquaintance.

Their origin has been already mentioned: they are the incidents of his late Weimar experience transfigured into Roman reminiscences. But after they had once, as finished poems, gained for themselves an independent existence, Goethe, who never again forgot the teachings of the classic masters, subjected them to a most unmerciful polishing. They must be wholly detached from himself, and be able to stand on their own merits. He makes them undergo the severest schooling. He gives them into the hands of strangers, that nothing may cling to them indicative of any personal relations; and the result is that these verses have an individuality quite unlike any of his former productions. We do not think of Goethe as entertaining us with mere fictions, but these hexameters excite our imagination so powerfully as to have the effect of immediate realities. Even knowing, as we do, that they are only the Weimar events transferred to Rome, we still waive this knowledge, and enjoy the "Elegies" as *Roba di Roma*, without wishing any one to tell us about their origin. It is the same spirit which makes Homer's Iliad seem to us so like a verbal narration of actual facts, and leads us to seek to-day for the Scæan gates and the fountain and fig-tree whose situation Homer so clearly and unmistakably points out. The scholar will ever, with the Iliad and Odyssey in hand, recognize anew the plains of Troy, and explore the cavern of Ithaca in which lay the sleeping Odysseus; and readers of the "Elegies" will never cease to visit in Rome the tavern where Goethe met with his adventure. Goethe's imagination here created a living reality, as Propertius had done before him, whose nightly adventures in the streets of Rome seem as genuinely true as if the statements of a reporter had been put into hexameters who was utterly incapable of drawing on his fancy, and whose sole business it was to relate the facts as literally as language would permit.

Where now lay this art of writing in the classic sense,

so as to produce the effect of what I term *reality*? This might have been asked when we spoke of the Roman remodelling of " Iphigenia," and of the final reason for the decided change which Goethe's artistic creations underwent in Rome, and what the secret which was unveiled to him there that now made the works and writings of the Greeks indispensable to him as models. If we would give it the correct name, we should say that Goethe won in Italy what we call " style."

The " style " of a work is often enough discussed. Every one speaks of it. We say a work has " style," or that it " wants style ; " but not every one at the first glance would be able to explain what is meant by "style," or, at the second, what he meant by it in this particular instance. Yet the distinction is made again and again, and the word, however vague its meaning may be, is indispensable to us.

What is " style " ? What distinguishes the last form of " Iphigenia " from the earlier ones ?

To answer these questions, I will now carry further the expression which I used before. Goethe wished that the " Roman Elegies " should live independent of their author.

You know how important the knowledge of the development of a child is from its first conception. In place of " child," we will now say "work of art."

We believe that we are able to follow the growth of more than one of Goethe's artistic creations from the moment when it flashed upon his mind. We watch the first mysterious movements : it exists, and, at the same time, it is not in existence. We see it grow, and finally, with perfectly formed members, come into the world. Now it is here, and lives. The study of this genesis, this development out of nothing into personality, seems with the work of art, as with the child, the most important thing. So soon as one, like the other, comes to the light of day, a living thing, mystery ceases. But in a spiritual sense it only now begins. The climax in the career of a child is not the moment when he enters on his individual life, but the epoch when, his education accomplished, in spiritual independence even of his parents he begins a life directed by his own free-will, — when the boy has become a man.

In the old world the Greeks alone, and in succeeding generations those who have caught their secret, have been able to give to works of art this power of sustaining an independent spiritual existence. As with the grown man father and mother are lost sight of, so with these works of art, the artist is forgotten in his creation. With Shakspeare's, Dante's, and Leonardo's figures, as well as those achieved in the youth of Raphael and Michael Angelo, the question of who was their creator always forces itself upon us as of the higher importance. It is Dante, Shakspeare, Leonardo, the young Raphael, and Michael Angelo themselves whom we see in their works. They are their children, but children not of age; and the father still holds the first place, without whom we should only partly understand his creations. But the characters of Homer, Sophocles, and Æschylus live their individual life: the father disappears by the side of his works.

And so, likewise, Goethe's works written before the Roman period are only dissevered parts of a personality as dear to us as the works themselves; and only what he wrote after his Italian journey no longer require Goethe's person, but are perfect creations, with their own aim and action. This is the reason why the works of the young Goethe fall into the background in comparison with the Goethe who, in Rome, had learned from the Greeks the secret of "style."

Moreover, the Greek artists created not only a natural but an ideal humanity, whose physical form never quite corresponded to Nature's, but who seemed like a distinct people of bronze or marble with forms of their own. The body, as the Greek artist newly created it, was simpler than the natural body; only the noblest lines and curves were brought into play, blending in artistic harmony such as Nature never produced. The physician or the natural philosopher sees in the human body a complex combination of matter and motion, never wholly fathomed. He makes no distinction between inward and outward; and the more acutely he observes, the more new and unexpected intricacies are discernible. But the Greek artist will only represent what appears to the practised eye of his people as the most desirable in outward form, and moulds his figures as all men and women would best like to be formed. And while generations of artists, with this aim, made the taste of the public and the means to gratify it ever anew their study, they at last succeeded in personifying the most ideal beauty in so lifelike a manner that it seemed as though Nature herself had produced it. The Greek artist grew up among traditions which took away his freedom. This marble people seemed to perpetuate themselves from generation to generation. The Zeus of Phidias, even though Phidias alone could create it, was to all Greeks the very image of the god,—as if Zeus had been present in the marble, and Phidias had only received the injunction from the people to chisel and polish the block of stone until at last the necessary form arose out of it.

And now, this people of statues is not dumb. They still speak; and their language is that of Greek poetry.

The verse of these Greek poets is suited to these marble lips.

Only those figures in a poem really speak whose words move in the simplest cadence, but which yet are as far beyond the accidental emphasis of common talk as the marbles are superior to the forms of real life. Poetical language gives to words a clear, sharply-defined value, but lends to them at the same time the melody which inspires the highest thoughts humanity is capable of uttering. It apparently limits language, confines it within rules, and excludes certain words in which the ideal accent is wanting. Only the Greeks have known how to lend to their whole language this tone and cadence in such a measure as to make it a system. Other nations have only attained to single sounds, and to words of a poetical language. In presence of the works of the Greek artists in Italy, Goethe's "Iphigenia" received this form and language, and he subsequently also rewrote "Tasso" and "Egmont." Every trace of subjective relation to the author must be erased. Iphigenia and Orestes have no longer anything to do with Frau von Stein and Goethe. No personal experience, by whose shock they had been called into being, clings now to the characters. They are of age, and no longer subject to the power of him who formed them, and who, before he gave them their highest finish in Rome, could guide them here and there at will.

But one incongruity even Goethe could not remove. These characters in their original conception had been different from what they finally became. In the earlier plot the subjective origin was not to be denied; and even in the "Roman Elegies" there was a certain last appearance of a connection all too near with Goethe's person, since he introduces himself as the hero of the adventures recounted. In order to realize how perfectly Goethe understood how to write after classic models, we must recall a number of poems in which the contents and form are still more striking, — "The Bride of Corinth," " God and the Bajadere," " The New Pausias," and "The Flower Maiden ; " but, above all, " Alexis and Dora." These poems (I mention only the most distinguished) are in the true sense of the word masterpieces ; by which is meant, the works of a poet who has attained the mastery of his art. Unlike his earlier characters, — who were distant, heavenly connections of the poet through a traceable pedigree, — we may say without exaggeration of these figures who meet us unexpectedly as in a beatific vision, that they are a combination of Greek sculpture, Raphaelistic drawing, and Titianesque coloring. These comparisons are forced upon us, because such an immense access of power in plastic drawing and coloring is here noticeable in Goethe. He knows exactly what effects he wishes to produce, and with what means they are to be attained ; and, finally, how to lend to the work a kind of finish which destroys every trace of the labor he has bestowed on it. " Alexis and Dora " is unsurpassed, — not as if it were a translation from the Greek, but as if an old Greek had known how to write German. Goethe had so thoroughly identified himself with the antique world, as if it were indeed a real living world, that he added a song to the Iliad at this time, — which it would seem he was quite justified in doing by the new theory that the Iliad is composed of songs only accidentally welded together. Goethe's " Achilleïs " is scarcely known, and is usually looked upon as a failure. I do not agree with this opinion. I consider this poem deserving of equal rank with his most successful ones : unfortunately, it was left unfinished.

Nevertheless, this manner of working might have been

regarded as an indication of a decline of power, if Goethe had not united all the advantages of this new method in perfection in one noble work, which in an artistic sense appears the most beautiful and faultless, and in a human sense the truest, of all his productions, — " Hermann and Dorothea."

The triumph of a work of art, as we have seen, from an æsthetic point of view, is so to affect the imagination, that before the work itself the creator is forgotten, and that only after a while, and as if recovering from an enchantment, we say to ourselves that the picture or the poem owes its existence to some hand without which it could never have been. This triumph was Goethe's in " Hermann and Dorothea." He seems to have discovered, in the form he gave to this poem, the innate rhythm of the German language ; and in the subject he glorifies the source of all German strength and excellence, — a healthy, temperate, domestic life. If the " Roman Elegies " sprung from the joy felt by a soul, long wandering in solitude, which has attained the possession of a beloved one, we have here the picture of quiet home life, which, as an outgrowth from the former, is painted in the most charming manner imaginable.

I will first speak of its form.

Klopstock was the creator of modern German prosody. Attempts had been made before him, which proved to be only attempts. Klopstock wrote the first real German odes ; he constructed true German hexameters, and, so to say, drilled our language in the classic measures by imitation of classic syntax, and by creating new combinations of words.

Klopstock would have done more if he had written less. He gained such facility in moving to antique measures that his art overstrained the natural capacities of the language. What he wrote was no longer German, but Klopstockian; and though the public found for a long time great pleasure in his verses, yet what was a mere fashion could have but a limited duration.

Ewald von Kleist (the elder Kleist, who fell in the Seven Years' War) made use of hexameters and fancy meters after the antique in a more discreet and therefore, to-day, more readable way. I mention Kleist among many who might be here named (for instance, Ramler, with whose odes Berlin resounded in the time of Frederick the Great), because he brings us directly to the man to whom we are indebted for the foundation of German hexameters, — to Voss. Kleist possessed something which is here of great importance, and which we look for in vain in Klopstock; he did little to change the language in which he wrote, but sought, so far as possible, to conform to its phraseology. Instead of forcing it, he coaxed it; instead of inventing new words, he adapted the existing material, while carefully avoiding the appearance of oddity. He expressly desired that his hexameters and other classic metres should be read as if they were simple prose.

Voss went further in this direction, and became the discoverer of the proper epic German. It must not be forgotten that, later, he tried to change his happily invented language into an artificial idiom, by which he forfeited the advantages it had possessed at first, and made his last works almost unintelligible. While Klopstock's most artificial productions offer difficulties which can be overcome, Voss's writings are stupid, rigid, wooden, or whatever adjectives one may choose to describe an insipid formalism.

But we here discuss Voss as the interpreter of Homer's poems to the Germans.

Homer's hexameter was the product of a dialect, — the Ionic. Never could such a tender measure be formed from the Attic, which was the language of the philosopher and of the statesman. The Attic narrator is, *par excellence*, Plato. He brings into play all the resources which the syntax of the language affords when he has anything to communicate, and thus produces a prose of the noblest kind, where every sentence has its own *rhythmus*.

It seems to me that Plato has made the grandest possible use of human language, — a harmony of dependent sentences, rising gradually to the highest climax of power, as for instance in his "Banquet," such as has never since even been attempted. All modern prose is, so far as concerns the appropriateness of the language to the matter, mere child's play compared with Plato's writings. Plato's periods require the utmost attention. One could drink in Homer's verse half asleep as compared with the strain this prose demands. The epic requires simplicity, with a tendency even to garrulousness, while the euphony of the words neutralizes the tediousness of the construction. The Ionic dialect was the language for the pleasurable recital of long-spun tales of adventure. It compares with the Attic as the soft guttural Sicilian with the keen staccato of the Tuscan, only that the Ionic has been elevated to the rank of a written language, which has never happened to the Sicilian. Homer was food for every one. The roughest palate and the most refined taste alike enjoyed him. The melodious movement of his verse lulled the one into sweet dreams, while it incited the other to a study of its subtleties. The nouns move slowly along in company with euphonious, oft-repeated, almost meaningless adjectives; but these adjectives, if one considers them closely, are as indispensable as the trains of princely garments which

BEAUTY OF THE IONIC DIALECT.

please the eye by their splendid though superfluous folds. The predominance of agreeable sounds in the very words themselves, which seem to strike the minor key, give to the narration a strong hold on the senses. We go on slowly as over a wide meadow strewn with flowers : it is always the same grass, indeed, which impedes our way, but it breathes a freshness over all, giving the feeling of easy, elastic progress, offering welcome delays, and turning the journey into a ramble, while the similarity of the flowers themselves is lost in their at first unnoticed but infinite diversity. Who has not picked the anemones growing in endless profusion, in the spring, upon the meadow plains surrounding the Roman Villas? At first one looks so much like another, it seems scarcely worth the trouble to pick more. By degrees, however, we notice that each has a form and color of its own, and then we are never tired of gathering them. So with Homer's repetition of simple words, each of which, in its special place, takes new form and tone.

The German language has a dialect which has much affinity with the Ionic, — the Platt Deutsch or Low German, which is spoken on the northern plains and along the northern coast. A crude but tender cadence, a rest of the voice upon broken vowels, with a capacity to be broad without being insipid, distinguish it. The Low Germans have had no Homer or Herodotus, and must allow this to be said. Perhaps, had they had ancestors of such power, Voss would have translated his Homer at once into Platt Deutsch. He, a Low German himself, struck the tone which rendered the Ionic of Homer in Hoch Deutsch. He knew how to give to his hexameters the tranquil flow which is indispensable to this measure. Voss, after having through his Homer opened the path to German prosody, ventured to attempt poems of his own.

He wrote the epic of "Luise," the story of a clergyman's daughter, who is married to a young "brother-in-office" of her father, which doubtless furnished the original for Goethe's "Hermann and Dorothea." Goethe frankly confessed the imitation, and the troop of his adversaries even accused him of having meant to compete with Voss.

Goethe *compete!*

Old Gleim, living in Halberstad, and no longer able to do anything else to help his friends but to fall into impotent rage whenever he thought them attacked (who in secret dubbed him a vain old fool), writes to Voss about "Hermann and Dorothea," that he had glanced over Goethe's "six-footers," for to read such stuff was simply impossible, and must call this "Hermann and Dorothea" a "sin against his holy Voss." "I will never be persuaded," he continues, "that it is anything but a godless satire. The fellow would cast derision on Voss's 'Luise.' Robespierre committed no greater piece of rascality! Here [in Halberstad, he means] all good souls are of my opinion." This was, of course, an extravaganza on the part of the good Canonicus, but, on the whole, it was the opinion that Goethe had only written hexameters such as had been the fashion twenty years ago; and even to-day, when Goethe's poem meets with unexceptional admiration, the hexameters are not suffered to pass wholly without blame.

I, on the other hand, take the liberty of asserting that the hexameter made by Voss a German metre was fully endowed with life only by Goethe. It is true that his first attempts, made in 1780, are hard to read. But in Italy the knowledge dawned upon him of the cadence of the elegiac, as well as the epic, hexameter. What had earlier been to him but the studied imitation of a dance motion became now his natural gait. He subjected

Voss's style to the right kind of drill, stripped the German hexameter of its academic stiffness, and suited it to the lips of the people. Goethe proceeded in this with the greatest caution and the finest instinct for the language. He recognized the failure in Klopstock's method, had seen his school come into fashion and disappear again, but detected with equal clearness Voss's dangerous tendency to a home-spun familiarity; the question, therefore, for Goethe became how to write a Hoch-Deutsch hexameter which should sound natural, be free from foreign accent, and which would adapt itself readily to the genius of the language. In this he succeeded. Goethe's hexameters excited the derision of the writers who had been captivated by Voss. One should read on this subject the exhaustive criticisms in the Jena literary paper for the year 1807. Certainly it is Goethe who has furnished the model verse which we needed, by his untiring polishing and correcting; by taking advice of others to whom he attributed a fine ear; by his hesitating choice of what seems to him best, with constant regard to the sound of the language when spoken.

It is well to consider that there is no correct versification in itself, any more than there is a correct language in itself. There are only verses which great poets have made, and a language which they have used. There have been very many attempts to outdo Goethe's hexameters and pentameters through so-called more correct ones. Platen, for example, has written, taken for all in all, a few hundred verses of this kind, which correspond in their construction to certain elegancies found in Greek hexameters. Platen's hexameters are excellent; but Goethe's are by no means inferior, though he did not take into consideration all the literary notions which influenced Platen. On the contrary, Goethe's so-called " incorrect " verses are the indispensable concessions which have given us freedom. Our ear to-day asks nothing beyond what Goethe has furnished us, and it is the same with our rhymes. Goethe writes : —

"Allein und abgetrennt von aller Freude
Seh ich aus Firmament nach jener Seite."

He is upbraided for trying to rhyme "Freude" with "Seite." I should like to ask where the men are to be found who have the right to decide whether Goethe may be allowed to rhyme "Freude" and "Seite"? Our whole German theory of versification at present groans under the pedantic pressure of unjustifiable restraints, owing to an unnecessary regard paid to certain peculiarities in the older languages, which it is quite superfluous to consider in our speech of to-day. These purists lay the foundation, not of an improvement, but of an injury, when, without taking counsel of the genius of the language, they would compel the external use of the Greek and Salic rules of prosody. How dull and labored sounds Wolf's model piece of German translation from Homer! how almost unintelligible the translations from Greek and Latin poets, in which attempts are made to reproduce all their prosodiac subtleties to such a degree that those unacquainted with the originals often cannot guess at the meaning of the German rendering! The discredit into which the pursuit of classic tongues has fallen in later times may possibly be ascribed, in a mild way, to these unintelligible productions. The insipidity of such artificial work is too plain. A language has a very tender growth. We must allow its tendrils to entwine where they will, and with practised eye observe where the richness of the sap causes them to spring forth. It is almost inconceivable to us, the groping, hesitating way in which Goethe worked, who pondered long years by himself, and consulted with others how to select one word, or how to form one cadence. I see a time coming when this care will be made the subject of minute study, the immense value of which to science it will be high treason to doubt. Goethe's hexameters, where they seem faulty in "Hermann and Dorothea," need only the accentuation of the right word in reading aloud, to resolve them into harmony. They are written for the ear, and not for the eye.

Concerning the *subject* of the poem, I remark, that Voss's " Luise " is, in its way, a great production. We recognize here, most plainly, the influence of classic models. It is a complete and finished picture which needs no accessories to make it understood and enjoyed. It has the peculiarity of a genuine classic work of art; of being, indeed, finished, using the word in its two senses. Goethe enjoyed reading the poem aloud, and showed himself touched by its beauty. The charms of Schleswig-Holstein scenery have been immortalized by Voss. Klaus Groth, in later times, has added what was left unsaid by him. Voss had, with marvellous truth, taken in with his eye the coloring of Nature, and learned from Homer to translate landscape into words. But, compared with Goethe's poem, Voss's is a pigmy. Who but Goethe could have given, as a background to such peaceful scenes, the hideous chaos of the Revolution, which at that time convulsed the world ?

Goethe had borne the material for this poem in his mind long years before the French Revolution was thought of. He hesitated about the form he should give to it. We see how both the form and the historical background, without which we can scarcely imagine the poem, occurred to him only at the last moment; perhaps, indeed, they were the final stimulant. Goethe finished the work in 1796 with the greatest rapidity: the correspondence with Schiller gives the dates of it exactly; afterward began the painful criticism which postponed the declaration that the poem was of age, ready to take its chance with the public.

Goethe in his old age said to Eckermann that "Hermann and Dorothea" was the only one of his poems which it still gave him pleasure to read. Dorothea, so far as my experience goes, stands more firmly on the soil of her native land than any other creation in German poetry. She has only one sister, of whom she reminds me, and who yet is one of the few characters in fiction which may not have been known to Goethe,— Gudrun, the heroine of the poem which, justly by the side of the Nibelungen, is valued as the German Odyssey. We find the same union of deep feeling with a certain reserve, the quiet, firmly-rooted convictions of duty, the almost philosophical moderation in joy as well as in grief. It is one of the charms of Goethe's poem that the moral conflicts grow out of the contrast between German character and the peculiar circumstances thrust upon our country by our nearest neighbors. Through these Dorothea receives a special mission. She is the interpreter of the highest thoughts which animated the minds of men at that time, though herself all unconscious of it. She is the representative of those healthy sentiments which are not shown by clinging to what is obsolete, but in cooperating to sustain what is good, and which lead us to seek repose of mind in that natural activity which is the prize of life. With what a firm step she moves along! There is a certain homely heroism in her conduct. Goethe's other characters, compared with Dorothea, have something ethereal in them, something not of flesh and blood, as if with one last fold of their garments they still clung to the clouds whence they descended. One would scarcely notice this if Dorothea were not there in contrast; and yet her form is the one which, more than all others, in the true sense was born solely of Goethe's imagination. The mother, in her relation to Hermann, suggests an approach to Goethe's mother. Yet such comparisons are futile, because the characters do not need them. To one thing I would call attention. While Goethe contrasted the well-established, undisturbed family life in the heart of Germany with that on the shores of the Rhine, — already disordered by the neighborhood of France, — he did not anticipate that the storm would ten years later sweep over the whole of Germany. The poem, as an historical monument, immortalizes the period between the beginning of the French Revolution and the wars of Napoleon, which for us was a comparatively peaceful time, marked by intellectual excitements and hopeful expectations which gave the tone in which Schiller's principal works were both written and received.

The unfavorable criticism with which, to a certain extent, " Hermann and Dorothea " was assailed had its rise in the " Xenien." To a man who had attempted such an outrage must be shown, even if it were Goethe, that people knew how to be angry. But all this went for nought; for in May, 1798, Cotta wrote to Schiller about the " immense circulation " of the work.

I would say nothing here of " Wilhelm Meister," were it not necessary to mention Schiller's influence upon it. The work was completed before Goethe's acquaintance with Schiller, who nevertheless, through his sympathy with it, urged Goethe to go to work upon it again vigorously, in order that the book might appear in print as a well-rounded-out and perfect whole. Schiller had undertaken to vindicate the work in this form. Above all, he quieted Goethe himself by some letters which are a masterpiece of criticism; and then in wider circles he created an excitement in favor of it, which if Goethe's romance had stood alone, without his support, it would never have produced.

"Wilhelm Meister" shows at their best all the peculiarities of Goethe's style. As a mountain at different heights may shelter the flora of different zones, so we here find specimens of Goethe's style in all its epochs. The narration opens in the very graphic Frankfort diction, moves on through the prose of the Ten Years, and winds up with a conclusion dashed off in a sketchy, hurried manner, which in language and composition lacks careful drawing and coloring, and gives only rough outlines. The romance begins with a firmly-woven plot, to be unravelled in time, but soon grows more disconnected, drops one thread after another, taking in new ones instead, and finally ends with a few hurried and almost enigmatical narrations. According to the idea which Goethe formed as the work went on, that he wished to exhibit life as it is, the romance ought never to have been finished, but like a memoir should have broken off suddenly at some one point. We lay aside the book with a feeling of disappointment, because Goethe has added a sequel in which a kind of revelation of the fate of the different persons is given, and an attempt made to establish a certain congruity in their relations one to the other. This was not demanded.

"Wilhelm Meister's" Lehrjahre is the home of Philina and Mignon, the two most original and lovely emanations of Goethe's genius. Neither of Mignon nor of Philina do we know, as I have said, whence they sprung. From different quarters conjectures have been made, which however are of no use to us, since all we know of the persons referred to is their names. Never was there such a realistic representation of a coquettish, versatile, irresistible *soubrette* as Philina, and never such a picture as in Mignon of a Southern child, dreamy, passionate, and crushed by fate, as is here painted with a pathos and beauty which insure it a place forever in the palace of memory.

A child drawn to her protector by a strange and irresistible attraction, Mignon feels all at once that she is no longer a child. With childlike confidence she steals to his side at night; like a dog she crouches at the feet of her master, presses herself unrecognized to his heart, and while she abandons herself to her suddenly-awakened passion, her being is consecrated to destruction. Henceforth she must consume herself, and her death is described with the most affecting truth and reality. After Marianna, who in the novelistic beginning had been the heroine, is left in the background, Mignon appears as the one for whose sake the whole fiction was written. Goethe says this himself, and reproached Madame de Staël for her criticism of "Wilhelm Meister," in which she spoke of the story of Mignon as only an episode, while in truth the other characters only revolve about her. What other, indeed, could have so moved Goethe that once, while pursuing his way alone from Erfurt to Gotha, lost in thoughts of the romance, he burst into tears? It was in the early days, and he wrote Frau von Stein of this. Mignon's fate, like a thin cobweb spun from flower to flower, destroyed by one breath of passion, must have been present to his soul.

Goethe, through association with Schiller, to whom he gave the manuscript of "Wilhelm Meister," was tempted, unfortunately, to mar this finest effect of his romance in declaring Philina, contrary to the clear development of the plot, to have been the one who ventured to go to the hero at night, and thus to destroy at the same time Philina's individuality. It is the peculiarity of her relation to Wilhelm, that, in spite of her wanton freedom, and the manifest opportunities she gives him to take liberties with her, he remains cold to her. She is herself cold by nature, and all her amorousness is only superficial. Through her consciousness of the utter lack of sentiment in her nature she is careless to excess in all moral matters, but incapable of passion.

"Wilhelm Meister," besides an enchanting variety of scenes, offers an amount of worldly wisdom which seems absolutely inexhaustible. With each repeated reading we find new traits which betray the keenest observation. Goethe gives us a kind of ironical foreknowledge regarding every new adventure of Wilhelm's, — that he will come out of it without true satisfaction, but yet with a whole skin. Human life appears as an eternal succession of feasts at which either the appetite or the guests are wanting, alternating with times when having the best appetite one must satisfy it with a crust of dry bread. Not long after the appearance of "Wilhelm Meister," a couple of young writers produced a criticism on it in a romance entitled "Charles' Efforts and Hindrances," a silly man who presents a comical figure, being eternally led about by the nose, as it would seem, by fate. But just this shows the deep meaning in Goethe's fiction, that Wilhelm Meister himself never appears ridiculous to us. In the same way Le Sage, in "Gil Blas of Santillana," leads his hero through innumerable, almost fruitless, adventures without making him ridiculous, even when he cuts the sorriest figure; for every reader says to himself, "It might have gone no better with me."

Goethe's romance is valuable also in the history of literature. It contains important information regarding Shakspeare's reception in Germany. The interpretation of Hamlet's character in it is celebrated and familiar to all.

The work has only one disadvantage: things are called and represented as they are, free from varnish of any kind, which led Schiller to foresee that such a *persiflage* on human nature could not be forgiven. Just because we know that man is so, it should not be said. Schiller estimated the world rightly. When Goethe's immorality is spoken of, special reference to " Wilhelm Meister " is intended.

We have now named and discussed the chief works belonging to the period of Goethe's co-labor with Schiller. If we compare them with the works of Schiller which at this time excited the enthusiasm of the German people, they are like a performance by a quartet of stringed instruments next door to the stormy orchestral music and loud voices ringing out from a great theatre, which can be heard only when some accident necessitates a pause. Goethe wrote for himself. The sudden sympathy which took the place of the former coldness of the public was Schiller's work. Scarcely was Schiller dead, however, when the old conditions reappeared. Again arose the voices of those who praised Goethe as a great man, but as one who had now done enough ; and again was Goethe just as indifferent to the cry as before. The pursuit of science seemed to him of more importance than the fate of his poetical works; and therefore this must be spoken of now as his chief interest.

LECTURE XXIII.

STUDY OF NATURAL SCIENCE. — "THE NATURAL DAUGH-
TER." — "ELECTIVE AFFINITIES."

AFTER Schiller's death, the natural means for Goethe to regain composure was through work. A glorious task seemed to offer itself, — the finishing of "Demetrius," Schiller's last drama, which was left lying on his table uncompleted.

Only Goethe could have finished the work in Schiller's spirit, — he who knew all the secrets and plans of the departed one. Indeed, at first he thought so himself, — considered himself called, and in duty bound, to do it. The public performance of the piece should be an imposing memorial service in honor of the dead. But, in spite of the best intentions, Goethe felt himself unable to fulfil the task. He did not even make the attempt to finish the piece. The only thing which Goethe wrote at that time in memory of Schiller was the epilogue to the "Song of the Bell," in which affecting elegy these words are found:

"Behind him, like a misty phantom, lay
The vulgar all that fills our earthly day.

This was written when, in memory of Schiller, the "Song of the Bell" was prepared for stage representation. Why was Goethe powerless before the "Demetrius"? Why sinks into the same grave with Schiller all that during their mutual labor seemed to have so absolutely engrossed him ? Goethe, in order to recover from the irreparable loss, takes refuge in his official labors ; or if he turns to literary work, chooses what least reminds him of Schiller. He reverts to Winckelmann's Letters. Schiller was, as it were, effaced. Goethe's art studies were what Schiller was least able to participate in, for want of previous training ; he took a lively interest in them, but stood related to them as an outsider, who in all haste seeks to learn as much as possible without making any pretension to an opinion of his own. On these Goethe now seemed to wish to concentrate his best powers. Already during Schiller's last years he had begun to do so. The political condition of Europe made the history of art a more and more conspicuous subject of public interest. The immense spoils of Bonaparte's Italian campaigns, which filled the Louvre in Paris, offered a collection of works of art such as had never before been gathered in any one place in the modern world.

This, as has been already remarked, happened while Schiller was yet living ; the principal reason, however, why Goethe after Schiller's death fell into such marked poetical inactivity was, that the reaction after his overstrained labor in this direction — symptoms of which had appeared during Schiller's life — now completely mastered him. The two great events which distinguished the close of the eighteenth century also produced a direct effect on him, — the end of the French Revolution in Imperialism under Napoleon ; and the overthrow of the German Empire, together with the Prussian Monarchy, by the decisive victories of the French, one of which was gained in the very neighborhood of Weimar. The times of moderate freedom which Schiller, in spite of the excesses of the French Revolution, hoped for till his last moment, had become to all nations only a dream. A frightful disenchantment united with terror, in presence of the monstrous, growing power of the one man who held everything in his hand, benumbed all other feelings. Goethe, standing on the threshold of old age, must have realized that constellations had begun to rule, in earthly as well as in spiritual spheres, for which the life he had hitherto pursued in no wise prepared him. He recognized that an important epoch was ended, and, withdrawing into himself, waited for the new world to be evolved out of this chaos.

And now we notice a peculiar development of his poetic ability. He begins, as it were, entirely anew. A romance grows in his imagination in the same way as " Werther " had arisen, — out of a mere inward impulse, as it would seem, simply to gratify his own heart, and without any thought of the public who might have a share in it ; just as " Werther " was written for the few people who were in the secret.

But yet this new work is in quite a different spirit from " Werther ; " notwithstanding the passion in it, the exciting personal element is wanting, which until now had been the distinguishing feature in Goethe's works, — his very last, " The Natural Daughter " excepted, in which this new spirit is likewise to be observed. We must not by any means attribute this to Goethe's having grown old, for he cannot be called an old man who was able to describe the passionate conflicts in " Elective Affinities." His changed manner of writing is to be ascribed to other causes.

To one of these we have already referred, and it must now be treated of in full, — the influence of Goethe's scientific studies on his writings and on his view of the world. Only now does the effect of these studies become obvious, although Goethe ever since his entrance into Weimar had devoted himself to natural science, especially after

SCIENTIFIC STUDIES AND DISCOVERIES. 445

his return from Italy, when he was so deeply engrossed in it that Schiller was forced to wrest him from its sway. For even what he produced freshly after the Italian epoch in the way of poetical works was, for the most part, only giving shape to conceptions which had long been hidden in his mind. "Hermann and Dorothea," "God and the Bajadere," "The Bride of Corinth," the "Achilleïs," had lain dormant in his imagination for years; but "The Natural Daughter" and "Elective Affinities" are entirely new, even in conception, and the date on the title-page points at the same time to the new century as the period of their birth.

Goethe, in many places in his works, has given a detailed account of his growing interest in the natural sciences. We can follow him step by step. An aptitude for these studies was born in him. We know how he listened in Leipsic to lectures on medicine and physics, and devoted himself as much to them in Strasburg as if they were his natural department; but all this and other occasional efforts in the Frankfort epoch must be regarded as only preliminary steps, amounting to little, for according to his own confession he knew nothing of natural science when he went to Weimar. His vocation there first opened the way to it. The care of the public forests led him to the study of botany; the superintendence of the collections in the University of Jena, to anatomy; the mining in Ilmenau, to geology; and his art studies, to physics. In each of these departments Goethe sought at first only to acquaint himself with the already known facts, but soon hastened on to pursue his own self-directed investigations; and ends with discoveries, the importance of which are only just beginning to be duly recognized.

Nothing can be more modest and graceful than Goethe's circumstantial description of the quite extraordinary way in which he partly forced himself, and in part was enticed, into the various departments of Natural Science. To a beginner of the ordinary cast the elements of all knowledge come as a well-regulated inheritance, which he has only to accept at a time when the human mind is best qualified for the mere reception of ideas. Goethe came to these studies as a full-grown man, in whom every new thing he sees awakens individual thoughts, and who is led on as it were indirectly and impulsively to his investigations. In pursuing his botanical studies he hunts up in the woods the forester, the herb-seeker, the essence-maker, and in obscure places the possessors of herbariums; reading at the same time an enormous amount concerning these subjects which he finds in the Weimar Library, making observations in his own garden, and soon proposing contradictory hypotheses to all found in the books, which he eagerly but quietly follows up. But only incidentally is time allowed him for this work. In imagination he forms the *typical plant* — the " Urpflanze," — out of which all other plants must be developed according to natural law, and to which all can be traced back. From time to time he is surprised by the continuance of dreams filled with this creation of his imagination; by degrees everything beside vanishes, and he lives in these thoughts as if his life had only this one interest. It is years, however, before he has advanced far enough to make his theories publicly known; and when he finally resolves to do so the professionals reject them with a shrug of the shoulders and a compassionate smile. But he waits for the applause of quite another public. With Christiane, after the Italian journey, he pursues these studies; for her he transforms his botanical theories into a poem, the chief contents of which are not indeed scientific, but bear reference to his secret happy intercourse with the beloved one.

HIS ORIGINAL IDEAS AND METHODS. 447

Professional people of the present day assert that Goethe's ideas contain the fundamental views on which modern botany rests.

Goethe's anatomical studies took a similar course. Here obtained in science, as then understood, an outward method of comparison to which Goethe opposed the high ideal unity which he had wrought out in his imagination. In botany a number of families were assumed in which all plants were included, — the criterion by which to distinguish them being the blossom. The difference in the families was supposed to have been pre-determined from the beginning, and to be in accordance with the plan of creation. Goethe's clearer insight was opposed to both premises.

He would not merely compare a plant bearing a certain kind of blossom with other plants of the same phase of development: he would not have any comparison instituted between individual plants, but would simply follow the successive phenomena of development from the very first moment. He takes up a plant as if there were only this one in the world, and tries to understand all the stages of its development. He examines the seeds, watches their germination, their growth, the influence of the soil, sun, light, and darkness, the richness or poverty of its leaves and blossoms, and the mounting of the sap. He examines into every detail of their individual relations, and seeks the laws according to which this incessant series of changes take place which are presented to his eye. He has no definite aim in view in making his researches that he should proceed like a police detective; but he follows with impartial eye all the different manifestations of life, and nothing escapes his loving look. By degrees, after he has gone from plant to plant, he thinks he discovers similarity of development, and ventures to assume the existence of laws. These laws lead him finally to his ideal formula for the constitution of all plants. His discovery is that the single parts of the plant — leaves, blossoms, stems, etc. — follow a common law of formation, and are only different manifestations of the same original type; so that Goethe's ideal typical plant, "Urpflanze," is in leaves, blossoms, stems, and root only an agglomeration of intrinsically the same parts which, under various influences, have taken various forms.

Goethe now tries to prove the existence of the same principle in the animal kingdom.

But we must not lose ourselves in specialties to follow Goethe's osteological discoveries. Enough that here, also, he did not succeed in the beginning in establishing his principle so as to convince others, but his discoveries, after having suffered from the disapprobation of the learned for decades, to-day are not only recognized as well founded, but as actually offering the basis for modern science. I refer you to the judgment of professional men on this subject. With the clear-sightedness of genius which made the poet, who pursued the subject only in his leisure hours, raise himself above the drudgery of all scientific investigation to grapple at once with the highest problems, he discerned the principles whose latest fruit is Darwin's wonderful theory, based on a grand idea, but radically false in its deductions. Goethe would have taken good care to avoid drawing the inferences of the Darwin school from the insight which he gained into the workings of Nature, yet would, perhaps, nevertheless have hailed with the deepest satisfaction the world-thrilling effect of conclusions to which his solitary and much-scoffed-at discoveries had helped to open the way.

We find Goethe occasionally giving vent to his joy at his successes as poet and author. But the expression of this feeling never rises above quiet content. He feels a cheerful complacency in what he had accomplished; but he is never filled with such absolute rapture as when, in the character of naturalist, he is able to impart to his friends a fresh discovery. Then his enthusiasm is passionate, — a joy thrills him which penetrates to his very marrow; he forgets everything else in such moments. It seems to us, on looking back to-day, that when the immense consequences involved in his new ideas flashed on him, he must have been penetrated with such overwhelming astonishment and awe as to be almost beside himself.

Concerning his geological studies, we will only remark that Agassiz ascribes to Goethe the first suggestion of the theory of the prevalence of an ice period on the earth, which is to-day of such momentous value.

It remains for us to speak of Goethe's most important scientific work, — the "Theory of Colors."

The disapprobation which all his scientific views at first encountered still continues on this subject, while in other departments opposition has yielded to the full sunshine of recognition. Goethe's "Theory of Colors" is not sustained by any competent authority. He starts with the same principle which he has everywhere else asserted. He will go back to the simple elements. He denies the diversity of colors, which he must regard as only intermediate steps between light and dark. It is not our task to decide this question; and I limit myself, as unprofessional, to the following observations, which scarcely touch the matter itself.

Considered as a book, as a product of words and thoughts, Goethe's "Theory of Colors" is truly enchanting. What it contains in historical material alone is sufficient to warrant what I have said of it. According to Goethe's principle, that in order to present a science one must give the history of this science, he has — while discussing what the learned as well as amateurs have said about colors in different ages — produced a book which no one can ever tire of reading who has once become acquainted with it.

Taking a survey of Goethe's scientific activity, and in view of his leading idea that creative Nature must be traced back to first principles, we perceive the relation of this idea to the fundamental principle of Greek art, which is to restore to the human body, and to human language, its simpler but more comprehensive forms. The task of the artist is not slavishly to copy accidental peculiarities which may distinguish individuals, but to invent simple forms under which all differences may be harmonized. We perceive Goethe's enthusiasm for Greek art to be intimately associated with his views of Nature; but we cannot here enlarge upon this. We have to discuss more important points, which make Goethe's method of observing Nature not only valuable to his own generation, but to the present as well.

Goethe's great idea is the limiting of all knowledge of Nature to the province of the "accessible," — the "Zugänglichen," as he expresses it.

We have seen what made Spinoza's philosophy so dear to him. It was not that he specially reverenced Spinoza's system, — Goethe even occasionally confessed that he did not know much about it; but it was because he saw in his works a connected mass of observations about human nature, in which only those things were brought under the severest scrutiny which could be comprehended by the observing, investigating, analyzing human intellect. No other philosophy had offered Goethe this. All had sought to formulate the incomprehensible as well.

Goethe insists that this same distinction shall be held

clear in the study of Nature. From the outset the "inaccessible" is recognized not only as the other but as the larger half of natural phenomena. The "inaccessible," which he also calls the "great mystery," prevails to such a degree that its inherent nature extends even to the "accessible;" so that he designates the "accessible" and the "inaccessible" together as the "great mystery." Again and again he declares that it is impossible for the individual to comprehend it, and denies to himself and others the right out of the known to construct the unknown. He looks upon himself, as it were, as a mariner who had sailed round a portion of the world in his ship, here and there making a landing, but who would not venture to draw general conclusions as to what might be contained in the heart of the country from what he had seen from the shore.

But while Goethe refuses to the understanding to take more for granted than can be grasped within the five fingers, he gives to the imagination of the poet all the more freely the right to create, with unconscious, dreamy power, images of what the mind wishes to perceive; only he preserves with great clearness the limits of the operation of both. Long since, in Goethe's youth, the great Laplace-Kantian hypothesis of the origin and future destruction of this earth had gained ground. Out of the rotating nebulæ (children learn this at school now-a-days) is formed the central gas-drop, which afterwards becomes the earth, and which as a congealing ball passes through all its phases, including the episode of its tenantry by the human race, until finally, as burned-out slag, it falls back into the sun, — a long, but to most people perfectly conceivable, process, for whose accomplishment no other agency is needed than some outside power to sustain an equal degree of heat in the sun.

No more hopeless perspective for the future can be thought of than this which is forced upon us to-day as a scientific necessity. A carcass which even a hungry dog would hesitate to approach is a refreshingly appetizing morsel compared with this last excrement of creation as which our earth is to be restored to the sun; and the scientific eagerness with which this generation accepts and believes such views is the sign of a morbid imagination, which learned men of the future will exert much ingenuity in explaining as a historical phenomenon.

Goethe never harbored any such dreary views. To fathom the indefinite past was to him a delight; but to grasp the indefinite future, except poetically, he was never tempted.

While in "Faust," where his imagination held sway, he did not hesitate to bring the distant heavenly spaces within the miserable limits of a theatre stage, as a man of science he did not even speculate on these subjects. It would have been contrary to his idea of freedom to try to dogmatize to-day on what will be in the future. Only vague anticipations are permissible here. Nature is to him ever wholly renewed, ever in her virgin state, whose future must remain veiled. What she does not herself impart cannot be won by force. All the names and numbers we may give are only labelled *phenomena*, which any drop of rain may efface.

Hence Goethe's unconcern at the incompleteness of his observations. He verifies the everlasting changeableness of things; he observes endless transitions from one condition to another: where then, he asks, is the moment in which an isolated particle of Nature, in the process of its development, may be considered as representing all the rest? The pregnant moment of a plant perhaps begins

THE VITAL UNITY OF NATURE. 453

at a time when no human eye observes it. Goethe believes nothing but what he has seen, nor accepts the observations of others until he has repeated them himself. His greatest enjoyment is in telling of what he has himself discovered. He looks upon himself as a traveller upon an exploring expedition, for whom every object has value and importance, and does not neglect to make a note of them even though the provisions give out and his people rebel. Right and left he stoops to pick up whatever attracts his eye, though another path may offer other objects. Goethe is the genuine *dilettante*. He never hopes in approaching Nature to overhear so many of her secrets as to be able to guess all the rest. He catches single sounds of an unknown language which strike on his ear, by means of which here and there a very simple sentence becomes clear to him. Goethe was persuaded that all phenomena stand in mutual relation, and that therefore nothing can be demonstrated by the study of isolated parts, however dexterous the treatment of them may be. This is the meaning of his axiom that Nature has neither kernel nor shell, neither an inward nor an outward, neither an essential nor a non-essential; but that each part must be looked upon as equally important to every other part.

Hence he turned with delight to the manifestations of Nature only when he was in the best mood for it. Indeed, he looks upon his own personality and its relation to outward things as so necessary an ingredient in his scientific labors that he will not separate these learned investigations from his every-day existence; he considers them as symptoms of his whole conduct of life, and of equal importance with everything else. Hence the stress he laid on his personal condition when pursuing his scientific studies. This manner of working seemed at last so momentous to him, that he regarded a scientific discovery as imperfectly communicated if he did not know the personal history of the discoverer. Hence, also, in his last days, when he turned his attention to meteorology and cloud formations, his singularly beautiful friendship for Howard, the English investigator, who was the first to furnish any definite conclusions on these subjects. He would not acknowledge the value of Howard's results until he had found out the relation of the man to his subject, had asked this question by letter, and received the most explicit and beautiful statements with regard to it. He afterwards published all this in translation as a biographical memorial in honor of this simple man.

With what eminent propriety this way of considering things may be designated as antique appears when we glance at the relation of man to Nature as it had been for centuries, and at the entire change it has undergone during the course of the last hundred years.

The Mosaic history of creation ends with man, who enters upon the stage endowed with the capacity to make useful to himself all that had been created before him. The Greek myths also introduce their gods and Titans as in a human sense terrestrial phenomena, so that they may be regarded as direct precursors of the human race. Even Aristotle himself could not imagine the world without making the Greeks the favored people, forming its centre; and Christianity elevates men to be the end and aim of creation in such a sense that without them the world would be meaningless.

Natural science rose to protest against these views. Astronomy opened the fight by proving the earth—which had been supposed to be the centre of the solar system —to be only a subordinate planet, whose sovereign inhabitants on this discovery must be satisfied to take a lower rank. Step by step, this theory by which the earth suf-tered degradation was followed out. It was proved that the earth had existed and passed through enormous periods of time before man was created. Forces were discovered whose effects are not known, much less directed, by the mind of man; and instead of the former godlike beings, standing in a comfortable proximity to him, man recognized mysterious forces operating from monstrous distances.

Nor to these forces did man feel himself in the same relation as formerly he felt to the Deity. The kingdoms of plants, minerals, and animals now share with man the mastery of the earth's surface: no more thought of submission as if their highest purpose was to be serviceable to mankind, but according to unknown constitutions they exist for themselves, speak a language unintelligible to man, and know nothing of him; while man himself, no longer knowing where he belongs, accepts gratefully the fact that in the vast animal kingdom a doubtful space has been allotted to him, where he modestly sits meditating with shame on his nearest of kin in the animal world, and is allowed laboriously to evolve from his feeble mind the conviction that there is no authoritative proof either of his own soul or of God as its creator and final refuge. This is the mental state of mankind, who have to-day such doubtful possession of this earth, which is at some future time to be converted into slag.

It was this view of things which, becoming universal in the second half of the last century, prepared the decline of the supremacy of the Romanic world. It was the sudden springing up of these theories which caused the unheard-of intellectual condition whose result was the French Revolution. A dissolution took place of convictions which had till then been universal, and upon which for thousands of years the structure of European life had rested. Everything was doubted, and there was no question which Science was not allowed to discuss, while the results so won were instantly applied to practical use. State and Church had long been sacrificed in thought before the tiniest flame had been kindled in the great brand of the French Revolution. Not merely free-thinking citizens, but high and low, held the new opinions, and neither Catholic nor Protestant clergy offered any resistance. Christianity and reverence for the antique mingled peacefully, for all eyes were dazzled by the new revelations from the realm of science which followed, flash upon flash. At the ascent of the first balloon a feeling actually possessed men that they were, in reality, flying into infinite space. From out the mouth of great Mother Nature men expected to receive the laws in conformity with which the new generations were to live.

One would suppose that Goethe, who without any teacher had been dragged by his own experience into the midst of this revolution in the world of thought, would have bowed a willing assent to these new views; but precisely here we see arise in him something which stands invincibly opposed to the despairing logic of the natural philosopher.

In Goethe's early years the disorganizing ideas on which Voltaire based his opinions, and which Rousseau labored to oppose, did not exist. Of his Frankfort writings he himself spoke later as mere poetical attempts. They paint only the inward man, and betray a pretty good understanding of the emotions of the soul. " Here and there," he continues, " we catch the sound of passionate delight in rural scenes and objects of Nature, as well as an earnest longing to find out the gigantic secret of the unceasing creation and destruction going on day by day around us." This impulse, however, at that time

ANTICIPATION OF DARWIN.

seemed to exhaust itself in a vague, "unsatisfactory sort of brooding."

In the first Weimar days his old view of the world pervaded all he wrote. But gradually, and quite independent of what is happening around him, Goethe changes his standpoint.

Indeed, the nearer he tries to come to the great Mystery, the more all impetuous feeling is restrained, while the study of what we may call the intercourse of Nature with herself holds a prominent place in his new way of looking at things. Under Herder's influence his view of history took another form. History became to Goethe a series of natural processes connected with the changes of the soil itself on which the history was enacted. Nations became individuals in his eyes, to observe whose movements formed part of the scientific investigation of Nature. Just so the life of the individual, the threads of man's destiny, became woven into the tissue of universal phenomena.

But it was chiefly through his own osteological discoveries that Goethe's views of the world gained a wholly new foundation. He finds that the material distinction firmly asserted by the learned men of his time between the skull of men and animals does not exist. Indeed, they would not believe that the intermaxillary bone, — rendered through him so famous, — which divides the upper jaw into several pieces, is peculiar to man also, because in man all the parts have so entirely grown together that in general the separation is only an imaginary one; for Goethe, however, the separation was there all the same, and by it the human skeleton proved to belong to the great series of Mammalia. In Europe he was literally the first to foresee the positive dethronement of the race which had formerly ruled.

Struggle as he might with his higher consciousness against carrying these intellectual hypotheses too far, the result of his new experiences was so great that they could not fail to produce a transformation in him. Goethe absolutely abandons his earlier standpoint. He recognizes mankind, and himself of course, as under the ban of a predestined servitude, which made the freedom that until that time had been allowed in whole departments entirely out of the question. His individual experiences and uninterrupted, quiet self-observation confirmed this to his own mind, even when he could not bring himself to accept the faith of others. With astonishment he had long marked within himself periodical moral alternations between good and evil, whose rotation he was anxious to calculate. Repeated examples teach him how powerless free-will seems against " the influences of the stars." He discovers constantly new chains whose ends disappear in mist, but whose pressure he feels only too palpably about him. Nothing would have been more natural than for him now to take the last step; but he does not do it. He willingly pursues the path to which the ever-increasing knowledge of physical science urges him; but he allows himself to be led only up to a certain point. With all his scientific subordination to the laws of Nature, Goethe's private personal bearing is remarkable.

Goethe never descends from his native, aristocratic standpoint; but, in spite of all which science might seem to prove to the contrary, regards man as the centre of creation, for whose sake everything else exists. It never occurs to him that he must first prove his claim to this proud position: he takes it as his right. We find him here to be in flagrant contradiction to the fundamental requirements of science, which demand radical and exact investigation of things. Chiefly for this reason may we call

Goethe a Greek, who could not surrender his inborn feeling of superiority even to philosophy. Under no circumstances will he consent to be a slave. Who will find fault with him for this? Where his personal, individual thought was not in place, he turned silently away.

Goethe, who was cramped by no obligations, made the most absolute use of his freedom. He labored in no university where he would have had to consider either colleagues or pupils; he was member of no academy which might impose upon him a certain social reserve: he was perfectly independent. No one dared question him, or turn his head in this or that direction so that he was forced to see what lay just there. In the possession of five healthy senses he regarded himself as the centre of all phenomena, and asserted that what was discernible to the *unassisted human eye* was the real standard for everything. This was the reason why he found no pleasure in astronomy, for which he needed a telescope, or in microscopic investigations. He even cherished a prejudice against Newton from the one circumstance that he operated with a prism instead of making a sufficient instrument of his healthy human eye.

It would by no means do to recommend Goethe's method as worthy of imitation. However, since such *was* his method, and since his example stands so distinctly before us, and since as a learned man he has contributed so much that is valuable, we will not cavil at those who in like manner follow the bent of their own genius from honoring Goethe as the patron and defender of this manner of pursuing the work. Goethe once incidentally declares science and art to be identical, and thus proclaims the inspiration of the favorable moment as the standard.

It is something refreshing to see the natural way in which, at a time when everything began to totter, he made firm ground under his own feet by this subjective treatment.

He had learned to look upon the development of mankind as only a part of the economy of Nature, and the fate of the individual as a wave in the great stream whose rising and sinking was governed by laws, the knowledge of which belongs to the realm of the "inaccessible." Goethe was much too practical to make the limit between freedom and necessity an arithmetical problem. He permits the foundation of things to rest undisturbed while he examines individual cases: he feels sure that, in some way, the law will manifest itself; and he finally discovers, starting from similitudes in Nature, the formula which is also adapted to the intellectual life.

This is contained in his doctrine of Necessarianism.

When almost the last of his old friends, Carl August, had died, and Goethe must greet as his new master the son whom he had known from his birth, he wrote a letter in which he formally proffered to him his homage. This letter, the style of which bears every mark of Goethe's "Orphic period," as Gervinus calls it, is written with the ceremonious elaboration peculiar to old age. It is often to be observed that aged men, clinging to a dear inheritance which they hope to perpetuate, adopt a curiously formal manner, because, through the experience of a long life, they are convinced of the importance of even trivial actions, and therefore, when something quite above the ordinary routine is to be done, feel compelled to be solemnly circumstantial. So it seems to have been with Goethe in this letter, from which I quote the following sentence:—

"The rational world is to be considered as a great immortal individual who steadily works out the Necessary, and thereby raises himself to be master even over Chance."

These words of a great sage are here given as the final result of all meditation.

We see from this that Goethe had arrived at a theory which brings the physical and moral world into the closest connection. In the physical world, the law of Necessity means that creative Nature has, so to say, a fixed budget of expenditure, the limits of which she never oversteps; so that if on one side in some of her forms there is a *plus*, it is counterbalanced in others by a *minus*. Goethe proceeds carefully by examples to illustrate this idea. In the moral world, on the other hand, the law of Necessity means the sequence of certain inevitable results from foregoing actions and conditions, not necessarily in a previously defined form, but unalterable in their dynamic manifestation. And here, for the smallest human action the same law serves as governs the deeds of the greatest masses : everywhere in the " Economy of Nature " proportionate compensation for all that happens. One might call this view of things a doctrine of Fatalism drawn from the past instead of applied to the future.

As I have said, we first encounter this view of things in " The Natural Daughter."

Goethe here lays aside any intention to surprise the public and to make his poetical creations swim about like fishes, gracefully playing " hide and seek " before the eyes of spectators, their golden scales gleaming brightest in the very spot where one would least expect to see them; he does not even give to his figures individual names, but only class names, such as King, Duke, etc., while as half-free, half-bound, they move on to their inevitable fate, representatives of partly historical, partly still existing, classes of society.

Goethe had learned from the Greeks, that in order to develop a real tragedy among human beings it was necessary to represent them in their highest moral potency, and then to urge them on to inevitable conflicts demanding the exercise of their whole strength. We know what simple, grand traits distinguish the characters of Antigone, Iphigenia, Creon, and the rest; and Goethe believes modern individualities should also be stripped of all that is petty and accidental, and represented only in their supreme moments: and he attempts it. In Eugenia, the heroine of the tragedy, he presents a maiden whose fate depends upon whether she is to pass henceforth for the distinguished daughter of a prince or for one picked up by chance, a waif, from the great mass of humanity. In the moment of trial she shows that she is nothing but a good-natured young maiden, vain and inquisitive; and her lot is decided. But these decisive scenes in the story develop with a cold necessity, as if one had set a pendulum in motion in an exhausted receiver to produce the most exquisite vibration possible.

It almost frightens one to see these crystallized figures appear and act, — their lives divorced from everything accidental, while only the free-will of the individual remains, as one might say, in its highest chemical purity, whose deliberate choice brings about the catastrophe.

Goethe never finished the Trilogy of which this piece formed a part, and in which, as he said, he hoped to symbolize the frightful events of the French Revolution. He relinquished the attempt because he found the public had no sort of comprehension of what he meant. We have only schedules of this sequel, which give no clear idea of it; but he tried to illustrate his views of the evolution of human destiny in another form in " Elective Affinities."

As he had undertaken in " The Natural Daughter " to represent the French Revolution, so in " Elective Affinities " his broken friendship with Frau von Stein was, at last, to receive poetic transfiguration. It had lain in his breast like an open wound which required healing, and it was only after long years that he succeeded in finding the right means for this.

We must not give an external interpretation to what I have said, as if Goethe strove to lay a poem, like a plaster, over the wound, in order, by so doing, to place matters on their old footing.

He had been, long since, if not absolutely restored to Frau von Stein's favor, at least on tolerable terms with her. His relation to her son had never changed; the young man clung to him with the old attachment: a number of letters prove this. In the first of these there is no mention of his parents; but soon after we find greetings to father and mother, and in a short time the intercourse with the family is renewed. In 1789 Herder met Goethe again at Frau von Stein's; yet this seems to have been only a formal meeting, and the mutual explanation came much later. This the Schillers were chiefly instrumental in bringing about. In 1796, as Frau von Stein was sitting, one morning, among the orange trees before her house, Goethe, with his little son by the hand, came across the path by the old way; and when he finally left her, she wrote in her diary: "How is it possible that I have so long misunderstood him!" When Frau Charlotte in the same year stood sponsor to Schiller's second son, she was surprised not to find Goethe at her side, who, through Schiller, sent her his greetings. Year by year the friendship regained more of its old tone, and we are not surprised at the beginning of the new century to find Goethe again in correspondence with his old friend. A pleasant confidence had once more grown up between them.

In this sense, then, no further reconciliation was necessary; neither was it intended in the romance to give explanation or excuse for the rupture, nor to glorify the former beloved one.

I say this emphatically, because there are some things which might lead to a different opinion. It would not have been unnatural for Goethe to represent the problem of what might have happened if he had married Frau von Stein after her husband's death; the romance even seems to begin with such an idea. A widower, still a young man, persuades a widowed friend of his own age, for whom he had earlier cherished a hopeless passion, to accept his hand for the sake of the old love. A marriage takes place. Soon after a young maiden of the name of Ottilie is introduced into this household, between whom and Edward the husband a passion is enkindled, by which Edward, Charlotte the wife, and Ottilie are all ruined.

Nothing would seem more natural than the supposition that Goethe's imagination had wrought out what, to human foresight, would have happened if Frau von Stein later had become his wife. The aim of the romance would then have been to show how wise it was in him to put an end to such a relation at the right time, even if he had to do it in a very hard way.

I almost believe Goethe intentionally sought to give this appearance, and therefore lent to Edward's wife, in a conspicuous way, Frau von Stein's Christian name. Perhaps he wished to mislead the critics. Weimar was too dangerous ground; there must no scandal arise. As soon as he had succeeded in diverting the scent of a gossiping world, Goethe might conceive his relation to Frau von Stein a second time in the same romance, and this time in its full pregnancy. Goethe, who was often questioned as to the special meaning of this fiction, and reproached with its immorality, once said, simply: "What the romance means is very clear. It is only an illustration of Christ's words, 'Whosoever looketh on a woman to lust after her hath committed adultery with her already in his heart.'" This could not refer to Frau von Stein at the time he left her, but to the beginning of their acquaintance, when he really coveted her.

Let us put into a few words Goethe's whole acquaintance during the Ten Years with Frau von Stein. A young man forms a friendship with a married woman which may be called a "spiritual marriage," and which if the husband had not been living would certainly have led to a real marriage. But even this spiritual marriage is opposed to the moral code of human intercourse as contained in the Ten Commandments, which receives its final emphasis from the words of Jesus Christ (Matthew v. 28).

Goethe accordingly takes a married pair who, though united by love, had yet outlived the first transports of passion on both sides, and who, like Herr von Stein and his wife, had been drawn together partly by external motives. Through Ottilie's advent now happens to these married people what befel Herr von Stein and his wife through Goethe.

Into their wedded life Ottilie enters, as Goethe once found his way into Frau von Stein's family. Not at once, but slowly like a moral polyp, Goethe attached himself to the Stein household. In the year 1780, four years after this friendship began, he writes to Lavater about Frau von Stein: "She has gradually succeeded to the position of mother, sister, beloved one; and a bond unites us which seems like these natural ties." To Frau von Stein Goethe had become son, brother, lover, all in one. All this in the romance must constitute the crime of the poor creature on whom Goethe imposes this burden. Ottilie's guilt is the growing into these relations with Edward which Goethe had borne to Frau von Stein. With all Ottilie's innocence, such as Goethe gave himself credit for when first drawn to Frau von Stein, she was yet guilty from the moment she gave room to the thought that Edward could, by a separation from Lotte, become free to make her his wife. As Goethe, by means of the intellectual element he brought into the Stein family, had gained such a vast ascendancy that a separation from him was inconceivable, he represents Ottilie by her spiritual superiority as occupying an unassailable position between Edward and Lotte. This maiden is endowed with a subtile capacity to enter into all human emotions against which we are powerless. Who can condemn Edward for his passion? And who blames Charlotte that she is ready, for Ottilie's sake, to consent to a divorce? Who ever blamed Frau von Stein for retaining such a mind as Goethe's in voluntary dependence upon her? It was Goethe who should have gone; and so Ottilie only, though innocent, is the cause of all the misfortune, and must atone for it all.

Not because Goethe wished to encroach upon Herr von Stein's rights was he guilty, but because he had offended against the command of God, to break whose laws is to interfere with the natural order of the world and insure destruction. In her individual relation to Charlotte Ottilie could scarcely be called guilty, because Charlotte herself wished to retreat in order to render Edward's marriage with Ottilie possible. Ottilie's guilt consisted in entertaining the thought of supplanting a married woman in the heart of her husband. In the same way Goethe in later years recognized his own guilt, in that he had persisted so long in holding a place which for him to have held was a sin against the holy ordinance on which rests the preservation of human society. All this shows the influence of Goethe's new view of the world on himself. With his eye fixed on the Universal, he now judges and condemns his peculiar case from the moral standpoint of the Universe.

To all this we find no allusion in Werther, — no hint that in his love for Lotte not only Albert's rights were invaded, but that he violated at the same time the fundamental laws of human society. Ottilie's love for Edward Nature herself finally opposes, who is bound to maintain her laws inviolate. The spiritual marriage of Ottilie and Edward, compared with the real marriage with Charlotte, was nothing but a finer kind of bigamy, against which the arm of Providence must ever be lifted. Such a spiritual marriage, as we have seen, had existed between Goethe and Frau von Stein. In that which had seemed to both an innocent and lawful compensation for all that had been denied them, Goethe now saw the unlawful, the criminal, the punishable.

If we take into consideration all the people who appear in " Elective Affinities," we see according to what consistent principles the composition is executed. In his earlier days Goethe was not accustomed to work in this way, but now he seems to have adopted Schiller's method. Every action is carefully thought out beforehand, every effect produced with conscious power, and the whole wrought up to a well-planned climax. A tragedy rises before our eyes in the form of a narration. There is not a trace of the early fragmentary, " fancy-free " style of writing.

The deliberation with which the romance is planned and executed, chief regard being shown to its effect as a whole, is visible even in its style. Goethe does not with restless hand file and polish anew each word, as he had done formerly, only to relinquish the task from sheer weariness; but he gives a certain amount of time to the handling, and lets that suffice. Hence, in some places there is a noticeable carelessness, while in others the wish is openly shown by a certain treatment to arrive at definite effects;—for instance, the intentionally short sentences in which we are informed of the death of the child through Ottilie's fault: here the breathless succession of the phrases is meant to excite the reader; and, lastly, the resort to a wholly external expedient for displaying Ottilie's mental wealth by attributing to her, under the name of a Diary, a rare amount of the finest observations on life, in the form of aphorisms: these could only belong, appropriately, to an older intellectual person, and would never have arisen even in the gifted soul of so young a maiden as Ottilie.

But in still other ways Goethe's new view of the universe is manifested in this romance. He endeavors to make plain the necessity of everything which happens by lending, as it were, a double value to each character in the romance. In the first place he represents each as an organic part of creation, acting instinctively according to fixed laws, as the die thrown on the table by higher spiritual powers has no choice how many spots shall turn up. And, in the second place, he treats the same characters as perfectly free, responsible beings, who must give an account of every thought of the soul. From this cause arises in the mind of the reader the same curious discord that enters into our judgment of long past events which we recognize as unavoidable, while at the same time we cannot give up the idea that some one was to blame for them.

In order to suggest this element of Fatalism, Goethe

has chosen an illustration from chemistry, which has given the name to the romance, and which has been the cause of so much misunderstanding.

He compares human beings to elements which attract or repel one another without any exercise of will in the matter. In order to understand him here, one must certainly be thoroughly conversant with his works. Spinoza, in his manner of treating human relations, had opened the way to these views. A parallel between personal and chemical attractions we find already in Goethe's letters to Schiller, as a simple comparison of which no special point is made. Only in the preface to " Elective Affinities " does this simile assume the fatalistic character so offensive to the reader, and which Goethe never intended that it should bear. The romance itself is a proof to the contrary. It would show how all this chemical force thrust upon man by the demoniac powers does not release him from personal responsibility. Goethe would say that whatever results from our own fault or that of others, however much unknown powers may seem to rule over and dispose the fate of mortals, it is, after all, given to man to escape their clutches. But this, indeed, the public was not able to find out. It would seem as if Goethe looked upon our moral actions as not free, but as emanations from an inexplicable force inherent in all substances, exciting all the emotions of the human soul; so that it appeared like the plaything of some dark spirits whose intention with regard to us, even if we could fathom them, we never could change.

A just exposition of his views has not been arrived at, because " Elective Affinities," after having been spoken of for fifty years as Goethe's most dangerous work, is to-day passed over and very little known.

If we may judge of the origin of " Elective Affinities "

from analogy with the rest of Goethe's works, the plot for it dates much farther back than the time at which he began to work on it. Goethe betrayed incidentally that in the beginning he had only intended to write a short story : indeed, the romance always retained this character ; it is planned for one grand consummation, and we notice in many places the interpolations and purposed extensions. Evidently the final execution of the work was long delayed, because Goethe, after having shaped out the whole in his imagination and detached it from the persons who first suggested it, stood in need of fresh experiences for the new characters developed in his fancy.

We know how he finally obtained them, and who served for Ottilie's prototype. In the same way in which Goethe's feeling for Frau von Stein has been discussed and disputed, the young maiden who was the original of Ottilie has also been the subject of much controversy. People have tried to decide by convincing proofs whether he really loved Minna Herzlieb, or whether his affection was restrained within the limits of an earnest but fatherly benevolence.

Here no one wishes to cast any aspersion on the fair fame of the beautiful, good, and lovable Minna Herzlieb, but rather to insure to her the honor due of having awakened in Goethe a real passion, and of having been the inspiration of some sonnets which Bettina, daughter of that Maximiliane Laroche who had married Brentano, claimed as addressed to herself alone.

As regards these sonnets, it is clearly established that Goethe gave away copies of them, made by his own hand, to several persons, and thus led Bettina to believe that she was the only one to whom spiritually they belonged. The contents are not very passionate : they are, as one would say to-day, more academic.

On the other hand, as regards Minna Herzlieb, it is not necessary to print either the manifold striking assertions of Goethe, or Minna's explicit declarations that love was never spoken of between them, or to test the credibility of their statements by the application of chemical affinities. The character of Ottilie in " Elective Affinities" shows clearly that it was no creation of passion. Goethe depicts the growing fancy of Edward and Ottilie for each other in the most vivid colors, and with masterly skill knows how to produce in the mind of the reader the utmost degree of sympathy. He stands above the characters like an unimpassioned narrator who does not write to relieve his mind in the storm of passion, but gives a tragic episode, with full observance of the rules of art. He displays Ottilie's character just as a father would that of his beloved daughter; and if Goethe later incidentally used the expression that " he had loved the maiden more than he should," the words do not in any way bear the stamp of a confession.

Ottilie is the result of the artistic reflections of a poet, who when he wrote this romance had the power to do anything but pour out his feelings passionately in a mere epic story, as he had formerly done. The words, " He had loved the girl more than he should have done," are explained by the would-be mysterious manner he occasionally adopted in his old age. He meant to express by it a very high degree of that friendly affection which, at this time of his life, he felt for many women and young girls. We know now that in the love-songs to Zuleika the passionate element was subsequently added.

Goethe's romance caused a tremendous excitement on its appearance, and elicited, together with the most unbounded admiration, the severest censures. Cotta considered it a treasure-house of the highest worldly wisdom;

the youthful generation found in Ottilie an ideal. This innocent maiden, standing alone in the world, who was so plainly cast into life by the heavenly powers to be tempted,— the combination of shrinking modesty with an extensive knowledge of the world ; a humble, submissive disposition united to an iron will,— seemed like a union of the greatest qualities. The older generation, on the other hand, saw with blank astonishment, in many places in the romance, earthly mysteries discussed with almost antique unreserve; while intimate friends sought to find out who had sat for the portraits of the different characters.

In regard to the latter, I need only remind you of what we know already concerning the genesis of Goethe's other creations to prove the fruitlessness of any attempts to give positive data. Although Minna Herzlieb is as certainly Ottilie as Lotte Buff was Werther's Lotte, this admission does not prevent Ottilie's origin from being shared by others. There were several Ottilies as there were indeed several Lottes ; and it does not help Minna much that at present she only is known, for an accident may any day reveal to us some one who must share with her the renown.

If Charlotte reminds us of Frau von Stein, it is but remotely. Luciane was thought by the Jacobi circle to represent Bettina ; Mittler, the friend who on all occasions speaks the truth and gives good advice, thereby only making mischief, is supposed to be Knebel. To trace out all these resemblances can be of real interest only to those who are acquainted with the whole amount of literary material, and who can positively assert that nothing has escaped their attention. Without such accurate knowledge, they would be mere suggestions which could not satisfy even the vaguest curiosity.

It has already been remarked how much the characters in "Elective Affinities" resemble those in "The Natural Daughter," in that all lack individuality to a certain degree. They are not what is commonly called interesting. They are types, like the figures in Greek tragedy. They have not the intrinsic genuineness, the air of familiarity, which charm us in "Werther" and in the first chapters of "Wilhelm Meister." Goethe has described even Nature more in general terms. While in "Werther" we recognize every tree of which he speaks, and are perfectly at home in Garbenheim, we nowhere get a distinct idea of the park of the laying out of which we hear so much in "Elective Affinities." They are the descriptions of an engineer. The pond in which the child is drowned lies nowhere clearly mirrored to our eye, while scattered bits of landscape painting which fill Goethe's letters give us in a few words the whole sentiment of the scene. Here the descriptions are more like scene-painting, and do not form an organic whole with the figures, but serve merely as background for them.

In "Elective Affinities," as has been already said, a tragedy is veiled in the guise of a narration in which the ethical motive is meant to predominate. If we could imagine Goethe to have chosen the dramatic form for the fiction, the characters would have borne still less of a personal stamp than in "The Natural Daughter." This may be the reason why more meaning has been attached to the chemical affinities in the book than should have been. The stress laid upon the purely human element is so conspicuous in the romance that it seems to have led to misinterpretation. Finally, each reader may have the same experience as the young woman who told Goethe that at first the book was unintelligible to her, but that suddenly, and without reading it a second time, the meaning flashed upon her: certain experiences were wanting which, falling into her later life, made things clear to her. Such experiences may not come to all.

The chief reason, however, why "Elective Affinities" made such a confused impression grew out of the general revolution of things in Germany and the rest of Europe — to which Goethe as man and poet stood opposed — in the year 1810, when the romance appeared. Without Goethe's being quite conscious of it, his work was received by a very different set of readers than that to which it was addressed. In imagination Goethe had written for a public which no longer existed. Herder and Schiller were dead; Knebel and Wieland old men; even Frau von Stein not far from seventy. Those for whom this apology for long past events was intended were no longer among the readers of new works. The Duchess, to whom Goethe had read the fiction and whose approbation had encouraged him to go on with it, was only one of the very few living representatives of a past time into which Goethe as poet had been transported.

When the book came out, as the latest novelty it was seized by the youthful generation, who hoped to find in it their own history. They were either wholly disappointed, or, inspired with enthusiasm for the genius felt along its pages, discerned things in it which were never intended. So the judgment of the day was only a strange echo of a voice which Goethe had sent in a wholly different direction from the one which received and re-echoed it.

But even this was not sufficient to characterize the strangely shifted stand-point from which "Elective Affinities" first made itself visible to the world. Not long before this, another work had appeared, the reflection of which had confused the judgment. Of this we will speak in the two following lectures.

LECTURE XXIV.

GOETHE AS A POLITICIAN. — NAPOLEON. — "FAUST."

WE know in Germany to-day what is meant by the dawn of a new era, and the rising of a fresh generation. As we compare our condition ten years ago with the present state of things, the world seems wholly changed. Former things are looked upon as antiquated; and it is accepted as a matter of course that every law must be rewritten to meet the wants of a new age, even though it has rendered good service under its old form for a hundred years and more: it no longer suits, because it is not new. Never, would it seem, was a leading generation so perfectly convinced as ours of the incompetency of all hitherto achieved. If a man between sixty and seventy years of age retires to-day, for the reason that he no longer understands men and things, it is only in rare cases deemed anything astonishing.

And yet what *we* experience is only an afterpiece to the European disturbance which began with the French Revolution and the subversion of the Roman-German Empire. Such a universal overthrow of all existing things took place at that time as had never happened before, and never could again; because all later revolutions have been but the continued agitation of elements which now and then dovetail together to form a basis apparently solid, but in reality of very superficial construction,—just as in great rivers the drifting blocks of ice unite and become firm again; though every one knows it can only last a short time, and that hot days will soon come, and set them floating once more. But the French Revolution was like the cracking of an enormous mass of ice which for thousands of years had been skated over: suddenly it appeared that the waters in the depth below had the power to rise to the surface. No one believed this, because no one could account for it. The thousand rifts which had appeared from time to time had not alarmed the motley company gliding along helter-skelter: they continued to laugh and dance, listening to the music of the old accustomed melodies. One day the abyss yawns, the waves rise and sweep over, and an unheard-of destruction sets in,— a destruction of men, property, and ideas. Then dawned a new era, in quite another sense from to-day, and a fresh generation was at the helm.

But the crash came, after all, much more gradually than one would imagine to-day.

In Germany the flood came much later than in France. It first reached us when, after the battle of Jena, the real heart of Germany was changed, as we say, from an Austrian to a French province. We too little realize now-a-days that Napoleon, in 1806, did not conquer Germany but Prussia, which, in spite of Frederick the Great's victories, was not yet wholly incorporated with Germany. Germany, which included Thuringia, had had no individual force with which to oppose foreign power: it had only been the gaming table at the service of strange hands who threw the dice. The French campaign against Prussia was to Germany like the explosion of a quickly-passing thunderstorm. The armies came suddenly hither from the West and the East, burst upon each other, and wheeled away conquerors and conquered together farther to the East. Germany previous to this had been politically quiet, — measured by the present standard, — and was so again after the whirlwind had swept by. Plundered Weimar was quietly set to rights once more, like a garden on the morning after a hailstorm, in which the sun begins to repair the injury of the previous night. People did not look upon the French as enemies: they were the champions of freedom, under the leadership of a hero who had crushed out the revolution in his own land. The pressure of French tyranny must more and more weigh upon Germany before the feeling could be roused in the heart of the people of what had been destroyed in Prussia, that their interests were one with Prussia, and that a new political existence must be inaugurated. These convictions grew up slowly, amid comparatively peaceful circumstances, and it required another series of years to mature them. It was in this transition period that the new school of poetry arose to which was given, without any just reason for it, the popular name of "Romanticist," which had distinguished the old Jena literary society, but whose patriotic aim was something quite new. During the time of the French supremacy this school reformed the German universities and gave new impulse to the sciences.

If in the face of these agitations a man like Goethe withdrew into himself, it was but natural. Moreover, the golden era of Jena and Weimar, in its hitherto exclusive sense, was now past. As Jena had once outshone Erfurt, so Halle now stepped into the foreground. Soon after this, also, the university was founded in Berlin. The older Romanticists, the Schlegels and Tieck, before the battle of Jena might still have been esteemed as appendages and emanations of the intellectual life of Weimar; but in the midst of the startling events of the time the rising men of talent, springing up everywhere on German soil, found their centres in Munich and Heidelberg, as well as in Jena. They thought of Goethe already with mere historic admiration, and, instead of calm æsthetic aims whose pursuit led them to the classics, they lived in passionate political thoughts of their own, whose ideal sphere was the poetry and history of their native-land, which was of greater value to them than all the treasures of ancient Greece. Nothing, therefore, was more natural than that Goethe should draw back ever more and more into himself.

Goethe could not fraternize with these youths, because he did not share in what characterized the new generation, — *hatred to France.* So little was his heart inoculated with this feeling, that he could not sympathize with it even when the war for independence broke out in Germany. For this he has been severely reproached.

We will attempt to state clearly how this accusation, which was only brought forward later, could have originated.

Enough has been said of Goethe's general view of the world to enable us to understand why the events which he was to witness between his sixtieth and seventieth years were accepted with the same philosophic calmness with which from this time he looked upon everything. This unimpassioned acceptance of whatever occurred would have been in itself sufficient to make it impossible for him to continue the "Demetrius" after Schiller's death, even if he had been inclined to conquer all other obstacles. Goethe was no active politician.

Schiller's stand-point was that of the French Revolution. He never, indeed, had an opportunity to engage with his own hands in the reformation of public affairs,

but, generally speaking, he was a radical. When he wrote
" Wilhelm Tell," which inculcates the murder of tyrants,
the character of Johann Parricida was not in the original
conception, and comes in at last to say to the public that
one may murder a sheriff, but not an emperor. The theory
of the sovereignty of the people was so mingled with
Schiller's blood that he instinctively makes it the basis
of all his dramas. Marie Stuart is a not less legitimate
rebel than the legitimate Elizabeth by whom she is murdered. The Maid of Orleans embodies in the form of
a shepherdess the invincible element in the lower orders
of the people, whose power expires as soon as a selfish
passion mingles with the pure love of country. Wallenstein is the genius of an army whose noblest exertions
evaporate in nothing, because they are made in the service of a miserable emperor whose adherents and ex-
ecutive officers are exhibited in their naked selfishness.
Schiller always represents great natures employed in a
struggle with political conditions which coil like snakes
about their feet. Goethe did not possess a spark of this
rebellious feeling against the facts of history. Even in
" Götz von Berlichingen " the political enthusiasm was only
a scholarly, æsthetic one. Goethe's peculiar creed is contained in " Egmont ; " Clärchen, in her despair wandering through the streets where the citizens only stare at
her without any sympathy, was Goethe's view as an historian of the people. How, as a practical statesman, in
his narrow circle he compassionated the lower classes and
studied to ameliorate their pitiful fate we have testimony
enough, which very probably might be increased to an
enormous degree by reference to the Weimar archives.
The people interested him only as moral objects, and he
pities individuals ; but ideas of universal reorganization,
such as the French Revolution introduced, and as are to-

day on everybody's tongue, Goethe did not then harbor. Politics, in the sense of to-day, did not exist for him.

How closely does he examine everything in Italy, so that not a movement of the national life escapes him! The horrible political condition of the people alone seems not to strike him as worthy of remark. He accepts it like the climate, soil, and so forth, as mere matter of fact. In view of the tyranny in the States of the Church, the thought never seems to come to him that the people will one day realize with shame their degradation, and rally in their own right.

It is true that the Duke in political affairs always desired Goethe's opinion, and that Goethe in the important transactions whose aim was the formation of the " Deutschen Fürstenbundes " drew up the protocol ; and we have a circumstantial letter from him to the Duke wherein he explains his views of the German conditions under Emperor Joseph. Many things of the kind are certainly still unpublished, and this side of Goethe's official labors may yet appear much wider than is generally believed. But what does this amount to ? For German, French, and Italian political conditions, in the present sense of progress, Goethe seems to have had no sympathy. The political movement at that time culminated in the interests of universal humanity. It was international, fostered only in educated circles, and had nothing to do with the governments.

I here recall the distinction, earlier explained, between the definitely-ended European history, which we call the Roman, and universal history, beginning in 1850 and embracing the five parts of the world, which is the Germanic. Of the latter Goethe had only a dim presentiment ; while he was fully at home in the former, for he had grown up in it.

HIS POLITICAL IDEAS UNPOPULAR. 481

Roman history never produced in the Germanic democratic sense a representation of the people. It had in an aristocratic sense an assembly of representatives to whom their rights were committed, but these were by no means deputies of the whole people. The people as a whole had only one advocate, the Emperor, who protected those of his subjects who had fewer rights against the more privileged ; the idea of a united nation and a body of people emanating from it — who, standing beside the Emperor, kept the welfare of their country ever in view, without whose yea and nay no legal enactment was possible — was as incomprehensible to Goethe as in the beginning it had been to the French, by whom during the Revolution this doctrine was first applied. They were enthusiastic in France over formulas whose scope they did not comprehend. The people, accustomed to being kept down by the mountainous weight of a government machine, were seized with a kind of giddiness when suddenly released from its pressure. An unheard-of self-maceration went on, until Napoleon in the most brutal way restored in part the former condition, and with his iron hand checked the further disintegration of old institutions.

Goethe, it is true, believed in Rousseau's doctrine of national sovereignty. He had seen the wholesome fermentation begin which these thoughts everywhere produced in the stagnant political life about him ; but never would the idea have entered his mind that such could really become the normal state of existence, nor would he have conceived it possible that what had been witnessed in France could ever take place in Germany. When Goethe joined in the campaign of 1793, he went in a private capacity, and as a spectator watched proceedings which could never profoundly awaken his sympathy in their ultimate aim. The Frenchmen who were seized, as it were, by patriotic spasms were to him objects of the greatest astonishment. He little dreamed that this people storming on from day to day would rise to such a terrific attack on sluggish Germany, infect her with their fever, and be the cause of revolutionary reforms. In Germany, Frederick the Great had made of Prussia a monarchy so sound in appearance as to guarantee stability to all; and the very thought of Prussia had a universally tranquillizing effect: he had only to raise his voice, and order was again restored. Even at that time there were circles which hailed with enthusiasm the thought of a Prussian emperor of Germany. In the heart of the land, therefore, people looked with perfect indifference upon what happened on the borders, and even when the French in their encounters with the South-German States came farther to the north, it did not excite the slightest anxiety. People were convinced that the experiences France was passing through would in a peaceful way benefit the whole world. For Schiller, as has just been said, these years were times of joyful hope to which he continued to abandon himself, even while in France and Italy the rotten supports of the old institutions were crashing to pieces with a sound that echoed and re-echoed over the wide earth. Schiller, while he glorified the French national spirit in the Jungfrau von Orleans, did not consider that French and Germans, as human beings, here did not mean the same thing. Schiller was flattered by the diploma of French citizen: " it might perhaps some day be of use to his children." No one saw in France an inimical element; and Knebel himself wished to celebrate in song Bonaparte's successes, whose exploits seemed fitted to be the inspiration of an heroic epic. At last came a time, when in spite of all this Prussia was forced to oppose the hero. We know what happened. Such a tremendous shock public opinion never before experienced. The iron colossus had not only stood upon clay feet, but had been wholly made of clay. **Prussia was not beaten,** — she ceased to exist. With satisfaction Austria and Saxony had offered a helping hand to achieve this : it was not fifty years since Frederick the Great had humbled them. Prussia was so hopelessly annihilated that the whole Prussian greatness, like a little episode in German history, seemed to be played out.

But this absolute destruction had a tranquillizing effect. Napoleon's victorious campaign in 1806 was hardly to be called a war. The fortresses surrendered without resistance. He marched into Berlin, and pushed on without meeting opponents. Germany, split at this time into three parts, remained so for nearly ten years, — the States of the Rheinbund, the true heart of Germany, almost belonging to France; Austria allied with France by marriage; and, far to the northeast, the down-trodden Prussian provinces whose life-blood was being drained by forced contributions. The wealth of the Prussian nobles vanished at this time.

This condition was all the more curious, that while Napoleon came by degrees to be hated more and more, the French individually were not hated. The good German families owed their solid culture to the French. German literature had something of the *parvenu* character, and did not offer the firm classic basis of the French. The Republic itself was also held in honor. The new privileges for the common people, which the Republic introduced, had put an end to innumerable deeply-rooted abuses and insufferable burdens, and created in their stead free national citizenship. The benefits of the French victories were perceived as vividly in Germany as the losses. We are indebted to the French for the rise of the German republican element. An era of economic reforms began ; and Western Germany, although cruelly depleted by the war, began to breathe freely under comfortable institutions which were modelled after the French.

Only gradually did the change of opinion gain ground, yet everywhere where the French came as conquerors it was to be observed how soon from agreeable companions they became insolent despots. If the police rule, operating through false reports and sustaining a deceitful peace by ever-increasing tyrannies, was felt to be intolerable in France, in Germany it became an oppression not to be endured. It was ever more and more clearly perceived that the systematic subjugation of Prussia was one and the same thing with the ruin of the German nation. The indignation with which the Prussian officials and nobles, as well as commoners, endured the ignominious part they were condemned to play was shared by the rest of Germany. In the minds of the younger and youngest generations awoke that feeling of resistance which was the beginning of the national up-rising in 1813, and which, as the real basis of our present political freedom, belongs among our most precious annals. But whence should Goethe — the statesman of the old school, the experienced witness of so much frailty in the highest circles — derive confidence in a popular agitation whose depth and force he was not able to appreciate?

Before all things, in Goethe's opinion, every change that was to amount to anything must be initiated by the Government; and as to the governments, Goethe knew too well how the matter stood with them. Nothing in his experience gave him any conception of a people who through their own undisciplined strength, trusting only to vague, ideal promptings, started an agitation of a purely private nature. In France they had guillotined the King, and put themselves in his place; but in Germany a noiseless upheaval was prepared, — not in opposition to the King and government, but with a quiet disregard of all existing authorities, — which, without special plan or resources, was expected to result in freedom, peace, and greatness for Germany. In order to take part in such an agitation it was necessary that one should be either a young enthusiast, an historical fanatic, an inexperienced beginner in life, or that as a Prussian he should be among those who were so frightfully oppressed by the existing state of things that to play *va banque* seemed the worthiest thing for him to do. These are the reasons why Goethe, who never had lived in Prussia, — whose first and second home lay on the map of Germany at that time far away from the Prussian boundary; who knew the helplessness of the court and the exhaustion of the land; who in Carlsbad must learn from hearsay how things were in Berlin, — necessarily looked upon our political condition as irremediable. Only one single war in the spirit of the new Germanic world had until now been known: this was the revolt of the American colonies from England. But even in this case it appeared doubtful if England, without the hostility of France under which she suffered at the same time, and without the monstrous distance which separated her from her colonies, would have yielded. The idea of an up-rising of Germany, an " insurrection of the whole people," never occurred to Goethe even in a dream. It seemed madness to oppose a " free, united Germany in arms " to the centralizing power of Napoleon, terrible even to the last. So it seemed to many of our noblest patriots, even when after the northern campaign signs appeared of the downfall of Napoleon, and York had already gone over to the Russians. It is interesting to read what Count Gesler writes to Caroline von Wolzogen, an enthusiastic patriot, as the people began to take up arms: Gesler had stood encouragingly at the side of the father of Theodore Körner in 1813:—

"An exultation has taken possession of the Germans which sometimes appears ridiculous to me. We are going to destruction like a crowd of Don Quixotes for our national honor. This is not inspiration from above, but comes entirely from among the people. How all the heterogeneous elements of which these patriot bands are composed under the most favorable circumstances could possibly be made homogeneous I cannot conceive. Nevertheless I have looked upon it as one looks upon a miracle, with a coolness and serenity which I must try to conceal."

Goethe also could not think otherwise. It was not want of patriotism, it was the impossibility of transforming himself at sixty-four into a youth of twenty. This secret doubt was also the cause why Goethe, when a volunteer corps was organized in Weimar, held his son back. Even if the Government had undertaken a war for freedom, Goethe could not have believed in any success of these volunteer elements, which, according to his war experiences in 1793, must give trouble on the field.

It only remains to us in this connection to speak of Goethe's predilection for Napoleon.

We know that Napoleon, on coming to Erfurt, sent for Goethe, and held the famous conversation with him, at the close of which the exclamation burst from his lips, "Voilà un homme!" which bears this translation: "At last a man who stands face to face with me in Germany!" Napoleon had fathomed Goethe; but Goethe also knew how to value Napoleon. In the midst of a confusion which appeared inextricable, Goethe had seen this youthful general rise like some ancient hero, who, one against a host, conquered whole nations with the stroke of a club.

But now Germany itself was to feel the power of Napoleon! The Prussian armies scattered like dust before this man, in whose hands the refractory French mob of the Revolution became well-disciplined troops, obedient to a wink. Goethe made the acquaintance of Napoleon surrounded by his marshals in the midst of their labors. He had never imagined anything like it. He saw fresh, genial, cultivated men, well versed in art and science, whose tremendous energy appeared even through a courteous manner, free from all prejudice, overflowing with health, power, and ambition, and accustomed to conquer wherever they appeared. Who could resist this unheard-of combination? What was even Frederick the Great, who swayed a well-organized, docile people, in comparison with Napoleon galloping on an unbridled horse, who tamed his own people (audacious to the point of brutality) at the same time that he subjugated foreign powers?

As an historical phenomenon the French emperor made such an impression on Goethe that no power on earth seemed great enough to confront him.

We know how universal this belief was in Europe, and how little even the Russian campaign tended to shake it. The emperor, hurrying alone from Moscow to Paris, was in his flight just as much an object of terror to the world as he had been at the beginning of the campaign. Therefore neither Goethe, nor others who thought as he did, should be reproached with want of patriotism. They were too far stunned by the events they had passed through to be able to judge them.

But now must be stated what is equally true.

Although, practically, Goethe did not think the right time had yet come; although he belonged to the statesmen who, even after the calamity in Russia, did not believe in any good result from this rising of the German people, — his heart always cherished the idea of what a free, united Germany might be. Of this we have proof. Naturally a man like Goethe must be reserved in his expression; but read what Dr. Kieser of Jena, who organized the volunteer corps in Weimar, told Luise Seidler of his conversation with Goethe at that time. With what fire Goethe could counsel when he really opened his heart! We imagine things in a much greater state of fusion at that time in Germany than they really were. We judge everything from the prevailing tone of mind in Berlin. We do not realize how disconnected, uninformed, and suspicious the rest of Germany was, — not knowing where to look for help. If they lifted their eyes to those above them they beheld vacillating characters by whom no encouraging word was ever spoken to the people; if on the other hand they looked down, they saw a people roused by a questionable political enthusiasm, who were conscious of their **weakness.**

These circumstances account for the manner in which Goethe subsequently accepted our victories and successes: he was surprised, and never concealed it. As a man of the old school who had seen the shipwreck of the Fürstenbund, he could only call to mind the dissensions among the princes who represented the people, and he looked upon the final conquest of France as simply an historical miracle. In December, 1813, he writes to Knebel that he has never known the Germans united except in their hatred of Napoleon. He would like to see what they would do next when they had driven him across the Rhine! It seems as if Goethe had foreseen all the pitifulness of the Vienna Congress, as well as how, after a short continuance of the intoxication of victory, the politically undisciplined people forced the Government to move on in a reactionary sense. Now for the first time, when

Goethe calculated on the necessary reaction of the people, did the conviction force itself upon him that a new era was about to begin. That feeling came over him of the utter worthlessness of the present which continued to the end of his days. His prophetic soul recognized that, after the frightful political struggles, the period of national exhaustion and stagnation which his last years witnessed was only an imperceptible preparation for new conflicts. Here again he was ahead of his contemporaries. At this time was roused in Goethe (since to him open liberal opposition seemed precipitate and unnecessary) the ironical spirit which prevails in the political passages in the second part of "Faust," and which may be compared to the often misunderstood opinions of Alexander von Humboldt at the court of Frederick William IV.

Goethe and Humboldt knew that the triumph of liberal ideas irresistibly drew on; but they also believed that the assistance of the private man could not hasten the approach of the world-historical agitations which were to convulse Europe. They satisfied themselves with playing the subordinate part of the political Mephisto and *pro virili parte*, — in view of the approaching storm to help to build the Noah's Ark in which during the time of high water all our intellectual work might safely be abandoned to the winds and waves. Goethe's conversations in the last ten years of his life reveal a clear understanding of the times; but he knew perfectly well that personally he should not witness the Revolution. The July French Revolution scarcely interested him : the strife pending at that time between Cuvier and Geoffroy St. Hilaire about matters of natural science seemed to him of vastly more importance than the street fights of Paris.

I have thus tried, in advance, to state concisely Goethe's political views. Let us now return to the point when some time after the battle of Jena, — forced to an involuntary peace by the omnipotent French emperor, — German youth sought refuge in the world of thought, there to find consolation for the bitter ignominy they had suffered, and to prepare for a brighter future.

It would never have occurred to any one at that time to interview Goethe for the purpose of finding out whether he was in secret friendly to France. Never were suspicions of this kind raised against him while he lived. They were first brought up during the thirty or forty years when the present German empire was slowly shaping itself in the minds of the people, and when all who had any pretension to renown or greatness of any kind had their political convictions inquired into, even posthumously. Then it looked as if Goethe in the years of oppression, and in the war for freedom, had not fulfilled his duty to his country. But in his own time it was otherwise regarded.

The thought of Goethe was an inspiring one for young and old. His name was written ineffaceably in the book of German glory. Did his labors as a poet seem ended? Goethe was nevertheless the "Altmeister." All rejoiced to see this mighty man still so hale and hearty. A pilgrimage to Weimar began to be among the things to be done; criticisms issuing from there won in importance. As in earlier times the older poets and authors for their own benefit had flattered the new power which rose in Goethe, so now the younger sought so to do. Goethe submitted as he formerly had done; but one day he proved to the people that he still intended to be a co-laborer, and that all he had hitherto produced had been only preliminary to his greatest achievement, with which he now surprised Germany.

Let us observe that until now the work has been but

THE APPEARANCE OF "FAUST." 491

cursorily mentioned on which is founded mainly, not only Goethe's fame, but that of our entire German literature, — " Faust." The fragments which had appeared in 1790 had passed almost unnoticed ; not until the first part was published complete in 1808 did "Faust" create an impression, but now in such measure that all Goethe had written hitherto was thrown into the shade by this new production.

We will now speak of "Faust," the work which as a dream transported him again into the midst of his youthful renown, and restored to him the first place among living poets, as if he were just entering on his career and as young as any of them ; from whose publication dates the world-wide fame which attended Goethe from that time until his death, and lives after him to-day.

Every one who names Goethe names Faust in spirit at the same time. "Faust" is Goethe's most beautiful, his greatest, and most important work ; that which he began the first, and which in conception reached on beyond his death. To no other can the expression *life-work* be applied with such truth. "Faust" would have sufficed to make Goethe our greatest poet, even if he had written nothing else.

"Faust" is the poem of poems. Put, not only all Goethe's other poems, but our entire poetic literature into the other scale and wait ! — which sinks ? The person of Faust appears to us to-day as a natural, indispensable product of German life, — I should say of German history, if history here were not an inadequate idea. History relates too exclusively to crude events ; the element out of which Faust arose is finer and more comprehensive. It embraces, beside the outward experiences of the people, also the creations of imagination : these are our immortals in the proper sense. Let me take some of our noblest names, — Charlemagne, Otto the Great, Frederick the Hohenstaufe, Frederick the Great; or, in another department, Frederick Schiller, Lessing, even Goethe himself, — and all contrasted with Faust strike us as imperfect and transitory, partly faded, partly grown dark with age. A feeling will steal over us that with all their immortality they are only long-buried, mortal, corruptible men, while Faust, who never lived, who in dreams was woven out of mist, — what a life-warmth radiates from his form!

Faust is to us Germans the sovereign in the host of all the creations of European literature. Hamlet, Achilles, Hector, Tasso, the Cid, Frithiof, Siegfrid, and Fingal, — all these forms seem to lose something of their lifelike freshness when Faust appears. The light which rests upon them is pale, like moonlight, while Faust stands in the full blaze of the sun. Their language has to our ears something of a foreign sound, while Faust speaks so as to be understood by every one in his faintest accents. The breath of those heroes is not the bracing mountain air which streams from the lips of Faust. Their spirit, however wide its scope, has not the expansive wing on which he soars above the world and its phenomena, that he may describe everything with his eagle glance. In order to test Schiller's knowledge of the world and dialectic acuteness, I feigned the possibility of his appearing to-day in the midst of our parliamentary debates. I chose this illustration, because when the question to decide is whether an appearance is real or not, we must apply the severest tests. A character in romance must bear the question of how should we regard him if he lived six months in our family. A picture must not lose in effect when we think of it as hanging on the walls of our own room; a warrior on the stage must remain a warrior to us if we transport him into the tumult of a real battle. Imagine any of those historic or fictitious heroes entering an assembly of the unrelenting critics, whom Germany has chosen to control in her name what are supposed to be the highest interests of the people, — would it not be perceived instantly that their language is no longer ours, their way of thinking obsolete, and their appearance among us altogether awkward? What would Achilles, or Cæsar, or even Frederick the Great, have to say to us to-day, which, without doing violence to themselves or to us, would be in harmony with our view of the present state of the world? But now, allow Faust to appear with Mephisto at his side, would not these two instantly perceive the significance of the moment, and in the twinkling of an eye, with a few incisive thoughts, be able to draw around them attentive listeners? To be sure, Faust is the youngest among the creations of poetic fancy which we have enumerated. He is chronologically nearer to us than the others. But we must consider how many long years have flown since the idea of Faust arose and since it was perfected; how little Goethe when he wrote his "Faust" knew of the world of to-day; how little the generation which was first inspired by it possessed the qualities which are now valued in political affairs. And yet Goethe succeeded in creating a character which is as full of life at this moment as if it were the creation of yesterday. Wholly different phases in Faust are illuminated to our eyes to-day from what were understood fifty years ago, yet we believe we see his character in the truer light. Who can say what they may discover who will judge it one or two hundred or a thousand years later, as we discuss Homer's heroes, who have already lived in story three thousand years?

And as Faust among men so is Gretchen among women.

Antigone, Iphigenia, Ophelia, Imogen, as regards intrinsic living power, must all yield precedence to her. Even Shakspeare's Juliet can not rival her. She stands more apart from us, and has many traits that have grown unfamiliar to us, while Gretchen says no word and takes no step which is not perfectly intelligible.

When speaking of Hermann and Dorothea, I placed Dorothea in contrast to all Goethe's other heroines, saying that none possessed, in my opinion, the reality of Dorothea. In the list of names enumerated, however, I purposely omitted Gretchen's, which among all Goethe's creations takes the highest place; for Gretchen has not only Dorothea's truth and reality in full measure, which draw us very near to her, but is at the same time, notwithstanding, separated from us by that ideal veil through which — though close before our eyes — she yet seems at an unapproachable distance from us. This blending of the most heartfelt sympathy with her, as if she were our sister, with the unfathomable mystery surrounding her as if she were a saint, lends to her in our eyes such an irresistible attraction that we place her without scruple — so far as our literary knowledge reaches — above all the beings that had ever sprung from the imagination of a poet. All the excellences are hers which Goethe's first youthful power lent to his earlier works, and, at the same time, all which mature years of criticism added to his original creative capacity. And these double advantages unite most naturally in Gretchen, since she is the first as well as the last of his creations. Through the entire life of a man he labored upon this his noblest work, and until the very last found something to add to or to improve in it.

Through Faust and Gretchen the Germans take the first rank in the poetry of all times and nations. This is granted them without grudging. Ever repeated English,

French, and Italian translations appear, whose authors from the outset offer their labor only as an attempt, since anything like the beauty of the original it is impossible to obtain. In the presence of no other work would they humble themselves so reverently. It is as if " Faust " were the common property of all modern nations, to which Germany had no special claim.

That under these circumstances " Faust" has already, as it were, become emancipated from Goethe as its author is not to be wondered at. In all Goethe's most finished works, those classic creations of his mature power which have an individuality of their own, his hand still remains visible, — if only so far, that no other artist save he could possibly have originated them. It was Goethe's language they all spoke. Goethe himself spread out like a great fruit-tree in the distance the branches on which these golden apples grew. Faust alone stands as if he had never grown anywhere on earth, but dropped finished from heaven.

And yet, separated as Faust seems from Goethe's other works, it is indispensable to them all. For now that we have at last come to Faust we may point out a fault in Goethe's manly types (Faust excepted) which I have hitherto passed over in silence, because I only wished to mention it at a time when I could explain it as inevitable.

In the contemplation of Goethe's poetic creations we have taken as our fundamental idea, that each should be interpreted as a personal confession, — the transmutation of his real life into poetry. Hence we derive the right to trace back especially the characters of his women into their living originals. Such an idea would never be suggested with regard to Homer's Penelope, or the women of Sophocles and Æschylus, and still less even with those of Molière, Shakspeare, or Schiller. The women of these poets lack wholly the intermixture of an individual element, which makes it so interesting for us to seek for the models of Goethe's characters. Shakspeare's Juliet has something elementary in her nature; one would never dream of wishing to decide how far personal fancy for any particular woman might have inspired Shakspeare, although as has been said by Lessing, "Love himself seems to have assisted in the work."

While Goethe's women have derived from this peculiarity the advantage of such fine shades of distinction as *life* alone can give, Goethe's manly types suffer a disadvantage from the fact that all of them had their origin in Goethe's own nature. It is always the same character — indefinitely outlined — returning in a new guise. Goethe often enough spoke of himself, — so to say, made an inventory of his qualities; and for the most part in his heroes we meet with a certain number of these elements which constituted his own nature. But while Goethe represented in his heroes now this, now that side of his nature, they all have something fragmentary, — they are never quite rounded out. They exhibit to us only the one side which is accidentally illuminated. If we consider Werther, Tasso, Edward, and the others as complete men, we find that the poet has left out of notice whole sides of their character. We should ask in vain with regard to Werther or Tasso, for instance, by what special fate their natures were so formed as to admit of their acting just as they do in the catastrophes depicted in the romance or the tragedy? Only the strangest experiences in life could have produced this immeasurable susceptibility. But what were they? Only through Goethe himself is their existence to be explained. All these figures come to life, as it were, only at the moments when Goethe brings them before us in action.

If however we understand them as incarnations of Goethe, who under ever-varying circumstances constantly reappears, they all lack a certain robust vitality without which a perfect man is inconceivable. These Goethean men have not the smell of actual man's flesh; they never eat and drink before our eyes; examined for recruits they would prove too thin-skinned, and to lack firmness of muscle.

But Goethe himself was quite otherwise. He could bear fatigue; retained his energy and elasticity under the most trying circumstances both by sea and land; had a good digestion; could be harsh if it was necessary, and stood his ground against any man when manliness was in question. Why have his ideal prototypes, collectively and individually, this touch of moonshiny paleness, while the poet himself went about so healthy and weather-tanned?

With all these characters we are obliged to think of Faust as their invisible counterpart. Faust — whom Goethe never laid out of his hands so long as he breathed — was the elder brother of this whole company, who always received beforehand the best morsels, and was responsible for them all.

At the side of Werther, Tasso, Wilhelm, Edward, Ferdinand, and the whole series Faust stands ever invisible, and asserts his birthright. He is the Crown Prince to whom the kingdom descends; the others are later born, and must be satisfied with what falls to their share by the way. Goethe has Faust always at his right hand: he treats the others according to his pleasure, and allots to them only their legitimate portions. Goethe himself stood in awe of Faust. This youngster too early grew over his head, and proved very refractory. For long years Goethe would not meddle with him at all, because he did not feel himself to be man enough to bring him up. But Faust outlived all the others, and remained with him after the others had long passed away. He represents to Goethe at the end of his days the sum of his entire poetical works. He alone survives the master, who so long as he lived would never have sent him out into the world as complete. Faust will in coming periods save all his weaker younger brethren — yes, even Goethe himself — from the sea of oblivion, as Moses saved the Israelites. For that the time may come when Goethe's works in their whole extent will be known only to a few it is very possible to imagine; but "Faust" will be an exception. The inheritors of the earth will never allow "Faust" to be snatched away from them again.

It is curious to observe how from first to last Goethe treated this poem with peculiar respect. I said just now that he shrank from it as being too mighty for him. We know his disinclination to declare his works of age. He always thinks they need more labor bestowed on them; nevertheless, sooner or later, he makes an effort to bring this hesitation, outwardly at least, to an end. With regard to "Faust," however, he could never conceive that it would end.

This work was to him the dearest from the beginning; and yet he constantly finds excuses for postponing it. From time to time he reads it aloud, but all the applause it excites cannot stimulate him to finish it. This continues until the Italian journey. For the first complete edition of his works he hopes now to master the "Faust." He packs up the manuscript and works occasionally upon it; but when all his other works are ready he has done mere nothing to this. At the close of the year 1787, when he thought seriously of returning home, he writes to the Duke that he will go at the "Faust" just at the last. "In order to finish the piece," he says farther on in the letter, " I must be specially collected. I must draw a magic circle around me ; for which may a kindly Fate prepare a favorable opportunity ! "

But this magic circle and this place were never granted Goethe. From year to year we notice his fear to meddle with the papers. The fragment published in 1790 almost seems like a further attempt to conceal the poem rather than to deliver it up. Schiller made the greatest efforts to incline Goethe to the work, and not without success ; but again and again Goethe let it drop from his hand. Even what in 1808 made such a prodigious sensation was, to Goethe, only a fragment. Finally he accustomed himself to the thought that so long as he lived he should continue to work upon it ; and he probably would never have allowed what was published after his death to have appeared in the form we have it, if his life had been continued.

LECTURE XXV.

"FAUST." — CONCLUSION.

FOR the comprehension of "Faust" we hold it necessary above all things to regard it as a whole. The first and second part — prologue, preliminary scene, and in short all that is published to-day as "Faust" — must be considered as a unit. Goethe says the poem rose before his view in its entirety when his imagination was first impressed with it.

Goethe states this explicitly in a letter which (like the one to the young Grand Duke wherein he treats of Necessarianism) is peculiarly solemn; concisely speaking, also, it may be said to have been the last thing he ever wrote. He composed this letter to Wilhelm von Humboldt, March 17, 1832, five days only before his death. It contains his last confession, — the simplest, grandest, fullest avowal with regard to himself which ever flowed from his lips. In it we have before us Goethe's literary testament, — yet not like the words of a dying man, but almost in the tone of one who, having already passed beyond the limits of earthly life, turns back, with one last thought, to the career he has just abandoned, and makes use of speech again that he may give an account of his earthly intentions.

To achieve anything of this nature two men were needed, — the one who communicates it, and the other who draws forth such a communication. It was for

Goethe and for us the most fortunate dispensation, that, in the latter half of his life, a man like Wilhelm von Humboldt was in friendly intercourse with him. Humboldt may be called the prince of critics; never have great poems been interpreted by a contemporary in the way that Schiller and Goethe's last works were by Wilhelm von Humboldt. It was owing to him, to begin with the least important of his efforts, that from the year 1790 everything that Schiller and Goethe produced was received and understood among us in the most deserving manner. Humboldt prevented August Wilhelm Schlegel — the most brilliant and talented of all the critics of that day, but at the same time capricious and vain to such a degree that his judgment was not to be relied on — from rising to be the standard critic. More valuable was Humboldt as the mediator who taught the German *savans* and philologists to appreciate and enjoy the works of Schiller and Goethe. Humboldt's greatest achievement, however, so far as Schiller and Goethe are concerned, was in assisting them to give the last touch of perfection to their style. There are no subtilties in language which have escaped him. He accepts untiringly all that is new, and holds fast to the old, subjecting it to ever fresh examination. Only to a man like Humboldt would Goethe have so fully given his last thoughts as he has done in this letter. I here quote merely what is of special interest to us.

In that high sense in which Aristotle makes man the subject of cold contemplation Goethe considers himself as, so to say, a " poetizing creature," and proceeds accordingly to criticise his development. He says : —

" The animals are taught through their organs. I add to this : men likewise, — only they have the advantage of teaching their organs in return.

" For every act and every talent something inborn is demanded which works of itself, and, bringing with it unconsciously the necessary ability, goes on working straight ahead; so that though it has a motive power of its own, it may yet run on without any definite aim or purpose. The earlier man becomes aware that there is a profession, that there is an art, which helps him to a methodical development of his natural talents, so much the happier will he be. Whatever he may receive from without will not endanger in the least his native idiosyncrasy. The finest genius is that which absorbs all into itself, and knows how to appropriate all without doing the slightest injury to its distinctive tendency, or to what is called character.

"But here come in the manifold relations between the conscious and the unconscious. Suppose one with a musical talent has an important score to prepare: consciousness and unconsciousness will be related to each other like note and envelope, — a simile I like to use. The organs of men, by practice, instruction, reflection, success and failure, assistance and opposition, and ever again *reflection*, unconsciously unite by spontaneous activity what has been acquired with what is inborn.

"For more than sixty years have I had before me my youthful conception of 'Faust,' — the whole series having been from the first clear to me, though not in all their details. I have always quietly kept my original plan in view, and have worked out, singly, those scenes which happened to interest me most; so that there remained gaps in the second part, only to be bridged over by investing them with an interest proportioned to the rest. Here now, indeed, the great difficulty showed itself, which was, — how to accomplish, by energy and resolution, what should have been the voluntary work of Nature. It would truly have been hard, however, if this had not been possible, after such a long, active, thoughtful life; and I do not allow myself to fear that a distinction will be made between the old and the new parts, — the earlier and the later work, — all of which we now commit to the gracious reader's future judgment."

This, then, is his testament concerning "Faust." He recognizes this work as the task for which his poetical talent was specially fitted. Goethe expressly demands that the work shall be considered as a whole, and rejects any critical distinction in the periods of its growth.

He gives in this letter the date of its beginning more than sixty years earlier than 1832, — therefore in 1772. In a propitious moment, suddenly, the work stood before his eyes! It was at the close of his student's course, when he had just been made " doctor " in Strasburg, and at the age of twenty-three.

From this time on we will now follow the work, and we shall see that its *history* is its best *explanation* and *interpretation.*

If Goethe says *the whole poem* rose at once and complete before his soul in 1772, he does not betray how much of it was at that time written down. He says, "the whole series, but less in detail." Are the additions which the published work gives in 1808 chiefly later additions, and has all contained in the first manuscript of 1790 been printed ? We may conclude so from Jacobi's casual remarks, but these are not wholly clear. Certainly the edition of 1790 contains passages which the manuscript of 1772 did not contain, or at least which Goethe did not read aloud to Jacobi. Did he omit these passages at that time, while he already harbored them in his imagination? Were the gaps so important of which Goethe writes to Humboldt? Thus we come to the question as to what serviceable material Goethe found in his surroundings and in his imagination in 1772. How wide was his horizon at that time ? What distinguishes the characters in the edition of 1808 from those which were brought on the stage in the fragment of 1790 ; and what from those which passed through his imagination in 1772?

And, finally, has a new light been shed over the whole work, changing its value, through the last additions and conclusions which were published after Goethe's death? Or had these very last ideas also been revealed to his mind as early as 1772?

Let us imagine that Goethe treated "Werther" as he treated "Faust," and instead of publishing it in 1793, and only revising it in 1786 for the complete edition of his works, had left it lying all the while in his desk and given it to the public first in 1786. As things were, "Werther" lay before Goethe at that time as a universally known fact, and therefore only to be altered with very great caution. Nevertheless, he made significant changes and additions, with the avowed purpose of giving a different turn to the course of the romance in many of its finer motives.

What would Goethe have done had "Werther" remained unprinted among his papers, and he could have proceeded with free hand to make the alterations? Would he have been satisfied with those, on the whole, very modest corrections?

Goethe would either have been obliged to leave the romance just as it was, and then it would have seemed as if he had the intention to represent times long past, which in writing the romance had not been thought of; or he must have adapted the events, conversations, and letters to the new state of the world. In this case the whole composition must have undergone reconstruction. Therefore we ask in the face of the "Faust" published in 1790, and further of the "Faust" published in 1808, what was the nature of the manuscript written in 1772 respecting not only the finer shades of difference but also its crude form? Were organic changes made? Have we the "Faust" in the same words as those read by Goethe

FREDERIKA THE ORIGINAL OF GRETCHEN.

in the Frankfort days to Jacobi, Klopstock, and the Duke?

To answer these questions we will examine the characters separately.

Let us look, first of all, at Gretchen.

Goethe, during the last part of his time in Strasburg when "Faust" was conceived, had in his soul the most painful remorse for having excited a passion in an unsuspicious being, and then faithlessly deserted her. Without doubt the origin of Gretchen is to be found in Frederika of Sesenheim. No suspicion must be herewith associated with what is in the vulgar sense meant by seduction; but in an ethical sense it was seduction in the highest degree. Goethe could not but feel that Frederika after having been forsaken in this way was widowed for ever. He knew what he had stolen and what he had destroyed. He had forced himself into the soul of a young maiden, had encouraged the idea that a tie had been formed between them which was eternal, and then one day given her to understand: "And now, enough, good-by; get over it as best you can!" Goethe conceived this frightful cruelty symbolically; his untrammelled poetic imagination followed out the love-affair to the most extreme consequences it admitted of in reality. In the artistic rendering actual seduction must be introduced to make fully palpable what the guilt might have been. All imaginable consequences must be represented; therefore was the crime of infanticide brought in. Goethe only needed to throw the reins over the neck of his fancy, and the way from Frederika to Gretchen was easily found. It was not even necessary that Goethe should actually have forsaken Frederika; just to have before him an image of his own faithlessness was enough to transform Frederika into Gretchen, who so plainly bears traits corresponding to Frederika's. We feel that when Goethe sketches Frederika herself later he wishes to indicate this analogy. The fascinating pertness of manner and perfectly confiding nature are conspicuous in his description of Frederika in " Dichtung und Wahrheit."

These traits also constitute in the first poetic vision the basis of Gretchen's character and her fate. In this therefore nothing might or could be changed. All future additions and omissions could not alter any of the essential lines in this picture of Gretchen; the few scenes which compose the fragment of 1790 contain the idea of Gretchen as perfectly as the edition of 1808, and in the very first manuscript it must have been the same.

But Gretchen in her glorified form as she appeared after her death among the angels, when she again met Faust, may have been a creation of later years. It is possible that this is one of the gaps subsequently filled up, to which Goethe alluded in his letter to Humboldt; yet here also the critic must proceed with great caution. Goethe, as we know, in his youth was very familiar with the religious ideas of the Mystics, to which, in another form, he returned quite naturally in his old age. So that this final rapturous scene is quite as likely to have been included in the first conception as to have been added in his later years. For if Faust's life in the first plan of the poem is brought to reconcilement, which we must assume, why exclude from it the last meeting with Gretchen?

And now let us confess that the scenes in the first part of " Faust," published in 1808, where Gretchen appears (here we include the scenes which without doubt belong to the original manuscript, though not in the 1790 edition), breathe a power and have a life-warmth which nothing else written by Goethe in this early period possesses.

Had they never subsequently been printed, which indeed some unlucky accident might easily have prevented, the best specimen of the fresh poetic power of the young Goethe would to-day seem to us to be wanting. These verses glow with a fire which touches us more directly than "Werther" or any other poems belonging to the first epoch. Not of the other works which at the time made Goethe's fame, but of "Faust," we think to-day when we read of the overwhelming impression he made on all who became acquainted with him in his youth; and yet "Faust" was known at that time only to very few. This youthful fire made the influence of "Faust" so tremendous on the younger generation that from this time they looked upon Goethe as belonging to them; and just as it had been after the appearance of "Götz" and "Werther," they expected new and still greater works of him. They confessed themselves at once outdone and vanquished by the newly-risen hero.

It was chiefly owing to this that when "Elective Affinities" appeared in 1809 it was seized upon with such avidity by the young people, among whom Goethe, when he wrote the novel, had least thought to find a public. It was to Ottilie's advantage that she now appeared as Gretchen's elder sister, as it were, in company with whom she outshone all Goethe's other heroines.

Gretchen has ever remained the same, through all the phases and stages of the poem, but of Mephistopheles the account is quite different.

Because Goethe identified Merck so strikingly and intentionally with Mephisto it has been usual to accept him as the origin of the character, and as being the only person who suggested it. But what did Goethe know of Merck when he composed the "Faust" in Strasburg; and how without Mephisto would the drama ever have been conceivable? We must seek other origin for this character.

Goethe was a perfectly self-sustained man when he went to Strasburg, and had long believed himself able to find the right path without guidance. He intended to study everything in turn,— jurisprudence, theology, and physics, just as they are enumerated in the opening of "Faust." He was accustomed to have every one he met yield to him, or at least treat him with special distinction; and, having been thus favored by fortune for so many years, he really thought a good deal of himself.

At this point he meets Herder. Concerning Herder we must recapitulate what has been already said.

He was the first man who had ever compelled Goethe to make the advances. He takes very little trouble to be gracious to him, even when Goethe humbles himself as he had never done before to any one. In fact Herder does not seem to care for Goethe at all; snubs him and subjects him to his moods and whims. He needed nothing that Goethe could possibly offer him, but had his established view of the world, which he had gained by his own experience. He opened to Goethe mental perspectives which he felt were vaster than any at which he could have arrived by himself. Herder first taught Goethe to study history from a universal standpoint.

And all this he did with an almost scornful rejection of Goethe's gratitude. Herder's ideas poured forth in a torrent; they were at the command of every one who came near him. But no one who stretched out his hand to receive them was spared the abuse which was wont to accompany his costly gifts.

Now it is just this that makes Mephisto's character so grand,— that he knows everything, not only the bad, but also the good, the great, the noble; that he shows every tact to have long existed in his all-embracing knowledge of the world; that he vastly exceeds Faust's knowledge in every direction; that he discloses to him the secrets of life, shows him one world after another, spreads out before him all the resources of humanity for both earthly and spiritual enjoyment, but only to scoff at them all, only to prove that good and bad, great and small, are identical, and the whole monstrous sum — *nothing*.

Of course Herder, this grand positive character, did not go so far; but he unconsciously seduced Goethe to this extreme. It was this which alarmed Goethe, — that Herder incessantly jingled the gold of ideas in his pocket, drew out handfuls of them that they might glisten for a moment in the sunshine, and then threw them aside as worthless coals. Herder's diabolical peculiarity was, first, to make his friends disclose to him their innermost soul; and then to annihilate the unsuspecting, open nature of his friends before their very eyes.

In Herder Goethe experienced for the first time the frightful power of the cold, disinterested, but merciless critic. How is it possible ever to disengage ourselves again from a man who we know has looked us through and through, and seen the good and the bad without any selfish motive for his examination? This explains why Faust instantly submits to Mephisto, and signs the contract with his blood. It is not merely for the sake of the promised enjoyment, but from the feeling that he was helplessly given over to this intellectual supremacy. Mephisto on his side has no other aim than to make Faust feel this power. In everything human he submits himself to Faust. Faust is the master, Mephisto the slave; Faust enjoys, Mephisto willingly panders to him and furnishes whatever can possibly give him pleasure: but he holds one thing ever in reserve, — the power to prove to

Faust at last that all was not worth the trouble. I repeat, Herder did not go so far, but his teachings incited Goethe on. As in Gretchen is realized what might have become of Frederika, so Mephisto shows whither Herder might have been led by his own doctrines. It was Herder who first taught Goethe to exercise his native gift of marring enjoyment by criticism, and in the very heat of passion to dream of desertion. As an illustration of this diabolical habit of destroying all pleasure in a work of art at the moment when it afforded the purest enjoyment, Goethe describes their reading together the "Vicar of Wakefield." [1]

Not till Herder had prepared the elements out of which Mephisto could grow, did Goethe meet with the man who supplied the wished-for personality, — Merck. We have seen how often Goethe worked in this way, — first, to bear in his imagination only the conception of a certain type of character, and then to wait till a chance meeting afforded him a model whose portrait he might copy. Mephisto now receives personality and that element of immeasurable grossness which distinguishes him.

Merck, high as Goethe placed him, did not by any means possess the positive attributes needed by a being who is to look down on things from such a height as Mephisto. Merck's criticisms were destructive, never constructive. Merck is only the spirit of negation, who can do nothing but deny because he lacks creative power. But Mephisto, whatever Goethe may say to the contrary, bears a whole creation within him. One has but to look narrowly into his assertions to discover that his negative criticisms contain a very positive meaning. Goethe, as has been said, denies this; nor was this in his plan: but here the character grew beyond Goethe's intentions, and

[1] See "Aus Meinem Leben." — Tr.

DEVELOPMENT OF MEPHISTOPHELES. 511

took on a nobler stature. If we could imagine Mephisto as taking his degree at a university, he would not merely chaff the professors, but prove to them at the same time that he understood more than all of them together of the subjects on which he was examined; that he was perfectly at home in literature, and that he was practically familiar with all theories. Merck was not great enough for Mephisto's later intellectual scope.

We see that for Mephisto an immeasurable increase was possible in the manifestation of his nature. Not so with Gretchen. All the experiences Goethe quietly gathered by himself, or through his friends, or from the world at large, he laid bare to Mephisto as the counterpart of his own mind, and to be unsparingly criticised by him. In all society Mephisto accompanies him, reads every book with him looking over his shoulder, and, as Goethe's acquaintances and experiences increase, and with them his capacity to strike the right tone in every grade of society, Mephisto also learns with him, and like a living reality constantly develops new traits. The aristocratic, self-possessed tone of a polished man of the world comes gradually into the character; he grows more and more refined and elegant. Out of the caricature of the musty old Master of Arts who had studied the profession he hated to the point of satiety, as which he probably would have been introduced to us in 1772, Mephisto by degrees develops into a caricature of a brilliant statesman of rank, who, after a mistaken career, has reluctantly retired from public life, and pours out unmercifully his trenchant satire upon all things.

A circumstance already mentioned helped to bring about this change. Goethe was destined to witness two great evolutions, — the former in the 18th century, when in the midst of tranquil hopes for the future a frightful insurrection broke forth; and, secondly, in the present century, after the struggle had begun in Germany, the transition from a storm of national enthusiasm to an enforced stagnation brought about by the pressure of the Government upon the people. This was the dulness which made him say, in 1820, that there prevailed among the people a feeling of the utter worthlessness of the present. Goethe was fundamentally a Liberal; but he not only understood the reactionary current which everywhere set in among us after the war for freedom, but felt obliged to recognize and sustain it as legitimate. To oppose it publicly was impossible; but equally impossible was it to suppress the criticism which recognized these political measures as mere palliatives, and prophesied to him with certainty a revolution to come. For this double *rôle* Mephisto was an excellent organ. His behavior as Faust's adjutant at the court of the Emperor gives, in an apparently inoffensive form, Goethe's criticism on what he saw around him. Goethe expresses it in general phrases, but each word cuts deeply. With Machiavellian pitilessness he scourges existing things through the mouth of Mephisto; and yet no one could reproach him for his verses.

Of course this phase came into Mephisto's character later; for in 1772 Goethe could have had but little experience in this direction.

After Gretchen and Mephisto it only remains for us to speak of Faust himself; the other characters and apparitions in the drama call for no further explanation. Wagner the Scholar, Valentin, Martha, and the rest are common types, about whose recognition there can be no doubt; while the allegorical and mythological personages in the second part offer difficulties to the interpreter only in so far that Goethe himself sometimes lends to them an enigmatical form by making them say and do things, part

FAUST IS THE HERO OF "FAUST." 513

of which have a double meaning, and part are incompre hensible for a time ; because he avowedly had intentions regarding them which it is impossible for this generation to fathom. Goethe wished to say many things which he could only say so veiled that they should not be immediately recognized ; and probably had before his mind in so doing the comprehension of a future more distant than ours. In Loeper's edition of " Faust " I find what is explainable explained and put together in the simplest manner, so as to afford the clearest commentary possible.

The all-important figure in the drama is he whose name it bears.

We said that the study of himself in which Goethe was constantly absorbed began in early life. Even as a boy he considered and treated himself objectively ; he was born with a two-fold nature, — one which acted, and the other which in the midst of the action reflected upon it.

Again, in Strasburg he must, through this self-criticism, have seemed to himself in a most trying state of discord. He had passed through the first stage of his youth ; the taking of his degree was soon to put an end to his years of study ; he felt the insufficiency of his own knowledge, and at the same time, also, that of his examiners. He was now to begin his so-called professional career, for which he felt himself in no wise prepared. Like Faust, he would teach, — and yet believed that he had discovered that what he had received as well as what he could impart was but a mass of empty formulas. Whichever way he might turn, his existence seemed to contain irreconcilable antagonisms. On one side he was surrounded by perfectly normal conditions. Belonging to a good and well-established family of honorable position, he had enjoyed a good education, had been trained in the most excellent principles, had passed successfully through the laborious study of a profession, and acquired extensive general culture ; but, as an offset to all these advantages, there rankled in him the feeling of isolation and forlornness in spite of his wide circle of acquaintances, the doubt whether he could ever endure any binding conditions, and, with insatiable scientific curiosity, the reproachful consciousness of superficiality. Goethe once confessed in his old age that he had never opened a book without imagining before he had read one page that he knew it all better than the author. In later years he was able to reflect upon this double nature of which he was so well aware more composedly than in early life, when this discovery agitated and surprised him. He saw that these contradictions formed an indelible peculiarity in his nature. However strong the good might be within him, the bad presented itself at the same time, and won the upper hand. The monstrous question before him, finally, was whether he must consider the bad as something positive, or whether it was to be thought of only as a phantom which at the day of judgment would collapse into nothing. The latter became Goethe's belief ; but he sought for certainty. This we know he found in Spinoza's theory ; and it was chiefly this that attracted him to Spinoza's writings. This is the special problem of "Faust." Goethe once said he could imagine he had committed every crime, and recognized in himself a capacity for all the vices, envy excepted. This should be embodied in "Faust;" and then, when at last the problem was solved, he would represent how all this earthly rubbish would drop away like a torment overcome, and man return sanctified to the hands of his Creator.

To these struggles and problems Goethe sought to give a symbolic form; he was filled with a longing to escape from himself, which increased to such a degree as even to suggest suicide. In Strasburg, at a time when this feeling came over him with insupportable power, he fell in with the "Old Folk's Comedy," which contained the story of Dr. Faustus. This was just the character he wanted. A sudden illumination flashed through his fancy. All that this rough play contained offered itself to him as a means of disengaging his thoughts from himself, and giving them form and expression in poetical visions. In magic pictures his past, his present, and his future life pass before his soul; all takes form, — the puerile scenes of the play are metamorphosed into parts of a grand drama full of high symbolic meaning. His tormenting thoughts are transferred to persons who suddenly come to view like very old acquaintances who until now have been hidden as it were in some enchanted mountain, from which, released by an earthquake, they suddenly stand before him, and are now dearer to him than his nearest relatives. He burdens these souls with all that he condemns in himself but cannot conquer, while his imagination shows him at the same time his feeling of indestructible self-reliance; and the incarnate triumph of this faith in the final solution of the drama may be considered as the gospel of the redemption of man through labor. How would it be possible to imagine this second part separated from the first? The conclusion of the second part *must* have originated at the same time with the first, — the mocking of Mephisto, and the rescue of Faust from his clutches, which suddenly lose all power to hold him. Colossal earthly achievements make this escape possible. Faust wrests from the sea a new tract of country. We see before us, in the consummation of Faust's life, the noblest glorification of human endeavor.

But if the character of Mephisto was enhanced by degrees during Goethe's life, the constant reconstruction of

Faust was even more necessary. How comprehensible that Goethe could never make up his mind to finish the poem, — the work and its principal character being from their very nature endless! Only after his own life on earth was finished could Faust be offered as a complete being.

We see that Goethe had dedicated to Faust his highest poetic power in preference to all the other children of his imagination; and this fact explains a certain lack of intrinsic force in the others. We have to take Werther as Werther *plus* Faust; Egmont as Egmont *plus* Faust; and so on through the whole series, — and we do this unconsciously. It is no artificial calculation; but it shows us at the same time, concerning Faust, why this most powerful of all Goethe's creations, viewed externally, is in a measure formless and vague. Faust's personality seems to refuse limitations; he feels, enjoys, and rushes through life without a firm footing on the earth, like a demon forced for a time to wear a human shape. That he is subject to human destiny is only an accident, a minor consideration with him. He flies hither and thither, resting nowhere permanently, — time and space, which we are all compelled to take into account, being alike indifferent to him.

This arises, as a necessary consequence, from his twofold existence. As Goethe's other characters demand an invisible complement, so Faust needs Goethe himself as his visible twin-brother. Faust represents Goethe's actual life. In the universality of Faust's existence Goethe became capable of growing old with him, and at the same time of remaining eternally young. Until his very last hours Goethe transfers to Faust his every thought. Faust is the incarnate spirit of Goethe, to whom no range is too vast, no experience impossible. We think of Faust as having written all Goethe's poems and all his scientific works. What Goethe has left behind in scattered verses and thoughts elicited by the moment's experience might all be considered as *paralipomena* to the " Faust."

We have now given the genesis of this character, together with the progressive development of the entire poem. In the degree in which Goethe's spiritual capacity increased he infused new power into this drama. In old age he grew dissatisfied with much he had written when young. He puts into verse what seems to him in its prosaic form to be too glaring. Revisions were constantly going on, new material being worked in, and fresh attempts made to round off the composition. He once said to Schiller that his work was like a heap of mushrooms which had all sprung up at the same time, and pressed close upon one another, while each was a thing in itself. He thus characterizes the agglutinative growth of the drama whose single parts, in spite of their individuality, are still to be recognized as members of the same family. Goethe could with justice say in his last letter, with reference to this work, that he had no fear of analytic criticism.

In his endeavor to give to this poem unity of coloring, the local element came in to help him in the happiest manner. It was not necessary for Goethe's imagination to travel far and wide in 1772; he only needed to combine what his most familiar recollections afforded him, and Faust's and Gretchen's native city was sketched. In this too there was nothing later to be changed or corrected.

Frankfort offered the groundwork, — the old German Reichstadt, walled in and exclusive, the last remnant of whose courts and alleys, nooks, passages, and corners, with the noise and smell of their various trades, are, today, fast disappearing. Our bare dwelling-houses are no longer the home-like nests of that time, which had been warmed by the presence of father, grandfather, and great grandfather; every scratch on whose timbers was known and reverenced,—the very sanctuaries of family life. In Goethe's youth all this was in its prime,—the mass of narrow houses occupied from garret to cellar, the churches in the midst of them centres of pomp and splendor, all straining upward in a thousand points because there was no room to unfold in breadth. Above lay the sun on roofs and chimneys, while below the air was musty and dim, even at high noon. There were narrow houses at the back with little gardens and walls, flowing fountains with chattering servant girls, massive gates through which on Sundays and holidays the crowd streamed toward the open country.

Goethe had had all this before his eyes in Frankfort, and found it again in Leipsic and Strasburg. Even in Weimar the fountain was not wanting before his house; in the centre of the little, irregular, three-cornered Platz where in the evening the maids stood to gossip.

All this gave to the figures in the drama their well defined characteristic accessories. The scenes at the court of the Emperor belong to the same historical epoch with the city scenes of the first act; and also the very last scenes where Faust becomes blind, are restricted to a certain period, a limitation which seems to clash with its contents. The pictures by the masters of the Renaissance in the sixteenth and seventeenth centuries furnish suitable decorations for the heavenly scenes; and even the classic parts have their prototypes in the conception of the antique as it was familiar to the masters of the sixteenth century.

This external scenic element comes to-day more into the foreground.

In the beginning "Faust" was looked upon simply as a poem: only the spiritual contents seemed of importance, and a stage for the drama existed but in imagination. Even the first part was considered so little suited for the actual theatre that its representation was not effected till 1828. For the celebration of Goethe's eightieth birthday the daring feat was undertaken, while it did not come into anybody's head that the second part *could* be represented, and still less that Goethe had ever really had practical, attainable stage effects in view. Goethe alone knew that the scenic representation of the whole poem was a work for the future. He occasionally asserted that some time a Frenchman would come who would make a " *spectacle* " of it; and there was truth in his joke. A French composer, not long since, transformed "Faust" into a grand magic opera; and a short while ago, in Leipsic, and again in Weimar, the second part, as a spoken drama, was given. Who looks at the work seriously will see that this could not succeed at the first attempt; only after many essays in the way of drama, opera, ballet, and spectacle will the right method of representation be found out; and only then will it appear what wonderfully grand effects for the stage Goethe had intended, visible to his mind alone, and the understanding of which he committed confidently to later times. I doubt not, a time will come when representations of the second part of " Faust " with the first will be made a dramatic national festival. This career of this greatest work of the greatest poet of all nations and times has just begun, and only the leading steps have been taken towards bringing to light the value of its contents.

The explanation and interpretation of " Faust " is one of our great scientific problems: the work contains beside its manifest poetic beauties a gigantic treasure of worldly wisdom, partly in such an enigmatical form as to challenge not only the acuteness of the ordinary reader, but also the ever-renewed study of the learned. We have a special literature whose aim it is to prove from "Faust" not only what Goethe's creed was, but the creed of his whole century.

"Faust" in 1808 made at once the impression of a literary revelation. In this work, in "Elective Affinities," and in his "Autobiography," which followed quickly, a new genius seemed to have arisen in familiar form authenticating himself as a citizen of the nineteenth century. As Goethe's first youthful days were mirrored in "Werther," to which his admirers who had been young with him always referred, so Goethe's new epoch — the Goethe of our century — began with "Dichtung und Wahrheit," with "Elective Affinities," and with "Faust," to which his earlier writings bear only, as it were, a pre-historic relation. Goethe's real popularity began with this work, but at the same time his more immediate private relations cease to be of moment in forming our judgment of him. Now when generation after generation, and all the intellectual life of Germany revolves about him, it becomes quite indifferent with whom out of this great circle he happened to stand in special connection. Goethe determined the career of many eminent men who never (or at most only once or twice) were permitted to come into personal contact with him. It would not only be unjust, but false to look upon the circumstances which day by day made the character of his life in the narrow Weimar surroundings as the framework for his biography. When the sun calls forth the enchantment of spring, the fertility of summer, and the wealth of autumn, thereby benefiting a whole people, it is not the most important consideration what clouds day by day surrounded the great luminary at its rising or setting. There might have been other clouds, or indeed there might have been none.

With this I conclude the analysis of Goethe in these lectures.

I said at the beginning that I would examine his works: they have been discussed.

Besides incessant productions of all kinds, poetic as well as scientific, which flowed from his pen so steadily that we can almost follow them day by day, another of his principal works was the " Westöstliche Divan." In this collection, together with new poems in oriental dress, is a memorial of his friendship for Marianne Willemer, whom he has celebrated in them as Zuleika. In the book of "Timur" on the other hand, Goethe has written out his final thoughts of Napoleon, his greatness, and his fall. The " Westöstliche Divan " is of special importance as showing a new phase of Goethean prosody, in which, turning away from antique metres, he gains new freedom in poetic expression. Once more hurrying on before his time, Goethe has struck the tone in which Rückert, Platen, and Heine wrote, and beyond which the lyric poetry of to-day has not risen.

After these poems, came the "Italian Journey," in 1817, as his last, great, finished work. Goethe next devoted himself to the careful preparation of a newly-collected edition of his works, as well as to that of many volumes of posthumous works which he did not wish to have published till he had retired from the stage of life.

But however many persons knew Goethe, or knew of him, he yet remained, to the German people, up to the time of his death, a half mythical being. Besides relatively small fragments of his correspondence nothing was known at that time of his letters, which are now the most excellent source of historical study. For even those men have nearly all passed away whose mental development the living Goethe influenced in his latter years. A fresh generation has arisen who never saw him face to face, but who know infinite details of his life, and who seek, so far as they are capable of doing, to understand his work.

If we take the last twenty years of Goethe's life together, according to the knowledge vouchsafed us today, we find in a time of political disintegration and gloomy silence in public life, that the reverence for Goethe was one of the few patriotic sentiments which all shared and ventured openly to acknowledge. In him alone Germany was united. This was Goethe's political influence in its highest sense.

He was the luminous point to which every eye turned in those sad days which dragged along between 1820 and 1830, seeming as if they would never end. It was this consciousness which led men to erect statues to him during his lifetime. Frankfort began, and other cities followed. The most beautiful among them in point of conception is the colossal figure by Steinhäuser, in the Weimar Museum (placed almost out of sight), executed according to the sketch which is in Berlin, designed and modelled by Bettina. Goethe sits, throned like Jupiter in antique dress, one hand rests, holding a wreath; the other holds a lyre raised aloft, on the strings of which a child-like genius standing between his knees is playing. It is a curious change to pass from this classic representation, which in Goethe's time was almost a matter of course, to the historic costume, which after his death became more and more the fashion. Rietschel made the beginning in the Weimar double statue. The one intended for Berlin by Schaper represents Goethe as a young man in the dress of the last century.

But another memorial to him still remains to be raised. It is incumbent on one of our German Universities to publish Goethe's works in a worthy form. Not until the hour approaches when solicitude for the German language and literature has become the interest of the whole nation, raising it above spasmodic efforts, will the German people derive the full measure of benefit from Goethe. Then, perhaps, his house which is to-day so drearily closed, in whose untrodden rooms his collections are awaiting a dubious fate, will stand open and accessible to all the world as in the days when Goethe lived; and as it was once it will again be entered as a sanctuary for remembrance.

Goethe's house in his last years became a place of pilgrimage. Weimar itself was no longer, as in Schiller's time, the fostering home of literary activities and the focus of intrigues and personal quarrels; it had become only Goethe's chosen retreat, where close beside Carl August's residence he peacefully fulfilled his own work. This undisturbed and at the same time stimulating life was for his nature a special gift of Providence. He reigned there with the most sovereign right, untroubled by the jealousy of any, and received with imperial benevolence all who knocked at his door. Weimar now formed the friendly boundary between North and South Germany. A certain solemn formality had impressed itself upon Goethe's air and bearing. He sometimes talked in an almost constrained way, and expressed his opinions in self-chosen phrases in a lapidary style one would gladly have exchanged for a more animated one. This is best shown in his correspondence with Zelter, the Berlin composer, for whom he cherished a sincere friendship.

If we desire a true picture of this Weimar life as it day by day glided by, through his last ten years, we shall specially enjoy reading "Eckermann's Reminiscences," together with those of the Chancellor von Müller. We realize, as if we had been eye-witnesses, how Goethe strove above all things to the very last to keep himself in contact with the young. He often said that this was the only means of keeping the heart young. His vitality was inexhaustible. Even in his seventieth year a young and beautiful maiden kindled in him a passion which it cost him a monstrous effort to subdue; and from this struggle arose some of his most ardent poems. Goethe, while enjoying all the privileges of age, seemed merely hiding the powers of his youth and not to have lost them. Finally all his friends were dead, — the Duke, Frau von Stein, even his son, had gone before him. But it did not crush him; to live was to him pure enjoyment. Until his very last days spring and sunshine always brought a fresh rapture to his soul, and tempted him to explore in all directions the fields and woods so dear to him; while the recollections of old friends springing up in his path refreshed him instead of making him sad. He looked forward to each new day with serene expectation and genuine human curiosity as to what it might bring forth.

On the 22d of March, 1832, he died.

He might have lived on like the patriarchs of the Old Testament for decades. Therefore his loss came at last like something so unexpected, and was so deeply felt. It seemed impossible that a man in the midst of the enjoyment of his best powers could be torn away.

The next morning after Goethe's death we read in Eckermann's Diary: —

"A deep longing seized me to look upon his earthly covering once more. His faithful servant, Friedrich, unlocked for me the chamber where they had laid him. Stretched upon his back he rested like a sleeper. Deep peace and serenity reigned on the features of his imposing and noble face. The mighty brow seemed still the home of thought. I wanted a lock of his hair, but reverence prevented me from cutting it off. The body lay naked, covered with a white cloth; great pieces of ice were about it. Friedrich removed the cloth. I was astonished at the godlike magnificence of his frame; the breast exceedingly broad and arched; the arms and legs full, soft, and muscular; the feet delicate and of the most perfect form; nowhere on the whole body a trace of fat, or emaciation, or decay. A perfect man lay in great beauty before me, and the rapture I felt allowed me to forget for a moment that the immortal spirit had quitted such a frame.

"I laid my hand upon his heart; all was still, and I turned away to give vent to my suppressed tears."

CHRONOLOGICAL TABLE.

1474–1533. Ariosto.
1544–95. Tasso.
1564–1616. Shakspeare.
1600–81. Calderon.
1606–84. Corneille.
1622–73. Molière.
1632–77. Spinoza.
1639–99. Racine.
1689. Birth of Richardson.
1694.   ,, ,, Voltaire.
1700.   ,, ,, Gottsched.
1710.   ,, ,, Johann Kaspar Goethe (Goethe's father).
1712.   ,, ,, Frederick the Great, and Rousseau.
1713.   ,, ,, Diderot.
1716.   ,, ,, Gellert.
1719.   ,, ,, Gleim.
1724.   ,, ,, Klopstock.
1728.   ,, ,, Oliver Goldsmith.
1729.   ,, ,, Lessing.
1730.   ,, ,, Hamann.
1731.   ,, ,, Elizabeth Textor, Goethe's mother.
1733.   ,, ,, Wieland.
1739.   ,, ,, Anna Amalia of Saxe-Weimar.
1741.   ,, ,, Lavater.
1742.   ,, ,, Merck, and Frau von Stein.
1743.   ,, ,, F. H. Jacobi.
1744.   ,, ,, Herder.

1748. The first Cantos of the "Messiah" are published. Birth of Gottfr. Aug. Bürger, and Christian Stolberg.
1749. Birth of Heinse.
1749. ,, ,, Goethe, August 28.
1750. ,, ,, Cornelia Goethe, Fred. Stolberg, and Caroline Flachsland.
1751. Birth of J. H. Voss.
1754. Restoration of the house of Goethe's father.
1755. Earthquake at Lisbon.
1756. Birth of Mozart and of Körner, Schiller's friend.
1757. ,, ,, Karl August.
1758. ,, ,, Zelter.
1759-61. The French in Frankfort. Fräulein von Klettenberg. Birth of Schiller. Death of Richardson.
1763-65. Coronation of Joseph II. "Christ's Descent into Hell." June 6, 1764, birth of Christiane Vulpius.
1765-68. Goethe in Leipsic. Oct. 19, 1765. Matriculation. "The Humors of the Lover." "The Guilty Confederates." Oeser. Publication of Lessing's Dramaturgy. Picture-gallery at Dresden. Hemorrhage. Leaves Leipsic, August 28, 1768. Death of Gottsched. Birth of Wilhelm von Humboldt, Charlotte Schiller, Aug. Wilh. Schlegel.
1768-70. Frankfort. "New Songs." Breitkopf und Sohn, Leipsic, 1770. Death of Gellert. Birth of Cuvier, Alex. von Humboldt, Napoleon, Beethoven.
1770-71. Strasburg. Arrival, April 2, 1770. Sesenheim: October, 1770. August 6, 1771, barrister's certificate. Leaves Strasburg, August 28, 1771. Birth of Hölderlin, 1770.
1771-72. Frankfort. Birth of Walter Scott, Friedrich Schlegel, and Geoffroy de St. Hilaire.
1772. Wetzlar. Charlotte Buff. Jerusalem. Journey on the Rhine. Ehrenbreitenstein. Mme. de Laroche. "On German Architecture." "Frankfort Critical Review."
1773. Publication of "Götz von Berlichingen." Cornelia

Goethe's marriage with Schlosser. The brothers Stolberg.

1774. "Pater Brey." "Gods, Heroes, and Wieland." "The fair at Plundersweilern." "Satyros." Maximiliane de Laroche's marriage with Brentano. "Faust." "The Sorrows of Werther." "Clavigo." Lavater's visit at Frankfort. Journey on the Rhine. Pempelfort. Fred. Jacobi. "Prometheus," "Mahomet," "The Wandering Jew." September: publication of "Werther." Klopstock and the Weimar princes in Frankfort. Death of Mlle. von Klettenberg.

1775. Engagement to Lilli. Journey to Switzerland with the Stolbergs. "Faust." Sept. 22, Charles August invites him to Weimar. Oct. 3, marriage of the Duke. Nov. 7, Goethe's arrival at Weimar. Wieland. Frau von Stein.

1776. Goes with the Duke to Leipsic. Lenz arrives at Weimar. Klopstock's letter. Councillor of Legation with a salary of 1200 Th'ls. Oct. 20, Herder's inaugural sermon. Nov. Lenzen's "Asiniana" (Eselei), "Stella," and "Claudine of Villa-Bella." Amateur-theatre. "Brother and Sister," "Proserpina." Goethe's portrait by Kraus, etching by Chodowiecki.

1777. Frau von Stein. "Wilhelm Meister." Trip to the Harz mountains. Birth of Clemens Brentano, and Hein. von Kleist.

1778. "To the Moon." Journey to Potsdam. "The Fisher." Death of Rousseau and Voltaire.

1779. March 28, First draft of the "Iphigenia" completed. April 6, First representation. Frederick the Great in camp in Silesia. Ettersburg. Jacobi's "Woldemar." Privy Councillor. Second journey to Switzerland, Sept. 12 to Jan. 13, 1780. Meeting with Frederika and Lilli. "Song of the Spirits above the Waters." "Jery and Bätely." Karl's School. Schiller. May's portrait of Goethe.

1780. "Letters from Switzerland," second part. "The Birds." Works on "Tasso." Schiller's "Essay on the Mutual Dependence of the Animal and Spiritual Nature of Man." Hard official duties in the commission on the war.

1781. "Erlking." "Only he who Longing Knows." Corona Schröter. Beginning of "Elpenor." At Dessau and Gotha. Anatomy and osteology. Death of Lessing. Birth of Achim von Arnim. Schiller's "Robbers."

1782. "Mieding's Death." Publication of "The Fishermaiden." Geological studies. Death of Goethe's father. Receives a diploma of nobility. Schiller's flight from Stuttgart.

1783. "Elpenor." Fred. Stein visits him. Birth of Charles Frederic of Saxe-Weimar. Second trip to the Harz. "Ilmenau." "Above all Heights is Peace." On the Brocken, Göttingen. "The Bard." "The Harpist." "Mignon." Schiller's "Fiesko."

1784. On the origin of the intermaxillary bone. "Ilmenau." Third trip to the Harz. "Secrets." "Jest, Trick, and Revenge." Death of Diderot. Marianne von Willemer born. "Cabal and Love."

1785. "Examination of my affairs." "What was wanting." With Knebel to the Fichtel mountains. Botanical studies, also osteological, mineralogical, and geological ones. Hamlet. Karlsbad. Schiller's arrival in Leipsic. Birth of Bettina.

1786. Practice in Italian. Revision of his writings. "Inclination." Death of Frederick the Great, August 17. Goethe leaves Karlsbad, Sept. 3. Passage of the Brenner, Sept. 9. Venice, Sept. 28 to Oct. 14. Rome, Oct. 29. Iphigenia in Tauris and in Delphi.

1787. 22d of Febr. to Naples. April 2 till May 14, Sicily. "Nausikaa." Bust by Trippel, portraits by Angelica Kauffmann, and Tischbein. "Goethe's Writings, with illustrations." Leipsic. Göschen. 1787-90. 4 vols. Birth of Uhland. Schiller's "Don Carlos." Heinse's "Ardinghello."

1788. "Faust." April 22. Departure from Rome. Florence. "Tasso." June 18, in Weimar. Sept. 7, Meeting with

CHRONOLOGICAL TABLE. 531

Schiller. Christiane Vulpius. "Roman Elegies." Maurice in Weimar. "Egmont" is published. Hamann's Death. Birth of Rückert.

1789. H. Meyer. "Tasso" is finished. Dec. 25, Birth of Goethe's son August.

1790. Superintendence of the government offices for Science and Art. "Metamorphosis of Plants" in print. Optic studies. Torquato Tasso. "Fragments of Faust" published. Journey to Venice. Epigrams. Off for Silesia. Giant Mountains, Galicia.

1791. Assumes the direction of the court theatre. "Prologue" on the 7th of May. "Contributions to Optics" published. Death of Merck and Mozart.

1792. Campaign to the Champagne. Valmy. To Pempelfort and Münster. Princess Gallitzin. "Great-Cophta" in print. Lips's portrait of Goethe.

1793. "The Civic General." "The Restless." "Conversations of the Emigrants." "Reinecke the Fox." Optic and Art studies with Meyer. Siege of Mayence. Death of Stein, Master-of-Horse.

1794. Arrangement with Schiller. Schiller's letter of Aug. 23. Schiller's fourteen days' visit to Goethe. " The Hours." Correspondence with Schiller. Publication of " Reinecke the Fox." Death of Bürger.

1795. Jan. 25, the first part of "The Hours." Voss's "Luise." "Epigrams." "Wilhelm Meister," vols. i. and ii. are published. Karlsbad.

1796. Translation of Benvenuto Cellini, for "The Hours." Schiller's treatment of "Egmont." "Alexis and Dora," "Wilhelm Meister," vols. iii. and iv., and "The Xenia," are published. Begins "Hermann and Dorothea." Platen is born.

1797. "Hermann and Dorothea" as Annual for 1798. Ballads. Work on "Faust." Third Swiss journey. "Euphrosyne." "Amyntas."

1798. "Theory of Colors." Discontinuance of "The Hours." Plan for "Achilleïs." Publication of the first part of "The Propylæa." Oct. 12, Opening of the new

Theatre. Schiller's "Prologue." "Wallenstein's Camp."

1799. Rehearsals of the Piccolomini, and Wallenstein's Death. Translation of Voltaire's "Mahomet." Schiller settles at Weimar. Birth of Heine.

1800. Work on "Faust." "Helena." "Palæophron and Neoterpe." "Tancred," after Voltaire. "Propylæa," last part. Schiller's "Wallenstein."

1801. "Terrible Disease." Work on "Faust." Representation of "Tancred" by Schiller. To Pyrmont. Göttingen. Art Exhibition at Weimar. Representation of Lessing's "Nathan." Death of Lavater. "Maria Stuart."

1802. Schiller's "Maid of Orleans," and "Turandot." Friedrich Schlegel's "Alarkos." "The Natural Daughter."

1803. Representation of the first part of "The Natural Daughter." April 2. Dismissal of Fichte. New Literary Gazette of Jena with Eichstädt. Mme. de Staël in Weimar. Death of Herder, Gleim, Klopstock, and Heinse. Schiller's "Bride of Messina." Kleist's "The Family Schroffenstein."

1804. Criticism of the Poems of Voss. "Götz von Berlichingen" arranged for the stage. Maria Paulowna in Weimar. "Wilhelm Tell." Brentano's "Ponce de Leon."

1805. Schiller dies, May 9. Will complete Schiller's "Demetrius." Epilogue to "The Lay of the Bell." Visits from Wolf, Fred. Jacobi, Zelter, Gall. Fourth Harz journey. Publication of Rameau's "Nephew" and "Winckelmann and his Age."

1806. "Theory of Colors." New draft of "Stella." Karlsbad. Geological and morphological labors. "Military Campaigns." Continued. Marriage with Christiane Vulpius, Oct. 19. "The Youth's Magic Horn."

1807. The Duchess Dowager dies. March. Bettina's Visit. Karlsbad. Plan to "Wilhelm Meister's Journeys." "The New Melusine." "Dangerous Wager." "Man of Fifty." "The Foolish Pilgrim." Hackert's Biography. Minna Herzlieb. " Elective Affinities." Zacharias Werner. " Sonet-mania." "Pandora's Return." New Edition of his "Works," Cotta. Vols. i.–iv.

1808. Karlsbad. Mme. Councillor dies. Audience at Napoleon's. "Works," vols. v.–xii.; vol. viii. contains the first part of "Faust." "Pandora's Return" published in the periodical "Prometheus."

1809. "Elective Affinities" published. Plan to "Fiction and Truth."

1810. Masquerades. "Theory of Colors" finished. Karlsbad. "Meister's Journeys." "The Nutbrown Maiden." Publication of "Theory of Colors." Portrait by Klügelgen. Arnim's "Dolores."

1811. Calderon's "The Firm Prince" played. "Hackert's Life" printed. Sulpice Boisserée at Weimar with Cornelius's drawings to the Nibelungs, and his own plans for the Cathedral of Cologne. Karlsbad. "Romeo and Juliet" adapted for the stage. Publication of the first part of "Fiction and Truth." Death of Kleist.

1812. Karlsbad. Teplitz. Writes "The Wager" for the Empress of Austria. Beethoven. Decides to arrange "Faust" for the stage. New revision of "Egmont." "Fiction and Truth," second part.

1813. Death of Wieland. Oration on Wieland. Disturbances caused by the war. Teplitz. "Shakspeare and no End." Works on "Fiction and Truth." Return to Weimar in August. Körner killed, August 26. Battle of Leipsic. Commencement of the "Westöstliche Divan."

1814. Westöstliche Divan "founded." Visit from Fr. A. Wolf. "Epimenides." Journey to the surroundings of the Main, Rhine, and Neckar. Prepares the "Italian Journey" for the press. Publication of the third part of "Fiction and Truth." Freimund Reimar's (Fr. Rückert) "German Poems."

1815. New edition of his works. Revision of the "Sicilian Journey." March 30: Representation in Berlin of "Epimenides." Frankfort and Wiesbaden. Marianne von Willemer. Work on the "Divan." The hundred days of Napoleon. Culminating period of the Weimar Theatre. Publication of Uhland's Poems. Death of Caroline Herder.

1816. June 6. Death of Christiane. Work on "Fiction and Truth," and the "Italian Journey." "Art and Antiquity," first part.

1817. Goethe's son marries Ottilie von Pogwisch. "Dog of Aubry." Criticism of Byron's "Manfred." "Divan." Art-studies. Portrait by Jagemann.

1819. Revision of the Yearly-and-Daily Journals. Publication of the "Divan." Karlsbad. Seventieth Birthday. Death of Fred. Jacobi and Fred. Stolberg.

1820. Karlsbad. "Wolkendiarium." Work on "Meister's Journeys." "Voss vs. Stolberg." Rauch's bust of Goethe.

1821. Revision of "Campaign in France." "Tame Xenia." Occupied on Byron, Scott, Calderon, Hindu poetry. Publication of the first part of "Meister's Journeys." Napoleon and Christ. Death of the Stolbergs.

1823. Eckermann. "To Lord Byron." Ulrike von Levetzow. "Marienbad, 1823."

1824. Revision of the "Correspondence with Schiller" and the "Annals." Byron's "Cain." Death of Byron. "Trilogy of Passion." Death of Lotte Schiller.

1825. Work on the second part of "Faust." New revision of "Meister's Journeys." Revision of the correspondence with Zelter. The "Annals" finished. Jubilee of Charles August. Goethe's Jubilee.

1826. "Helena" completed. Revision of the new edition of his works in forty volumes. Continuation of the revision of the "Journeys." Study of Dante. The porcelain painter Selbers paints Goethe on a cup. August 29: Return of the letters to Frau von

Stein. September 17: **Unveiling** of Dannecker's bust of Schiller. "While contemplating Schiller's Cranium." "Annals." Story of " The Child and the Lion." Death of Voss. Platen's "The Fateful Fork."

1827. Riemer. Göttling, Eckermann aid the new edition. Publication of vols. i.-x. The fourth volume contains the "Helena." Letter from Walter Scott. Visit from Ludwig of Bavaria on the 28th of August. On French, Czech, Serbian, Chinese, and German Poetry. Work on "Faust" and on "Meister's Journeys." Frau von Stein dies January 6. Death of Beethoven.

1828. Death of Carl August. Vols. xi.-xx. of the "Works" are published. Work on "Faust" and "Meister's Journeys." Seventieth birthday of Zelter. "Correspondence between Schiller and Goethe," Parts I. and II. in print. Portrait of Goethe by Stieler. Death of Lotte Kestner.

1829. Completion of "Meister's Journeys" and "My Second Residence at Rome." Soret translates "The Metamorphosis of Plants." Publication of " The Correspondence with Schiller," Part III., and vols. xx.-xxx. of "The Works." Paganini, Zelter in Weimar. Work on "Faust." The sculptor David makes a model of his bust at Weimar. Death of Fr. Schlegel.

1830. Death of the Grand-duchess Louise. In "Fiction and Truth" description of " the most wretched, sweetest year of my life." Felix Mendelssohn in Weimar. "Classical Walpurgisnight." French Revolution of July; controversy between Cuvier and Geoffroy de St. Hilaire. Publication of "The Works," vols. xxxi. -xl. August von Goethe dies at Rome on the 28th of October.

1831. New revision of "The Metamorphosis of Plants." Completion of "Faust," July 20. David sends from Paris the bust of Goethe in marble; unveiling of the same, August 28. Publication of Part IV. "Fiction and Truth." Disposition of his effects. Death of Achim von Arnim.

1832. Death of Cuvier. "On plastic Anatomy." On the "Principes de philosophie Zoölogique, par Geoffroy de St. Hilaire." "On the Rainbow." On the opera "The Women of Athens." Portrait by Schwerdgeburth. Death of Zelter and Walter Scott. Goethe's last letter of March 17. Commencement of the disease, March 16. He passes away on the 22d of March, at half-past eleven in the forenoon. *Postmortem* outline by Preller.

1832–34. Publication of Goethe's Posthumous Works, 15 vols.

1835. "Letters to a Child." Death of Platen.

1836, 1837. Publication of Goethe's Poetical and Prose Works, 2 vols.

1842. Publication of Goethe's Posthumous Works, 5 vols. Death of Clemens Brentano.

1843. Death of Hölderlin.

1844. Goethe Monument by Schwanthaler, at Frankfort.

1845. Death of A. W. Schlegel.

1852. Goethe Statue by Steinhäuser after Bettina's sketch.

1856. Death of Heine.

1857. Unveiling of the Goethe-Schiller Monument by Rietschel at Weimar.

1859. Death of Bettina.

1860. Death of Marianne von Willemer.

1862. Death of Uhland.

1866. Death of Rückert.

1872. Death of Goethe's daughter-in-law.

1880. Unveiling of the Goethe Monument at Berlin.

INDEX.

Academy of Sciences at Erfurt, 241.
Academy, an, 404.
Academic life of Goethe at Rome, 350.
Accessible and inaccessible, the, in nature, 450.
Achilles, 16, 492, 493.
Achilleïs, 427, 445.
Actors, Italian, 91.
"Adrastea," by Herder, 406.
Adultery, 252.
Æschylus, 424 ; his female characters, 495.
Agassiz ascribes to Goethe his first thought about the glacial period, 449.
"Agnes von Lilien," novel by Caroline Wolzogen, attributed to Goethe, 402.
Aim of humanity, 194.
Aja, Frau, nickname of Goethe's mother, 221.
Albani, Cardinal, 314.
Albert in "Werther," 467.
Alcibiades as prince of fable compared to Cæsar, 305.
Alexander the Great, 304.
"Alexis and Dora," 427.
Allegorical and mythological personages in the second part of "Faust," 510.
"Allwill," 185 ; "Allwill's collection of letters" (1774), 189 ; Julian Schmidt on "Allwill," *ibid.*
Allwine in Jacobi's "Woldemar," 190.

Alps, the, as represented by Goethe, 297.
Alsace, 60 *et seq.*, 261; Alsatian soldiers, 39 ; relation of Alsace to Germany, 39.
Amalia, Duchess of Saxe-Weimar, 226, 234 *et seq.*, 325, 390 ; her portraits, 238 ; intercourse with Wieland, 238.
America, 232, 311 ; separation from England, 485 ; colonization, 303.
Ancient conception of the universe, 451 ; poesy, 422 ; prose as example for the Germans, 431 ; the opera and the drama, 284.
Anemones in the plains surrounding the Roman villas, 431.
Antichrist, 314.
Antigone, 462 ; comparison with Gretchen, 493.
Antiques in Germany in Goethe's time, 315.
Antonio in "Tasso," 330.
"Ardinghello," by Heinse, 374.
Ariosto, 91, 150.
Aristotle, 305 ; his conception of the universe, 454.
Army, popular among the people, 197 *et seq.*
Art, 502 ; art and poetry with the Romans, 309.
Artistic moderation of the antique poets, 426.
Art-Meyer (Kunst-Meyer), 388, 410.
"Art-pope," Goethe called, 14.

Asiatics on European soil, 303.
Asia in the XVIIIth century the Arcadia of authors, 241.
Aspersion of Goethe in political relations, 490.
Attic dialect, 430.
Augsburger Allgemeine Zeitung, 1793 (Augsburg Public Gazette), 393, 408.
Aureæ arces Romæ, 309.
Austria, 483.

Bad, the, in Spinoza's writings, 514.
Balloon, the first, 456.
Bancroft, 225.
"Banquet" of Plato, 430.
Basedow and Lavater, 180 et seq.
Batsch at Jena, 395.
Battle of Jena, 477.
Beaulieu-Marconnay, Count of, on Anna Amalia, Carl August, and Minister von Fritsch, 234 et seq., 245.
Beaumarchais, Marie, in "Clavigo," 73.
Beautiful, the, as the aim of mankind, 200.
Belluomo troupe, 390.
Belvedere, near Weimar, 262.
Bembo, 211.
Berlin, 32, 488; Goethe on, 314; Berlin and Rome, 319; museum at, 186; University, 477.
Bernhard of Weimar, 191.
Bettina, 132, 470; her sketch for the Goethe statue in the museum at Weimar, 522.
Bible, the, in the XVIIIth century, 197.
Bigamy, in Goethe's "Stella," 214.
Bodmer, 240.
Boisserée, 186; Goethe speaks with Boisserée about Lilli, 1815, 225, 230.
Bologna, 300.
Book drama in Germany, 90.

Brackenburg, 370.
"Braut von Messina," 418.
Brentano, Clemens, 129.
Brentano, merchant at Frankfort, 138.
Breeze, among the Lindens in "Werther," 358.
Breeze, among the oaks in "Götz," 358.
"Bride of Corinth," 445.
Brion Family, 61, 69.
Brion, Frederika, 57 et seq., 113, 119, 217 et seq., 250, 506 et seq.; Goethe's grief about Frederika, 87; correspondence with Goethe, 66, 70; first appearance, 62; in Strasburg, 66; Frederika and Alsace, 261; Goethe's Frederika and the genuine Frederika, 57 et seq.; compared with Frau von Stein, 258.
Brother and Sister, the, 288.
Buff, Amtmann, 118.
Burkhardt, Dr., at Weimar, 248, 324.
Busts, as historical material, 173.
Byron, Lord, 392, 418.
Byron, Lord, the hero of Richardson's novels, 151.

Cæsar in the German Congress, 493.
Cagliostro, 106.
Calderon, 91.
Campaign of 1792, 390.
Cannonade of Valmy, 391.
Cantata for Gluck's niece, 286 et seq., 329.
Carriers of human culture, 194.
Cathedral of Cologne, 186.
Catullus, 339.
Celts, the, emigrate into Europe, 195.
Ceremonial observances of aged men, 460.
Carl August, 235 et seq., 264, 389 et seq., 500, 524; his iron will, 274; his feeling of an excess

of strength, 268; his greatness, 268; in political affairs, 480; his letters to Goethe written from below to one above him, 264; Goethe's "most gracious sovereign," 264; after Goethe's Italian journey, 353 *et seq.*; takes control of the government 1775, 226; correspondence between him and Goethe 1775–1828, 265; cultivates with Goethe the park at Weimar, 261; Carl August and "Tasso," 331; Carl August and von Fritsch, 245; his death, 460.

Charlemagne, contrasted with Faust, 492.

"Charles's Efforts and Hindrances," 440.

"Carlos, Don," 1785, put on the stage by Goethe, 394.

Characters in "Faust," 505.

Charlotte in the "Elective Affinities," 464 *et seq.*

China, in German Literature, 241.

Chinese, the, the great and just nation in the XVIIIth century, 241.

Christianity, 197; Christianity and modern thought, 455; Christianity and the creation of the world, 454.

Christiane Vulpius, 335 *et seq.*, 389 *et seq.*; her eccentricities, 341; in the "Roman Elegies," 338, 340; foster-sister of the princesses in "Tasso," 340; Christiane and the ladies of Weimar, 403; her death, 1816, 340.

Cicero, his periods, 177.
Cid, the, 492.
"Cid," Corneille's, 157.
Cinquecento, Italy of the, 332.
Citizen's estate, its use through the example of France, 483.
Clara, in "Egmont" (Clärchen), 16, 277, 370, 479.

"Claudine of Villabella," 163, 216, 327.
"Clavigo," 18, 50, 73, 163, 362.
Clergy, the European, 312.
Clerical language in the XVIIIth century, 197.
Cologne, 129, 182, 186, 314.
Colors, theory of, 391, 449 *et seq.*
Comédie larmoyante, 50, 93.
Conclusion of European History, 1850, 480.
"Confessions, The," of Rousseau, 25.
Confession, Goethe's last, 500.
Connection of all phenomena, 453.
Conscious and the unconscious, 502.
Consecration to Psyche, 87.
Constantin, Prince of Saxe-Weimar, 226, 235.
Continuation of and controversial writings about "Sorrows of Werther," 165.
"Contributions to Optics," 391.
Corneille, 32, 93 *et seq.*, 157, 165, 264; his heroes, 95; his "Menteur," 35, 98.
Corpus Juris, 310.
Correct versification in itself, 433.
Costumes for antique plays in the XVIIIth century, 295.
Cotta, 359, 412; Cotta makes Goethe's acquaintance through Schiller, 408.
Cotta, Baron von, 393.
Council, Goethe begs for relief in the, 278.
"Countess, Swedish, The," of Gellert, 33.
Court Theatre, the, 1791, 390.
Creon, 462.
Crime, 514.
Criticism of the Gospels, 199.
Cuvier, 489.

Dannecker, 173.
Dante, 4, 157 *et seq.*, 352, 424.
Dante for the Romanic world what Homer was for that of Greece, 310.

Darmstadt, 234; Darmstadt, friendships, 117; society in 1772, 86.
Darwin, 448.
Death of the child in the "Elective Affinities" related by Goethe in breathless sentences, 468.
"Demetrius," by Schiller, 418, 442, 478.
Demon, 206; Demoniac powers, 469.
Descartes, the teacher of Spinoza, 202 *et seq.*
Descriptions by Goethe, 358.
Desor, on the motion of Glaciers, 204.
Dialect, expression of feelings void of — required in the "Iphigenia," 293.
Dialogues and Duets, 285.
Diaries of Goethe, 20, 70.
Diary of Ottilie, 468.
"Dichtung und Wahrheit," 22 *et seq.*, 55, 67, 82, 110, 128, 132, 168, 180, 187, 506, 520; concluded with Goethe's arrival at Weimar, 247; on Lilli, 217.
Didactic purpose of the "Nouvelle Heloise," 156.
Diderot, 50 *et seq.*; in Germany, 93; Diderot and the English drama, 151.
Dido, the subject of a tragedy by Frau von Stein, 256.
Doctrine of Fatalism, 461.
Dog on the stage, 265.
Dorothea, 16, 435 *et seq.*, 494.
Drama, 148; in connection with literature, 285.
Drama, the German, in the XVIIIth century, 94; Trifles by Goethe, 390.
Dramatizations of "Sorrows of Werther," 164.
Dressing-gown of the Schiller statues, 404 *et seq.*
Dumas, Alex., translates "Hamlet," 58.

"Dumme Jungen" (silly boys) of 1772, 211.
Düntzer, 216, 250, 385; on Goethe's official activity, 248; on the three oldest arrangements of "Iphigenia," 295.
Düsseldorf, 129, 184.

Earliest songs of Goethe, 35.
Eckermann, 84, 211, 328, 414, *et seq.*; at Goethe's funeral, 524.
Ecclesiastical States, 480.
Ecclesiastical education, 198.
"Economy of Nature," 461.
Education, modern, of girls, 401.
Edward, in the "Elective Affinities," 464 *et seq.*; as compared to "Faust," 497.
"Egmont," 16, 18, 263, 369 *et seq.*, 385, 391, contains Goethe's peculiar creed, 479; the Regent in, 370; Egmont *plus* Faust, 516; arranged by Schiller, 407.
Ehrenbreitenstein, 130, 181.
Einhardt, 91.
"Elective Affinities," the plot dating before the commencement of the work, 470.
"Elective Affinities," 444, 462, 520; publication of the "Elective Affinities," 1809, 507; why it made a confused impression, 474; a tragedy in the guise of a narration, 473.
Electra, in the "Iphigenia," 300.
Elizabeth, in "Götz," 162; in "Marie Stuart," 479.
Emerson, 387.
"Emile" of Rousseau, 111, 152, 212.
Emigrations from Asia into Europe in pre-historic times, 194.
Emperor and people, 481.
Emperor in "Faust," 518.
Engagements in the XVIIIth century, 65.
England, 51; English poetry and morals, 155; the family-novel,

151; English novel in Germany in the XVIIIth century, 152.
Enlightenment, 210.
Envy, 514.
Epistle, Goethe's to Frederika Oeser, 1768, 151.
Erfurt, 477; became Prussian only, 1802; ancient seat of mental life, 241 *et seq.*; large place compared to Weimar, 232.
Ernst August Constantine, Duke of Saxe-Weimar, father of Carl August, 235.
Estrangement, complete, never took place between Schiller and Goethe, 394.
"Ethics," the, of Spinoza, 201 *et seq.*
Ettersburg, 191.
Eugenia in "The Natural Daughter," 462.
Evangels (Gospels), 199.
Events of Goethe's life systematically arranged, printed by Gödeke, 279.

Fanny, 161.
Farewell, in "Iphigenia," 289, 296.
Fatalistic character in the "Elective Affinities," 469.
"Faust," 10, 16, 18, 19, 41 *et seq.*, 452, 489, 491 *et seq.*; gradual growth of, 503; as stage play, 519; as grand magic opera, 519.
Faust's "two souls," 205.
Faust, demon in human shape, 516; the youngest of all classic poetic fancies, 493; the poetic work *per se*, 491; the special problem of Faust, 514; impression of Faust in 1808, 520; development of the person in poetry, 514; the explanation of Faust one of our great scientific problems, 519; first conception of Faust, 502, 515; first and second part of Faust originated at the same time, 500; first representation of Faust in Weimar, 1828, 519, Frankfort and Faust, 518; printed in 1790, 391; the history of Faust its best explanation, 503; Goethe's chief work, 491, 507; in the world of to-day, 493; in Strasburg, 88; in a thousand years, 493; international poetical property, 495; the local element in Faust, 517; without conclusion in Goethe's thoughts, 498, 515; possible without Goethe as originator, 495; paralipomena to Faust, 335; represents Goethe's actual life, 516.
Faust's salvation, 515.
"Faust," scenes in, of 1790 and 1808; in regard to Gretchen, 505; and the real stage, 519; and German history, 491; and Gretchen occupying the first place, 493; and Mephistopheles, 507; the invisible counterpart of all of Goethe's male characters, 495.
Faust's immortality, 498; reconciliation in Faust, 514; Dr. Faustus in "Old Folk's Comedy," 515; its completion after Goethe's death, 516.
"Faust," the, of 1772, 503 *et seq.*; of 1787, 498; of 1790, 491, 499, 503 *et seq.*; of 1808, 491, 503 *et seq.*; only a fragment, 499; its second part, 515; on the stage, 519.
Ferdinand in "Stella," 497.
Ferrara, 331.
Fichte, 394.
Fingal, 492.
Flachsland, Caroline, 82, 114, 161, 242, 276, 389; letters to Herder, 87 *et seq.*; her judgment of Madame La Roche, 131.
Florence, 348; Boboli Garden in Florence, 28.
Folk-songs, their influence on Goethe's language, 291.
Formation of clouds, 454.

Forum, Roman, 313.
Frau Rath, 80 et seq.
Frankfort, 24 et seq., 314, 385; "Anzeigen," 122 et seq., 175, 372; in Goethe's time, 408; contrasted with Weimar, 232; North-German, 357; Frankfort and Lavater, 1774, 178.
France, 33.
Free Will, 458.
Frederick the Great, 2, 90, 107, 476, 482 et seq., 487, 492 et seq.; against Stella, 213; in the world of to-day, 493; bears much from Voltaire, 265; Frederick and the Jesuits, 313; glorified by Wieland in the epos "Cyrus," 240.
Frederick the Hohenstaufe, 492.
Frederick William IV., 489.
Freedom, 359; freedom in the XVIIIth century, 51; Freedom dwells on the mountains in the XVIIIth century, 176.
French, the, as conquerors, 484; in Germany in 1806, 476.
French culture in Germany, 483; classic tragedy in England, 93; "French form" of the drama, 286; literature, 1770, 43; national spirit, 482; republic honored in Germany, 483; revolution, 10, 105, 435 et seq., 443, 456, 475 et seq., 478 et seq.; benefit of the French Revolution in Germany, 483; playwrights in Germany, 98; tyranny, 1806, 477; verses by Goethe, 35.
Friday receptions, 390.
Friendship, 387; indestructible friendship between Goethe and Carl August, 265; between Goethe and Schiller, 397.
Frithiof, 492.
Fritsch, von, 235 et seq., 331; Fritsch and Goethe, 244 et seq.; his opposition, 272.
Future of the world, 451 et seq.

Gallantry, 34 et seq., 217.
Gall, 205.
Garbenheim, 164, 473.
Garda, Lago di, 298.
Gellert, 33 et seq., 40, 133, 151.
Genius, 502.
Geniuses in the XVIIIth century, 239.
Geoffroy de St. Hilaire, 489.
George, innkeeper's son in Drusenheim, 64.
German, the, of "Götz von Berlichingen," 98, 293; of the XVIth and XVIIth centuries, 291; in "Iphigenia," 293, 323.
German character, 436; family life, 162, 437; Frau, 401; war for independence, 478; league of princes, 479, 488; the "Marquis Posas" of German birth, 265; Goethe's knowledge of German history, 110; Goethe, member of the German Society at Strasburg, 42; German house in Wetzlar, 118, 135; hexameter, 432; emperor, 101 et seq.; criticism, 501; life in the XVIth century, 104; Odyssey, 436; philology, 501; prose, 3; Schiller's prose, 399; public, 277, 385, 412; German public on Frau von Stein, 251 et seq.; German public on Götz, 372; German public and the history of art in the XVIIIth century, 317; opinion organized by Schiller and Goethe, 408; German purists, 434; judicial procedure in the XVIIIth century, 77; Reformation, 28, 103 et seq., 108; Imperial cities, 518; cavaliers, 107; chivalry, 102; language, 2, 251; care for the German language a concern of the people, 523; cities, 27 et seq.; a German national theatre impossible in the XVIIIth century, 94: history of the German stage, 93 et seq.; ver-

sification, 434; German verse of Moritz, 377; popular rising, 1813, 484 et seq.; conditions, 1813, 488.
"German Mercury," the, 189, 239 et seq., 243, 393.
Germany, 105, 110, 312; 1806, 476 et seq.; clergy in, 106 et seq.; Middle, 232; in pre-historic times, 305; political disintegration of, 522.
Germans, 195, 304 et seq.; emigrate into Europe, 195; German Empire in Rome, 308; universal history beginning in 1850, 480.
Gervinus, 94, 460.
Gesler, Count, 485.
"Gil Blas of Santillana," 440.
Glacial motion, 204.
Glass clocks, 168.
Gleim, 184.
Gluck, 286 et seq.; niece, 286.
Göchhausen, Fräulein von, 295.
Goedeke, 279, 379.
Golden heart, Lilli's present, 223.
"Golden Mirror," the, by Wieland, 241.
Görz, Count, 226.
God, 200; Spinoza's, 207.
"Gods, heroes, and Wieland," 243.
Gottsched, 33 et seq., 133.
Gottschedism, 99.
"Götz von Berlichingen," 18, 40, 86 et seq., 98 et seq., 135, 148, 157, 175, 358, 370, 507; as politician and soldier, 105 et seq.; as political play, 479; George in, 115; in Strasburg, 98, 109; his life, 99 et seq.; his little son, 162; completed, 115.

GOETHE. 1749-1775.
Goethe's law business in Frankfort, 73 et seq.; admiration for Herder, 193; visit to the Socratian cobbler at Dresden, 61; visit to Mme. La Roche, 128 et seq.; visit to Lavater, 222; hemorrhage, 36; parting with Lilli, 225; the "splendid boy," 292; dissertation for degree, 74; doctor's degree, 73; first journey to Switzerland, 221; adversaries, 90; happy circumstances, 1774, 215; good party in Frankfort, 1774, 216; hates the parental mansion, 1772, 135; horizon, 1772, 503 et seq.; in the years 1771-72, 88 et seq.; in Heidelberg, 1775, 227; in Leipsic, 445; in Strasburg, 38 et seq., 445, 503, 513 et seq.; childhood, 30; mystic religious views in his youth, 41; contemplated journey to Italy, 1775, 227; journey to the Rhine with Lavater, 181; renown gained by "Werther," 215; sends "Werther" to Lotte Kestner, 143; studies in Strasburg, 508; Goethe and Jacobi in Pempelfort, 186; Goethe and Kestner's first meeting in Wetzlar, 158; and Klopstock, 210; and Werther, 520; paternal mansion, 25; leaves Frederika, 66; attempts to break with Lilli, 219; intends to become doctor, 1771, 60; intends to go to Strasburg, 37; two portraits in Lavater's "Physiognomie," 175.

1775–1832.
Goethe abdicates as poet and author, 1776, 283; aversion to Schiller, 1788, 373; "Altmeister," 490; from 1780, to 1793, 391; official activity, 248; engaged in 1780 on a life of Bernhardt of Weimar, 281; government official, 266, et seq., 282, 480; acknowledges his wrong towards Jacobi, 191 et seq.; visits Schiller in Jena, 394; considers his co-operation with Schiller the greatest outward event of his life, 415; statue at

Weimar, 522; discontinues in 1776 his literary labors, 248; indispensable to Carl August, 264; thinks in his deepest soul differently from Schiller, 410; the "fat privy councillor," 392; the "most polished man of the age," 407; the "cold gray man of art," 407; the "aristocratic Roman," 364; entrance at Weimar, 1, 244; discovers the intermaxillary, 457; delight at physical discoveries, 449; first winter in Weimar, 244 et seq.; first Weimar times, 275; son of a Frankfort patrician as against the Thuringian nobility, 233; friendship with Schiller, 397; in awe of Faust, 497; Goethe's garden-house in the park of Weimar, 266 et seq.; garden in Weimar, 266; avoids Herder, 407; designs a frontispiece to a work of Schiller's, 394; called "Smooth and Cold," 323; belief in Napoleon, 486; Gleim enraged, 432; Hartz journey, 61; house in Weimar, 390; closed, 523; marriage, 335; ideal of the literary German public, 1800, 417; in the campaign of 1793, 481; Eckermann's description of his appearance after death, 524 et seq.; in the last ten years of his life, 489; in Silesia, 390; in Weimar, 231 et seq.; sick when Schiller died, 419; artist and *savan*, 1786, 282; Councillor of Legation with a salary of 1200 thalers, 231; passion in his seventieth year, 524; last twenty years, 522; reads "Hermann and Dorothea" to Jacobi's son, 192; "abused" by Schiller; how to be understood, 414; contributor to "The Hours," 393 et seq.; after Schiller's death, 417 et seq., 441 et seq., 478; new in

Weimar, 238; superintendence of the government institutions for science and art, 1790, 389; "orphic period," 460; contrasted with Faust, 492; personal meeting with Wieland, 243; production from 1776–86 scanty, 248; "Professor," 400; secretary at the discussions on the formation of the league of German princes, 480 et seq.; counsel to Eckermann how to manage as a poet, 414; Goethe goes to Switzerland with the Duke, 268 et seq.; coffin in the prince's tomb, 265; authorship, 1785, 282; plays Alceste in his "Mitschuldigen," 274; the greater force beside the duke, 264; strict official, 273; templar at the ball, 273; will, regarding "Faust," 502; theatrical manager in Weimar, 274; sorrow for Christiane, 341; engaged in botany with Christiane, 446; separation from Herder in later times, 406 et seq.; arrives at Weimar Nov. 7, 1775, 227; Goethe and the son of Frau von Stein, 254; and the rising of 1813, 484 et seq.; and the families of his old friends and the "young poets," 411, 184; and popular representation, 481; and a united Germany, 488; and Herder, 508; after his Italian journey, 353 et seq.; and Napoleon, 486; and Schiller, 392 et seq.; their meeting, 1794, 395; relation to Frau von Stein, disinterested friendship of the noblest kind, 251; at Jena, 394; marriage, 383 et seq.; glorifies Thuringia, 261; intercourse with Carl August after 1786, 279; mediator between the duke and the duchess, 267; Life at Weimar, 520; resolves to complete Schiller's "Demetrius," 442; his literary testament, 500; typical plant, 446 *et seq.*; hesitating progress on his "Faust," 497; ten years in Weimar, 247, 465; return to Weimar from Italy in the summer of 1788, 353, 364; connection with the literary production of Germany, 420; acquaintance with Schiller "a ten years' marriage," 413 *et seq.*; dies March 22, 1832, 524.

ITALY.

Goethe's journey to Italy, 18; autumn 1786 to Italy, 279; visit at the house of the Balsamo in Palermo, 61; first appearance in Rome, 312; passage across the Brenner, 297; house in Rome, 347; longing for home, 351; in Italy when Schiller came to Weimar, 255; thirty-seven years old when he arrived at Rome, 314; an inn in Rome, 348; "Circle" in Rome, 321; arrival at Rome, 1786, 302; with the Duchess Dowager in Italy, 1790, 390; Roman life of, 1787–88, 347; tavern in Rome, 422; leaves Rome in April, 1788, 353; for the first time his own master at Rome, 315.

FAMILY.

Goethe's family, 196; the young, 400; mother, 80 *et seq.*, 231; on the first representation of "Iphigenia," 295; mother and Christiane Vulpius, 337; Goethe's mother and "Hermann and Dorothea," 437; reverence for Lavater, 178.

LETTERS.

Goethe's farewell letter to Frau von Stein, 383; notes to Frau von Stein in the summer of 1783, 367 *et seq.*; letters to Wilhelm von Humboldt of the 17th of March, 1832, 500; to Frau von Stein of Nov. 1, 1786, 302; last letter to Humboldt, 500, 506; to Schiller of Aug. 27, 1794, 398 *et seq.*; letter to Philip Seidel of May, 1787, 326; from Saarbrücken, 1771, 160; letters to Gustchen Stolberg, 217; earliest letters to Jacobi, 188 *et seq.*; to Kestner, 125 *et seq.*; to Lotte, 125 *et seq.*; to Frau von Stein, edited by A. Schöll, 250; from Italy to Carl August, 279; first letter from Italy, 297; later revision of his letters from Italy, 316; from Sicily, 343; the most perfect in the "Italian Journey," 343; correspondence with Frau von Stein, 193, 249; with Jacobi, 186; with Lavater, 167.

OPINIONS.

Goethe to Carl August on "Faust," 1787, 498; to his mother on his entrance into service at the Saxon court, 231; to Frau von Stein in September 1780, on his writings, 280; on "Wilhelm Meister," 439; to Herder on Lavater in later times, 178; to Lavater on Spring in 1781, 263; on Lilli, 224; to Kestner on his (Goethe's) writing, 1780, 280; on "Faust" as a stage play, 519 *et seq.*; characterization of Hamlet in "Wilhelm Meister," 440; of his father, 79; construes Wieland historically, 242; criticism of verses received, 411; calls Klopstock's "Republic of Learned Men" the most important writing of the century, 213; *promemoria* of Schiller's professorship of Dec. 3, 1788, 375; criticises Fräulein von Sternheim, 131; Lavater, 178; Wieland's "Golden Mirror," 242; predicts the revolution in the second half of the XIXth century, 512 ; later sayings about Schiller, 414 ; Goethe on Carl August to Eckermann, 268 ; on "Faust" to Schiller, 517 ; on Schiller's criticism of "Egmont," 373 ; on Wieland's "Oberon," 244.

IDIOSYNCRASIES.

Goethe's obtuseness and penetration, 205 ; humility, 334 ; double existence, 205, 514 ; impulse to confess, 255 ; obtuseness, 126 ; inclination to incognito, 61 ; youthful elegance, 233 ; could be pithy, 497 ; bodily bearing, 395 ; somnambulism, 360 ; severity to himself, 206 ; doctrine of Fatalism, 461 ; self-criticism, 513 ; self-reliance, 234 ; suicidal thoughts, 135, 514 ; speaks in parables, 205 ; stiffness in intercourse, 395 ; leaning to the universal, 315 ; unapproachableness, 387 ; secretiveness, 247.

STYLE, LANGUAGE, METRE.

Hexameter, 422 ; written for the ear, not for the eye, 435 ; ridiculed, 433 ; condemned by Gleim, 432 ; before and after the Italian journey, 432 ; Iambics, 329 ; imitation of Lavater's style, 175 ; so-called "incorrect" verses, 433 ; unrhymed rhymes, 434 ; language, 15 ; in "Tasso," 329 ; in "Werther," 165 ; in "Iphigenia," "Tasso," "Egmont," 426 ; from a spoken becomes a written, 292 ; style in the "Elective Affinities," in the last period, 523.

GENERAL.

Goethe, genuine disciple of Spinoza, 269 ; nobility, 334 ; anatomical studies, 447 ; other male characters beside Faust, 495 *et seq.* ; aristocratic standpoint in his view of the cosmos, 458 ; well versed in the Bible, 197 ; adopts everywhere the medium, 75 ; botanical studies, 385 ; Christian education, 200 ; representation of Spinoza, 207 ; democracy, 335 ; monuments, 522 ; the "Great Heathen," 208 ; poetry an everlasting confession, 495 ; poetry in contrast with Schiller's, 358 *et seq.* ; a Greek, 459 ; origin of his poems, 423 ; enthusiasm for Greek art in close connection with his views of Nature, 450 ; successes, 417 ; plots of his writings never mere repetitions of experiences, 468 ; fragmentary style of writing, 467 ; female characters, 496 ; scientific activity, 421, 453 ; belief in God and immortality, 207 ; both articles of faith, 200 ; " Paganism," Goethe's, 208 ; historian, 82 *et seq.* ; 479 ; ideal stage, 333 ; incarnations, 497 ; inclination to incognito, 61 ; artistic-historical studies, 385 ; lives always outside of Prussia, 485 ; learns of the classic masters, 422 ; literary landscape painter, 158 ; fragmentary male characters, 496 ; laborious poetic work, 434 ; nature, 207 ; never in Paris, London, Vienna, 314 ; never dissipated, 335 ; osteological studies, 385 ; patriotism, 486 ; his want of when suspected, 490 ; Goethe's physical appearance, 273 *et seq.*, 497 ; politician in the wars of liberty, 477 ; political views, 47 *et seq.*, no active politician, 478 ; result, 522 ; popularity, 520 ; as novel writer, compared with Rousseau, 154 ; his collective works to be taken as a *paralipomena* to Faust, 517 ; so-called immorality, 441, 465 ; statesman of the old school, 484; subjective point of view, 461; many things not in his journals, 267; sense of independence, 415; Goethe and the German Nation, 481 *et seq.*, 488, 521 *et seq.*; and astronomy, 459; botany, 446 *et seq.*; marriage, 464; geology, 449; meteorology, 454; natural sciences, 445 *et seq.*; osteology, 448, 457; and Spinoza's system, 201; relation to the history of literature, 385; to philology, 385; works in future epochs, 498; two great changes in his political opinions, 511.

WORKS.

Goethe's earliest poem "Christ's descent into hell," 198; "Memory of vanished joy," 223 *et seq.*; to Lida, 299; "Eyes, my eyes, what weighs you down?" 223; "God and the Bajadere," 445; epilogue to the "Song of the Bell," 442; first complete edition of his writings, 1785, 282, 384; collection of his poems, 384; Erwin of Steinbach, 137, 160; poems of his first sojourn at Weimar, 291; complete edition of his works, 521; "High up on the tower old," 181; Ilmenau, poem to Carl August, 269; "In the field I wander, still and gloomy," 229; "In the sweet vale, on snow-crowned height," 228; works of his youth, 36; "Thou didst know each motive of my being," 259; Odes, 210; Goethe's and Pindar's odes, 160; romances and ballads, 291; criticisms in the "Gelehrten Frankfurter Anzeigen," 131; translation of Corneille's "Menteur," 98; "It is impossible to show the day to the day," 413; "Wherefore so resistlessly dost draw me?" 217;

works before and after his Italian journey 424.
[Works not mentioned above under their proper letter.]
Greeks, 110, 195 *et seq.*, 454; poetical works of the Greeks, 411.
Greece, its connection with Asia, 304.
Greek art, 320, 424 *et seq.*; sea, 359; myths of the creation, 454; Greek and Roman culture, 386; tragedy, 473; versification, 426.
Gretchen, 16, 493 *et seq.*; to be referred back to Frederika, 505; origin of, 505 *et seq.*; first and last creation of Goethe, 494; in glorified form, 506.
Grimm, Jacob, 152; birthday, January 6th, 169.
Grimm, Jacob and Wilhelm ("Wörter Buch"), 33.
Groth, Klaus, 435; and the low German dialect, 176.
Gudrun, 436.
Guillard's libretto of "Iphigenia" for Gluck, 288.
Günderode, 129.
Gutzkow, 202.

Hapsburg dynasty, 95.
Hackert, Philipp, 344 *et seq.*
Hadrian, his times at Rome, 339.
Halle, 477.
Hamann, 44 *et seq.*
Hamlet, 16, 58, 492.
Händel, 286.
Haugwitz, Count, 222.
Haym on Herder and Merck, 85.
Heavenly scenes in "Faust," 518.
Hector, 492.
Heidelberg, 478.
Heine and the "Westöstliche Divan," 521; and Goethe, 407.
Heinse, 374.
Hennes, Dr., 222.
Henrietta in Jacobi's "Woldemar,' 190.

Herder, 3, 9, 33, 37, 67, 75, 87 *et seq.*, 114 *et seq.*, 163, 192, 239, 336, 380, 389, 406 *et seq.*, 421, 457, 463 ; call from Bückeburg to Weimar, 275 ; bride, 161 ; character, 354 *et seq.;* Christianity, 198 ; "conversion," 89 ; wife, 276, 389 ; historical view, 457 ; Haym's book on Herder, 85 ; in Bückeburg, 212 ; in Strasburg, 43 *et seq.;* in Weimar, 276 *et seq.;* cold, disinterested, merciless critic, 509 ; "Die kritischen Wälder," 46 ; on Wieland, 242 ; writings, 406 ; called as professor to Göttingen, 276 ; language, 54 ; always preacher, 54 ; quarrel with Wolf, 406 ; seeks to overpower Goethe, 167 ; on the Roman church, 312 ; on Goethe's Italian letters, 364 ; Herder and Mephisto, 508 *et seq.;* leaves Strasburg, 60.

Herder's capacity for loving, 355.

"Hermann and Dorothea," 19, 428, 432, 494 ; 1796, 192 ; the only large poem giving pleasure to Goethe in his old age, 436 ; envious criticisms, 437 ; its "immense circulation," 437.

Herodotus, 431.

Heroes, 409.

Herzlieb, Minna, 470 *et seq.*

Hexameter, Franks and Vandals make Latin hexameter, 90 ; high German (Hoch Deutsch) hexameter, 433 ; Homer's hexameter, 430.

Heyne writes about Wieland's "Golden Mirror," 241.

Highest ideas, 200 ; interest of humanity, 200.

Himburg's unauthorized edition of Goethe's works, 296.

Hirzel, Solomon, 21, 25, 169 ; catalogue, 36, 248.

History, 83, 454, 491 ; historians, 413 ; historical heroes in dramas, 370 ; hypotheses, 195 ; truth in works of fiction, 103 *et seq.*

History of art exciting public interest about 1800, 443.

History of Europe, 304 *et seq.;* of the world about 1700, 47.

"History of Mankind," 276.

Homer, 4 *et seq.*, 16, 26, 157, 194 *et seq.*, 305, 310, 422, 424 ; as poet of his nation, 430 *et seq.;* the first great phenomenon of Europe, 302 ; influence on Goethe, 196 ; Homer's heroes, 493.

"Hours," the, by agreement with Cotta, 393.

Howard, 454.

Human skulls, 457 ; culture immeasurable, 194.

Humboldt, Alex. von, 4, 489 *et seq.*

Humboldt, Wilhelm von, 4, 394, 408 ; prince of German critics, 501 *et seq.;* makes Schiller's and Goethe's works accessible to German *savans* and philologists, 501.

Hutten, 102.

Ideal kingdom of Rousseau, 212.

"Ideas of the Philosophy of the History of Mankind," by Herder, 276, 356.

Iliad, 422.

Ilm, the, 261.

Immortality, 207 ; literary, 165, Goethe's belief in immortality, 200 *et seq.*

Imogen and Gretchen, 494.

Infanticide, the, by Wagner, 41, 505.

Innate rhythm of the German language, 428.

Intended effects in the "Elective Affinities," 467.

Interpolations and extensions in the "Elective Affinities," 470.

Intrigue to separate Goethe and Schiller, 409.

Ionic dialect, 430.

INDEX. 549

"Iphigenia," 16, 18, 26, 263, 356 *et seq.*, 421, 462; as stage performance, 328; work on "Iphigenia," 290 *et seq.*; originated from Gluck's cantata, 287; read again to Carl August in 1785, 296; German and Roman "Iphigenia," 283 *et seq.*; a Hellenistic play, 323; a step backward, 284; first representation of, 277; date of its origin, March, 1779, 287; first reading in Rome, 322; Goethe's child of pain, 296; "Iphigenia" in the first draft or sketch, 295 *et seq.*; in Italy, 297 *et seq.*; rehearsals, 1779, 295; Roman remodelling, 326, 423 *et seq.*; to be printed in 1786, 296; "Iphigenia" and the Italian librettos, 285; and Frau von Stein, 426; and Schiller, 327, 328; fourth act written March 18, 1779, 287; arranged for the stage by Schiller, 407; reading refused by Goethe, 1792, 328; Iphigenia at Delphi, 300; "Iphigenia in Aulis" by Gluck, 286, 328; "Iphigenia in Tauris" by Gluck, 293, 294, 328; libretto by Guimard de la Touche, 288.
Islands of the blest, 75.
Italians of the XVIth century, 244.
"Italian Journey" of Goethe, 25, 377; false judgment of it, 316.
Italy as a political body according to Goethe's view, 480; home of the opera, 284.
Ithaca, 422.

Jabach's house at Cologne, 186.
Jacobi, Fritz, 167 *et seq.*, 184 *et seq.*, 192, 328 *et seq.*, 333, 392 *et seq.*, 396; to Goethe on "Woldemar's" execution, 191; view on Spinoza's doctrine, 192; grandchild, 192; family, 184 *et seq.*; wife, 185 *et seq.*; "Iphigenia" sent to Jacobi, 191; error concerning Goethe, 208 *et seq.*; circle, 472; posthumous papers, 186; novel "Allwill," 185; writes in Goethe's style, 189; son at Goethe's, 192; on "Faust," 503; on Herder, 1788, 354; transcendental tendencies increase, 192; Jacobi and Spinoza, 207; and Wieland, 243; "Woldemar,' 189.
Jacobi, George, 184.
Jacobi, Helen, 185.
Jacobi, Max, 186.
Jahn, Otto, 36.
Jaxthausen, the real and the poetical, 104.
Jean Paul, 5; heroines, 161; novels, 82.
Jena, 12, 375, 386, 445; zenith, 477; *savans*, 417; literary paper of Jena, 433; boasters of Jena and Halle, 34; battle of Jena, 337; Jena people and Goethe, 407.
Jerusalem, 135 *et seq.*
Jesuits in Rome, 320.
Jew, poems of a Polish, — 1772, 122.
Jews, 201; their emigration from Portugal, 201; in Amsterdam opposed to Spinoza, 202; Jewish spirit, 203.
Johannes Secundus, 339.
Joseph II., Emperor, 241.
Juan Don, 216.
Juliet, of Shakspeare, 16, 494, 496.
Julie, of Rousseau, 154.
July, revolution of, 489.
Jung Stilling, 14 *et seq.*; his Christianity, 199.
Just, the, as the aim of mankind, 200.
Justi, Wilhelm, 317.

Kant, 393 *et seq.*, 451.
Kauffmann, Angelica, 321 *et seq.*
Keil at Weimar, 70, 248.
Kernel and shell of Nature, 453.

Kestner, 118 *et seq.*, 134; his letter to Hennig on "Werther," 146; receives a copy of the "Iphigenia," 296; sensitiveness at the appearance of "Werther," 143.
Kieser, Dr., in Jena, 488.
Kleist, Ewald von, 429.
Klettenberg, Fräulein von, 175.
Klopstock, 161, 226, 286, 505; visit in Frankfort, 1774, 210; letter to Goethe, May, 1776, 245; his German, 211, 213; Fanny, 161; "Republic of Learned Men," 212; hexameter, 433; "Messiah," 211; adoring pupils, 222; compared with Wieland, 239, 240; creator of modern German prosody, 428 *et seq.;* Klopstock and German fiction, 211 *et seq.*
Knebel, 226, 277, 472; Schiller displaces him at Goethe's, 406; reads "Iphigenia," 296; wishes to chant Bonaparte's victories, 482.
Kochberg, 262.
Körner, Councillor, 360, 363, 365, 394; Körner and Schiller, 408; Theodore, 486.
Kotzebue, 396; in Weimar, 409.
Kriegk, 31; picture of German culture, 76 *et seq.*

Lahnstein, 181.
Lake of Lucerne, 223.
Landscape painting, 343 *et seq.*
Landscapes, description of, 159 *et seq.*, 345.
Language, Goethe's in his Frankfort times, 291 *et seq.;* language of Spinoza hardly to be called language, 204; language of Stolberg, 222; philosophy, and history, 201.
Laplace, 451.
Laroche, privy councillor, 130; Maximiliane von Laroche, 134,
470; marries Brentano, 136; Sophie von Laroche (born Guterman), 130 *et seq.*, 240, 243.
Late acquaintance of Schiller and Goethe, 399.
Lavater, 167 *et seq.*, 194 *et seq.*, 217, 385, 396, 465; "Glimpses into Eternity," 170; deceived himself and others, 173; bust by Dannecker, 173 *et seq.;* Goethe's characterization of, 179; Christianity, 200 *et seq.;* the "prophet," 178; influence on Goethe's diction, 291; employs his spiritual — yes, his clerical — power for worldly purposes, 187; dialect, 175; in Coblentz, 181; in Frankfort, 1774, 176; childhood, 170 *et seq.;* oracular speech, 175; "Physiognomical Fragments," 1775–1778, 172 *et seq.;* style, 181; the hero of Goethe's "Mahomet," 178; described by Goethe, 177, 178; some one gave Goethe in Strasburg the silhouette of Frau von Stein for Lavater's work, 258.
Law of necessity in Nature, 461.
Lebrun, painter, 186.
Leipsic, 32 *et seq.*, 232, 314, 518; maidens of, 35; gallantry, 34; girls, 215.
Lenz, 40, 329 *et seq.*
Leonardo da Vinci, 424.
Lerse, 40.
Le Sage, 440.
Lessing, 9, 31, 33, 45, 50, 99, 163, 312, 492; as dramatic poet, 96 *et seq.;* in Wolfenbüttel, 212; compared to Wieland, 239; on Shakspeare's Romeo and Juliet, 496; and Spinoza, 207; scientifically construed for the first time by Gervinus, 94.
Lilli Schönemann, 215 *et seq.*, 246, 250, 258; character, 217; Goethe at her window on the last evening

before leaving for Weimar, 227 ; Goethe, 1830, on Lilli, 230 ; Countess Egloffstein Lilli's confidante, 230 ; marries Türckheim, 229 ; her children and Goethe, 230.
Literary workers of the second class, 184.
Loeper, G. von, 22, 69, 216 ; edition of "Faust," 513 ; on Merck, 85.
London in Shakspeare's time, 95.
"Lorelei," 129.
Lotte Buff, 70, 118 et seq., 217, 262 et seq.; Lotte Kestner, 140 ; her grandchildren and Goethe, 161 ; has blue eyes, Werther's Lotte black ones, 144 ; Lotte Kestner and Werther's Lotte, 138; Lotte in "Werther," 161, 466 ; Werther's Lotte, 472 ; Werther's Lotte Goethe's most renowned creation, 160 ; Werther and Lotte and Klopstock, 211; Werther's Lotte and Rousseau's Julie, 160.
Lotte Schiller's belief in Goethe, 402.
Louis XIV., 95.
Louis XV., 49.
Louise, Duchess, 474 ; confidante of Frau von Stein in her relation with Goethe, 252.
Luciane represents Bettina, 472.
Lucinda in Strasburg, 59.
"Luise," by Voss, 435.
Luther, 102, 196 et seq.; in Erfurt, 241 ; death, 162.
Lyric poetry of to-day, 521.

Madrid, 95.
Mahomet, 169.
"Mahomet," Goethe's tragedy of, 178, 210.
Maid of Orleans, 479, 482.
Manuscript of the "Iphigenia" accompanies Goethe, 296 et seq.
Marcellus Theatre, 348.

Marianna in "Wilhelm Meister," 277, 439.
"Marquis Posas," Germans are all born, 265.
Martha in "Faust," 512.
"Marie Stuart," 418, 479.
"Master-singing" (Meistersängerei) in the construction of Greek verses, 411.
Medici, Giuliano and Lorenzo dei, 103.
Meer, Jan van der, 174.
Memoir, 438.
Mengs, 322.
Mephisto, 86, 515 ; development of the character, 507 et seq.; in the world of to-day, 493 ; part of the political Mephisto, 489 ; growth of in Goethe's mind, 511.
Merck, 83 et seq., 116, 134, 173, 177, 510 et seq.; gets Goethe out of Wetzlar, 128 ; printing-office in Langen, 86 ; and Mephisto, 134, 507, 510 et seq.; characterized by Goethe, 83 et seq.
Merkel in Weimar, 409.
"Messiah" of Klopstock, 161, 240.
Metastasio's librettos, 286.
Meyer, 388.
Michael Angelo, 103, 196 et seq., 312, 315, 319, 424.
Mignon, 438 et seq.
"Minna von Barnhelm," 97.
"Mitschuldigen," 98, 274 ; earliest form, 35.
Mittler in the "Elective Affinities" supposed to be Knebel, 472.
Modern prose compared with Plato's, 430.
Modern translations of classic verse, 434.
Molière, 32, 91.
Monologues and arias, 285.
Montesquieu, 276.
Moral organization of humanity, 200.

Morbid imagination of the present generation, 452.
Moritz, 388; letters from Italy, 377; in Weimar, 378; and "Iphigenia," 377.
Mosaic history of creation, 454.
Moses, 498.
Moscow, 487.
Mountains awaken poetical thoughts in Goethe, 297.
Mozart, 216, 418.
Müller, Johannes von, 83.
Müller, Chancellor, 206, 212.
Müller, Wilhelm, 339.
Munich, 478.
Murat, 347.
Music, influence of on Goethe while writing "Iphigenia," 292.
Myth of every man's life formed in his own recollection, 247.
Mythical, the, in history, 304 *et seq.*

Naked human eye, the, — the true measure of things, 459.
Naples, 343, 347.
Napoleon, 443, 476 *et seq.*, 482, 485 *et seq.;* his interview with Goethe, 486; marshals, 487 *et seq.;* victorious campaign, 1806, 483.
National, the, as compared to the purely human, 196.
"Natural Daughter, The," 444, 461 *et seq.*, 473 *et seq.*
Natural sciences, 489.
Nature, descriptions of, in "Werther," 158.
"Natur (Die) der Dinge," heroic poem by Wieland, 240.
Necessarianism, 460 *et seq.*, 500.
Necessity of the events in the "Elective Affinities," 468.
New generation in Germany, 475.
Newspapers, no, in the XVIIIth century, 262.
Newton, 459.
Nibelungen, 436.

Nicolai's novel, "Sebaldus Nothanker," 197.
"Noachide" by Wieland, 240.
Nobility in Thuringia, 400; in the XVIIIth century, 233.
Nobility, position of the, in Germany, 272; no nobleman among Goethe's friends in his youth, 234.
Noble, the, in opposition to the Common, 89 *et seq.*
North Germany, 409, 523.
"Nouvelle Heloise" of Rousseau, 152 *et seq.*
Novel, history of the, 149 *et seq.*
Novel writers, their rise in Jena, 477 *et seq.;* romantic school, 417 *et seq.;* romances and ballads of Goethe, 291.

Objectivity of the Hebrew mind, 203.
Odes the, of Klopstock, 428; of Ramler, 429.
Odyssey, 422.
Oeser, 317; Frederika Oeser, 151.
Olympia, excavations in, 320.
"Once upon a time there was," in Greek history, 305.
Opera, genesis of the, 284; difference of the beginnings of the opera and the drama, 284; librettos, 285.
Ophelia and Gretchen, 494.
Orestes, character in "Iphigenia," 289, 426.
Oriental legend, 250.
Ossian, 159.
Ottilie, 464 *et seq.*, 470; as Gretchen's elder sister, 507; fatal effect of her fault, 468.
Otto the Great, 492.

Padua, 298, 348.
Paintings of Mary, 103, 162.
Palaces of the cardinals places of resort for the learned, 313.

INDEX. 553

Palatinate, 319.
Palazzo, Farnese in Rome, 349 *et seq.*
Palm-tree, Goethe's in Padua, 348; in Villa Malta, 348; palm-trees in Germany, 305.
Pamela, 1740, 151.
Paris, 37, 350; Goethe's intended journey to Paris and Italy, 37; Voltaire and Parisian society, 51.
Partnership, Schiller and Goethe, 405, 416.
Passionate element not intentionally expressed in "Elective Affinities," 471.
"Pausias, The New," and "The Flower Maiden," 427.
Peasants' War, the, 101.
Pempelfort, 186.
Penelope, 495.
Personal events, 426.
Petrarch, 165.
Phidias, 305, 425.
Philanthropists in the XVIIIth century, 167 *et seq.*
Philina, 277, 438 *et seq.*
Philosophers, 207; in the XVIIIth century, 51.
Philosophy, why we study, 201.
Photographic portraits, 57.
Phrenology, 205.
Physicians and the public, 171.
"Physiognomical Fragments" of Lavater, 183.
Pindar, 160, 210, 305.
Pisa, 351.
Plants of glass, 169.
Platen's hexameter, 433; Platen and the "Westöstliche Divan," 521.
Plato, 196, 305; the Attic narrator, 430.
Platt Deutsch, 176, 431 *et seq.*
Plautus, 91, 310.
Plessing, 61.
Pliny, 310.

Poetical language, 426.
"Poetizing creature," 501.
Poetry, the, of Homer, 430.
Police, assistance of the, desired on account of personal insult to Schiller, 416; and the public, 171.
"Political Treatise," by Spinoza, 203.
Popes, 309; the Papal government in Rome, 349.
Popular epic, 150.
Popular element in "Egmont," 373.
Pre-historic inhabitants of Europe, 304.
Present, the, feeling of its small worth, 1820, 413, 512.
Preux, St., 153 *et seq.*
Princesses in "Tasso," 340.
Professional poetry, 410, 502.
Progress, national, 483.
Propertius, 339, 422.
Prose of the Ten Years, 438; of "Werther," 291; Plato's, 430.
Protestants, 312.
Prototype of Charlotte in the "Elective Affinities," 472; of Ottilie, 470 *et seq.*
Prussia, 482 *et seq.*; 1806, 476; nobility, 1806, 483.
Prussian emperor, 481.
Public of Schiller, 358; the public and the "Elective Affinities," 469, 471.
Punch in the XVIIIth century, 87.
Pylades in Frankfort, 68.

Quadroons of America, 305.
Quietude of life in the XVIIIth century, 262.

Racine, 32, 92, 95.
Ramler, 429.
Ranke, L. von, on Ferrara in history, 332.

Raphael, 194 *et seq.*, 208, 312, 315, 319, 418, 427; his influence on Goethe, 194; youth, 36; age of, 91.
Reading passion of the Spanish public in the XVIth century, 150.
Reality of a poem, 422.
Reception of Shakspeare in Germany, 440.
Reflection, the power of, in Goethe, 193.
Reformation, the age of the, 102.
Relation of modern humanity to the cosmos, 454.
Religion, 170, 197; religious needs of our time, 199.
Rembrandt's portraiture of the Jews, 202.
Renown of Goethe after the publication of "Werther," 164.
Revolution, general, of matters in Germany and Europe in 1810, 474.
Rhine, the, 129; the river of Goethe's home, 232; song of the, 232.
Rhine, confederation of the, 483.
Rhine, country of the, 129.
Rhine, falls of the, compared to Lavater, 169.
Rhine, journey of the, with Lavater, 181 *et seq.*
Rhine poetry, 129.
Rhine, valley of the, 359; Celts and Germans in the, 303.
Richardson's novels, 151 *et seq.*
Richelieu finds a lack of *esprit de suite* in Corneille, 264.
Riemer, 22.
Rietschel's statues of Goethe and Schiller, 404, 522.
Rigi, Goethe on its summit, 223.
Rinaldo Rinaldini, 341.
Rising, the, of 1813, 484.
Robespierre, 432.
Robinson Crusoe, 49.
Robinson, Goethe's old adorer, 341.
"Roman Elegies," the, 334, 339, 391, 421, 423; the, and Christiane, 338.
Romans, 109; they lack the fabulous, 305; figure of the Roman ladies, 338; fall of the Roman-German empire, 475; Roman citizen, 307; comedy in the middle ages, 91; literature, 309; politics, 307; world, 475; history of the world, 480; the old, 195, 304 *et seq.*
Romantic experiments of the first French Republic, 75.
Rome, 208, 338 *et seq.;* the history of, our world history, 306 *et seq.;* Goethe's Rome existing no more, 318; Goethe's second sojourn in, 347; metropolis of the world, 302, 308, 313; of to-day, 311; contemplated second flight of Goethe to, 415; ruins of, 309; as a city, 311; the Rome of 1786, 311; the most brilliant period of its history, 309, 314.
Romeo and Juliet, 58, 104, 496.
Rousseau, 50 *et seq.*, 75, 111, 456; "Contrat Social," 43; "Émile," 1762, 152; the originator of the idea of national sovereignty, 481; his spirit in Lavater, 170; "Nouvelle Heloise," 1760, 152; and Christianity, 54; and the novel, 151 *et seq.;* and the Germans, 52.
Rückert and the "Westöstliche Divan," 521.
Rugantino, Crugantino, 216.
Rural, the, in the "Elective Affinities," 473.
Russian campaign, 487.
Russian officers at Werther's grave, 1814, 164.

Sachsenhausen, South German, 357.
Salzmann, 40 *et seq.;* correspondence with Goethe, 40, 70.

INDEX.   555

"Sampson, Miss Sarah," by Lessing, 50.
San-Gallo, 349.
Savigny, 3.
Saxony, 483.
Scala di Spagna in Rome, 349.
Schaper's statue of Goethe for Berlin, 523.
Schelling, 3.
Scherer, Wilhelm, on Jacobi, 190.
Schiller, 3, 9 *et seq.*, 31, 389, 474, 501; as a poet influenced by Goethe, 412; as a politician, 393, 478 *et seq.*, 482; as professor in Jena, 392; as a writer for the stage, 412; manner of treating his subjects, 410; acquaintance with the bookseller Cotta, 392; realizes his enormous capacities, 361; bitter criticism on Goethe, 1788, 372 *et seq.;* needs a faction, 359; letter to Goethe of August 23, 1794, 397 *et seq.;* of Aug. 31, 1794, 399; letters 392; letters to Goethe, 398; correspondence with Cotta, 359, 392; bust of, by Dannecker one of the best German busts, 173; correspondence, 418; visit of thanks at Goethe's in Dec. 1788, 375 *et seq.;* the conscious master of German prose, 399; his writing and Goethe's, 410; rapid manner of working, 418; his entry at Weimar, 255; encourages Goethe to work, 408; conquers Goethe, 394; first meeting with Goethe, in the summer of 1788, 368; 372; certificate of French citizenship, 482; wife, 392, 401 *et seq.;* Frau, and Charlotte von Stein, 256, 403; and Goethe in their later intercourse, 404; female characters, 495; friendship with Goethe the date of Goethe's separation from Herder, 406; goes to

Jena, 1789, 380; historical writing, 393; Schiller, Goethe, and Herder, 406; grand expectation, — the meeting with Goethe, 1788, 361; wooes Lotte von Lengefeld, 397; marriage, 400; his hopes of theatrical success, 362; iambics, 329; in the imperial diet, 397, 492; in Darmstadt with Carl August, 1785, 362; gets "Iphigenia" and "Egmont" ready for the stage, 407; in Folkstädt at Goethe's return from Italy, 364; in Weimar, 360 *et seq.;* events of his youth, 391; bodily carriage, 396; adaptiveness, 396; literary cleverness, 410; method in composition, 467; to Leipsic, 1785, 363; to Weimar, 1787, 363; calls his youth "dreary," and "joyless," 357; new call to Weimar, 405 *et seq.;* not able to participate in Goethe's art studies, 443; organizes a party in Jena, 417; smokes and takes snuff, 396; criticises " Egmont," 370 *et seq.;* rhetoric, 414; his ruined health, 417; saw Goethe the first time in 1779, 361; debts, 361; mother-in-law, 397 *et seq.;* plays a part in "Clavigo," 1779, 362; death, 418; on Frau von Stein, 255; on her "Dido," 256; on Goethe to Körner, 368, 375; and the people, 478 *et seq.;* and the young poets, 411; and Goethe, 19, 364 *et seq.;* and Goethe as a literary firm, 416; and Goethe's separation a preparatory time of trial for both, 399; and Goethe's weaknesses, 255; and Moritz on Goethe, 377 *et seq.;* and "Wilhelm Meister," 437 *et seq.;* father, 357, 397; vain expectation of a meeting with Goethe in the summer of 1788, 365 *et seq.;* marriage, 380;

intercourse with Goethe, 409; Works, 358; tries to lead Goethe to "Faust," 499; ten years younger than Goethe, 357; invited by Goethe, September 4, 1794, 400; recommended to a professorship at Jena, 375; criticised by Goethe twenty years after his death, 414; second son, 463.
Schlegel, August Wilhelm von, 3, 396, 501; his iambics, 329.
Schlegel, Frederick, abdicates North Germany, 409.
Schleswig-Holstein, 176, 435.
Schlosser, engaged to Goethe's sister, 134.
Schmidt, Julian, on Jacobi, 189.
Schmoll, 182.
Schöll, 186; on Goethe's official activity, 248, 266.
Schroeter, Corona, 277.
Science and art identical, 459.
Secret, the great, of Nature, 450 et seq.; the gigantic, of Nature, 456.
Sects, in the XVIIIth century, 197.
Seidel, Philip, 324, 334; the only person in Weimar who knew about Goethe's journey to Italy, 326.
Seidler, Luise, 488.
Semitics, 195.
Sesenheim, 58 et seq., 127; Goethe's behavior at, and his own account of it, 69; love affair at, 70; visit in, 1779, 71 et seq.
Several Ottilies and several Lottes, 472.
Shakspeare, 4 et seq., 16, 32, 34, 43, 90, 105, 114, 168, 196 et seq., 424; his influence on Goethe, 194; modern tendency to detract from, 168; translated by Wieland, 240.
Sicily, 343, 346.
Sidonius Apollinaris, 90.
Siegfrid, 492.
Siege of Mentz, 1793, 390.

Sienna, 351.
Simrock, 129.
Situation of the "Nouvelle Heloise" in "Faust," 158.
Sclaves emigrate into Europe, 195.
Somnambulist, Goethe shows himself a, 206.
Sonnets to Bettina, 470.
Sophocles, 424; female characters of, 495.
South German, Goethe a, 232; Schiller a, 357.
South Germany, 232, 523.
Sovereignty the, of the people, 479.
Spanish Theatre, 91.
Spinoza, 192 et seq.; 269, 450, 469, 514; his influence on Goethe, 196; ethics, 201; born 1632 at Amsterdam, 201; Latin, 204; "Political Treatise," 203; dies at the age of 45, 203; system, 201; banished from Amsterdam, 202.
Spiritual marriage, 190.
Spring, 169; of 1781, 263.
Staël, Mme. de, her opinion of "Wilhelm Meister," 439.
Stahr, the oldest edition of "Iphigenia," 295.
"Stein, Charlotte von, Goethe's friend," by Düntzer, 250.
Stein, Frau von, 247 et seq., 275, 335, 365, 383 et seq., 389, 403, 524; notices the change in Goethe after his return from Italy, 366 et seq.; the "Hausfrau," 262; an old woman, 1810, 474; Goethe to, about Frederika, 73; Goethe's letters to, 256 et seq.; criticism on her intercourse with Goethe, 251, 257 et seq.; after her rupture with Goethe, 256; after Goethe's Italian journey, 353; her silhouette, 258; that she was to have been Goethe's mistress, an unnecessary hypothesis, 251; her interest

in Goethe's creations, 262 ; change in the relation of Goethe to her, 257, 260 ; and Calypso, 249 ; and the "Elective Affinities," 462 *et seq.*; and "Iphigenia," 288, 327; and "Tasso," 331 ; Goethe's relation to her in latest times, 254 ; reconciliation with Goethe, 463.
Stein, Fritz von, 254.
Stein, Herr von, 465 *et seq.*
Steinhäuser's collossal statue of Goethe at Weimar, 522.
Stella, 213 *et seq.*
Sternheim, Fräulein von, 131.
Stolberg, the counts of, 221 *et seq.*, 292 ; their language, 222 ; and Klopstock, 246 ; Augusta countess of (Gustchen), 217, 220, 222 ; Goethe's letter to her in 1776, 246 ; Leopold von, 333.
Strasburg, 196, 215, 314, 518; Archbishop de Rohan of, 106 ; French theatre at, 98 ; the inn, "Zum Geist," at, 38 ; Goethe on the cathedral of, 359 ; Götz von Berlichingen at, 105 ; Miss Lauth in, 40, 42 ; life in, 38 ; costumes of the girls in, 39 ; times of, 210.
Stuart, Mary, 104.
Study of the classic languages today in poor repute, 434.
Study of philosophy, 201.
Stuttgard, 362 ; Dannecker's works in, at present, 173.
Style, 423 *et seq.*; carelessness of, in the "Elective Affinities," 468 ; finished, in Schiller's and Goethe's works, 501 ; the, of Schiller, 358 ; Lotte Schiller's epistolary, 402.
Suabian, Schiller a, 357.
Substantives in Homer, 430.
Success, 411.
Suetonic phrases in Einhardt, 91.
Suicide, 156 ; Goethe's suicidal thoughts, 514.
Supreme court at Wetzlar, 117.

Swiss, 176.
Swiss dialect of Lavater, 176.
Syntax of Plato, 430.

Tacitus, 83, 177, 194.
"Tasso," 18, 150, 263, 328 *et seq.*, 340, 385, 391, 426, 492 ; work on, 1780, 281 *et seq.*; construction of, 332 ; "Tasso" in prose, 328 ; the fruit of Goethe's longing for Italy, 328 ; compared to "Faust," 496 *et seq.* ; a perfect work, 332.
Tasso, "an enhanced Werther," 330.
"Tell, Wilhelm," 418, 479.
Ten Years, the, 18, 247, 264, 278, 385 ; the, no invention of the critics, 249.
Theatre, English, 91 ; French, 91 ; heroes in the, 492 ; in Italy in the XVth and XVIth centuries, 285 ; modern European, 90 ; of San Crisostomo in Venice, 300 *et seq.*
Theology, 207, 212 ; princely theologic-literary position of Klopstock, 211.
"Thirty-years War," 28, 47.
Thoas and Carl August, 289.
Thucydides, 305.
Thuringia, 232 ; Goethe's new country, 261 ; forest of, 261.
Tibullus, 339.
Tischbein, 348.
Titania, 330.
Titian, 427.
"To lard the fat" (Speck spicken), 268.
Translations of "Faust," 494.
Trilogy in "The Natural Daughter," 462.
Triumvirs of love, 339.
Trojan plains, 422.
Türckheim, von, 230.
Turn in Goethe's cosmic views, 457 *et seq.*, 467.
Twistings of moral qualities, 458.

Tyrants, the blood of, 221.
Uncertainty in Goethe's treatment of language after 1776, 292.
Universal, the, Goethe's impulse to go into, 315.
Universities, 459.
"Uriel Acosta," by Gutzkow, 202.

Vagabondism in German fiction, 216.
Valentin in "Faust," 512.
Vatican, 319.
Vega, Lope de, 91.
Venice, 299.
"Venetian Epigrams," 390.
Verona, 298.
Vesuvius, 316.
"Vicar of Wakefield," 59, 62, 69 et seq., 151, 162, 165, 510.
Vicenza, 298.
Vienna, 32; Congress of, 488; and Rome, 319.
Villa Ludovisi, 349.
Villa Pamphili Doria, 349.
Virtue, 34,
Vogt, Carl, 204.
"Voilà un homme," 486.
Voltaire, 3 et seq., 50 et seq., 93 et seq., 165, 456; as a historian, 51; writes poetry at the age of twelve, 239; his "Henriade" placed higher than Homer's songs, 211; tragedies of, 92; and the Germans, 52; and Schiller, 359.
Voss, 435; the discoverer of epic German, 429; his "Luise,"432; and the German hexameter, 429, 431 et seq.; visit of his son at Schiller's, 418.
Vulpius, Goethe's brother-in-law, 341.

Wagner in "Faust," 512.
Wagner, Heinrich Leopold, 41 et seq.
"Wahrheit und Dichtung," 22.

"Wallenstein," 418, 479.
"Wanderer's Storm Song,"
Wartburg, 262.
Watteau, 258.
Weimar, 12, 347, 486, 522; fountain in front of Goethe's house at, 518; plundered, 1806, 477; Goethe's appearance in, 24; Goethe's chosen retreat, 523; Goethe's real university, 386, Court Theatre at, 390; compared to Frankfort, 232; park of, 261; castle and theatre of, destroyed by fire, 283; and Goethe, 275; and Jena, 386; the friendly boundary between South and North Germany, 523; pilgrimages to, 490; archives of, 235; library, 446; existence, 335; first days of Goethe at, 277; friends of Goethe, 352; society, 244; princes at Frankfort, 226; theatre under Goethe, 407.
Weimar, Bernhardt von, 281.
Weislingen, 110, 113.
Wentzel's "Goethe in Silesia," 390.
"Werther," 117 et seq., 142, 358, 467, 473, 507; 1786, 504; first beginnings of, 136; fragmentary compared with "Faust," 496 et seq.; "Werther" and the German public, 146 et seq.; and Rousseau's "Nouvelle Heloise," 152; refused by a bookseller, 142.
Werther, character of, 154; dress of, copied by young Germans, 164; plus "Faust," 516; compared with St. Preux, 154 et seq.
"Werther's Well" in Wetzlar, 164.
"Westöstliche Divan," 521 et seq.
Wetterau, 261.
Wetzlar, 117, 215; and "Sorrows of Werther," 164.
Wiedermann, Freiherr von, 36.
Wieland, 3, 35, 130, 160, 185, 393, 421, 474; always an imitator, 240; at Bodmer's in Zürich, 240;

letter to Gluck, July 14, 1776, 286 ; letters, 239 ; born, 1733, 239 ; in Bern, 240 ; in Biberach, 240 ; in the history of German literature, 239 *et seq.*; in Erfurt, 240 ; settles at Weimar, 1772, 243 ; "Oberon," 244 ; editor of the "German Mercury," 239 ; translates Shakspeare, 240 ; and Carl August, 242 ; at Weimar when Goethe arrives, 238.
"Wilhelm Meister," 18, 216, 263, 421, 437 *et seq.*, 473 ; origin of, 438 ; Goethe, in August, 1782, on, 281 ; contents of, 274 *et seq.*
Wilhelmsthal, 262.
Willemer, Marianne, 521.
Winckelmann, 3, 31, 312 ; letters to Berendis, 313 ; letters published by Goethe, 316, 443 ; murder of, 317 ; in Rome, 315 *et seq.*; life by Justi, 317 ; his influence, 317.
Wine and beer, 232.
"Woldemar," Jacobi's novel, 189 *et seq.*; nailed to a tree in Ettersburg, 191 ; carried off by the devil, 191.
Wolfram of Eschenbach as a delineator of Nature, 159.

Wolf and the Homeric question, 406 ; his translation of Homer, 434.
Wolmar, Von, in the "Nouvelle Heloise," 162.
Wolzogen, Caroline von, 485.
World-wide fame of Goethe dates from the appearance of his "Faust," 491.
Worship of reason in France, 75.
Worthlessness of the present (1820), 489.

Xantippe, 342.
"Xenien," 437 ; "Xenienkampf," 416 *et seq.*
Xerxes, 304.

York, 485.
Youthful Goethe, the ("Jungen Goethe"), 21.
Youthful powers of Goethe, 506.
Youths endowed with the rhyming faculty, Goethe and Schiller's different treatment of, 411.

Zöppritz, 186.
Zuleika, 471, 521.
Zürich dialect, 175.

www.ingramcontent.com/pod-product-compliance
Lightning Source LLC
Chambersburg PA
CBHW031938290426
44108CB00011B/597